The Ethics of the Family

The Ethics of the Family

Edited by

Stephen Scales, Adam Potthast and Linda Oravecz

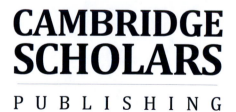

The Ethics of the Family,
Edited by Stephen Scales, Adam Potthast and Linda Oravecz

This book first published 2010

Cambridge Scholars Publishing

12 Back Chapman Street, Newcastle upon Tyne, NE6 2XX, UK

British Library Cataloguing in Publication Data
A catalogue record for this book is available from the British Library

ISBN (10): 1-4438-2057-1, ISBN (13): 978-1-4438-2057-8

TABLE OF CONTENTS

ACKNOWLEDGEMENTS

This volume came about as a result of the 10th International Conference of the Society for Ethics Across the Curriculum (SEAC). The three of us co-organized the conference and worked to see this volume through to completion. We would like to thank the members of the Executive Committee of SEAC for having confidence in the idea that the subject of family ethics would generate some exciting work in applied ethics; I think we were all surprised at just how fertile this ground proved to be. We owe a deep debt of gratitude to the Secretary-Treasurer of SEAC, Donna Werner, for her attention to the organizational details of the peer-review process for the conference. We would also like to thank the College of Liberal Arts of Towson University and the Department of Arts, Languages, and Philosophy of Missouri University of Science and Technology for their support of our work on this project. Our thanks as well to Scarlett Huffman at Harvard University Press and Amy Shapiro for their granting of permissions for the use of excerpts in Chapter One. But this volume is mainly the result of a great deal of work on the part of the contributing authors. We would like to thank them all for their patience and generosity during the editorial process.

We would also like to thank Ana Maria Soto, Duncan Scales, and Wolfgang (Walt) Fuchs for their love, support, and wisdom.

—Stephen Scales,
(Department of Philosophy, Towson University)
—Linda Oravecz,
(Department of Family Studies and Community Development,
Towson University)
—Adam Potthast,
(Department of Arts, Languages, and Philosophy, Missouri University of
Science and Technology)

CONTRIBUTORS

Jeff Buechner is a member of the Department of Philosophy, Rutgers University-Newark, and Director of the Rutgers-Merck Summer Institute in Bioethics (whose participants are students in the Newark area public high-school system) He is a Visiting Distinguished Research Fellow at the Saul Kripke Center, CUNY, The Graduate Center. He is the author of *Godel, Putnam and Functionalism: A New Reading of Representation and Reality* (MIT Press, 2008) and *Ways of Reasoning: Tools and Methods for Thinking Outside the Box* (Oxford University Press, forthcoming). He is also a partner in e4 Educational Technology (designing critical thinking and ethical reasoning packages for use in computer video-games, such as Second Life)

Kristie Bunton is professor and chair of the Department of Communication and Journalism at the University of St. Thomas in St. Paul, Minn. She earned a doctoral degree in mass communication ethics and law from Indiana University, and master's and bachelor's degrees from the University of Missouri School of Journalism. Her research has been published in academic journals that include Public Integrity, Journal of Mass Media Ethics, Journalism and Mass Communication Quarterly, Journalism Educator and American Journalism.

Suk Choi is Assistant Professor in the Department of Philosophy and Religious Studies at Towson University in Baltimore. His research specialties and teaching interests include East Asian philosophy, comparative philosophy, ethics, and aesthetics. He earned a Ph.D. in philosophy at University at Buffalo, the State University of New York, with a dissertation on Chu Hsi's Neo-Confucianism. He also holds M.A. and B.A. degrees in philosophy (aesthetics) from Seoul National University in Korea.

Hallie Liberto is currently a graduate student working on her PhD in philosophy at the University of Wisconsin- Madison. She specializes in ethics and political philosophy and is writing her dissertation on the moral foundation of laws pertaining to the alienation of bodily rights.

Ernâni Magalhães is Visiting Assistant Professor of Philosophy at West Virginia University. His primary focus is in metaphysics and his work has appeared in such journals as *Philosophia* and the *Australasian Journal of Philosophy*.

Michael McFall is an IHUM Post-Doctoral Fellow at Stanford University. He received his Ph.D. in Philosophy from Syracuse University, and he is the author of *Licensing Parents: Family, State, and Child Maltreatment* (Lanham, MD: Lexington Books, 2009).

Elizabeth Meade is Chair of the Department of Humanities and Professor of Philosophy at Cedar Crest College, in Allentown, Pennsylvania. She has published on the topics of moral judgment and teaching ethics and presented on numerous issues in theoretical and applied ethics. She teaches courses in theoretical ethics, applied and professional ethics, reproductive technology and gender studies.

Robert L. Muhlnickel, Ph.D. is Visiting Assistant Professor of Christian Ethics at Colgate Rochester Crozer Divinity School in Rochester, New York. He received his M. Div. from St. Bernard's Institute for Theology and Ministry, his M.S.W. from SUNY Buffalo, and his Ph. D. in Philosophy from the University of Rochester in 2008. His doctoral dissertation was on the compatibility of consequentialist moral theories with the commonsense distinction between doing harm and allowing harm. Before earning his doctorate, he was a social worker at Strong Memorial Hospital.

Paul F. Newhouse is an adjunct professor of philosophy at Towson University in Maryland. He received an M.A. in philosophy from the Johns Hopkins University, and a J.D. from the University of Maryland Law School. He maintains a civil litigation practice in Towson, Maryland, and is especially interested in the intersection of philosophical ethics and law.

Kathryn J. Norlock is an Associate Professor of Philosophy at St. Mary's College of Maryland, and affiliated faculty with Women, Gender, and Sexuality Studies and Environmental Studies. She specializes in ethical theory and feminist philosophy, and is the author of *Forgiveness from a Feminist Perspective* and co-editor of *Evil, Political Violence and Forgiveness*. Although feminism and good sense prevent her from endorsing all of Kant's views, she finds him indispensible in interpersonal and political theory.

Linda Oravecz is an Assistant Professor in Family Studies and Community Development at Towson University. Her research interests include family and community violence, ethnic families and family policy.

Laura Osinski in an Instructor at Madison Area Technical College, where she teaches ethics, applied ethics, logic and critical thinking, and philosophy of religion. She earned her doctorate under the supervision of Professor Andrew Levine, concentrating in social and political philosophy. Her dissertation examined the tension between free speech and political equality in campaign finance reform. Prior to studying philosophy, Laura was a program analyst for the Wisconsin state legislature.

Yvette E. Pearson is an Assistant Professor in the Department of Philosophy and Religious Studies and the Co-director of the Institute for Ethics and Public Affairs at Old Dominion University. Her research interests include grappling with the myriad moral issues surrounding human reproduction, whether it is done via assisted reproductive technology or the old-fashioned way. She has also written on ethical issues related to practices and public policies regarding genetic testing and embryonic stem cell research. Dr. Pearson has been teaching bioethics and other applied ethics courses for undergraduates for the past 13 years and occasionally teaches graduate-level applied ethics courses as well. She is also the Senior Associate Editor for the *Journal of Philosophy, Science, and the Law*.

James J. Ponzetti, Jr., Ph.D., D.Min., C.F.L.E., C.C.F.E. is an Associate Professor of Family Studies in the Department of Sociology, Faculty of Arts, The University of British Columbia., Vancouver, B.C. Canada. In 2002, he became a Faculty Fellow of Green College, a center for advanced interdisciplinary scholarship at the University of British Columbia. He has previously served on the faculty at the University of New Mexico, Central Washington University and Western Illinois University. He founded and directed the Oregon Family Nurturing Center, Inc. before moving to UBC. As a Certified Family Life Educator in both Canada and the United States (C.C.F.E., Family Services Canada, and C.F.L.E., National Council on Family Relations), he is committed to the promotion of family life education. He is currently involved in numerous research projects, such as premarital rituals, computers and family life, the use of theater in sexuality education, and moral philosophy in family science. He is on the editorial board for the *Family Science Review*, and the *Journal of Intergenerational Relationships*, and regularly serves as a reviewer for several professional journals including *Personal Relationships*, and *Journal of Social and Personal Relationships*.

Adam Potthast is an Assistant Professor of Professional Ethics at Missouri University of Science and Technology in Rolla, MO where he teaches courses in ethics, political philosophy, and the meaning of life. He also co-wrote *Ethics for Dummies* (forthcoming June 2010) with Christopher Panza of Drury University.

Karen Rice is a licensed Social Worker in the state of Pennsylvania and received her master's degree from Temple University. Currently, she is a doctoral student at the University of Maryland School of Social Work and works as an Adjunct Professor at Millersville University. Ms. Rice's practice experience includes working as a child welfare caseworker and supervisor for 14 years in a public child welfare agency in Pennsylvania. Ms. Rice is a trainer for the Pennsylvania Child Welfare Competency-Based Training Program where she collaborates on developing training curriculum and instructs casework staff on various child welfare related topics.

Wade L. Robison is the Ezra A. Hale Professor of Applied Ethics at the Rochester Institute of Technology. He received his Ph.D. in philosophy from the University of Wisconsin-Madison, with a minor in law. He directed a National Endowment for the Humanities Institute on David Hume at Dartmouth in 1990, has received several NEH fellowships, including a year-long fellowship in Political Science at UC-Santa Barbara, and has directed numerous conferences, the most recent the 29th conference on David Hume in Helsinki. He was President of the Hume Society for sixteen years and was the first President of the Society for Ethics Across the Curriculum. He has published extensively in philosophy of law, David Hume, and practical and professional ethics. His book *Decisions in Doubt: The Environment and Public Policy* (University Press of New England, 1994) won the Nelson A. Rockefeller Prize in Social Science and Public Policy. He has co-edited anthologies in Hume, medical ethics, business and professional ethics, and his most recent book, with L. Reeser, is on *Ethical Decision Making in Social Work* (Allyn & Bacon, 2000). Among his more recent articles is "Representation and Misrepresentation: Tufte and the Morton Thiokol Engineers on the

Challenger" with two of his students, David Hoeker and Stefan Young, and Roger Boisjoly.

Sangeeta Sangha is a graduate student in the Philosophy Department at Bowling Green State University. Sangeeta's research interests lie in moral psychology and virtue ethics. Her dissertation examines tragic dilemmas from a neo-Aristotelian perspective.

Stephen Scales is Associate Professor of Philosophy at Towson University in Towson, Maryland. Dr. Scales received his B.A. in Liberal Arts from The New School for Social Research in 1986, and earned his Ph.D. in philosophy from The University of California, San Diego in 1995. Dr. Scales currently sits on the Executive Committee of the Society for Ethics Across the Curriculum. He has published on family ethics and ethics pedagogy.

Eric J. Silverman is Assistant Professor of Philosophy and Religious Studies at Christopher Newport University. He earned a Bachelor of Arts from Rutgers University and a Master of Arts from Baylor University before receiving his doctoral degree from Saint Louis University. His research interests include medieval philosophy, ethics, and philosophy of religion. His first monograph is *The Prudence of Love: How Possessing the Virtue of Love Benefits the Lover* (Rowman and Littlefield's Lexington Books, 2010).

Mark Strasser is Trustees Professor of Law at Capital University Law School in Columbus, Ohio. Much of his work focuses on the intersection of constitutional law and family law, especially insofar as the law adversely impacts the families of sexual minorities.

Michael Taber is Assistant Professor of Philosophy at St. Mary's College of Maryland, where he is also Director of the Paul H. Nitze Scholars Program. His teaching and research interests are in Ancient Greek philosophy, as well as in ethics, and he has written "Concern for Others in Socrates" (in *Desire, Existence, and Identity*) "Cultural Pluralism in the Philosophy Classroom: The One and the Many Again" *Teaching Philosophy* and various book reviews.

Steven Weimer is a graduate student in the Philosophy Department at Bowling Green State University. Steven's primary research interests lie in political philosophy and applied ethics. He is writing his dissertation on the political implications of social and cultural diversity.

Prof. **Steven Weiss** is an Associate Professor in the Department of History, Anthropology and Philosophy at Augusta State University; he also serves as an adjunct faculty member in the clinical medicine program for medical students at the Medical College of Georgia. He taught at the University of Madras, India from 1996-97 as part of the Fulbright Abroad Program, and has published in the areas of Nietzsche studies and environmental ethics. He is currently doing research on medical-ethical issues related to the use of cognitive and performance enhancement drugs for the healthy general population.

Diane Williamson received her Ph.D. in philosophy from Vanderbilt University in 2009. She works on the relationship between Kantian moral theory and the psychological construct of emotional intelligence. She has taught at Colgate University and Le Moyne College. With her next project she seeks to apply Kantian virtue ethics to the relationship between humans and animals, as well as the environment.

Charles Zola, Ph.D. earned his bachelor's degree in philosophy from the University of Scranton and his master's and doctoral degrees in philosophy, with distinction, from The Institute of Philosophy of the Katholieke Universiteit, Belgium. He has taught philosophy and ethics at the University of Scranton, Wilkes University, and Penn State Hazleton. He has also been the Executive Director of the Ethics Institute of Northeastern Pennsylvania at Misericordia University, Dallas, Pennsylvania. Currently is Assistant Professor of Philosophy at Mount Saint Mary College, Newburgh, New York. His areas of interest are ethics and applied ethics, especially elder care ethics.

CHAPTER ONE

INTRODUCTION

WHAT IS A FAMILY?

While the word "family" is recognizable to everyone, paradoxically, it can be difficult to come to a consensus on its definition for many reasons. Individuals tend to define family based on what they are familiar with. Experiences in our families of origin, the families we are born into, or families of procreation, those we form through marriage and the birth of children, color how we view what a family should be. For example, an only child raised by a grandparent is more likely to consider such a family structure as "normal" than someone from a more traditional, two-parent family.

Additionally, there are social and cultural biases concerning what a family is. In the United States, the cultural icon of family is that of the two parent household, male as breadwinner, female as homemaker and caregiver, and the preferred number of children, which is two.[1] While this family structure actually makes up less than 7%[2] of families in the US, it is viewed as the cultural norm, and therefore a bias exists for the families falling outside of this "norm".

The meaning of family has varied over time and among groups. Cultures place different importance on a variety of family structures. Polygamy is commonly practiced in many Asian, Arabic and African nations. Asians are more likely than Anglo-Americans to live with their extended families.[3] Similarly, Latino infants and children are more likely than their Anglo counterparts to have active contact with multiple extended family members.[4]

Family is also a political symbol, with both sides of the aisle claiming "pro-family" policies, in effect implying that the other party does not promote "family values". Conservatives favor policies that promote marriage among heterosexuals and discourage single parent families. Conversely, liberals are more likely to include gay and single parent

---

[1] Townsend, J. (2003). Reproductive behavior in the context of global population. *American Psychologist, 58.* 179-204.

[2] United States Census Bureau (2002). *Current Population Survey.* Retrieved February 8, 2009 from   http://www.census.gov/cps/

[3] Knox, D., & Schacht, C. (2008). *Choices in Relationships: An introduction to marriage and the family.* (9th Edition). CA: Wadsworth Publishing.

[4] Garcia, C. (1993). What do we mean by extended family? A closer look at multigenerational Hispanic families. *Journal of Cross-Cultural Gerontology, 8,* 137-146.

families, although even the current presidential administration is loathe to define marriage as anything other than that between a man and a woman.

There are several different bases of definitions for "family". One of the most common is the biological ties we have to another. We often refer to someone as a "blood" relative, and research suggests that in times of crisis, we are more likely to seek and receive assistance from biological family. [5] Other family members may be defined by their legal ties, i.e.: through marriage or adoption. According to this definition, a man and a woman are not family until they have a marriage license, and adoptive parents and child are not legally family until a judge finalizes the process.

Other bases by which family may be defined, but are much less recognized by those who are the gatekeepers of rights and responsibilities granted to family members, are emotional and affective, or how we feel about someone. For example, in African American and Hispanic communities, fictive kin, or non-relatives who are regarded as family members, often enjoy ties as strong or stronger than those established by blood or marriage.[6] Emotionally, we feel they are family, so therefore, they are. Interaction patterns may also determine who is considered family, or "we do things for one another that only a family member would do".

While discussing the definition of family, it is important to contrast it with that of marriage. Marriage involves two individuals who usually choose one another, a monogamous sexual relation between spouses is expected, as is procreation. The marriage ends when one spouse dies or there is a divorce. On the other hand, family, according to some definitions, usually involves more than two people, and is the consequence of procreation. As any newlywed couple can attest, one of the questions that they will be asked repeatedly is "when are you going to start a family?", implying that a married couple in and of itself is not yet quite a family. Members are born or adopted into the family, by no choice of their own (as many an angry child will remind their parents), and the family continues beyond the life of the individual. Sex between near kin is neither expected nor approved.

Lastly, family is often defined on the basis of household arrangement. This classification has an Anglo bias, literally defining family by who is

---

[5] Burnstein, E., Crandall, C., & Kitayama, S. (1994). Some neo-Darwinian decision rules for altruism: Weighing cues for inclusive fitness as a function of the biological importance of the decision. *Journal of Personality and Social Psychology*, 67, 773-779.

[6] Dilworth-Anderson, P., Burton, W.., & Turner, W. (1993). The importance of values in the study of culturally diverse families. *Family Relations, 42,* 238-42.

living under one roof. It is important to note that The U.S. Census Bureau
defines family as: two or more people living together who are related by
birth, marriage or adoption. Such a definition clearly excludes many who
consider themselves to be family, and today we find many groups fighting
to have their relationships recognized as such.

Definitions of family have important consequences for individuals,
often determining which rights and obligations of family members are
recognized.   These definitions have both economic and social
consequences. Economic benefits and assets are only available to those
legally defined as family by the provider, i.e.: social security benefits or
the ability to be on another's health insurance policies. If a family
member dies intestate, the assets of that person will usually be distributed
among legal or biological relatives, such as spouses or children. Social
implications of family definition include the ability to make decisions for
another, for example whether to continue life support measures.
Additionally, how we define family as a society affects the ability of a
child to believe that their family, regardless of form, is "normal".

Federal and State definitions of marriage and family have a critical
impact on policies affecting families. According to the 2000 Census, there
are 594,000 same sex partner households, with children living in 27
percent of those households. Most of these families are unable to have
married heads of household.   The Defense of Marriage Act of 1996
defined marriage under federal law as exclusively heterosexual, while
declaring that states are not required to recognize same sex marriages
performed in other states. At this writing, only the states of
Massachusetts, Connecticut and Iowa recognize same sex marriage, while
Vermont, New Jersey and New Hampshire offer legal unions which allow
the same state (but not federal) rights and responsibilities of marriage to
same sex couples. By not allowing same sex couples to marry, individuals
are unable to: access partners Medicare or Social Security; file joint taxes;
obtain death benefits when a partner dies; obtain health/retirement
benefits; sponsor partner for immigration to the US; and divorce.
Additionally, same sex partners are at risk of losing access to their
children if only one partner has legal rights to the child and the couple
separates.

One can imagine the challenge of defining family will only grow more
complex as family structures continue to change and birth technologies
progress. For example, in 2008, a transgendered male gave birth to a child,
allowing the possibility for him to be the child's mother, father, or even

both.[7] Reproductive technologies allow children to have multiple parents, often blurring the lines of "family" members, while gay people continue to fight for the right to both marry and adopt children. As these and other changes occur in the American family, it will become increasingly important to define what a family is.

---

[7] Reuters. (2008). *Transgender man reportedly gives birth.*
http://www.reuters.com/article/newsOne/idUSN0326774720080704

AN INTRODUCTION TO ETHICS:
SOME BASIC CONCEPTS

We begin to look at the place of ethics in the family with a brief explanation of some basic and important concepts in ethics. **Moral Intuitions** are our prephilosophical or prereflective views or feelings about rightness and wrongness (perhaps transmitted at mother's knee). For example[1], suppose I live in a rather sleazy part of town, and as I'm walking home one day, I come around a corner and suddenly see a bunch of young hoodlums pouring gasoline on a live cat and lighting it ablaze! "Oh, that is so wrong!", I say to myself. I have an immediate reaction of moral disapproval, a feeling of moral nausea or disgust. This is a moral intuition. Even if I can't yet say *why* what they are doing is wrong, I have the feeling that what they are doing is wrong. Moral intuitions are these gut reactions of approval or disapproval that we have to the various situations we encounter. Except, perhaps for some extreme sociopaths who are described as "without any conscience", we all have moral intuitions. According to some views, these intuitions provide the basic data that ethical theories are constructed to explain and/or revise. **Considered Moral Judgments** are particular moral judgments justifiable by appeal to principles. If I say, "It would be wrong to set that cat on fire because it's an instance of causing unnecessary suffering", then I have a particular moral judgment. More general moral rules like, "Don't kill people for profit", or "It's wrong to cause unnecessary suffering" are used to justify such judgments. But what will we use to justify such general rules? For this, we appeal to **Ethical Principles**, the most general ultimate or first principles of ethical theories. For example, "Maximize net aggregate social utility" is the first principle of utilitarianism. Or, the first principle of Kantian ethics tells us that we must "Always act so that you could at the same time will that the maxim of your action should become a universal law of nature". Finally, **Ethical Theories** are these principles, rules, and judgments together (hopefully in some kind of agreement with our most fundamental moral intuitions) and the arguments in support of

---

[1] The example is due to Gilbert Harman's description in *The Nature of Morality* (Oxford UP, 1977), chapter 1; reprinted as "Ethics and Observation" in James Rachels, ed. *Ethical Theory, vol. 1* (Oxford UP, 1998).

them. Some examples of ethical theories that we will look at include Utilitarianism, Contractarianism, Divine Command Moral Theory, etc.

Finally, before moving on to a map of the most prominent ethical theories, we ought to say something about "**Reflective Equilibrium**". "Reflective Equilibrium" is a term which comes out of a particular ethical theory we will examine (the contractarian approach of John Rawls). But it is useful to introduce it at the beginning of our investigation because it may serve as a kind of check on which ethical theories we are willing to accept. In discussing his own contractarian view, Rawls points out that our thinking about ethics may often lead us into what might be termed, "**Cognitive/Emotional Dissonance**". This is a sort of disharmony between the moral intuitions I actually feel (my gut) and the principles I am prepared to rationally defend (my head). It is the grappling with this sort of disharmony that constitutes a great deal of the work we do in ethics. How does Rawls say that we ought to overcome such cognitive/emotional dissonance? He says that we move back and forth between intuitions and principles, sometimes altering principles in order to hold onto our most fundamentally felt intuitions, sometimes giving up weakly held intuitions in order to hold onto powerful and useful principles.

For example, suppose that one of the ethical theories we will look at (a crude version of act utilitarianism) tells us that the right thing to do is whatever will maximize happiness in a given situation. That doesn't sound like a crazy theory right off the bat. Now let's say that you are a doctor, and that there are three very sick patients on your ward in the hospital. One needs a new heart; one needs a new liver, and one needs a new pancreas. Each one is dying and their families and friends are extremely distraught. Suppose that in off the street comes a new patient, Adam. After a brief examination, you discover that Adam has a mild ear infection, which should be cleared up with a course of antibiotics. But suppose that you also discover that Adam just happens to be a perfect genetic match for all of the three dying patients on your ward. Let's also suppose that you could do whatever you want to Adam and there's almost no likelihood that anyone will ever find out about it. Now you have a choice. You could give Adam the antibiotics and send him on his way. This option would increase utility slightly: Adam will feel better and he'll stop complaining to his friends and family. Alternatively, you could knock Adam out with a sedative, carve him up and distribute his parts to the other patients on your ward. This would increase utility greatly: Sadly, Adam will meet his untimely demise (all lives are presumed to have positive utility value), and his friends and family will be distraught, but the other three patients on your ward will now become healthy, happy, productive members of society. All of their family and friends will be overjoyed! What would the crude act utilitarian say is the right thing to do? Carve Adam up! If we were ever tempted to become crude act utilitarians, I hope that this case illustrates just why we shouldn't. Here, the practical entailments of the theory are in such violent conflict with some of our most fundamental moral intuitions that the theory simply has to give way to the power of our intuitions. My conviction that murdering people in order to distribute their organs to others is wrong is simply too fundamental for me ever to give it up. Hence, what we've discovered is that crude act utilitarianism is a terrible ethical theory according to the requirement to move to a reflective equilibrium.

On the other hand, there may be cases where I would be willing to give up weak intuitions in order to save a theory. For example, suppose that initially, I have a weak prephilosophical intuition against physician-assisted suicide; it makes me feel morally queasy. But suppose that I come upon a very powerful theory in medical ethics which allows me to explain lots of other intuitions I have, and provides guidance on a host of difficult cases, but which also entails that physician assisted suicide is morally permissible. It may be that I would be willing to give up my weak intuition against physician assisted suicide in order to hang on to this powerful and fruitful theoretical approach. Hence, Rawls instructs us to move back and forth between intuitions and principles, sometimes giving up theory to save deeply held intuitions, and sometimes giving up weakly held intuitions in order to save theory, until we arrive at a fit between them. This peace between intuition and theory is the state that Rawls refers to as "reflective equilibrium". It is the solution to the cognitive/emotional dissonance discussed above, and it requires both that we learn the principles of various ethical theories and that we work through real-world applications in order to achieve the goal of peace between our (cognitive) heads and our (emotional) guts.

It may be that this peace is the best we can hope for in evaluating the ethical theories we will look at and in applying them to the world of the family. This is our goal for all students of ethics: to achieve internal consistency, coherence, conciliance, and excellence of theory (to overcome cognitive/emotional dissonance), to become better able to rationally defend your ethical views (to learn to make an argument for your position), and to become better able to understand and respect other ethical views (by seeing which principles and arguments lie behind them). Now we will look at some of the major ethical theories that have been advanced in the history of ethics.

AN INTRODUCTION TO SOME PROMINENT ETHICAL THEORIES

There are a number of ways to divide and categorize ethical theories; here is what we think is a useful way to do so. We can divide all ethical theories into two major camps: the consequentialist camp, and the nonconsequentialist camp.

In ethical deliberation, it is common to think that what make my actions right or wrong are the consequences of those actions. If one tends to act in ways that create large amounts of bad consequences (suffering) for no good reason, it is hard to defend these actions as ethical. Similarly, the great ethical triumphs of the past (good consequences such as ending legalized slavery, limiting infectious disease and hunger, giving citizens a say in their government) tend to be those that limit suffering and lead to greater happiness. Broadly consequentialist theories all evaluate conduct as right or wrong based solely on the value of the consequences of the conduct. On this approach, the Right is defined in terms of the Good; the right thing to do is to aim at maximizing good consequences. An Egoist approach says that the right thing to do is to maximize my own good; a tribalist approach says that the right thing to do is to maximize the good of some group, and a utilitarian approach says that the right thing to do is to maximize the good of all. Broadly nonconsequentialist views evaluate conduct as right or wrong based on factors in addition to the value of the consequences of the conduct. On this approach, the Right is defined independently of the Good (Rightness depends on motives, procedures, divine will, etc). Here is an outline of the major consequentialist and nonconsequentialist positions we will touch upon:

Consequentialist Views

1) **Ethical Egoism**: The right thing to do is to maximize my own good.
   a) **Crude Hedonistic Egoism:** Always act so as to maximize my own short-term pleasure
   b) **"Enlightened" Egoism:** Always act so as to maximize my own long-term rational self-interest
2) **Tribalism:** The right thing to do is to maximize the good of some group (nation, family, etc.)

3) Utilitarianism: The right thing to do is to maximize the good of all (net aggregate social utility).

a) **Act Utilitarianism**: Always act so as to maximize net aggregate social utility (e.g., maximize the net balance of pleasure over pain for all: The Greatest Happiness Principle).

b) **Rule Utilitarianism:** Always act in accordance with a rule (set of rules, moral code, etc.) which, if generally followed, would maximize net aggregate social utility.

Nonconsequentialist Views

1) Divine Command Moral Theory: The right thing to do is to obey the will of God.

2) Kantian Deontological Ethics: The right thing to do is to act only upon maxims that we could will to serve as universal laws

3) Contractarianism: The right thing to do is to abide by principles which free and rational individuals would enter into from some initial contract situation

4) Virtue Ethics: The right thing to do is to display virtuous states of character in our actions

5) The Ethics of Care: The right thing to do is to build caring relationships and to respond to the needs of those with whom we stand in relationship

Egoism and Tribalism

The view that the right thing to do is to maximize one's own good is known as ethical egoism. To some people, this sounds like just the opposite of ethics, but it is a possible position in ethics and has been advocated by a rather famous author (Ayn Rand, who refers to her view as "objectivism", but it is really a form of enlightened egoism). Hence, we would rather discuss its strengths and weaknesses rather than simply ignoring the view altogether. There are two possible varieties of this approach: one could adopt either a "crude" or an "enlightened" version of egoism. On the crude version, the right thing to do is to maximize one's own short-term pleasure. It's easy to see why there are no famous advocates of this position. After all, shooting heroin is said to produce very intense short-term pleasure for those who do it. But the long-term outcome of such an approach is often deadly. Hence, despite the fact that this sometimes seems to be the preferred ethical theory of certain college students, we will pass over any further discussion of it.

The enlightened egoist urges that the right thing to do is to maximize one's own long-term rational self-interest. This view promotes selfishness as a virtue, and condemns altruism (the view that the right thing to do is to be willing to sacrifice one's own interests for the interests of others). There are several arguments that might be offered in support of this view.

Arguments for Ethical Egoism[1]

1) Altruism is self-defeating: Since we know our own interests best, we are well suited to pursue them. But since we know the interests of others only imperfectly, we would likely bungle the job of pursuing theirs. Furthermore, the policy of looking out for others may be seen as an offensive intrusion into their privacy. And charity may be degrading to other people; it robs them of their individual dignity and self-respect.

But is giving food to starving children really inept, intrusive, or degrading? Most of us (including, especially the starving children) would say that it isn't. Hence, although we ought to be careful to be competent and sensitive when we take the interests of others into consideration in our moral deliberations, it doesn't seem that the best policy in every case is to ignore them completely.

2) Ayn Rand's Argument: One's life as a rational being is all one has; it is supremely valuable. The ethics of altruism regards the life of the rational individual as something that one must be ready to sacrifice for the good of others; it does not take seriously the value of the human individual. Ethical egoism does take that (highest) value seriously. Hence, we should be egoists.

But this argument presents egoism and altruism as the only two possible ethical positions. Perhaps both are false. Maybe neither one's own interests nor the interests of others should be ignored in ethical reasoning. This leads us into a problem which can be seen to trouble all consequentialist positions other than utilitarianism: **The Problem of Arbitrary Distinction**.

Let us first try to explain this problem as a criticism of some tribalist views, and then perhaps we can see how it applies to egoism as well. Racists and sexists draw a circle around a certain group of people and then claim that the interests of the people inside the circle count for more

---

[1] Summarized from Rachels, James, *The Elements of Moral Philosophy (Fourth Edition)*, Chapter 6 (Boston, McGraw Hill, 2003)

(morally) than the interests of the people outside of the circle. Since moral claims are always supposed to be backed by good reasons, we may ask the sexist, for example, just *why* the interests of men are more morally important than the interests of women. At first, the sexist might try to present some reasons why we ought to take men's interests are more important than women's interests. He might say that men are always more intelligent than women, or that women are incapable of rational thought at all. Or he might say that all and only men are capable of guiding their lives according to moral principle, and that women are simply incapable of being moral agents. All of these claims have actually been advanced in the history of sexist thought. But eventually, all of these claims have been shown to be empirically false. Now what is the sexist left to do? If he wants to remain a sexist (giving greater moral weight to the interests of men over those of women), all he is left to say is that men's interests ought to be given greater moral weight *simply because we are men*. But that is not a reason at all; it is just a restatement of sex (or gender) differences. Hence, the sexist is trapped: he wants to make a moral distinction, but his distinction is entirely arbitrary; there is no reason behind it at all! The same problem plagues many other tribalist views, e.g., racism, nationalist chauvinism, etc.

Returning to the egoist, we might ask: why should my interests be weighted more heavily than the interests of others in my moral deliberations? What is the egoist going to say here? What possible trait that I have could justify giving greater weight to my interests than to the interests of every other person in the world? I mean I realize that I am devastatingly handsome, have a quick wit, and cook wonderful lasagna. But Jude Law is more handsome; Steve Martin is funnier, and Julia Child makes better lasagna. What is the egoist left to say here? It seems that he is in the same position as the sexist discussed above; all he has left to say is, "Just because they're *my* interests". But again, that is not a reason at all; just like the tribalist views, egoism seems to fall prey to the problem of arbitrary distinction.

Utilitarianism

This problem leads us naturally into consideration of one of the major ethical theories we will look at: utilitarianism. Utilitarianism makes no arbitrary distinction between the interests of groups of people. According to utilitarianism, every person's interests are to be weighed equally in our moral deliberations. Everyone is to count for one and none for more than one. Like the varieties of egoism discussed above, utilitarianism also requires that we **maximize expected utility**, but instead of doing so for oneself or one's tribe, we are required to do it for everyone.

So if one can ultimately alleviate more suffering by helping strangers than one could by helping family members, we are required to help the strangers. (This assumes that one has a stark choice between the two options. Often in real choices this is not the case.) Of course the other side of the coin to this decision holds as well: if one can ultimately alleviate more suffering by helping family members than one could by helping strangers, then one is required to help those family members. And in fact we find that this will often be the case, since ordinary people's actions frequently have a greater effect on those close to them than those who are farther away. We can send money to aid organizations who help those starving overseas, but we can cook someone a meal or teach them to cook if they are closer to home. Utilitarian ethical theories tend to be very sensitive to the facts of particular situations. Occasionally this may mean overriding traditionally accepted obligations when the results will lead to greater happiness and reduced suffering overall.

We've already seen a thought experiment involving one form of utilitarianism: act-utilitarianism in the example of Adam going into the hospital. Jeremy Bentham was an early advocate of the act utilitarian approach. He developed what has been called the **Hedonic Calculus**, according to which we ought to take the intensity, duration, speed, fruitfulness, purity, and extension of pleasures into account in our moral thinking, and we should aim to maximize expected utility or happiness (for Bentham, this was just pleasure and the absence of pain) in all of our actions.

Since we've already discussed a case that seems to show this form of act utilitarianism to be seriously faulty (the doctor case above), let us move ahead to look at John Stuart Mill's rule utilitarian position. In the selection from Utilitarianism excerpted below, John Stuart Mill says, "In the case of abstinences indeed- of things which people forbear to do from moral considerations, though the consequences in the particular case might be beneficial- it would be unworthy of an intelligent agent not to be consciously aware that the action is of a class which, if practised generally, would be generally injurious, and that this is the ground of the obligation to abstain from it.." In other words, Mill is aware that there are times when I could generate more expected utility by carving Adam up, but that this action is of a class (murder) which, if people generally practice it, would cause utility to go down, which is a good reason we shouldn't do it. Hence, Mill is adopting what is referred to as **a rule utilitarian** approach.

We ought to conform our actions to those rules which, if generally practiced would maximize utility for all.

According to Mill, we should conform our actions to rules which, if generally practiced, would maximize net noble pleasures. That is, aside from being a rule utilitarian, Mill also makes a qualitative distinction between **higher and lower pleasures**. According to Mill, some pleasures are base and some are noble. Those pleasures which make use of what Mill calls our "higher faculties" (these being reason and sensibility) are nobler or better pleasures than those which do not. Mill says, "It is better to be a human being dissatisfied than a pig satisfied; better to be Socrates dissatisfied than a fool satisfied. And if the fool, or the pig, is of a different opinion, it is because they know only their side of the question." How do we decide which pleasure is better, according to Mill? He says that we should ask people who have experienced both pleasures; whatever the majority of these people choose is the better (higher, nobler) pleasure. What matters for Mill is the amount of noble pleasure which can reasonably be expected to result from the adoption of a particular rule, or set of rules. He tells us that these rules are "signposts" on the way to utility. In the following selection, Mill addresses some criticisms of his view and explains it in more detail.

One possible criticism of rule utilitarianism to keep in mind when reading Mill is what has been called **The Collapse or Rule-Worship Problem**. Suppose that the rule-utilitarian urges that we should follow the rule "Don't lie" because if such a rule were generally followed, then the net aggregate social utility would be greater than if it were not followed. And suppose that we come upon a case where my lying to a mad nuclear bomber would save millions of lives. Now the rule utilitarian can either A) urge that we modify our rule (to something like "Don't lie unless you can save millions of lives by doing so"), or he can B) say "bite the bullet", accept the counter-intuitive implications of the claim and urge us to stick with the original rule.

If he urges that we modify the rule because we can get more utility in this one case, then what about saving 10 lives? What about one life? What about just making someone feel better (by telling a "white" lie)? If the reason that we should modify the rule in the first case is that we will achieve greater utility, then (by the same reasoning) we should modify our rules in every case where we can get more utility by doing so. But this kind of thinking seems to have collapsed into act utilitarianism, which is what rule utilitarians were trying to get away from in the first place.

On the other hand, if he urges that we should refuse to modify the rule, then this rule utilitarian can be accused of "rule worship" at the expense of what utilitarianism is all about: utility. Indeed, in such a case, it is not even clear that he deserves to be called a utilitarian anymore. After all, rules are supposed to be merely "signposts" on the road to greater utility for the rule utilitarian. If we can clearly see that a sign that says "This way to Disneyland" will actually lead us away from Disneyland into a big ditch full of mud, we would be foolish to follow it.

FROM *UTILITARIANISM* BY JOHN STUART MILL[1]

The creed which accepts as the foundation of morals, Utility, or the Greatest Happiness Principle, holds that actions are right in proportion as they tend to promote happiness, wrong as they tend to produce the reverse of happiness. By happiness is intended pleasure, and the absence of pain; by unhappiness, pain, and the privation of pleasure. To give a clear view of the moral standard set up by the theory, much more requires to be said; in particular, what things it includes in the ideas of pain and pleasure; and to what extent this is left an open question. But these supplementary explanations do not affect the theory of life on which this theory of morality is grounded- namely, that pleasure, and freedom from pain, are the only things desirable as ends; and that all desirable things (which are as numerous in the utilitarian as in any other scheme) are desirable either for the pleasure inherent in themselves, or as means to the promotion of pleasure and the prevention of pain.

Now, such a theory of life excites in many minds, and among them in some of the most estimable in feeling and purpose, inveterate dislike. To suppose that life has (as they express it) no higher end than pleasure- no better and nobler object of desire and pursuit they designate as utterly mean and grovelling; as a doctrine worthy only of swine, to whom the followers of Epicurus were, at a very early period, contemptuously likened; and modern holders of the doctrine are occasionally made the subject of equally polite comparisons by its German, French, and English assailants.

When thus attacked, the Epicureans have always answered, that it is not they, but their accusers, who represent human nature in a degrading light; since the accusation supposes human beings to be capable of no pleasures except those of which swine are capable. If this supposition were true, the charge could not be gainsaid, but would then be no longer an imputation; for if the sources of pleasure were precisely the same to human beings and to swine, the rule of life which is good enough for the one would be good enough for the other. The comparison of the Epicurean life to that of beasts is felt as degrading, precisely because a beast's pleasures do not satisfy a human being's conceptions of happiness. Human beings have faculties more elevated than the animal appetites, and when once made conscious of them, do not regard anything as happiness which

---

[1] Excerpted from http://www.gutenberg.org/ebooks/11224

does not include their gratification. I do not, indeed, consider the Epicureans to have been by any means faultless in drawing out their scheme of consequences from the utilitarian principle. To do this in any sufficient manner, many Stoic, as well as Christian elements require to be included. But there is no known Epicurean theory of life which does not assign to the pleasures of the intellect, of the feelings and imagination, and of the moral sentiments, a much higher value as pleasures than to those of mere sensation.

It must be admitted, however, that utilitarian writers in general have placed the superiority of mental over bodily pleasures chiefly in the greater permanency, safety, uncostliness, etc., of the former- that is, in their circumstantial advantages rather than in their intrinsic nature. And on all these points utilitarians have fully proved their case; but they might have taken the other, and, as it may be called, higher ground, with entire consistency. It is quite compatible with the principle of utility to recognise the fact, that some kinds of pleasure are more desirable and more valuable than others. It would be absurd that while, in estimating all other things, quality is considered as well as quantity, the estimation of pleasures should be supposed to depend on quantity alone.

If I am asked, what I mean by difference of quality in pleasures, or what makes one pleasure more valuable than another, merely as a pleasure, except its being greater in amount, there is but one possible answer. Of two pleasures, if there be one to which all or almost all who have experience of both give a decided preference, irrespective of any feeling of moral obligation to prefer it, that is the more desirable pleasure. If one of the two is, by those who are competently acquainted with both, placed so far above the other that they prefer it, even though knowing it to be attended with a greater amount of discontent, and would not resign it for any quantity of the other pleasure which their nature is capable of, we are justified in ascribing to the preferred enjoyment a superiority in quality, so far outweighing quantity as to render it, in comparison, of small account.

Now it is an unquestionable fact that those who are equally acquainted with, and equally capable of appreciating and enjoying, both, do give a most marked preference to the manner of existence which employs their higher faculties. Few human creatures would consent to be changed into any of the lower animals, for a promise of the fullest allowance of a beast's pleasures; no intelligent human being would consent to be a fool, no instructed person would be an ignoramus, no person of feeling and conscience would be selfish and base, even though they should be persuaded that the fool, the dunce, or the rascal is better satisfied with his lot than they are with theirs. They would not resign what they possess more than he for the most complete satisfaction of all the desires which they have in common with him. If they ever fancy they would, it is only in cases of unhappiness so extreme, that to escape from it they would exchange their lot for almost any other, however undesirable in their own eyes. A being of higher faculties requires more to make him happy, is capable probably of more acute suffering, and certainly accessible to it at more points, than one of an inferior type; but in spite of these liabilities, he can never really wish to sink into what he feels to be a lower grade of existence. We may give what explanation we please of this unwillingness; we may attribute it to pride, a name which is given indiscriminately to some of the most and to some of the least estimable feelings of which mankind are capable: we may refer it to the love of liberty and personal independence, an appeal to which was with the Stoics one of the most effective means for the inculcation of it; to the love of power, or to the love of excitement, both of which do really enter into and contribute to it: but its most appropriate appellation is a sense of dignity, which all human beings possess in one form or other, and in some, though by no means in exact, proportion to their higher faculties, and which is so essential a part of the happiness of those in whom it is strong, that nothing which conflicts with it could be, otherwise than momentarily, an object of desire to them.

Whoever supposes that this preference takes place at a sacrifice of happiness- that the superior being, in anything like equal circumstances, is not happier than the inferior- confounds the two very different ideas, of happiness, and content. It is indisputable that the being whose capacities of enjoyment are low, has the greatest chance of having them fully satisfied; and a highly endowed being will always feel that any happiness which he can look for, as the world is constituted, is imperfect. But he can learn to bear its imperfections, if they are at all bearable; and they will not make him envy the being who is indeed unconscious of the imperfections, but only because he feels not at all the good which those imperfections qualify. It is better to be a human being dissatisfied than a pig satisfied; better to be Socrates dissatisfied than a fool satisfied. And if the fool, or the pig, are a different opinion, it is because they only know their own side of the question. The other party to the comparison knows both sides.

It may be objected, that many who are capable of the higher pleasures, occasionally, under the influence of temptation, postpone them to the lower. But this is quite compatible with a full appreciation of the intrinsic superiority of the higher. Men often, from infirmity of character, make their election for the nearer good, though they know it to be the less valuable; and this no less when the choice is between two bodily pleasures, than when it is between bodily and mental. They pursue sensual indulgences to the injury of health, though perfectly aware that health is the greater good.

It may be further objected, that many who begin with youthful enthusiasm for everything noble, as they advance in years sink into indolence and selfishness. But I do not believe that those who undergo this very common change, voluntarily choose the lower description of pleasures in preference to the higher. I believe that before they devote themselves exclusively to the one, they have already become incapable of the other. Capacity for the nobler feelings is in most natures a very tender plant, easily killed, not only by hostile influences, but by mere want of sustenance; and in the majority of young persons it speedily dies away if the occupations to which their position in life has devoted them, and the society into which it has thrown them, are not favourable to keeping that higher capacity in exercise. Men lose their high aspirations as they lose their intellectual tastes, because they have not time or opportunity for indulging them; and they addict themselves to inferior pleasures, not because they deliberately prefer them, but because they are either the only ones to which they have access, or the only ones which they are any longer capable of enjoying. It may be questioned whether any one who has remained equally susceptible to both classes of pleasures, ever knowingly and calmly preferred the lower; though many, in all ages, have broken down in an ineffectual attempt to combine both.

From this verdict of the only competent judges, I apprehend there can be no appeal. On a question which is the best worth having of two pleasures, or which of two modes of existence is the most grateful to the feelings, apart from its moral attributes and from its consequences, the judgment of those who are qualified by knowledge of both, or, if they differ, that of the majority among them, must be admitted as final. And there needs be the less hesitation to accept this judgment respecting the quality of pleasures, since there is no other tribunal to be referred to even on the question of quantity. What means are there of determining which is the acutest of two pains, or the intensest of two pleasurable sensations, except the general suffrage of those who are familiar with both? Neither pains nor pleasures are homogeneous, and pain is always heterogeneous with pleasure. What is there to decide whether a particular pleasure is worth purchasing at the cost of a particular pain, except the feelings and judgment of the experienced? When, therefore, those feelings and judgment declare the pleasures derived from the higher faculties to be preferable in kind, apart from the question of intensity, to those of which

the animal nature, disjoined from the higher faculties, is suspectible, they
are entitled on this subject to the same regard.

I have dwelt on this point, as being a necessary part of a perfectly just
conception of Utility or Happiness, considered as the directive rule of
human conduct. But it is by no means an indispensable condition to the
acceptance of the utilitarian standard; for that standard is not the agent's
own greatest happiness, but the greatest amount of happiness altogether;
and if it may possibly be doubted whether a noble character is always the
happier for its nobleness, there can be no doubt that it makes other people
happier, and that the world in general is immensely a gainer by it.
Utilitarianism, therefore, could only attain its end by the general
cultivation of nobleness of character, even if each individual were only
benefited by the nobleness of others, and his own, so far as happiness is
concerned, were a sheer deduction from the benefit. But the bare
enunciation of such an absurdity as this last, renders refutation
superfluous.

According to the Greatest Happiness Principle, as above explained, the
ultimate end, with reference to and for the sake of which all other things
are desirable (whether we are considering our own good or that of other
people), is an existence exempt as far as possible from pain, and as rich as
possible in enjoyments, both in point of quantity and quality; the test of
quality, and the rule for measuring it against quantity, being the preference
felt by those who in their opportunities of experience, to which must be
added their habits of self-consciousness and self-observation, are best
furnished with the means of comparison. This, being, according to the
utilitarian opinion, the end of human action, is necessarily also the
standard of morality; which may accordingly be defined, the rules and
precepts for human conduct, by the observance of which an existence such
as has been described might be, to the greatest extent possible, secured to
all mankind; and not to them only, but, so far as the nature of things
admits, to the whole sentient creation.

I must again repeat, what the assailants of utilitarianism seldom have
the justice to acknowledge, that the happiness which forms the utilitarian
standard of what is right in conduct, is not the agent's own happiness, but
that of all concerned. As between his own happiness and that of others,
utilitarianism requires him to be as strictly impartial as a disinterested and
benevolent spectator. In the golden rule of Jesus of Nazareth, we read the
complete spirit of the ethics of utility. To do as you would be done by, and
to love your neighbour as yourself, constitute the ideal perfection of
utilitarian morality. As the means of making the nearest approach to this
ideal, utility would enjoin, first, that laws and social arrangements should

place the happiness, or (as speaking practically it may be called) the interest, of every individual, as nearly as possible in harmony with the interest of the whole; and secondly, that education and opinion, which have so vast a power over human character, should so use that power as to establish in the mind of every individual an indissoluble association between his own happiness and the good of the whole; especially between his own happiness and the practice of such modes of conduct, negative and positive, as regard for the universal happiness prescribes; so that not only he may be unable to conceive the possibility of happiness to himself, consistently with conduct opposed to the general good, but also that a direct impulse to promote the general good may be in every individual one of the habitual motives of action, and the sentiments connected therewith may fill a large and prominent place in every human being's sentient existence. If the impugners of the utilitarian morality represented it to their own minds in this its, true character, I know not what recommendation possessed by any other morality they could possibly affirm to be wanting to it; what more beautiful or more exalted developments of human nature any other ethical system can be supposed to foster, or what springs of action, not accessible to the utilitarian, such systems rely on for giving effect to their mandates.

The objectors to utilitarianism cannot always be charged with representing it in a discreditable light. On the contrary, those among them who entertain anything like a just idea of its disinterested character, sometimes find fault with its standard as being too high for humanity. They say it is exacting too much to require that people shall always act from the inducement of promoting the general interests of society. But this is to mistake the very meaning of a standard of morals, and confound the rule of action with the motive of it. It is the business of ethics to tell us what are our duties, or by what test we may know them; but no system of ethics requires that the sole motive of all we do shall be a feeling of duty; on the contrary, ninety-nine hundredths of all our actions are done from other motives, and rightly so done, if the rule of duty does not condemn them. It is the more unjust to utilitarianism that this particular misapprehension should be made a ground of objection to it, inasmuch as utilitarian moralists have gone beyond almost all others in affirming that the motive has nothing to do with the morality of the action, though much with the worth of the agent. He who saves a fellow creature from drowning does what is morally right, whether his motive be duty, or the hope of being paid for his trouble; he who betrays the friend that trusts him, is guilty of a crime, even if his object be to serve another friend to whom he is under greater obligations. But to speak only of actions done from the motive of duty, and in direct obedience to principle: it is a misapprehension of the utilitarian mode of thought, to conceive it as implying that people should fix their minds upon so wide a generality as the world, or society at large. The great majority of good actions are intended not for the benefit of the world, but for that of individuals, of which the good of the world is made up; and the thoughts of the most virtuous man need not on these occasions travel beyond the particular persons concerned, except so far as is necessary to assure himself that in benefiting them he is not violating the rights, that is, the legitimate and authorised expectations, of any one else. The multiplication of happiness is, according to the utilitarian ethics, the object of virtue: the occasions on which any person (except one in a thousand) has it in his power to do this on an extended scale, in other words to be a public benefactor, are but exceptional; and on these occasions alone is he called on to consider public utility; in every other case, private utility, the interest or happiness of some few persons, is all he has to attend to. Those alone the influence of whose actions extends to society in general, need concern themselves habitually about so large an object. In the case of abstinences indeed- of things which people forbear to do from moral considerations, though the consequences in the particular case might be beneficial- it would be unworthy of an intelligent agent not to be consciously aware that the action is of a class which, if practised generally, would be generally injurious, and that this is the ground of the obligation to abstain from it. The amount of regard for the public interest implied in this recognition, is no greater than is demanded by every system of morals, for they all enjoin to abstain from whatever is manifestly pernicious to society.

Again, defenders of utility often find themselves called upon to reply to such objections as this- that there is not time, previous to action, for calculating and weighing the effects of any line of conduct on the general happiness. This is exactly as if any one were to say that it is impossible to guide our conduct by Christianity, because there is not time, on every occasion on which anything has to be done, to read through the Old and New Testaments. The answer to the objection is, that there has been ample time, namely, the whole past duration of the human species. During all that time, mankind have been learning by experience the tendencies of actions; on which experience all the prudence, as well as all the morality of life, are dependent. People talk as if the commencement of this course of experience had hitherto been put off, and as if, at the moment when some man feels tempted to meddle with the property or life of another, he had to begin considering for the first time whether murder and theft are injurious to human happiness. Even then I do not think that he would find the question very puzzling; but, at all events, the matter is now done to his hand. It is truly a whimsical supposition that, if mankind were agreed in considering utility to be the test of morality, they would remain without any agreement as to what is useful, and would take no measures for having their notions on the subject taught to the young, and enforced by law and opinion. There is no difficulty in proving any ethical standard whatever to work ill, if we suppose universal idiocy to be conjoined with it; but on any hypothesis short of that, mankind must by this time have acquired positive beliefs as to the effects of some actions on their happiness; and the beliefs which have thus come down are the rules of morality for the multitude, and for the philosopher until he has succeeded in finding better.

That philosophers might easily do this, even now, on many subjects; that the received code of ethics is by no means of divine right; and that mankind have still much to learn as to the effects of actions on the general happiness, I admit, or rather, earnestly maintain. The corollaries from the principle of utility, like the precepts of every practical art, admit of indefinite improvement, and, in a progressive state of the human mind, their improvement is perpetually going on. But to consider the rules of morality as improvable, is one thing; to pass over the intermediate generalisations entirely, and endeavour to test each individual action directly by the first principle, is another. It is a strange notion that the acknowledgment of a first principle is inconsistent with the admission of secondary ones. To inform a traveller respecting the place of his ultimate destination, is not to forbid the use of landmarks and direction-posts on the way. The proposition that happiness is the end and aim of morality, does not mean that no road ought to be laid down to that goal, or that persons going thither should not be advised to take one direction rather than another. Men really ought to leave off talking a kind of nonsense on this subject, which they would neither talk nor listen to on other matters of practical concernment. Nobody argues that the art of navigation is not founded on astronomy, because sailors cannot wait to calculate the Nautical Almanack. Being rational creatures, they go to sea with it ready calculated; and all rational creatures go out upon the sea of life with their minds made up on the common questions of right and wrong, as well as on many of the far more difficult questions of wise and foolish. And this, as long as foresight is a human quality, it is to be presumed they will continue to do. Whatever we adopt as the fundamental principle of morality, we require subordinate principles to apply it by; the impossibility of doing without them, being common to all systems, can afford no argument against any one in particular; but gravely to argue as if no such secondary principles could be had, and as if mankind had remained till now, and always must remain, without drawing any general conclusions from the experience of human life, is as high a pitch, I think, as absurdity has ever reached in philosophical controversy.

The remainder of the stock arguments against utilitarianism mostly consist in laying to its charge the common infirmities of human nature, and the general difficulties which embarrass conscientious persons in shaping their course through life. We are told that a utilitarian will be apt to make his own particular case an exception to moral rules, and, when under temptation, will see a utility in the breach of a rule, greater than he will see in its observance. But is utility the only creed which is able to furnish us with excuses for evil doing, and means of cheating our own conscience? They are afforded in abundance by all doctrines which recognise as a fact in morals the existence of conflicting considerations; which all doctrines do, that have been believed by sane persons. It is not the fault of any creed, but of the complicated nature of human affairs, that rules of conduct cannot be so framed as to require no exceptions, and that hardly any kind of action can safely be laid down as either always obligatory or always condemnable. There is no ethical creed which does not temper the rigidity of its laws, by giving a certain latitude, under the moral responsibility of the agent, for accommodation to peculiarities of circumstances; and under every creed, at the opening thus made, self-deception and dishonest casuistry get in. There exists no moral system under which there do not arise unequivocal cases of conflicting obligation. These are the real difficulties, the knotty points both in the theory of ethics, and in the conscientious guidance of personal conduct. They are overcome practically, with greater or with less success, according to the intellect and virtue of the individual; but it can hardly be pretended that any one will be the less qualified for dealing with them, from possessing an ultimate standard to which conflicting rights and duties can be referred. If utility is the ultimate source of moral obligations, utility may be invoked to decide between them when their demands are incompatible. Though the application of the standard may be difficult, it is better than none at all: while in other systems, the moral laws all claiming independent authority, there is no common umpire entitled to interfere between them; their claims to precedence one over another rest on little better than sophistry, and unless determined, as they generally are, by the unacknowledged influence of considerations of utility, afford a free scope for the action of personal desires and partialities. We must remember that only in these cases of conflict between secondary principles is it requisite that first principles should be appealed to. There is no case of moral obligation in which some secondary principle is not involved; and if only one, there can seldom be any real doubt which one it is, in the mind of any person by whom the principle itself is recognised.

Broadly Nonconsequentialist Views: The Divine Command Moral Theory

At a Michigan campaign event on January 14th, 2008, presidential candidate, Governor Mike Huckabee explained why he wanted to amend the Constitution of the United States in order to outlaw abortion and gay marriage. He said, "I have opponents in this race who do not want to change the Constitution. But I believe it's a lot easier to change the Constitution than it would be to change the word of the living God. And that's what we need to do is amend the Constitution so it's in God's standards rather than trying to change God's standards so it lines up with some contemporary view of how we treat each other and how we treat the family."[1]. Huckabee obviously believes that his religious views tell him what is the right thing to do. He may subscribe to a view called **Divine Command Moral Theory (DCMT).** According to this view, the right thing to do is to follow (obey) the will of God. And Huckabee isn't the only one who might believe this; on the contrary, it seems to be an extremely popular view in America in the 21st century. According to Pew Research Center, almost 50% of Americans say that belief in God is necessary to be a moral person[2], 61% say that children are more likely to become moral adults if they have a religious upbringing, 51% say that the biggest lesson of the 9/11 attacks is that there is too little religion in the world[3], and 25% believe that "The government should take special steps to make our country a Christian country"[4].

---

[1] http://firstread.msnbc.msn.com/archive/2008/01/15/579265.aspx
[2] "News Release: Americans Struggle with Religion's Role at Home and Abroad" at http://pewforum.org/publications/reports/poll2002.pdf. For an interesting contrast to this popular opinion in the U.S., see Gregory Paul's article, "Cross-National Correlations of Quantifiable Societal Health with Popular Religiosity and Secularism in the Prosperous Democracies" in *The Journal of Religion and Society* (Volume 7, 2005), where Paul establishes that, "In general, higher rates of belief in and worship of a creator correlate with higher rates of homicide, juvenile and early adult mortality, STD infection rates, teen pregnancy, and abortion in the prosperous democracies".
[3] News Release: Americans Struggle with Religion's Role at Home and Abroad at http://pewforum.org/publications/reports/poll2002.pdf
[4] "Separation of Church and State," Pew Research Center, 2007-OCT-05, at: http://pewresearch.org/

In the following excerpt from John Arthur's "Does Morality Depend on Religion?", Arthur considers three ways in which some people might think that religion is necessary for morality: some see it as necessary for moral motivation; some see it as necessary for moral guidance; and some see it as necessary in order for objective morality to exist at all. Arthur first defines a moral code as "a tendency to evaluate (perhaps without even expressing it) the behavior of others and to feel guilt at certain actions when we perform them." And he defines religion as "A system of belief in supernatural power(s) that created and perhaps also control nature, along with a tendency to worship and pray to those supernatural forces or beings." Arthur then considers the three ways in which people might think that religion is necessary for morality.

With regard to moral motivation, he points out that there are other motives which might (and actually do) lead us to do the right thing. Although Arthur provides no empirical data to back up his claim that "When it really gets down to it, most of us don't give much of a thought to religion when making moral decisions", this claim does seem to be borne out by casual unscientific surveys we take in our classes.

With regard to using religion for moral guidance, he points out that in order to follow Divine Command Moral Theory (DCMT), we would need to know what the will of God is. In order to know this, we would have to answer three questions which seem to make this a very difficult task. First, we would have to answer the question: **"Which God should we follow?"** There are perhaps thousands of Gods that have been described and worshipped by human societies over the centuries of recorded history. Which one is the true God of the universe? Note that this wouldn't be a problem if all the Gods told us to do the same thing. But they don't: some command that we not eat certain kinds of meat; some command that we pray five times every day; and some demand human sacrifices to the Sun. Of all the Gods that have been described, which one is the God that we should follow? In answering this question, it won't do to simply follow the God that my parents followed. I mean my parents are perfectly nice people, but neither one of them has any special insight into which is the true God of the universe. Hence, it seems that, until we can find a principled and reasonable way to figure out which is the God that DCMT instructs us to follow, it's useless to us as a moral guide.

But suppose that we could (somehow!) solve this "Which God?" problem. The second problem for DCMT to overcome might be summed up in the question, **"Which expression of His will?"** Even people who agree that (for example) Jesus is the true God of the universe disagree about which set of signs we ought to take as the true expression of His will. Some say that the Holy Bible is enough; others say that certain apocryphal writings which were excluded from the Bible ought to have been included; others say that the Holy Bible plus the Book of Mormon is the true expression of God's will; still others think that natural signs (hurricanes, rainbows, etc.) are part of the communication of God's will. Here, again, it seems that we need a principled and reasonable method to determine which set of signs we ought to take as the true expression of God's will.

But suppose that we could (somehow!) solve that problem. The third question that Arthur raises might be summarized as **"Which interpretation?"** Even people who agree that (again, for example) Jesus is the true God and who also agree that (for example) the Holy Bible together with the Book of Mormon are the veridical signs of God's will may still disagree about how to interpret those signs. The Bible tells us, "Thou shalt not kill." But what does it mean? Does it mean that we shouldn't kill people? What about other animals? Insects? Microbes? If it is referring to killing people, does it mean that we can't kill even in self-defense? What about during a time of war? What about killing as a form of capital punishment? The point is that even people who agree about which is the true God and which set of signs is the true expression of His will still have serious disagreements about how to interpret those signs. When we put these three questions together, it begins to look as if DCMT does not provide the simple moral guidance that we thought it might give us. Indeed, Arthur suggests that we would probably be better off trying to figure out right and wrong on our own, rather than trying to figure out how to answer all of these metaphysical questions in order to get any reliable moral guidance.

Arthur also addresses the view that religion is needed in order for there to be any objective morality at all. According to this view, if there is a moral Law, then there must be a moral Legislator, the originator of the moral Law, and this moral legislator is God. In response to this view, Arthur raises what might be called **The Problem of the Euthyphro**. This is a problem which comes from the Platonic dialogue, *Euthyphro*, in which Socrates and Euthyphro are discussing piety (or holiness). Since Euthyphro is a sort of priest, Socrates first asks him if he knows what piety is. Euthyphro responds that he does, and Socrates asks him for a definition of piety. To the question "What is piety?", Euthyphro offers various answers, but finally settles on saying that "piety is what all the gods love." To this, Socrates asks Euthyphro whether the gods love pious things because they are pious, or whether the pious things are pious because the gods love them. Arthur suggests that a similar question may be raised against those who see God as a moral legislator. With regard to the things that God commands, are they commanded by God because they are right, or are they right because he commands them? If these things are commanded by God because they are (independently) right, then it would seem that rightness exists independently of the will of God and that DCMT is leading us in the wrong direction by pointing us to God's will for moral guidance. On this view, God seems to become an unnecessary middleman between us and morality. If, on the other hand, the things that are right are right just because God commands them, then it looks as if God's commands must be absolutely arbitrary and that God could change his mind and make murder and rape right if he chooses to do so. Hence, either way, Arthur suggests that DCMT has some serious questions to answer.

FROM "DOES MORALITY DEPEND ON RELIGION?" BY JOHN ARTHUR [1]

The issue which I address in this paper is the nature of the connection, if any, between morality and religion. I will argue that although there are a variety of ways the two can be connected, in fact religion is not necessary for morality, either logically or psychologically. First, however, it will be necessary to say something about the subjects: just what are we referring to when we speak of morality and of religion?

A useful way to approach the first question—the nature of morality—is to ask what it would mean for a society to exist without a moral code. What would such a society look like? How would people think? And behave? The most obvious thing to say is that its members would never feel any moral responsibilities or any guilt. Words like duty, rights, fairness, and justice would never be used, except in the legal sense. Feelings such as that I ought to remember my parents' anniversary, that he has a moral responsibility to help care for his children after the divorce, that she has a right to equal pay for equal work, and that discrimination on the basis of race is unfair would be absent in such a society. In short, people would have no tendency to evaluate or criticize the behavior of others, nor to feel remorse about their own behavior. Children would not be taught to be ashamed when they steal or hurt others, nor would they be allowed to complain when others treat them badly.

Such a society lacks a moral code. What, then, of religion? Is it possible that a society such as the one I have described would have religious beliefs? It seems clear that it is possible. Suppose every day these same people file into their place of worship to pay homage to God (they may believe in many gods or in one all-powerful creator of heaven and earth). Often they can be heard praying to God for help in dealing with their problems and thanking Him for their good fortune. Whenever a disaster befalls them, the people assume that God is angry with them; when things go well they believe He is pleased. Frequently they give sacrifices to God, usually in the form of money spent to build beautiful temples and churches.

---

[1] From *Morality and Moral Controversies*, 2nd edition, John Arthur, ed. (Prentice-Hall, Inc., 1986), pp. 10-15. Copyright John Arthur 1986, reprinted by permission of Amy Shapiro, ashapiro@hhk.com.

To have a moral code, then, is to tend to evaluate (perhaps without even expressing it) the behavior of others and to feel guilt at certain actions when we perform them. Religion, on the other hand, involves beliefs in supernatural power(s) that created and perhaps also control nature, along with the tendency to worship and pray to those supernatural forces or beings. The two—religion and morality—are thus very different. One involves our attitudes toward various forms of behavior (lying and killing, for example), typically expressed using the notions of rules, rights, and obligations. The other, religion, typically involves a different set of activities (prayer, worship) together with beliefs about the supernatural.

We come, then, to the central question: What is the connection, if any, between a society's moral code and its religious beliefs? Many people have felt that there must be a link of some sort between religious beliefs and morality. But is that so? What sort of connection might there be? In what follows I distinguish various ways in which one might claim that religion is necessary for a moral code to function in society. I argue, however, that such connections are not necessary, and indeed that often religion is detrimental to society's attempt to encourage moral conduct among its members.

One possible role which religion might play in morality relates to motives people have. Can people be expected to behave in any sort of decent way towards one another without religious faith? Religion, it is often said, is necessary so that people will DO right. Why might somebody think that? Often, we know, doing what is right has costs: you don't cheat on the test, so you flunk the course; you return the lost billfold, so you don't get the contents. Religion can provide motivation to do the right thing. God rewards those who follow His commands by providing for them a place in heaven and by insuring that they prosper and are happy on earth. He also punishes with damnation those who disobey. Other people emphasize less selfish ways in which religious motives may encourage people to act rightly. God is the creator of the universe and has ordained that His plan should be followed. How better to live one's life than to participate in this divinely ordained plan? Only by living a moral life, it is said, can people live in harmony with the larger, divinely created order.

But how are we to assess the relative strength of these various motives for acting morally, some of which are religious, others not? How important is the fear of hell or the desire to live as God wishes in motivating people? Think about the last time you were tempted to do something you knew to be wrong. Surely your decision not to do so (if that was your decision) was made for a variety of reasons: "What if I get caught? What if somebody sees me—what will he or she think? How will I feel afterwards? Will I regret it?" Or maybe the thought of cheating just doesn't occur to you. You were raised to be an honest person, and that's what you want to be—period. There are thus many motives for doing the right thing which have nothing whatsoever to do with religion. Most of us in fact do worry about getting caught, about being blamed and looked down on by others. We also may do what is right just for that reason, because it's our duty, or because we don't want to hurt others. So to say that we need religion to act morally is mistaken; indeed it seems to me that most of us, when it really gets down to it, don't give much of a thought to religion when making moral decisions. All those other reasons are the ones which we tend to consider, or else we just don't consider cheating and stealing at all. So far, then, there seems to be no reason to suppose that people can't be moral yet irreligious at the same time.

Another oft-heard argument that religion is necessary for people to do right questions whether people would know how to do the right thing without the guidance of religion. In other words, however much people may want to do the right thing, it is only with the help of God that true moral understanding can be achieved. People's own intellect is simply inadequate to this task; we must consult revelation for help.

Again, however, this argument fails. Just consider what we would need to know in order for religion to provide moral guidance. First we must be sure that there is a God. And then there's the question of which of the many religions is true. How can anybody be sure his or her religion is the right one? After all, if you had been born in China or India or Iran your religious views would almost certainly not have been the ones you now hold. And even if we can somehow convince ourselves that the Judeo-Christian God is the real one, we still need to find out just what it is He wants us to do. Revelation comes in at least two forms, according to theists, and not even Christians agree which form is real. Some hold that God tells us what He wants by providing us with His words: the Ten Commandments are an example. Many even believe, as Billy Graham once said, that the entire Bible was written by God using 39 secretaries. Others doubt that every word of the Bible is literally true, believing instead that it is merely an historical account of the events in history whereby God revealed Himself. So on this view revelation is not understood as statements made by God but, instead as His intervening into historical events, such as leading His people from Egypt, testing Job, and sending His son as an example of the ideal life. But if we are to use revelation as a guide we must know what is to count as revelation—words given us by God, events, or both? Supposing that we could somehow solve all those puzzles, the problems of relying on revelation are still not over. Even if we can agree on who God is and on how and when He reveals Himself we still must interpret that revelation. Some feel that the Bible justifies various forms of killing, including war and capital punishment, on the basis of such statements as "An eye for an eye." Others, emphasizing such sayings as "Judge not lest ye be judged" and "Thou shalt not kill," believe the Bible demands absolute pacifism. How are we to know which interpretation is correct?

Far from providing a short-cut to moral understanding, looking to revelation for guidance just creates more questions and problems. It is much simpler to address problems such as abortion, capital punishment, and war directly than to seek answers in revelation. In fact, not only is religion unnecessary to provide moral understanding, it is actually a hindrance. (My own hunch is that often those who are most likely to appeal to Scripture as justification for their moral beliefs are really just rationalizing positions they already believe.)

Far from religion being necessary for people to do the right thing, it often gets in the way. People do not need the motivation of religion; they for the most part are not motivated by religion as much as by other factors, and religion is of no help in discovering what our moral obligations are. But others give a different reason for claiming morality depends on religion. They think religion, and especially God, is necessary for morality because without God there could BE no right or wrong. The idea was expressed by Bishop R. C. Mortimer: "God made us and all the world. Because of that He has an absolute claim on our obedience.... From [this] it follows that a thing is not right simply because we think it is.... It is right because God commands it."[2]

What Mortimer has in mind can best be seen by comparing moral rules with legal ones. Legal statutes' we know, are created by legislatures. So if there had been no law passed requiring that people limit the speed they travel then there would be no such legal obligation. Without the commands of the legislature statutes simply would not exist. The view defended by Mortimer, often called the divine command theory, is that God has the same relation to moral law as the legislature does to statutes. Without God's commands there would be no moral rules.

Another tenet of the divine command theory, besides the belief that God is the author of morality, is that only the divine command theory is able to explain the objective difference between right and wrong. This

---

[2] R. C. Mortimer, *Christian Ethics* (London: Hutchinson's University Library, 1950), pp. 7-8.

point was forcefully argued by F. C. Copleston in a 1948 British Broadcasting Corporation radio debate with Bertrand Russell.

RUSSELL. But aren't you now saying in effect "I mean by God whatever is good or the sum total of what is good—the system of what is good, and, therefore, when a young man loves anything that is good he is loving God." Is that what you're saying, because if so, it wants a bit of arguing.

COPLESTON I don't say, of course, that God is the sum total or system of what is good . . . but I do think that all goodness reflects God in some way and proceeds from Him, so that in a sense the man who loves what is truly good, loves God even if he doesn't advert to God But still I agree that the validity of such an interpretation of man's conduct depends on the recognition of God's existence, obviously.... Let's take a look at the Commandant of the [Nazi] concentration camp at Belsen. That appears to you as undesirable and evil and to me too. To Adolph Hitler we suppose it appeared as something good and desirable. I suppose you'd have to admit that for Hitler it was good and for you it is evil.

RUSSELL. No, I shouldn't go so far as that. I mean. I think people can make mistakes in that as they can in other things. If you have jaundice you see things yellow that are not yellow. You're making a mistake.

COPLESTON. Yes, one can make mistakes, but can you make a mistake if it's simply a question of reference to a feeling or emotion? Surely Hitler would be the only possible judge of what appealed to his emotions.

RUSSELL. ... you can say various things about that; among others, that if that sort of thing makes that sort of appeal to Hitler's emotions, then Hitler makes quite a different appeal to my emotions.

COPLESTON. Granted. But there's no objective criterion outside feeling then for condemning the conduct of the Commandant of Belsen, in your view.... The human being's idea of the content of the moral law depends certainly to a large extent on education and environment, and a man has to use his reason in assessing the validity of the actual moral ideas of his social group. But the possibility of criticizing the accepted moral code presupposes that there is an objective standard, that there is an ideal moral order, which imposes itself. . . . It implies the existence of a real foundation of God.[3]

God, according to Copleston, is able to provide the basis for the distinction, which we all know to exist, between right and wrong. Without that objective basis for defining human obligation we would have no real reason for condemning the behavior of anybody, even Nazis. Morality would be little more than an expression of personal feeling.

---

[3] This debate was broadcast on the Third Program of the British Broadcasting Corporation in 1948.

Before assessing the divine command theory, let's first consider this last point. Is it really true that only the commands of God can provide an objective basis for moral judgments? Certainly many philosophers . . . have felt that morality rests on its own, perfectly sound footing; to prejudge those efforts or others which may be made in the future as unsuccessful seems mistaken. And, second, if it were true that there is no nonreligious basis for claiming moral objectivity, then perhaps that means there simply is no such basis. Why suppose that there must be such a foundation?

What of the divine command theory itself? Is it reasonable, even though we need not do so, to equate something's being right with its being commanded by God? Certainly the expressions "is commanded by God" and "is morally required" do not mean the same thing; atheists and agnostics use moral words without understanding them to make any reference to God. And while it is of course true that God (or any other moral being for that matter) would tend to want others to do the right thing, this hardly shows that being right and being commanded by God are the same thing. Parents want their children to do the right thing, too, but that doesn't mean they, or anybody else, can make a thing right just by commanding it!

I think that, in fact, theists themselves if they thought about it would reject the divine command theory. One reason is because of what it implies. Suppose we grant (just for the sake of argument) that the divine command theory is correct. Notice what we have now said: Actions are right just because they are commanded by God. And the same, of course, can be said about those deeds which we believe are wrong. If God hadn't commanded us not to do them, they would not be wrong. (Recall the comparison made with the commands of the legislature, which would not be law except for the legislature having passed a statute.)

But now notice this. Since God is all-powerful, and since right is determined solely by His commands, is it not possible that He might change the rules and make what we now think of as wrong into right? It would seem that according to the divine command theory it is possible that tomorrow God will decree that virtues such as kindness and courage have become vices while actions which show cruelty and cowardice are the right actions. Rather than it being right for people to help each other out and prevent innocent people from suffering unnecessarily, it would be right to create as much pain among innocent children as we possibly can! To adopt the divine command theory commits its advocate to the seemingly absurd position that even the greatest atrocities might be not only acceptable but morally required if God were to command them.

Plato made a similar point in the dialogue Euthyphro. Socrates is asking Euthyphro what it is that makes the virtue of holiness a virtue, just as we have been asking what makes kindness and courage virtues. Euthyphro has suggested that holiness is just whatever all the gods love.

SOCRATES. Well, then, Euthyphro, what do we say about holiness? Is it not loved by all the gods, according to your definition?
EUTHYPHRO. Yes.
SOCRATES. Because it is holy, or for some other reason?
EUTHYPHRO. No, because it is holy.
SOCRATES. Then it is loved by the gods because it is holy: it is not holy because it is loved by them?
EUTHYPHRO. It seems so.
SOCRATES.... Then holiness is not what is pleasing to the gods, and what is pleasing to the gods is not holy as you say, Euthyphro. They are different things.
EUTHYPHRO. And why, Socrates?
SOCRATES. Because we are agreed that the gods love holiness because it is holy: and that it is not holy because they love it.[4]

Having claimed that virtues are what is loved by the gods why does Euthyphro so readily agree that the gods love holiness because it's holy? One possibility is that he is assuming whenever the gods love something they do so with good reason, not just arbitrarily. If something is pleasing to gods, there must be a reason. To deny this and say that it is simply the gods' love which makes holiness a virtue would mean that the gods have no basis for their opinions, that they are arbitrary. Or to put it another way, if we say that it is simply God's loving something that makes it right, then what sense does it make to say God wants us to do right? All that could mean is that God wants us to do what He wants us to do. He would have no reason for wanting it. Similarly "God is good" would mean little more than "God does what He pleases." Religious people who find this an unacceptable consequence will reject the divine command theory.

But doesn't this now raise another problem? If God approves kindness because it is a virtue, then it seems that God discovers morality rather than inventing it. And haven't we then suggested a limitation on God's power, since He now, being a good God, must love kindness and command us not to be cruel? What is left of God's omnipotence?

But why should such a limitation on God be unacceptable for a theist? Because there is nothing God cannot do? But is it true to say that God can

---

[4] Plato, Euthyphro, tr. H. N. Fowler (Cambridge, Mass.: Harvard University Press, 1947).

do absolutely anything? Can He, for example, destroy Himself? Can God make a rock so heavy that He cannot lift it? Or create a universe which was never created by Him? Many have thought that God's inability to do these sorts of things does not constitute a genuine limitation on His power because these are things which cannot logically be done. Thomas Aquinas, for example, wrote that, "whatever implies contradiction does not come within the scope of divine omnipotence, because it cannot have the aspect of possibility. Hence it is more appropriate to say that such things cannot be done than that God cannot do them."[5] Many theists reject the view that there is nothing which God cannot do.

But how, then, ought we to understand God's relationship to morality if we reject the divine command theory? Can religious people consistently maintain their faith in God the Creator and yet deny that what is right is right because He commands it? I think the answer to this is "yes." First, note that there is still a sense in which God could change morality (assuming, of course, there is a God). Whatever moral code we decide is best (most justified), that choice will in part depend on such factors as how we reason, what we desire and need, and the circumstances in which we find ourselves. Presumably, however, God could have constructed us or our environment very differently, so that we didn't care about freedom, weren't curious about nature, and weren't influenced by other's suffering. Or perhaps outr natural environment could be altered so that it is less hostile to our needs and desires. If He had created either nature or us that way, then it seems likely that the most justified moral code might be different in important ways from the one it is now rational for us to support. In that sense, then, morality depends on God whether or not one supports the divine command theory.

In fact, it seems to me that it makes little difference for ethical questions whether a person is religious. The atheist will treat human nature simply as a given, a fact of nature, while the theist may regard it as the product of divine intention. But in any case the right thing to do is to follow the best moral code, the one that is most justified. Instead of relying on revelation to discover morality, religious and nonreligious people alike can inquire into which system is best.

In sum, I have argued first that religion is neither necessary nor useful in providing moral motivation or guidance. My objections to the claim that without God there would be no morality are somewhat more complex. First, it is wrong to say that only if God's will is at its base can morality be objective. The idea of the best moral code—the one fully rational persons

---

[5] Thomas Aquinas, Summa Theologica, Part 1, Q. 25, Art. 3.

would support—may prove to provide sound means to evaluate one's own code as well as those of other societies. Furthermore, the divine command theory should not be accepted even by those who are religious. This is because it implies what clearly seems absurd, namely that God might tomorrow change the moral rules and make performing the most extreme acts of cruelty an obligation we all should meet. And, finally, I discussed how the theist and atheist might hope to find common ground about the sorts of moral rules to teach our children and how we should evaluate each other's behavior. Far from helping resolve moral disputes, religion does little more than sow confusion. Morality does not need religion and religion does not need morality.

KANTIAN ETHICS

Often when people think about ethics, they think about what cannot possibly be justified. Torture, for instance, is completely abhorrent to some people. It doesn't matter to them if great happiness could be gained or great suffering alleviated by torturing another human being; it simply should not be done. This kind of non-consequentialist ethical thinking finds its most systematic defense in the system detailed by Immanuel Kant starting in his *Groundwork for the Metaphysics of Morals*. Kantian ethical theories are **deontological**, concentrating on the concepts of duty and obligation as opposed to the consequences of an action (though modern forms of Kantian ethics often make some room for consequences alongside duty and obligation).

In the *Groundwork*, Kant defends the view that what is truly valuable in human life is a **good will**. The moral worth of an action depends not on its consequences but on whether the action arises from the **motive of duty**, which shows that the action comes from a good will. Kant contrasts the motive of duty with what he calls "inclination", or simple desire. One acts from **inclination** when one helps someone across the street solely because it makes one happy, for instance, but that does not yet give one's action moral worth. Kant believed that unlike acting from inclinations, duty arose from the faculty of practical reason, which moved the will by invoking principles rather than simple desire. Thus, for Kant the principle behind the action—Kant calls this a "maxim"—is the source of morality.

It is not enough, though, to say that moral worth lies in principles rather than consequences. Kant must also say what kind of principle behind an act gives that act moral worth. Not just any principle can count as the motive of duty. Kant believed that the only principle sufficiently compelling to serve as the source of all moral action is the so-called **Categorical Imperative**. Two main formulations of the Categorical Imperative are worth covering here:

The Universal Law Formulation: Act only according to that maxim whereby you can at the same time will that should become a universal law. (G 421)

The Formulation of Humanity: Act in such a way that you treat humanity, whether in your own person or in the person of another, always at the same time as an end and never simply as a means. (G 429)

Kant believed these were essentially formulations of the same command, but it can be difficult to see why he believed that. The first formulation expresses the idea that the principle behind one's action should be a principle that could serve as an actual law of nature. This was important to Kant because laws of nature were universal—binding on everyone regardless of individual circumstances—and the moral laws we give ourselves resemble natural laws in their universality. Thus, the principles behind our actions should be principles that everyone could have behind their own actions. They should be what ethicists call **universalizable**.

Many people find Kant's second formulation more intuitive. What makes the will so valuable for Kant is its ability to set ends for itself. Robbing it of this ability, then, whether the will is yours or another's, will be forsaking something of ultimate value. This is supposed to amount to the same set of morally acceptable actions as the first formulation. Ultimately treating someone else as a mere means to your own ends is trying to force a principle of action that he or she could not reasonably accept. As illustrated below, making a false promise seems to be a clear example of a case where a borrower completely disregards whatever purpose the lender has for his or her money, thus treating the lender as a mere means. Considering everyone as an end rather than a mere means is considering what would happen if one's maxim were to become a universal law.

Kant believed that the categorical imperative gave us two kinds of duties. If an action's maxim could not be universalized at all, Kant believed we were never allowed to act on it. He called duties like these **perfect duties**. Some maxims may be universalizable, on the other hand, but still unable to be *willed* to be universal laws. These duties he called **imperfect duties**. We are still required to act on imperfect duties, but not with the kind of rigidity that perfect duties require.

Kant's critics point out that taking a hard line like this on morality would lead to extremely undesirable states of affairs, like the consequences of **rule worship** described above. If lying to someone prevents them from murdering a friend or family member and has no other bad consequences, it can be difficult to appreciate Kant's point. Kant himself considered this objection in a short piece called *On a Supposed Right to Lie from Philanthropic Concerns* and famously holds tight to the idea that one should not lie even to thwart someone planning a murder. Most modern Kantians do not consider a hard line like this to be required by Kant's system.

Christine Korsgaard, for instance, argues that a Kantian could adopt two sets of rules: one for the non-ideal world and one for the ideal world. In the non-ideal world, she thinks, we do not commit a moral wrong by lying to the murderer. In the ideal world, though, we would not be permitted to lie.

Others have raised concerns that Kant's ethical system places too much emphasis on the dictates of reason as opposed to feelings and emotions, leading to the problem of **inappropriate motives**. Recall the example above about helping someone to cross the street because it makes one happy. According to Kant, the good nature of the action does not give the action moral worth. It is a choice with moral worth only if it comes from the motive of duty—if the motive behind it is that one *must* help. This foundational part of Kant's theory is in tension with common-sense views of morality that see positive emotions as contributing to the moral worth of an action. Visiting a sick family member or friend at a hospital because one figures it is one's duty seems somehow worse than doing it out of love for the person. Since familial bonds are frequently based on complicated sets of emotion, this can make Kantian perspectives on ethics difficult to integrate into discussions of ethics and the family.

In Kant's defense, he does not say that actions done from inclination are worthless, just that they lack *moral* worth. Kant associates moral worth with the idea of moral obligation and whether or not one agrees with this association, it would be even stranger to argue that one is morally obligated to have particular feelings when acting. So visiting someone out of a sense of duty has moral worth whether or not one likes it. If it makes one feel good, so much the better.

In the following excerpts, Kant lays out the two formulations of the categorical imperative and applies them to particular situations:

FROM *FUNDAMENTAL PRINCIPLES OF THE METAPHYSICS OF MORALS* BY IMMANUEL KANT[1]

Everything in nature works according to laws. Rational beings alone have the faculty of acting according to the conception of laws, that is according to principles, i.e., have a will. Since the deduction of actions from principles requires reason, the will is nothing but practical reason. If reason infallibly determines the will, then the actions of such a being which are recognised as objectively necessary are subjectively necessary also, i.e., the will is a faculty to choose that only which reason independent of inclination recognises as practically necessary, i.e., as good. But if reason of itself does not sufficiently determine the will, if the latter is subject also to subjective conditions (particular impulses) which do not always coincide with the objective conditions; in a word, if the will does not in itself completely accord with reason (which is actually the case with men), then the actions which objectively are recognised as necessary are subjectively contingent, and the determination of such a will according to objective laws is obligation, that is to say, the relation of the objective laws to a will that is not thoroughly good is conceived as the determination of the will of a rational being by principles of reason, but which the will from its nature does not of necessity follow.

The conception of an objective principle, in so far as it is obligatory for a will, is called a command (of reason), and the formula of the command is called an imperative.

All imperatives are expressed by the word ought [or shall], and thereby indicate the relation of an objective law of reason to a will, which from its subjective constitution is not necessarily determined by it (an obligation). They say that something would be good to do or to forbear, but they say it to a will which does not always do a thing because it is conceived to be good to do it. That is practically good, however, which determines the will by means of the conceptions of reason, and consequently not from subjective causes, but objectively, that is on principles which are valid for every rational being as such. It is distinguished from the pleasant, as that which influences the will only by means of sensation from merely

---

[1] Excerpted from http://www.gutenberg.org/ebooks/5682 . Translated by Thomas Kingsmill Abbott (1829-1913).

subjective causes, valid only for the sense of this or that one, and not as a principle of reason, which holds for every one.

A perfectly good will would therefore be equally subject to objective laws (viz., laws of good), but could not be conceived as obliged thereby to act lawfully, because of itself from its subjective constitution it can only be determined by the conception of good. Therefore no imperatives hold for the Divine will, or in general for a holy will; ought is here out of place, because the volition is already of itself necessarily in unison with the law. Therefore imperatives are only formulae to express the relation of objective laws of all volition to the subjective imperfection of the will of this or that rational being, e.g., the human will.

Now all imperatives command either hypothetically or categorically. The former represent the practical necessity of a possible action as means to something else that is willed (or at least which one might possibly will). The categorical imperative would be that which represented an action as necessary of itself without reference to another end, i.e., as objectively necessary.

Since every practical law represents a possible action as good and, on this account, for a subject who is practically determinable by reason, necessary, all imperatives are formulae determining an action which is necessary according to the principle of a will good in some respects. If now the action is good only as a means to something else, then the imperative is hypothetical; if it is conceived as good in itself and consequently as being necessarily the principle of a will which of itself conforms to reason, then it is categorical.

Thus the imperative declares what action possible by me would be good and presents the practical rule in relation to a will which does not forthwith perform an action simply because it is good, whether because the subject does not always know that it is good, or because, even if it know this, yet its maxims might be opposed to the objective principles of practical reason.

Accordingly the hypothetical imperative only says that the action is good for some purpose, possible or actual. In the first case it is a problematical, in the second an assertorial practical principle. The categorical imperative which declares an action to be objectively necessary in itself without reference to any purpose, i.e., without any other end, is valid as an apodeictic (practical) principle.

Whatever is possible only by the power of some rational being may also be conceived as a possible purpose of some will; and therefore the principles of action as regards the means necessary to attain some possible purpose are in fact infinitely numerous. All sciences have a practical part, consisting of problems expressing that some end is possible for us and of imperatives directing how it may be attained. These may, therefore, be called in general imperatives of skill. Here there is no question whether the end is rational and good, but only what one must do in order to attain it. The precepts for the physician to make his patient thoroughly healthy, and for a poisoner to ensure certain death, are of equal value in this respect, that each serves to effect its purpose perfectly. Since in early youth it cannot be known what ends are likely to occur to us in the course of life, parents seek to have their children taught a great many things, and provide for their skill in the use of means for all sorts of arbitrary ends, of none of which can they determine whether it may not perhaps hereafter be an object to their pupil, but which it is at all events possible that he might aim at; and this anxiety is so great that they commonly neglect to form and correct their judgment on the value of the things which may be chosen as ends.

There is one end, however, which may be assumed to be actually such to all rational beings (so far as imperatives apply to them, viz., as dependent beings), and, therefore, one purpose which they not merely may have, but which we may with certainty assume that they all actually have by a natural necessity, and this is happiness. The hypothetical imperative which expresses the practical necessity of an action as means to the advancement of happiness is assertorial. We are not to present it as necessary for an uncertain and merely possible purpose, but for a purpose which we may presuppose with certainty and a priori in every man, because it belongs to his being. Now skill in the choice of means to his own greatest well-being may be called prudence, in the narrowest sense. And thus the imperative which refers to the choice of means to one's own happiness, i.e., the precept of prudence, is still always hypothetical; the action is not commanded absolutely, but only as means to another purpose.

Finally, there is an imperative which commands a certain conduct immediately, without having as its condition any other purpose to be attained by it. This imperative is categorical. It concerns not the matter of the action, or its intended result, but its form and the principle of which it is itself a result; and what is essentially good in it consists in the mental disposition, let the consequence be what it may. This imperative may be called that of morality.

There is a marked distinction also between the volitions on these three sorts of principles in the dissimilarity of the obligation of the will. In order to mark this difference more clearly, I think they would be most suitably named in their order if we said they are either rules of skill, or counsels of prudence, or commands (laws) of morality. For it is law only that involves the conception of an unconditional and objective necessity, which is consequently universally valid; and commands are laws which must be obeyed, that is, must be followed, even in opposition to inclination. Counsels, indeed, involve necessity, but one which can only hold under a contingent subjective condition, viz., they depend on whether this or that man reckons this or that as part of his happiness; the categorical imperative, on the contrary, is not limited by any condition, and as being absolutely, although practically, necessary, may be quite properly called a command. We might also call the first kind of imperatives technical (belonging to art), the second pragmatic (to welfare), the third moral (belonging to free conduct generally, that is, to morals).

Now arises the question, how are all these imperatives possible? This question does not seek to know how we can conceive the accomplishment of the action which the imperative ordains, but merely how we can conceive the obligation of the will which the imperative expresses. No special explanation is needed to show how an imperative of skill is possible. Whoever wills the end, wills also (so far as reason decides his conduct) the means in his power which are indispensably necessary thereto. This proposition is, as regards the volition, analytical; for, in willing an object as my effect, there is already thought the causality of myself as an acting cause, that is to say, the use of the means; and the imperative educes from the conception of volition of an end the conception of actions necessary to this end. Synthetical propositions must no doubt be employed in defining the means to a proposed end; but they do not concern the principle, the act of the will, but the object and its realization. E.g., that in order to bisect a line on an unerring principle I must draw from its extremities two intersecting arcs; this no doubt is taught by mathematics only in synthetical propositions; but if I know that it is only by this process that the intended operation can be performed, then to say that, if I fully will the operation, I also will the action required for it, is an analytical proposition; for it is one and the same thing to conceive something as an effect which I can produce in a certain way, and to conceive myself as acting in this way.

If it were only equally easy to give a definite conception of happiness, the imperatives of prudence would correspond exactly with those of skill, and would likewise be analytical. For in this case as in that, it could be said: "Whoever wills the end, wills also (according to the dictate of reason necessarily) the indispensable means thereto which are in his power." But, unfortunately, the notion of happiness is so indefinite that although every man wishes to attain it, yet he never can say definitely and consistently what it is that he really wishes and wills. The reason of this is that all the

elements which belong to the notion of happiness are altogether empirical,
i.e., they must be borrowed from experience, and nevertheless the idea of
happiness requires an absolute whole, a maximum of welfare in my
present and all future circumstances. Now it is impossible that the most
clear-sighted and at the same time most powerful being (supposed finite)
should frame to himself a definite conception of what he really wills in
this. Does he will riches, how much anxiety, envy, and snares might he not
thereby draw upon his shoulders? Does he will knowledge and
discernment, perhaps it might prove to be only an eye so much the sharper
to show him so much the more fearfully the evils that are now concealed
from him, and that cannot be avoided, or to impose more wants on his
desires, which already give him concern enough. Would he have long life?
who guarantees to him that it would not be a long misery? would he at
least have health? how often has uneasiness of the body restrained from
excesses into which perfect health would have allowed one to fall? and so
on. In short, he is unable, on any principle, to determine with certainty
what would make him truly happy; because to do so he would need to be
omniscient. We cannot therefore act on any definite principles to secure
happiness, but only on empirical counsels, e.g. of regimen, frugality,
courtesy, reserve, etc., which experience teaches do, on the average, most
promote well-being. Hence it follows that the imperatives of prudence do
not, strictly speaking, command at all, that is, they cannot present actions
objectively as practically necessary; that they are rather to be regarded as
counsels (consilia) than precepts of reason, that the problem to determine
certainly and universally what action would promote the happiness of a
rational being is completely insoluble, and consequently no imperative
respecting it is possible which should, in the strict sense, command to do
what makes happy; because happiness is not an ideal of reason but of
imagination, resting solely on empirical grounds, and it is vain to expect
that these should define an action by which one could attain the totality of
a series of consequences which is really endless.

   When I conceive a hypothetical imperative, in general I do not know
beforehand what it will contain until I am given the condition. But when I
conceive a categorical imperative, I know at once what it contains. For as
the imperative contains besides the law only the necessity that the
maxims[2] shall conform to this law, while the law contains no conditions

---

[2] A maxim is a subjective principle of action, and must be distinguished from the
objective principle, namely, practical law. The former contains the practical rule
set by reason according to the conditions of the subject (often its ignorance or its
inclinations), so that it is the principle on which the subject acts; but the law is the

restricting it, there remains nothing but the general statement that the maxim of the action should conform to a universal law, and it is this conformity alone that the imperative properly represents as necessary.

There is therefore but one categorical imperative, namely, this: Act only on that maxim whereby thou canst at the same time will that it should become a universal law.

Now if all imperatives of duty can be deduced from this one imperative as from their principle, then, although it should remain undecided what is called duty is not merely a vain notion, yet at least we shall be able to show what we understand by it and what this notion means.

Since the universality of the law according to which effects are produced constitutes what is properly called nature in the most general sense (as to form), that is the existence of things so far as it is determined by general laws, the imperative of duty may be expressed thus: Act as if the maxim of thy action were to become by thy will a universal law of nature.

We will now enumerate a few duties, adopting the usual division of them into duties to ourselves and ourselves and to others, and into perfect and imperfect duties.[3]

1. A man reduced to despair by a series of misfortunes feels wearied of life, but is still so far in possession of his reason that he can ask himself whether it would not be contrary to his duty to himself to take his own life. Now he inquires whether the maxim of his action could become a universal law of nature. His maxim is: "From self-love I adopt it as a principle to shorten my life when its longer duration is likely to bring more evil than satisfaction." It is asked then simply whether this principle founded on self-love can become a universal law of nature. Now we see at once that a system of nature of which it should be a law to destroy life by means of the very feeling whose special nature it is to impel to the improvement of life would contradict itself and, therefore, could not exist

---

objective principle valid for every rational being, and is the principle on which it ought to act that is an imperative.

[3] It must be noted here that I reserve the division of duties for a future metaphysic of morals; so that I give it here only as an arbitrary one (in order to arrange my examples). For the rest, I understand by a perfect duty one that admits no exception in favour of inclination and then I have not merely external but also internal perfect duties. This is contrary to the use of the word adopted in the schools; but I do not intend to justify there, as it is all one for my purpose whether it is admitted or not.

as a system of nature; hence that maxim cannot possibly exist as a universal law of nature and, consequently, would be wholly inconsistent with the supreme principle of all duty.

2. Another finds himself forced by necessity to borrow money. He knows that he will not be able to repay it, but sees also that nothing will be lent to him unless he promises stoutly to repay it in a definite time. He desires to make this promise, but he has still so much conscience as to ask himself: "Is it not unlawful and inconsistent with duty to get out of a difficulty in this way?" Suppose however that he resolves to do so: then the maxim of his action would be expressed thus: "When I think myself in want of money, I will borrow money and promise to repay it, although I know that I never can do so." Now this principle of self-love or of one's own advantage may perhaps be consistent with my whole future welfare; but the question now is, "Is it right?" I change then the suggestion of self-love into a universal law, and state the question thus: "How would it be if my maxim were a universal law?" Then I see at once that it could never hold as a universal law of nature, but would necessarily contradict itself. For supposing it to be a universal law that everyone when he thinks himself in a difficulty should be able to promise whatever he pleases, with the purpose of not keeping his promise, the promise itself would become impossible, as well as the end that one might have in view in it, since no one would consider that anything was promised to him, but would ridicule all such statements as vain pretences.

3. A third finds in himself a talent which with the help of some culture might make him a useful man in many respects. But he finds himself in comfortable circumstances and prefers to indulge in pleasure rather than to take pains in enlarging and improving his happy natural capacities. He asks, however, whether his maxim of neglect of his natural gifts, besides agreeing with his inclination to indulgence, agrees also with what is called duty. He sees then that a system of nature could indeed subsist with such a universal law although men (like the South Sea islanders) should let their talents rest and resolve to devote their lives merely to idleness, amusement, and propagation of their species- in a word, to enjoyment; but he cannot possibly will that this should be a universal law of nature, or be implanted in us as such by a natural instinct. For, as a rational being, he necessarily wills that his faculties be developed, since they serve him and have been given him, for all sorts of possible purposes.

4. A fourth, who is in prosperity, while he sees that others have to contend with great wretchedness and that he could help them, thinks: "What concern is it of mine? Let everyone be as happy as Heaven pleases, or as he can make himself; I will take nothing from him nor even envy him, only I do not wish to contribute anything to his welfare or to his assistance in distress!" Now no doubt if such a mode of thinking were a universal law, the human race might very well subsist and doubtless even better than in a state in which everyone talks of sympathy and good-will, or even takes care occasionally to put it into practice, but, on the other side, also cheats when he can, betrays the rights of men, or otherwise violates them. But although it is possible that a universal law of nature might exist in accordance with that maxim, it is impossible to will that such a principle should have the universal validity of a law of nature. For a will which resolved this would contradict itself, inasmuch as many cases might occur in which one would have need of the love and sympathy of others, and in which, by such a law of nature, sprung from his own will, he would deprive himself of all hope of the aid he desires.

These are a few of the many actual duties, or at least what we regard as such, which obviously fall into two classes on the one principle that we have laid down. We must be able to will that a maxim of our action should be a universal law. This is the canon of the moral appreciation of the action generally. Some actions are of such a character that their maxim cannot without contradiction be even conceived as a universal law of nature, far from it being possible that we should will that it should be so. In others this intrinsic impossibility is not found, but still it is impossible to will that their maxim should be raised to the universality of a law of nature, since such a will would contradict itself It is easily seen that the former violate strict or rigorous (inflexible) duty; the latter only laxer (meritorious) duty. Thus it has been completely shown how all duties depend as regards the nature of the obligation (not the object of the action) on the same principle.

If now we attend to ourselves on occasion of any transgression of duty, we shall find that we in fact do not will that our maxim should be a universal law, for that is impossible for us; on the contrary, we will that the opposite should remain a universal law, only we assume the liberty of making an exception in our own favour or (just for this time only) in favour of our inclination. Consequently if we considered all cases from one and the same point of view, namely, that of reason, we should find a contradiction in our own will, namely, that a certain principle should be objectively necessary as a universal law, and yet subjectively should not be universal, but admit of exceptions. As however we at one moment regard our action from the point of view of a will wholly conformed to reason, and then again look at the same action from the point of view of a will affected by inclination, there is not really any contradiction, but an antagonism of inclination to the precept of reason, whereby the universality of the principle is changed into a mere generality, so that the practical principle of reason shall meet the maxim half way. Now, although this cannot be justified in our own impartial judgement, yet it proves that we do really recognise the validity of the categorical imperative and (with all respect for it) only allow ourselves a few exceptions, which we think unimportant and forced from us...

The question then is this: "Is it a necessary law for all rational beings that they should always judge of their actions by maxims of which they can themselves will that they should serve as universal laws?" If it is so, then it must be connected (altogether a priori) with the very conception of the will of a rational being generally. But in order to discover this connexion we must, however reluctantly, take a step into metaphysic, although into a domain of it which is distinct from speculative philosophy, namely, the metaphysic of morals. In a practical philosophy, where it is not the reasons of what happens that we have to ascertain, but the laws of what ought to happen, even although it never does, i.e., objective practical laws, there it is not necessary to inquire into the reasons why anything pleases or displeases, how the pleasure of mere sensation differs from taste, and whether the latter is distinct from a general satisfaction of reason; on what the feeling of pleasure or pain rests, and how from it desires and inclinations arise, and from these again maxims by the co-operation of reason: for all this belongs to an empirical psychology, which would constitute the second part of physics, if we regard physics as the philosophy of nature, so far as it is based on empirical laws. But here we are concerned with objective practical laws and, consequently, with the relation of the will to itself so far as it is determined by reason alone, in which case whatever has reference to anything empirical is necessarily excluded; since if reason of itself alone determines the conduct (and it is the possibility of this that we are now investigating), it must necessarily do so a priori.

The will is conceived as a faculty of determining oneself to action in accordance with the conception of certain laws. And such a faculty can be found only in rational beings. Now that which serves the will as the objective ground of its self-determination is the end, and, if this is assigned by reason alone, it must hold for all rational beings. On the other hand, that which merely contains the ground of possibility of the action of which the effect is the end, this is called the means. The subjective ground of the desire is the spring, the objective ground of the volition is the motive; hence the distinction between subjective ends which rest on springs, and objective ends which depend on motives valid for every rational being. Practical principles are formal when they abstract from all subjective ends; they are material when they assume these, and therefore particular springs of action. The ends which a rational being proposes to himself at pleasure as effects of his actions (material ends) are all only relative, for it is only their relation to the particular desires of the subject that gives them their worth, which therefore cannot furnish principles universal and necessary for all rational beings and for every volition, that is to say practical laws. Hence all these relative ends can give rise only to hypothetical imperatives.

Supposing, however, that there were something whose existence has in itself an absolute worth, something which, being an end in itself, could be a source of definite laws; then in this and this alone would lie the source of a possible categorical imperative, i.e., a practical law.

Now I say: man and generally any rational being exists as an end in himself, not merely as a means to be arbitrarily used by this or that will, but in all his actions, whether they concern himself or other rational beings, must be always regarded at the same time as an end. All objects of the inclinations have only a conditional worth, for if the inclinations and the wants founded on them did not exist, then their object would be without value. But the inclinations, themselves being sources of want, are so far from having an absolute worth for which they should be desired that on the contrary it must be the universal wish of every rational being to be wholly free from them. Thus the worth of any object which is to be acquired by our action is always conditional. Beings whose existence depends not on our will but on nature's, have nevertheless, if they are irrational beings, only a relative value as means, and are therefore called things; rational beings, on the contrary, are called persons, because their very nature points them out as ends in themselves, that is as something which must not be used merely as means, and so far therefore restricts freedom of action (and is an object of respect). These, therefore, are not merely subjective ends whose existence has a worth for us as an effect of our action, but objective ends, that is, things whose existence is an end in itself; an end moreover for which no other can be substituted, which they should subserve merely as means, for otherwise nothing whatever would possess absolute worth; but if all worth were conditioned and therefore contingent, then there would be no supreme practical principle of reason whatever.

If then there is a supreme practical principle or, in respect of the human will, a categorical imperative, it must be one which, being drawn from the conception of that which is necessarily an end for everyone because it is an end in itself, constitutes an objective principle of will, and can therefore serve as a universal practical law. The foundation of this principle is: rational nature exists as an end in itself. Man necessarily conceives his own existence as being so; so far then this is a subjective principle of human actions. But every other rational being regards its existence similarly, just on the same rational principle that holds for me: so that it is at the same time an objective principle, from which as a supreme practical law all laws of the will must be capable of being deduced. Accordingly the practical imperative will be as follows: So act as to treat humanity, whether in thine own person or in that of any other, in every case as an end withal, never as means only. We will now inquire whether this can be practically carried out.

CONTRACTARIANISM

According to the contractarian tradition, the right thing to do is to abide by principles that rational people (would) have freely adopted (contracted into) from within some initial situation. The early advocates of this view are referred to as social contract theorists. Some of the most prominent social contract theorists were Thomas Hobbes (1588-1679), John Locke (1632-1704), and Jean-Jacques Rousseau (1712-1778). We present a very attenuated overview of the views of Hobbes and Locke solely in order to introduce the work of one of the greatest contractarian thinkers of the 20th century, John Rawls (1921-2002).

Thomas Hobbes (1588-1679)

Thomas Hobbes lived through some very turbulent times in the history of England, including the English Civil War (1642-1649). Hobbes was struck by the contrast between the sharp disagreement in political matters all around him, as compared to the vast and deep agreement on mathematical and scientific matters in his era. Hobbes had a thoroughly materialistic view of humanity and of the rest of nature. For him, everything is just matter in motion. In his mechanistic and deterministic view, there are no immaterial Gods or ghosts or souls or spirits. His materialistic philosophy of mind led him to want to construct a materialistic political philosophy. He reasoned that if he could formulate a political theory with the same logical precision found in the sciences (explaining the cause of the state in terms of the motions of bodies, making politics into a branch of physics), then men would be more likely to agree and achieve **peace and order**. Hence, in 1651, he produced his most well-known book, *Leviathan*.

Leviathan gives us a description of what Hobbes called **The State of Nature** (the condition of men before there is any government or civil society). He describes this state as a state of (rough) equality between men, and of relative scarcity. According to Hobbes, these characteristics lead to competition and diffidence between men. Indeed, without a common power to overawe them all, men exist in a state of war of all against all. Since they have nothing to fear from violating the covenants they might make with one another, such covenants are void (meaningless) in the state of nature. Hence, according to Hobbes, people existing in this amoral and warlike state miss out on all of the advantages that could come from cooperative living, and their lives are, "solitary, nasty, poor, brutish, and short." Given the obvious incentive to try to escape from the state of nature, it's fortunate that reason suggests a path by which they can do so; the institution of a commonwealth. Their desire for a better (more cooperative) life leads them to give up all of their rights to a ruler (sovereign) who can keep the peace and enforce order among them. Hobbes says, "Before the names of just and unjust can have place, there must be some coercive power to compel men equally to the performance of their covenants, by the terror of some punishment, greater than the benefit they expect by the breach of their covenant....and such power there is none before the erection of a COMMONWEALTH." According to Hobbes, the social contract has the following form: "I authorize and give up my right of governing myself, to this man, or to this assembly of men, on this condition, that thou give up thy right to him, and authorize all his actions in like manner." This renunciation is absolute: he says that the only way to secure ourselves is to give **all** of our rights to the Sovereign; the Sovereign will give us back whatever he thinks best for the preservation of peace and security. Hence, Hobbes is sometimes called the father of modern totalitarianism; we might contrast the view of John Locke, according to whom, because we lack security in the State of Nature, we would be rational to give up some of our rights to a State, but the government should be limited in its powers and we should retain the right of revolt if it fails to protect our lives, liberty, or property. Locke's view, according to which the legitimacy of government can only be founded upon the (express or tacit) consent of the people, became the basis of social and political philosophy for generations, and we can see his influence in the founding documents of the United States government.

John Rawls: *A Theory of Justice* (1971)

In 1971, John Rawls, a professor at Harvard University published a book which has since caused a revolution in the fields of political philosophy and ethics. The book is entitled *A Theory of Justice*, and its main aim, according to Rawls was "To present a conception of justice which generalizes and carries to a higher level of abstraction the familiar theory of the social contract as found, say, in Locke, Rousseau, and Kant." Although Rawls is grounded in the contractarian tradition, the hypothetical contract that he describes is not a contract to set up a particular civil society, but rather, an agreement on the principles of justice for the basic structure of society. Rawls' argument relies upon an claim that we should all accept principles which free and rational persons would accept in an initial position of equality, but these principles are not the particular laws of a civil society; they are the principles of distributive justice which can be used to judge the worth of any civil society.

What is it that Rawls is concerned with the distribution of? He refers to the goods he is focusing on as "**primary goods**". These are things that any rational person is presumed to want because the possession of these primary goods makes it easier to get anything else. There are two kinds of primary goods, according to Rawls: natural primary goods, and social primary goods. Natural primary goods include things like health and vigor, native intelligence and imagination, strength, beauty, etc.. It may be that one day we will have it in our power to determine the distribution of these goods (i.e., if we perfect genetic screening techniques so that we become able to produce "designer babies"), but since we don't (yet) have the power to determine the distribution of these goods, we can put them to the side and focus upon the social primary goods. There are four categories of **social primary goods** that Rawls outlines. They are **rights and liberties, powers and opportunities, wealth and income, and the social bases of self-respect (forms of social recognition)**. Now how does Rawls suggest that we determine a just distribution of these social goods?

The name that Rawls gives to his theory is "Justice as Fairness"; though this is not meant to imply that justice and fairness are to be equated in Rawls' view. There are two central parts to this theory:

1) A description of the initial contract situation and of the problem of choice we face there.

2) A set of principles which (he argues) would be agreed to.

Part One: The Original Position

Rawls refers to the first part of this scheme as "The Original Position." This is a hypothetical situation of equality, in which rational deliberators are to choose principles of justice upon which to base a society. The people in the OP are narrowly rational beings (they choose the most effective means to given ends), and mutually disinterested (they are just looking out for their own interests. Rawls describes them as having all the knowledge we possess about what people are like, what they desire, what they fear, etc. They might be described as knowing all we know about people except one thing; which one they are. Rawls says that in order that the people in the OP will choose principles of justice in a fair and unbiased way, they should choose from behind what he calls "**The Veil of Ignorance**." Hence, people in the O.P. are to be deprived of knowledge of their place in society, class, position or social status, natural assets and abilities, intelligence, strength, conception of the good, and special psychological propensities. This ignorance is meant to exclude bias from the choice of principles of justice in the original position.

Which principles does Rawls believe would be chosen from within this elaborate hypothetical situation? He argues that his two principles of justice would be chosen. Here is one formulation of those two principles.

Part Two: The Two Principles of Justice as Fairness

1)   The Principle of Equal Rights and Liberties: "Each person is to have an equal right to the most extensive basic liberty compatible with a similar liberty for others."

2)   The Difference Principle and the Principle of Fair Equality of Opportunity: "Social and economic inequalities are to be arranged so that they are both (a) to the greatest benefit of the least advantaged, and (b) attached to offices and positions open to all under conditions of fair equality of opportunity."

Rawls stresses that we are to understand these two principles as lexically ordered. That is, the first principle must be fulfilled before we go on to the second one; it won't be allowed to sacrifice the rights and liberties guaranteed under the first principle in order to give citizens a greater share, for example, of wealth and income.

Why would rational deliberators in the original position choose these two principles? Rawls argues that under conditions of uncertainty as to the probabilities of outcomes, where the risk is high and I may not get what I want, rational deliberators would employ the **Maximin Strategy**: This strategy of rational choice ranks alternatives by their worst possible outcome, and prescribes that we are to adopt the alternative the worst possible outcome of which is superior to the worst outcomes of the others.

As an example of this "play it safe" strategy at work, consider **The Prisoner's Dilemma:** You and your drug-dealing partner are arrested in possession of a very tiny amount of cocaine. The police only have enough evidence to send you both away for one year each. The guards put you in separated rooms and offer you the following deal (and they tell you that they are offering your partner the same deal). "Squeal" means that you confess, tell the police where your stash is, and testify against your partner. You don't know what your partner is going to do (you haven't known him that long and in the world of high-stakes drug-dealing, people often find it healthier to maintain a "strictly business" relationship). Thus, you must choose under conditions of uncertainty. What do you do?

Assume that there are no adverse consequences connected to the act of "squealing" itself (i.e., your partner won't send some of his friends after you or your family, you won't have to drop out of the drug-dealing business, etc.).

Prisoner A

	Squeal	Don't Squeal
Squeal	A: 5 Years B: 5 Years	A: 20 Years B: Probation

Prisoner B

	A: Probation	A: 1 Year
Don't Squeal	B: 20 Years	B: 1 Year

Rational choice theory tells us that when we are confronted with a dangerous and uncertain situation like this, the rational strategy to employ is maximin strategy. Since the worst thing that can happen to me if I squeal is 5 years in prison, and the worst thing that can happen if I don't squeal is 20 years in prison, the rational thing for me to do under these circumstances is to squeal. Of course, my partner, if he is rational, will employ the same kind of thinking. Notice that this does not yield the optimal outcome for my partner and me: if we both were to choose not to squeal, we would spend a total of 2 years in prison, whereas if we both squeal, we spend a total of 10 years in prison. And, indeed, in situations where we imagine people playing this game more than once in succession, different strategies might be more rational (e.g., a retaliation strategy where I don't squeal until my partner does, then squeal in retaliation, then go back to not squealing, etc.). But the choice that Rawls outlines in the OP is made only once, and the deliberators behind the veil of ignorance have no knowledge of any likelihood that they might be rich, poor, male, female, etc.; furthermore, they know that some possible outcomes would be simply unacceptable for them (a set of principles which allowed some people to be slaves, for example). Hence, Rawls argues that this kind of "play it safe" strategy would be the one that the deliberators would employ and it would lead them to his two principles of justice.

The theory Rawls that outlines has proven to be an extremely powerful one for analyzing many different moral issues. One especially strong application of the theory concerns the problem of intergenerational justice.

If we imagine people in the original position as ignorant not only about their race, sex, social status, etc., but also about to which generation they belong, we may be able to arrive at a new understanding of what would be required by intergenerationally just policies regarding the use of renewable and nonrenewable environmental resources. The applications to the ethics of the family may also be particularly useful, as some of the pieces in this collection demonstrate.   Here is an excerpt from Rawls major work, *A Theory of Justice*.

FROM *A THEORY OF JUSTICE* BY JOHN RAWLS[1]

1. The Role of Justice

Justice is the first virtue of social institutions, as truth is of systems of thought. A theory however elegant and economical must be rejected or revised if it is untrue; likewise laws and institutions no matter how efficient and well-arranged must be reformed or abolished if they are unjust. Each person possesses an inviolability founded on justice that even the welfare of society as a whole cannot override. For this reason justice denies that the loss of freedom for some is made right by a greater good shared by others. It does not allow that the sacrifices imposed on a few are outweighed by the larger sum of advantages enjoyed by many. Therefore in a just society the liberties of equal citizenship are taken as settled; the rights secured by justice are not subject to political bargaining or to the calculus of social interests. The only thing that permits us to acquiesce in an erroneous theory is the lack of a better one; analogously, an injustice is tolerable only when it is necessary to avoid an even greater injustice. Being first virtues of human activities, truth and justice are uncompromising.

These propositions seem to express our intuitive conviction of the primacy of justice. No doubt they are expressed too strongly. In any event I wish to inquire whether these contentions or others similar to them are sound, and if so how they can be accounted for. To this end it is necessary to work out a theory of justice in the light of which these assertions can be interpreted and assessed. I shall begin by considering the role of the principles of justice. Let us assume, to fix ideas, that a society is a more or less self-sufficient association of persons who in their relations to one another recognize certain rules of conduct as binding and who for the most part act in accordance with them. Suppose further that these rules specify a system of cooperation designed to advance the good of those taking part in it. Then, although a society is a cooperative venture for mutual advantage, it is typically marked by a conflict as well as by an identity of interests. There is an identity of interests since social cooperation makes possible a better life for all than any would have if each were to live solely by his

[1] Reprinted by permission of the publisher from A THEORY OF JUSTICE (REVISED EDITION) by John Rawls, pp, 3-4, 6-7, 10-19, 52-56, Cambridge, Mass.: The Belknap Press of Harvard University Press, Copyright © 1971, 1999 by the President and Fellows of Harvard College.

own efforts. There is a conflict of interests since persons are not indifferent as to how the greater benefits produced by their collaboration are distributed, for in order to pursue their ends they each prefer a larger to a lesser share. A set of principles is required for choosing among the various social arrangements which determine this division of advantages and for underwriting an agreement on the proper distributive shares. These principles are the principles of social justice: they provide a way of assigning rights and duties in the basic institutions of society and they define the appropriate distribution of the benefits and burdens of social cooperation...

2. The Subject of Justice

Many different kinds of things are said to be just and unjust: not only laws, institutions, and social systems, but also particular actions of many kinds, including decisions, judgments, and imputations. We also call the attitudes and dispositions of persons, and persons themselves, just and unjust. Our topic, however, is that of social justice. For us the primary subject of justice is the basic structure of society, or more exactly, the way in which the major social institutions distribute fundamental rights and duties and determine the division of advantages from social cooperation. By major institutions I understand the political constitution and the principal economic and social arrangements. Thus the legal protection of freedom of thought and liberty of conscience, competitive markets, private property in the means of production, and the monogamous family are examples of major social institutions. Taken together as one scheme, the major institutions define men's rights and duties and influence their life-prospects, what they can expect to be and how well they can hope to do. The basic structure is the primary subject of justice because its effects are so profound and present from the start. The intuitive notion here is that this structure contains various social positions and that men born into different positions have different expectations of life determined, in part, by the political system as well as by economic and social circumstances. In this way the institutions of society favor certain starting places over others. These are especially deep inequalities. Not only are they pervasive, but they affect men's initial chances in life; yet they cannot possibly be justified by an appeal to the notions of merit or desert. It is these inequalities, presumably inevitable in the basic structure of any society to which the principles of social justice must in the first instance apply. These principles, then, regulate the choice of a political constitution and the main elements of the economic and social system. The justice of a social scheme depends essentially on how fundamental rights and duties are assigned and on the economic opportunities and social conditions in the various sectors of society ...

3. The Main Idea of The Theory of Justice

My aim is to present a conception of justice which generalizes and carries to a higher level of abstraction the familiar theory of the social contract as found, say, in Locke, Rousseau, and Kant. In order to do this we are not to think of the original contract as one to enter a particular society or to set up a particular form of government. Rather, the guiding idea is that the principles of justice for the basic structure of society are the object of the original agreement. They are the principles that free and rational persons concerned to further their own interests would accept in an initial position of equality as defining the fundamental terms of their association. These principles are to regulate all further agreements; they specify the kinds of social cooperation that can be entered into and the forms of government that can be established. This way of regarding the principles of justice I shall call justice as fairness.

Thus we are to imagine that those who engage in social cooperation choose together, in one joint act, the principles which are to assign basic rights and duties and to determine the division of social benefits. Men are to decide in advance how they are to regulate their claims against one another and what is to be the foundation charter of their society. Just as each person must decide by rational reflection what constitutes his good, that is, the system of ends which it is rational for him to pursue, so a group of persons must decide once and for all what is to count among them as just and unjust. The choice which rational men would make in this hypothetical situation of equal liberty, assuming for the present that this choice problem has a solution, determines the principles of justice.

In justice as fairness the original position of equality corresponds to the state of nature in the traditional theory of the social contract. This original position is not, of course, thought of as an actual historical state of affairs, much less as a primitive condition of culture. It is understood as a purely hypothetical situation characterized so as to lead to a certain conception of justice? Among the essential features of this situation is that no one knows his place in society, his class position or social status, nor does anyone know his fortune in the distribution of natural assets and abilities, his intelligence, strength, and the like. I shall even assume that the parties do not know their conceptions of the good or their special psychological propensities. The principles of justice are chosen behind a veil of ignorance. This ensures that no one is advantaged or disadvantaged in the choice of principles by the outcome of natural chance or the contingency of social circumstances. Since all are similarly situated and no one is able to design principles to favor his particular condition, the principles of justice are the result of a fair agreement or bargain. For given the circumstances of the original position, the symmetry of everyone's relation to each other, this initial situation is fair between individuals as moral persons, that is, as rational beings with their own ends and capable, I shall assume, of a sense of justice. The original position is, one might say, the appropriate initial status quo, and the fundamental agreements reached in it are fair. This explains the propriety of the name "justice as fairness": it conveys the idea that the principles of justice are agreed to in an initial situation that is fair. The name does not mean that the concepts of justice and fairness are the same, any more that the phrase "poetry as metaphor" means that the concepts of poetry and metaphor are the same.

Justice as fairness begins, as I have said, with one of the most general of all choices which persons might make together, namely, with the choice of the first principles of a conception of justice which is to regulate all subsequent criticism and reform of institutions. Then, having chosen a conception of justice, we can suppose that they are to choose a constitution and a legislature to enact laws, and so on, all in accordance with the principles of justice initially agreed upon. Our social situation is just if it is such that by this sequence of hypothetical agreements we would have contracted into the general system of rules which defines it. Moreover, assuming that the original position does determine a set of principles (that is, that a particular conception of justice would be chosen), it will then be true that whenever social institutions satisfy these principles those engaged in them can say to one another that they are cooperating on terms to which they would agree if they were free and equal persons whose relations with respect to one another were fair. They could all view their arrangements as meeting the stipulations which they would acknowledge in an initial situation that embodies widely accepted and reasonable constraints on the choice of principles. The general recognition of this fact would provide the basis for a public acceptance of the corresponding principles of justice. No society can, of course, be a scheme of cooperation which men enter voluntarily in a literal sense; each person finds himself placed at birth in some particular position in some particular society, and the nature of this position materially affects his life prospects. Yet a society satisfying the principles of justice as fairness comes as close as a society can to being a voluntary scheme, for it meets the principles which free and equal persons would assent to under circumstances that are fair. In this sense its members are autonomous and the obligations they recognize self-imposed.

One feature of justice as fairness is to think of the parties in the initial situation as rational and mutually disinterested. This does not mean that the parties are egoists, that is, individuals with only certain kinds of interests, say in wealth, prestige, and domination. But they are conceived as not taking an interest in one another's interests. They are to presume that even their spiritual aims may be opposed, in the way that the aims of those of different religions may be opposed. Moreover, the concept of rationality must be interpreted as far as possible in the narrow sense, standard in economic theory, of taking the most effective means to given ends. I shall modify this concept to some extent, as explained later (§25), but one must try to avoid introducing into it any controversial ethical elements. The initial situation must be characterized by stipulations that are widely accepted.

In working out the conception of justice as fairness one main task clearly is to determine which principles of justice would be chosen in the original position. To do this we must describe this situation in some detail and formulate with care the problem of choice which it presents. These matters I shall take up in the immediately succeeding chapters. It may be observed, however, that once the principles of justice are thought of as arising from an original agreement in a situation of equality, it is an open question whether the principle of utility would be acknowledged. Offhand it hardly seems likely that persons who view themselves as equals, entitled to press their claims upon one another, would agree to a principle which may require lesser life prospects for some simply for the sake of a greater sum of advantages enjoyed by others. Since each desires to protect his interests, his capacity to advance his conception of the good, no one has a reason to acquiesce in an enduring loss for himself in order to bring about a greater net balance of satisfaction. In the absence of strong and lasting benevolent impulses, a rational man would not accept a basic structure merely because it maximized the algebraic sum of advantages irrespective of its permanent effects on his own basic rights and interests. Thus it seems that the principle of utility is incompatible with the conception of social cooperation among equals for mutual advantage. It appears to be inconsistent with the idea or reciprocity implicit in the notion of a well-ordered society. Or, at any rate, so I shall argue.

I shall maintain instead that the persons in the initial situation would choose two rather different principles: the first requires equality in the assignment of basic rights and duties, while the second holds that social and economic inequalities, for example inequalities of wealth and authority, are just only if they result in compensating benefits for everyone, and in particular for the least advantaged members of society. These principles rule out justifying institutions on the grounds that the hardships of some are offset by a greater good in the aggregate. It may be expedient but it is not just that some should have less in order that others may prosper. But there is no injustice in the greater benefits earned by a few provided that the situation of persons not so fortunate is thereby improved. The intuitive idea is that since everyone's well-being depends upon a scheme of cooperation without which no one could have a satisfactory life, the division of advantages should be such as to draw forth the willing cooperation of everyone taking part in it, including those less well situated. The two principles mentioned seem to be a fair basis on which those better endowed, or more fortunate in their social position, neither of which we can be said to deserve, could expect the willing cooperation of others when some workable scheme is a necessary condition of the welfare of all. Once we decide to look for a conception of justice that prevents the use of the accidents of natural endowment and the contingencies of social circumstance as counters in a quest for political and economic advantage, we are led to these principles. They express the result of leaving aside those aspects of the social world that seem arbitrary from a moral point of view....

The Original Position and Justification

I have said that the original position is the appropriate initial status quo which insures that the fundamental agreements reached in it are fair. This fact yields the name "justice as fairness." It is clear, then, that I want to say that one conception of justice is more reasonable than another, or justifiable with respect to it, if rational persons in the initial situation would choose its principles over those of the other for the role of justice. Conceptions of justice are to be ranked by their acceptability to persons so circumstanced. Understood in this way the question of justification is settled by working out a problem of deliberation: we have to ascertain which principles it would be rational to adopt given the contractual situation. This connects the theory of justice with the theory of rational choice.

If this view of the problem of justification is to succeed, we must, of course, describe in some detail the nature of this choice problem. A problem of rational decision has a definite answer only if we know the beliefs and interests of the parties, their relations with respect to one another, the alternatives between which they are to choose, the procedure whereby they make up their minds, and so on. As the circumstances are presented in different ways, correspondingly different principles are accepted. The concept of the original position, as I shall refer to it, is that of the most philosophically favored interpretation of this initial choice situation for the purposes of a theory of justice.

But how are we to decide what is the most favored interpretation? I assume, for one thing, that there is abroad measure of agreement that principles of justice should be chosen under certain conditions. To justify a particular description of the initial situation one shows that it incorporates these commonly shared presumptions. One argues from widely accepted but weak premises to more specific conclusions. Each of the presumptions should by itself be natural and plausible; some of them may seem innocuous or even trivial. The aim of the contract approach is to establish that taken together they impose significant bounds on acceptable principles of justice. The ideal outcome would be that these conditions determine a unique set of principles; but I shall be satisfied if they suffice to rank the main traditional conceptions of social justice.

One should not be misled, then, by the somewhat unusual conditions which characterize the original position. The idea here is simply to make vivid to ourselves the restrictions that it seems reasonable to impose on arguments for principles of justice, and therefore on these principles themselves. Thus it seems reasonable and generally acceptable that no one should be advantaged or disadvantaged by natural fortune or social circumstances in the choice of principles. It also seems widely agreed that it should be impossible to tailor principles to the circumstances of one's own case. We should insure further that particular inclinations and aspirations, and persons' conceptions of their good do not affect the principles adopted. The aim is to rule out those principles that it would be rational to propose for acceptance, however little the chance of success, only if one knew certain things that are irrelevant from the standpoint of justice. For example, if a man knew that he was wealthy, he might find it rational to advance the principle that various taxes for welfare measures be counted unjust; if he knew that he was poor, he would most likely propose the contrary principle. To represent the desired restrictions one imagines a situation in which everyone is deprived of this sort of information. One excludes the knowledge of those contingencies which sets men at odds and allows them to be guided by their prejudices. In this manner the veil of ignorance is arrived at in a natural way. This concept should cause no difficulty if we keep in mind the constraints on arguments that it is meant to express. At any time we can enter the original position, so to speak, simply by following a certain procedure, namely, by arguing for principles of justice in accordance with these restrictions.

It seems reasonable to suppose that the parties in the original position are equal. That is, all have the same rights in the procedure for choosing principles; each can make proposals, submit reasons for their acceptance, and so on. Obviously the purpose of these conditions is to represent equality between human beings as moral persons, as creatures having a conception of their good and capable of a sense of justice. The basis of equality is taken to be similarity in these two respects. Systems of ends are not ranked in value; and each man is presumed to have the requisite ability to understand and to act upon whatever principles are adopted. Together with the veil of ignorance, these conditions define the principles of justice as those which rational persons concerned to advance their interests would consent to as equals when none are known to be advantaged or disadvantaged by social and natural contingencies.

There is, however, another side to justifying a particular description of the original position. This is to see if the principles which would be chosen match our considered convictions of justice or extend them in an acceptable way. We can note whether applying these principles would lead us to make the same judgments about the basic structure of society which we now make intuitively and in which we have the greatest confidence; or whether, in cases where our present judgments are in doubt and given with hesitation, these principles offer a resolution which we can affirm on reflection. There are questions which we feel sure must be answered in a certain way. For example, we are confident that religious intolerance and racial discrimination are unjust. We think that we have examined these things with care and have reached what we believe is an impartial judgment not likely to be distorted by an excessive attention to our own interests. These convictions are provisional fixed points which we presume any conception of justice must fit. But we have much less assurance as to what is the correct distribution of wealth and authority. Here we may be looking for a way to remove our doubts. We can check an interpretation of the initial situation, then, by the capacity of its principles to accommodate our firmest convictions and to provide guidance where guidance is needed.

In searching for the most favored description of this situation we work from both ends. We begin by describing it so that it represents generally shared and preferably weak conditions. We then see if these conditions are strong enough to yield a significant set of principles. If not, we look for further premises equally reasonable. But if so, and these principles match our considered convictions of justice, then so far well and good. But presumably there will be discrepancies. In this case we have a choice. We can either modify the account of the initial situation or we can revise our existing judgments, for even the judgements we take provisionally as fixed points are liable to revision. By going back and forth, sometimes altering the conditions of the contractual circumstances, at others withdrawing our judgments and conforming them to principle, I assume that eventually we shall find a description of the initial situation that both expresses reasonable conditions and yields principles which match our considered judgments duly pruned and adjusted. This state of affairs I refer to as reflective equilibrium. It is an equilibrium because at last our principles and judgments coincide; and it is reflective since we know to what principles our judgments conform and the premises of their derivation. At the moment everything is in order. But this equilibrium is not necessarily stable. It is liable to be upset by further examination of the conditions which should be imposed on the contractual situation and by particular cases which may lead us to revise our judgments. Yet for the time being we have done what we can to render coherent and to justify our convictions of social justice. We have reached a conception of the original position.

I shall not, of course, actually work through this process. Still, we may think of the interpretation of the original position that I shall present as the result of such a hypothetical course of reflection. It represents the attempt to accommodate within one scheme both reasonable philosophical conditions on principles as well as our considered judgments of justice. In arriving at the favored interpretation of the initial situation there is no point at which an appeal is made to self-evidence in the traditional sense either of general conceptions or particular convictions. I do not claim for the principles of justice proposed that they are necessary truths or derivable from such truths. A conception of justice cannot be deduced from self-evident premises or conditions on principles; instead, its justification is a matter of the mutual support of many considerations, of everything fitting together into one coherent view.

A final comment. We shall want to say that certain principles of justice are justified because they would be agreed to in an initial situation of equality. I have emphasized that this original position is purely hypothetical. It is natural to ask why, if this agreement is never actually entered into, we should take any interest in these principles, moral or otherwise. The answer is that the conditions embodied in the description of the original position are ones that we do in fact accept. Or if we do not, then perhaps we can be persuaded to do so by philosophical reflection. Each aspect of the contractual situation can be given supporting grounds. Thus what we shall do is to collect together into one conception a number of conditions on principles that we are ready upon due consideration to recognize as reasonable. These constraints express what we are prepared to regard as limits on fair terms of social cooperation. One way to look at the idea or the original position, therefore, is to see it as an expository device which sums up the meaning of these conditions and helps us to extract their consequences. On the other hand, this conception is also an intuitive notion that suggests its own elaboration, so that led on by it we are drawn to define more clearly the standpoint from which we can best interpret moral relationships. We need a conception that enables us to envision our objective from afar: the intuitive notion of the original position is to do this for us.....

Two Principles of Justice

I shall now in a provisional form the two principles of justice that I believe would be agreed to in the original position. The first formulation of these principles is tentative. As we go on I shall consider several formulations and approximate step by step the final statement to be given much later. I believe that doing this allows the exposition to proceed in a natural way.

The first statement of the two principles read as follows.

First: each person is to have an equal right to the most extensive scheme of equal basic liberties compatible with a similar scheme of liberties for others.

Second: social and economic inequalities are to be arranged so that they are both (a) reasonably expected to be to everyone's advantage, and (b) attached to positions and offices open to all....

These principles primarily apply, as I have said, to the basic structure of society and govern the assignment of rights and duties and regulate the distribution of social and economic advantages. Their formulation presupposes that, for the purposes of a theory of justice, the social structure may be viewed as having two more or less distinct parts, the first principle applying to the one, the second principle to the other. Thus we distinguish between the aspects of the social system that define and secure the equal basic liberties and the aspects that specify and establish social and economic inequalities. Now it is essential to observe that the basic liberties are given by a list of such liberties. Important among these are political liberty (the right to vote and to hold public office) and freedom of speech and assembly; liberty of conscience and freedom of thought;

freedom of the person, which includes freedom from psychological oppression and physical assault and dismemberment (integrity of the person); the right to hold personal property and freedom from arbitrary arrest and seizure as defined by the concept of the rule of law. These liberties are to be equal by the first principle.

The second principle applies, in the first approximation, to the distribution of income and wealth and to the design of organizations that make use of differences in authority and responsibility. While the distribution of wealth and income need not be equal, it must be to everyone's advantage, and at the same time, positions of authority and responsibility must be accessible to all. One applies the second principle by holding positions open, and then, subject to this constraint, arranges social and economic inequalities so that everyone benefits.

These principles are to be arranged in a serial order with the first principle prior to the second. This ordering means that infringements of the basic equal liberties protected by the first principle cannot be justified, or compensated for, by greater social and economic advantages...

The two principles are rather specific in their content, and their acceptance rests on certain assumptions that I must eventually try to explain and justify. For the present, it should be observed that these principles are a special case of a more general conception of justice that can be expressed as follows.

All social values – liberty and opportunity, income and wealth, and the social bases of self-respect – are to be distributed equally unless an unequal distribution of any, or all, of these values is to everyone's advantage.

Injustice, then, is simply inequalities that are not to the benefit of all. Of course, this conception is extremely vague and requires interpretation.

As a first step, suppose that the basic structure of society distributes certain primary goods, that is, things that every rational man is presumed to want. These goods normally have a use whatever a person's rational plan of life. For simplicity, assume that the chief primary goods at the disposition of society are rights, liberties, and opportunities, and income and wealth. (Later on in Part Three the primary good of self-respect has a central place.) These are the social primary goods. Other primary goods such as health and vigor, intelligence and imagination, are natural goods; although their possession is influenced by the basic structure, they are not so directly under its control. Imagine, then, a hypothetical initial arrangement in which all the social primary goods are equally distributed: everyone has similar rights and duties, and income and wealth are evenly shared. This state of affairs provides a benchmark for judging improvements. If certain inequalities of wealth and differences in authority would make everyone better off than in this hypothetical starting situation, then they accord with the general conception.

Now it is possible, at least theoretically, that by giving up some of their fundamental liberties men are sufficiently compensated by the resulting social and economic gains. The general conception of justice imposes no restrictions on what sort of inequalities are permissible; it only requires that everyone's position be improved. We need not suppose anything so drastic as consenting to a condition of slavery. Imagine instead that men forego certain political rights when the economic returns are significant. It is this kind of exchange which the two principles rule out; being arranged in serial order they do not permit exchanges between basic liberties and economic and social gains...

For the most part, I shall leave aside the general conception of justice and examine instead the special case of the two principles in serial order. The advantage of this procedure is that from the first the matter of priorities is recognized and an effort made to find principles to deal with it. One is led to attend throughout to the conditions under which the absolute weight of liberty with respect to social and economic advantages, as defined by the lexical order of the two principles, would be reasonable. Offhand, this ranking appears extreme and too special a case to be of much interest; but there is more justification for it than would appear at first sight. Or at any rate, so I shall maintain (§82). Furthermore, the distinction between fundamental rights and liberties and economic and social benefits marks a difference among primary social goods that suggests an important division in the social system. Of course, the distinctions drawn and the ordering proposed are at best only approximations. There are surely circumstances in which they fail. But it is essential to depict clearly the main lines of a reasonable conception of justice; and under many conditions anyway, the two principles in serial order may serve well enough.

The fact that the two principles apply to institutions has certain consequences. First of all, the rights and liberties referred to by these principles are those which are defined by the public rules of the basic structure. Whether men are free is determined by the rights and duties established by the major institutions of society. Liberty is a certain pattern of social forms. The first principle simply requires that certain sorts of rules, those defining basic liberties, apply to everyone equally and that they allow the most extensive liberty compatible with a like liberty for all. The only reason for circumscribing basic liberties and making them less extensive is that otherwise they would interfere with one another.

Further, when principles mention persons, or require that everyone gain from an inequality, the reference is to representative persons holding the various social positions, or offices established by the basic structure. Thus in applying the second principle I assume that it is possible to assign an expectation of well-being to representative individuals holding these positions. This expectation indicates their life prospects as viewed from their social station. In general, the expectations of representative persons depend upon the distribution of rights and duties throughout the basic structure. Expectations are connected: by raising the prospects of the representative man in one position we presumably increase or decrease the prospects of representative men in other positions. Since it applies to institutional forms, the second principle (or rather the first part of it) refers to the expectations of representative individuals. As I shall discuss below (§14), neither principle applies to distributions of particular goods to particular individuals who may be identified by their proper names. The situation where someone is considering how to allocate certain commodities to needy persons who are known to him is not within the scope of the principles. They are meant to regulate basic institutional arrangements. We must not assume that there is much similarity from the stand-point of justice between an administrative allotment of goods to specific persons and the appropriate design of society. Our common sense intuitions for the former may be a poor guide to the latter.

Now the second principle insists that each person benefit from permissible inequalities in the basic structure. This means that it must be reasonable for each relevant representative man defined by this structure, when he views it as a going concern, to prefer his prospects with the inequality to his prospects without it. One is not allowed to justify differences in income or in positions of authority and responsibility on the ground that the disadvantages of those in one position are outweighed by the greater advantages of those in another. Much less can infringements of liberty be counterbalanced in this way...

ARISTOTELIAN VIRTUE ETHICS

Almost all contemporary ethicists believe that having excellent psychological traits, or *virtues* is important. But the ethical theories we have seen so far emphasize that virtues are valuable because they promote good actions. A growing number of ethicists do not believe that actions are the kind of things that belong at the center of ethics. They believe that what is really valuable are actually the **virtuous character traits**. According to virtue ethicists, assessing individual actions as right or wrong is secondary to assessing these character traits, exemplifying the good ones (virtues), and refraining from the bad ones (vices). Virtuous character traits are not rigid beliefs but dispositions to act in certain ways.

Perhaps the most classically grounded ethical theory, virtue ethics receives its most famous treatment in Aristotle's *Nicomachean Ethics*. In this series of chapters, Aristotle defends the idea that virtuous behavior is the path to happiness and thus the proper center of ethical thinking

What we mean by "happiness" in today's world may lead one to believe that a happy life cannot possibly be all there is to ethics. But Aristotle does not use the idea of happiness to refer to the fun, carefree life. Aristotle is saying that virtue is the path to what Greeks called *eudaimonia* or a life of **human flourishing** including prosperity and material goods.

For Aristotle, a virtue conducive to happiness is a habit that aims at **the mean between two extremes**: an excess and a deficiency. The courageous person, for instance, does not have the habit of running rashly into battle, throwing caution to the wind. But he or she does not shrink from battle either. Courage is thus the mean between the extremes of rashness and cowardice. The same can be said for the virtue of temperance, which is the mean between self-indulgence and self-deprivation. The following chart lays out the virtues that Aristotle mentions in the *Ethics*:

Doctrine of the Mean:

Feeling/Action	Vice of Deficiency	Virtue	Vice of Excess
Fear	Foolhardiness		Courage
Cowardice	Conciliance		Surliness
Friendliness	Flattery		Pleasure
Insensitivity	Temperance		Intemperance
Spending	Meanness		Liberality
Prodigality	Self-regard		Poor-spiritedness
Proper Pride	Vanity		Anger
Wimpiness?	Gentleness		Irascibility
Sociability	Boorishness		Wittiness Buffoonery

He is also careful to distinguish a virtue of character from a virtue of thought. Intellectual virtues can be learned from teaching and experience. Aristotle believed this is not how we mainly acquire virtues of character, which must be practiced if they are going to be learned as habits. Furthermore, since virtues are embodied psychological states as opposed to the kinds of principles or rules invoked by utilitarians and Kant, then it will make sense to think of **following the example of virtuous people** rather than simply following impartial rules. If one is not virtuous, one can still become virtuous by practicing virtuous behavior as displayed by others. The more one acts virtuously, the more one falls into a habit of doing so, feels pleasure from doing so, and implants the disposition to do so in one's character (and hence, the easier it is to perform virtuous actions):

ACT

**HABIT
(VIRTUE or VICE)**

DISPOSITION

PLEASURE

So a virtuous person will not observe certain rules about being virtuous. Rather the virtuous person is worth emulating in his or her own right because he or she possesses *phronesis* (**prudence** or **practical wisdom**).

Prudence, unlike rules, cannot always be written down. Instead, like the virtues, it must be practiced and lived to be developed. One becomes brave by doing brave actions and avoiding cowardly ones. Here, Aristotle enjoys a common-sense advantage over utilitarianism and Kantian ethics. Kant believed lying was never morally acceptable, but a person with practical wisdom might be comfortable with the idea that lying is required of a virtuous person in certain extreme circumstances, but not in ordinary life. Similarly, utilitarianism emphasizes treating all people as counting equally in difficult choices between helping family members or close friends and strangers. The prudent person might understand at a more intuitive level that there are times when friendship should trump equal treatment and other times when equal treatment should trump friendship. We may not be able to codify *phronesis* about when we should let friendship guide us in exact terms, but we can get better at making tough decisions by making decisions and amassing life experience.

Virtue ethics can be seen as very well integrated into typical family life, as at least one essay in this volume tries to show. Often one's first moral education comes from the example set by one's family members, not abstract moral rules. While utilitarians and Kantians seem uncomfortable with ethical views arising in some families, virtue ethics captures the idea that our moral lives are continuous with early moral education within a family.

There are, of course, important criticisms of thinking about ethics in terms of virtue as well. It is fairly easy to see how utilitarian and Kantian theories give guidance in extremely novel situations. If virtue ethicists consider *phronesis* central to ethical deliberation, it is not clear it will be able to give guidance in settings with which the deliberator has very little experience. Though perhaps no ethical theory can give guidance in all possible situations.

Finally, virtue ethics seems to do a good job of explaining how ethics integrates with individual lives, but some philosophers believe a good ethical theory should give an account of what larger groups should do. Since virtues are states of particular people, it is hard to see how virtue ethics deals with the ethical evaluation of public policies for instance.

In the following excerpt from *Nicomachean Ethics*, Aristotle discusses how virtue is acquired, and what kinds of states are virtuous.

FROM *NICOMACHEAN ETHICS*[1] BY ARISTOTLE TRANSLATED BY W. D. ROSS

Book 2.

1

Virtue, then, being of two kinds, intellectual and moral, intellectual virtue in the main owes both its birth and its growth to teaching (for which reason it requires experience and time), while moral virtue comes about as a result of habit, whence also its name (ethike) is one that is formed by a slight variation from the word ethos (habit). From this it is also plain that none of the moral virtues arises in us by nature; for nothing that exists by nature can form a habit contrary to its nature. For instance the stone which by nature moves downwards cannot be habituated to move upwards, not even if one tries to train it by throwing it up ten thousand times; nor can fire be habituated to move downwards, nor can anything else that by nature behaves in one way be trained to behave in another. Neither by nature, then, nor contrary to nature do the virtues arise in us; rather we are adapted by nature to receive them, and are made perfect by habit.

Again, of all the things that come to us by nature we first acquire the potentiality and later exhibit the activity (this is plain in the case of the senses; for it was not by often seeing or often hearing that we got these senses, but on the contrary we had them before we used them, and did not come to have them by using them); but the virtues we get by first exercising them, as also happens in the case of the arts as well. For the things we have to learn before we can do them, we learn by doing them, e.g. men become builders by building and lyreplayers by playing the lyre; so too we become just by doing just acts, temperate by doing temperate acts, brave by doing brave acts.

This is confirmed by what happens in states; for legislators make the citizens good by forming habits in them, and this is the wish of every legislator, and those who do not effect it miss their mark, and it is in this that a good constitution differs from a bad one.

Again, it is from the same causes and by the same means that every virtue is both produced and destroyed, and similarly every art; for it is

---

[1] Excerpted from http://classics.mit.edu/Aristotle/nicomachaen.2.ii.html (translated by W. D. Ross, 1908)

from playing the lyre that both good and bad lyre-players are produced. And the corresponding statement is true of builders and of all the rest; men will be good or bad builders as a result of building well or badly. For if this were not so, there would have been no need of a teacher, but all men would have been born good or bad at their craft. This, then, is the case with the virtues also; by doing the acts that we do in our transactions with other men we become just or unjust, and by doing the acts that we do in the presence of danger, and being habituated to feel fear or confidence, we become brave or cowardly. The same is true of appetites and feelings of anger; some men become temperate and good-tempered, others self-indulgent and irascible, by behaving in one way or the other in the appropriate circumstances. Thus, in one word, states of character arise out of like activities. This is why the activities we exhibit must be of a certain kind; it is because the states of character correspond to the differences between these. It makes no small difference, then, whether we form habits of one kind or of another from our very youth; it makes a very great difference, or rather all the difference.

2

Since, then, the present inquiry does not aim at theoretical knowledge like the others (for we are inquiring not in order to know what virtue is, but in order to become good, since otherwise our inquiry would have been of no use), we must examine the nature of actions, namely how we ought to do them; for these determine also the nature of the states of character that are produced, as we have said. Now, that we must act according to the right rule is a common principle and must be assumed-it will be discussed later, i.e. both what the right rule is, and how it is related to the other virtues. But this must be agreed upon beforehand, that the whole account of matters of conduct must be given in outline and not precisely, as we said at the very beginning that the accounts we demand must be in accordance with the subject-matter; matters concerned with conduct and questions of what is good for us have no fixity, any more than matters of health. The general account being of this nature, the account of particular cases is yet more lacking in exactness; for they do not fall under any art or precept but the agents themselves must in each case consider what is appropriate to the occasion, as happens also in the art of medicine or of navigation.

But though our present account is of this nature we must give what help we can. First, then, let us consider this, that it is the nature of such things to be destroyed by defect and excess, as we see in the case of strength and of health (for to gain light on things imperceptible we must use the evidence of sensible things); both excessive and defective exercise destroys the strength, and similarly drink or food which is above or below a certain amount destroys the health, while that which is proportionate both produces and increases and preserves it. So too is it, then, in the case of temperance and courage and the other virtues. For the man who flies from and fears everything and does not stand his ground against anything becomes a coward, and the man who fears nothing at all but goes to meet every danger becomes rash; and similarly the man who indulges in every pleasure and abstains from none becomes self-indulgent, while the man who shuns every pleasure, as boors do, becomes in a way insensible; temperance and courage, then, are destroyed by excess and defect, and preserved by the mean.

But not only are the sources and causes of their origination and growth the same as those of their destruction, but also the sphere of their actualization will be the same; for this is also true of the things which are more evident to sense, e.g. of strength; it is produced by taking much food and undergoing much exertion, and it is the strong man that will be most able to do these things. So too is it with the virtues; by abstaining from pleasures we become temperate, and it is when we have become so that we are most able to abstain from them; and similarly too in the case of courage; for by being habituated to despise things that are terrible and to stand our ground against them we become brave, and it is when we have become so that we shall be most able to stand our ground against them.

3

We must take as a sign of states of character the pleasure or pain that ensues on acts; for the man who abstains from bodily pleasures and delights in this very fact is temperate, while the man who is annoyed at it is self-indulgent, and he who stands his ground against things that are terrible and delights in this or at least is not pained is brave, while the man who is pained is a coward. For moral excellence is concerned with pleasures and pains; it is on account of the pleasure that we do bad things, and on account of the pain that we abstain from noble ones. Hence we ought to have been brought up in a particular way from our very youth, as Plato says, so as both to delight in and to be pained by the things that we ought; for this is the right education.

Again, if the virtues are concerned with actions and passions, and every passion and every action is accompanied by pleasure and pain, for this reason also virtue will be concerned with pleasures and pains. This is indicated also by the fact that punishment is inflicted by these means; for it is a kind of cure, and it is the nature of cures to be effected by contraries.

Again, as we said but lately, every state of soul has a nature relative to and concerned with the kind of things by which it tends to be made worse or better; but it is by reason of pleasures and pains that men become bad, by pursuing and avoiding these- either the pleasures and pains they ought not or when they ought not or as they ought not, or by going wrong in one of the other similar ways that may be distinguished. Hence men even define the virtues as certain states of impassivity and rest; not well, however, because they speak absolutely, and do not say 'as one ought' and 'as one ought not' and 'when one ought or ought not', and the other things that may be added. We assume, then, that this kind of excellence tends to do what is best with regard to pleasures and pains, and vice does the contrary.

The following facts also may show us that virtue and vice are concerned with these same things. There being three objects of choice and three of avoidance, the noble, the advantageous, the pleasant, and their contraries, the base, the injurious, the painful, about all of these the good man tends to go right and the bad man to go wrong, and especially about pleasure; for this is common to the animals, and also it accompanies all objects of choice; for even the noble and the advantageous appear pleasant.

Again, it has grown up with us all from our infancy; this is why it is difficult to rub off this passion, engrained as it is in our life. And we measure even our actions, some of us more and others less, by the rule of pleasure and pain. For this reason, then, our whole inquiry must be about these; for to feel delight and pain rightly or wrongly has no small effect on our actions.

Again, it is harder to fight with pleasure than with anger, to use Heraclitus' phrase', but both art and virtue are always concerned with what is harder; for even the good is better when it is harder. Therefore for this reason also the whole concern both of virtue and of political science is with pleasures and pains; for the man who uses these well will be good, he who uses them badly bad.

That virtue, then, is concerned with pleasures and pains, and that by the acts from which it arises it is both increased and, if they are done differently, destroyed, and that the acts from which it arose are those in which it actualizes itself- let this be taken as said.

4

The question might be asked,; what we mean by saying that we must become just by doing just acts, and temperate by doing temperate acts; for if men do just and temperate acts, they are already just and temperate, exactly as, if they do what is in accordance with the laws of grammar and of music, they are grammarians and musicians.

Or is this not true even of the arts? It is possible to do something that is in accordance with the laws of grammar, either by chance or at the suggestion of another. A man will be a grammarian, then, only when he has both done something grammatical and done it grammatically; and this means doing it in accordance with the grammatical knowledge in himself.

Again, the case of the arts and that of the virtues are not similar; for the products of the arts have their goodness in themselves, so that it is enough that they should have a certain character, but if the acts that are in accordance with the virtues have themselves a certain character it does not follow that they are done justly or temperately. The agent also must be in a certain condition when he does them; in the first place he must have knowledge, secondly he must choose the acts, and choose them for their own sakes, and thirdly his action must proceed from a firm and unchangeable character. These are not reckoned in as conditions of the possession of the arts, except the bare knowledge; but as a condition of the possession of the virtues knowledge has little or no weight, while the other conditions count not for a little but for everything, i.e. the very conditions which result from often doing just and temperate acts.

Actions, then, are called just and temperate when they are such as the just or the temperate man would do; but it is not the man who does these that is just and temperate, but the man who also does them as just and temperate men do them. It is well said, then, that it is by doing just acts that the just man is produced, and by doing temperate acts the temperate man; without doing these no one would have even a prospect of becoming good.

But most people do not do these, but take refuge in theory and think they are being philosophers and will become good in this way, behaving somewhat like patients who listen attentively to their doctors, but do none of the things they are ordered to do. As the latter will not be made well in body by such a course of treatment, the former will not be made well in soul by such a course of philosophy.

5

Next we must consider what virtue is. Since things that are found in the soul are of three kinds- passions, faculties, states of character, virtue must be one of these. By passions I mean appetite, anger, fear, confidence, envy, joy, friendly feeling, hatred, longing, emulation, pity, and in general the feelings that are accompanied by pleasure or pain; by faculties the things in virtue of which we are said to be capable of feeling these, e.g. of becoming angry or being pained or feeling pity; by states of character the things in virtue of which we stand well or badly with reference to the passions, e.g. with reference to anger we stand badly if we feel it violently or too weakly, and well if we feel it moderately; and similarly with reference to the other passions.

Now neither the virtues nor the vices are passions, because we are not called good or bad on the ground of our passions, but are so called on the ground of our virtues and our vices, and because we are neither praised nor blamed for our passions (for the man who feels fear or anger is not praised, nor is the man who simply feels anger blamed, but the man who feels it in a certain way), but for our virtues and our vices we are praised or blamed.

Again, we feel anger and fear without choice, but the virtues are modes of choice or involve choice. Further, in respect of the passions we are said to be moved, but in respect of the virtues and the vices we are said not to be moved but to be disposed in a particular way.

For these reasons also they are not faculties; for we are neither called good nor bad, nor praised nor blamed, for the simple capacity of feeling the passions; again, we have the faculties by nature, but we are not made good or bad by nature; we have spoken of this before. If, then, the virtues are neither passions nor faculties, all that remains is that they should be states of character.

Thus we have stated what virtue is in respect of its genus.

6

We must, however, not only describe virtue as a state of character, but also say what sort of state it is. We may remark, then, that every virtue or excellence both brings into good condition the thing of which it is the excellence and makes the work of that thing be done well; e.g. the excellence of the eye makes both the eye and its work good; for it is by the excellence of the eye that we see well. Similarly the excellence of the horse makes a horse both good in itself and good at running and at carrying its rider and at awaiting the attack of the enemy. Therefore, if this is true in every case, the virtue of man also will be the state of character which makes a man good and which makes him do his own work well.

How this is to happen we have stated already, but it will be made plain also by the following consideration of the specific nature of virtue. In everything that is continuous and divisible it is possible to take more, less, or an equal amount, and that either in terms of the thing itself or relatively to us; and the equal is an intermediate between excess and defect. By the intermediate in the object I mean that which is equidistant from each of the extremes, which is one and the same for all men; by the intermediate relatively to us that which is neither too much nor too little- and this is not one, nor the same for all. For instance, if ten is many and two is few, six is the intermediate, taken in terms of the object; for it exceeds and is exceeded by an equal amount; this is intermediate according to arithmetical proportion. But the intermediate relatively to us is not to be taken so; if ten pounds are too much for a particular person to eat and two too little, it does not follow that the trainer will order six pounds; for this also is perhaps too much for the person who is to take it, or too little- too little for Milo, too much for the beginner in athletic exercises. The same is true of running and wrestling. Thus a master of any art avoids excess and defect, but seeks the intermediate and chooses this- the intermediate not in the object but relatively to us.

If it is thus, then, that every art does its work well- by looking to the intermediate and judging its works by this standard (so that we often say of good works of art that it is not possible either to take away or to add anything, implying that excess and defect destroy the goodness of works of art, while the mean preserves it; and good artists, as we say, look to this in their work), and if, further, virtue is more exact and better than any art, as nature also is, then virtue must have the quality of aiming at the intermediate. I mean moral virtue; for it is this that is concerned with passions and actions, and in these there is excess, defect, and the intermediate. For instance, both fear and confidence and appetite and anger and pity and in general pleasure and pain may be felt both too much and too little, and in both cases not well; but to feel them at the right times, with reference to the right objects, towards the right people, with the right motive, and in the right way, is what is both intermediate and best, and this is characteristic of virtue. Similarly with regard to actions also there is excess, defect, and the intermediate. Now virtue is concerned with passions and actions, in which excess is a form of failure, and so is defect, while the intermediate is praised and is a form of success; and being praised and being successful are both characteristics of virtue. Therefore virtue is a kind of mean, since, as we have seen, it aims at what is intermediate.

Again, it is possible to fail in many ways (for evil belongs to the class of the unlimited, as the Pythagoreans conjectured, and good to that of the limited), while to succeed is possible only in one way (for which reason also one is easy and the other difficult- to miss the mark easy, to hit it difficult); for these reasons also, then, excess and defect are characteristic of vice, and the mean of virtue;

For men are good in but one way, but bad in many.

Virtue, then, is a state of character concerned with choice, lying in a mean, i.e. the mean relative to us, this being determined by a rational principle, and by that principle by which the man of practical wisdom would determine it. Now it is a mean between two vices, that which depends on excess and that which depends on defect; and again it is a mean because the vices respectively fall short of or exceed what is right in both passions and actions, while virtue both finds and chooses that which is intermediate. Hence in respect of its substance and the definition which states its essence virtue is a mean, with regard to what is best and right an extreme.

But not every action nor every passion admits of a mean; for some have names that already imply badness, e.g. spite, shamelessness, envy, and in the case of actions adultery, theft, murder; for all of these and suchlike things imply by their names that they are themselves bad, and not the excesses or deficiencies of them. It is not possible, then, ever to be right with regard to them; one must always be wrong. Nor does goodness or badness with regard to such things depend on committing adultery with the right woman, at the right time, and in the right way, but simply to do any of them is to go wrong. It would be equally absurd, then, to expect that in unjust, cowardly, and voluptuous action there should be a mean, an excess, and a deficiency; for at that rate there would be a mean of excess and of deficiency, an excess of excess, and a deficiency of deficiency. But as there is no excess and deficiency of temperance and courage because what is intermediate is in a sense an extreme, so too of the actions we have mentioned there is no mean nor any excess and deficiency, but however they are done they are wrong; for in general there is neither a mean of excess and deficiency, nor excess and deficiency of a mean.

7

We must, however, not only make this general statement, but also apply it to the individual facts. For among statements about conduct those which are general apply more widely, but those which are particular are more genuine, since conduct has to do with individual cases, and our statements must harmonize with the facts in these cases. We may take these cases from our table. With regard to feelings of fear and confidence courage is the mean; of the people who exceed, he who exceeds in fearlessness has no name (many of the states have no name), while the man who exceeds in confidence is rash, and he who exceeds in fear and falls short in confidence is a coward. With regard to pleasures and pains- not all of them, and not so much with regard to the pains- the mean is temperance, the excess self-indulgence. Persons deficient with regard to the pleasures are not often found; hence such persons also have received no name. But let us call them 'insensible'.

With regard to giving and taking of money the mean is liberality, the excess and the defect prodigality and meanness. In these actions people exceed and fall short in contrary ways; the prodigal exceeds in spending and falls short in taking, while the mean man exceeds in taking and falls short in spending. (At present we are giving a mere outline or summary, and are satisfied with this; later these states will be more exactly determined.) With regard to money there are also other dispositions- a mean, magnificence (for the magnificent man differs from the liberal man; the former deals with large sums, the latter with small ones), an excess, tastelessness and vulgarity, and a deficiency, niggardliness; these differ from the states opposed to liberality, and the mode of their difference will be stated later. With regard to honour and dishonour the mean is proper pride, the excess is known as a sort of 'empty vanity', and the deficiency is undue humility; and as we said liberality was related to magnificence, differing from it by dealing with small sums, so there is a state similarly related to proper pride, being concerned with small honours while that is concerned with great. For it is possible to desire honour as one ought, and more than one ought, and less, and the man who exceeds in his desires is called ambitious, the man who falls short unambitious, while the intermediate person has no name. The dispositions also are nameless, except that that of the ambitious man is called ambition. Hence the people who are at the extremes lay claim to the middle place; and we ourselves sometimes call the intermediate person ambitious and sometimes unambitious, and sometimes praise the ambitious man and sometimes the unambitious. The reason of our doing this will be stated in what follows; but now let us speak of the remaining states according to the method which has been indicated.

With regard to anger also there is an excess, a deficiency, and a mean. Although they can scarcely be said to have names, yet since we call the intermediate person good-tempered let us call the mean good temper; of the persons at the extremes let the one who exceeds be called irascible, and his vice irascibility, and the man who falls short an inirascible sort of person, and the deficiency inirascibility.

There are also three other means, which have a certain likeness to one another, but differ from one another: for they are all concerned with intercourse in words and actions, but differ in that one is concerned with truth in this sphere, the other two with pleasantness; and of this one kind is exhibited in giving amusement, the other in all the circumstances of life. We must therefore speak of these too, that we may the better see that in all things the mean is praise-worthy, and the extremes neither praiseworthy nor right, but worthy of blame. Now most of these states also have no names, but we must try, as in the other cases, to invent names ourselves so that we may be clear and easy to follow. With regard to truth, then, the intermediate is a truthful sort of person and the mean may be called truthfulness, while the pretence which exaggerates is boastfulness and the person characterized by it a boaster, and that which understates is mock modesty and the person characterized by it mock-modest. With regard to pleasantness in the giving of amusement the intermediate person is ready-witted and the disposition ready wit, the excess is buffoonery and the person characterized by it a buffoon, while the man who falls short is a sort of boor and his state is boorishness. With regard to the remaining kind of pleasantness, that which is exhibited in life in general, the man who is pleasant in the right way is friendly and the mean is friendliness, while the man who exceeds is an obsequious person if he has no end in view, a flatterer if he is aiming at his own advantage, and the man who falls short and is unpleasant in all circumstances is a quarrelsome and surly sort of person.

There are also means in the passions and concerned with the passions; since shame is not a virtue, and yet praise is extended to the modest man. For even in these matters one man is said to be intermediate, and another to exceed, as for instance the bashful man who is ashamed of everything; while he who falls short or is not ashamed of anything at all is shameless, and the intermediate person is modest. Righteous indignation is a mean between envy and spite, and these states are concerned with the pain and pleasure that are felt at the fortunes of our neighbours; the man who is characterized by righteous indignation is pained at undeserved good fortune, the envious man, going beyond him, is pained at all good fortune, and the spiteful man falls so far short of being pained that he even rejoices. But these states there will be an opportunity of describing elsewhere; with regard to justice, since it has not one simple meaning, we shall, after describing the other states, distinguish its two kinds and say how each of them is a mean; and similarly we shall treat also of the rational virtues.

8

There are three kinds of disposition, then, two of them vices, involving excess and deficiency respectively, and one a virtue, viz. the mean, and all are in a sense opposed to all; for the extreme states are contrary both to the intermediate state and to each other, and the intermediate to the extremes; as the equal is greater relatively to the less, less relatively to the greater, so the middle states are excessive relatively to the deficiencies, deficient relatively to the excesses, both in passions and in actions. For the brave man appears rash relatively to the coward, and cowardly relatively to the rash man; and similarly the temperate man appears self-indulgent relatively to the insensible man, insensible relatively to the self-indulgent, and the liberal man prodigal relatively to the mean man, mean relatively to the prodigal. Hence also the people at the extremes push the intermediate man each over to the other, and the brave man is called rash by the coward, cowardly by the rash man, and correspondingly in the other cases.

These states being thus opposed to one another, the greatest contrariety is that of the extremes to each other, rather than to the intermediate; for these are further from each other than from the intermediate, as the great is further from the small and the small from the great than both are from the equal. Again, to the intermediate some extremes show a certain likeness, as that of rashness to courage and that of prodigality to liberality; but the extremes show the greatest unlikeness to each other; now contraries are defined as the things that are furthest from each other, so that things that are further apart are more contrary.

To the mean in some cases the deficiency, in some the excess is more opposed; e.g. it is not rashness, which is an excess, but cowardice, which is a deficiency, that is more opposed to courage, and not insensibility, which is a deficiency, but self-indulgence, which is an excess, that is more opposed to temperance. This happens from two reasons, one being drawn from the thing itself; for because one extreme is nearer and liker to the intermediate, we oppose not this but rather its contrary to the intermediate. E.g. since rashness is thought liker and nearer to courage, and cowardice more unlike, we oppose rather the latter to courage; for things that are further from the intermediate are thought more contrary to it. This, then, is one cause, drawn from the thing itself; another is drawn from ourselves; for the things to which we ourselves more naturally tend seem more contrary to the intermediate. For instance, we ourselves tend more naturally to pleasures, and hence are more easily carried away towards self-indulgence than towards propriety. We describe as contrary to the mean, then, rather the directions in which we more often go to great lengths; and therefore self-indulgence, which is an excess, is the more contrary to temperance.

9

That moral virtue is a mean, then, and in what sense it is so, and that it is a mean between two vices, the one involving excess, the other deficiency, and that it is such because its character is to aim at what is intermediate in passions and in actions, has been sufficiently stated. Hence also it is no easy task to be good. For in everything it is no easy task to find the middle, e.g. to find the middle of a circle is not for every one but for him who knows; so, too, any one can get angry- that is easy- or give or spend money; but to do this to the right person, to the right extent, at the right time, with the right motive, and in the right way, that is not for every one, nor is it easy; wherefore goodness is both rare and laudable and noble.

Hence he who aims at the intermediate must first depart from what is the more contrary to it, as Calypso advises- Hold the ship out beyond that surf and spray.

For of the extremes one is more erroneous, one less so; therefore, since to hit the mean is hard in the extreme, we must as a second best, as people say, take the least of the evils; and this will be done best in the way we describe. But we must consider the things towards which we ourselves also are easily carried away; for some of us tend to one thing, some to another; and this will be recognizable from the pleasure and the pain we feel. We must drag ourselves away to the contrary extreme; for we shall get into the intermediate state by drawing well away from error, as people do in straightening sticks that are bent.

Now in everything the pleasant or pleasure is most to be guarded against; for we do not judge it impartially. We ought, then, to feel towards pleasure as the elders of the people felt towards Helen, and in all circumstances repeat their saying; for if we dismiss pleasure thus we are less likely to go astray. It is by doing this, then, (to sum the matter up) that we shall best be able to hit the mean.

But this is no doubt difficult, and especially in individual cases; for or is not easy to determine both how and with whom and on what provocation and how long one should be angry; for we too sometimes praise those who fall short and call them good-tempered, but sometimes we praise those who get angry and call them manly. The man, however, who deviates little from goodness is not blamed, whether he do so in the direction of the more or of the less, but only the man who deviates more widely; for he does not fail to be noticed. But up to what point and to what extent a man must deviate before he becomes blameworthy it is not easy to determine by reasoning, any more than anything else that is perceived by the senses; such things depend on particular facts, and the decision rests with perception. So much, then, is plain, that the intermediate state is in all things to be praised, but that we must incline sometimes towards the excess, sometimes towards the deficiency; for so shall we most easily hit the mean and what is right.

THE ETHICS OF CARE

In the 1970's, a psychologist named Lawrence Kohlberg was working at Harvard University, trying to develop a theory regarding the moral development of children. Kohlberg and his staff would ask children of various ages about moral dilemmas and problems, and categorize their answers in order to try to find similar stages of moral thinking that each child was exhibiting at a certain age. After an extensive longitudinal study of many children, Kohlberg developed the following scale of moral maturity:

Level I: Preconventional Morality (age 1-10)
    Stage 1: Obedience and Punishment Orientation (age 1-5):
The right thing to do is to obey those with superior power and thus avoid punishment.
Moral judgment is motivated by a need to avoid punishment.
    Stage 2: Instrumental Relativist Orientation (age 5-10):
The right thing to do is whatever would get me what I want.
Moral judgment is motivated by a need to satisfy my own desires.

Level II: Conventional Morality (age 10-13)
    Stage 3: "Good Boy/Nice Girl" Orientation (age 8-16):
The right thing to do is whatever will gain the approval of others: Conform to the expectations of others.
Moral judgment is motivated by a need to avoid rejection or disapproval from others.
    Stage 4: Law and Order Orientation (age 16-→):
The right thing to do is to obey the rules of society. Anyone breaking the (positive) law deserves to be punished.
Moral Judgment is motivated by a need not to be criticized by a true authority figure (e.g., the sheriff).

Level III: Postconventional Morality (adolescence-adulthood)
    Stage 5: Contractarian Orientation (only about 20-25% of adults reach this stage, and then usually only after their mid-twenties):
The right thing to do is to obey the laws, but only if they were established in a fair manner and fulfill an ethical purpose.
Moral judgment is motivated by respect for all, respecting democratic social order, and living under fairly determined laws.

Stage 6: Universal, Ethical Orientation:
The right thing to do is to act on principles which are autonomously chosen by me and for which I can stand up as a responsible and reasonable individual.
Moral judgment is motivated by one's own conscience.

Hence, Kohlberg presented moral development as a process of growing abstraction and impartiality in moral thinking, leading ultimately to an entirely impartial universalist viewpoint in stage six. One of Kohlberg's Graduate Assistants named Carol Gilligan noticed something strange about the way children fit into this scale. The girls in the study scored consistently lower (in every age group) than the boys. And many of the girls seemed to get "stuck" at stage three. Since, according to Piaget, a theory of development does not stand on its base, but hangs from its apex (i.e., hinges upon what we take the top of the scale to be), Gilligan decided to use mature women as the standard of complete moral maturity. This led her to an amazing discovery. According to Gilligan, in general, men and women think morally differently. They see moral problems from radically different perspectives

According to Gilligan, women (typically) have a different conception of moral problems. They tend to see conflicting responsibilities rather than competing rights. They focus on helping other members of a community (joined by bonds of relationship) who are in need rather than respecting other autonomous and separate individuals. Gilligan gave a name to these two ways of seeing moral problems: The Ethics of Justice, and the Ethics of Care.

Ethics of Justice vs.	**Ethics of Care**
Focus on Rights	Focus on responsibilities (responding to the needs of those with whom I am in relationship).
Adhering to rules	Nurturing caring relationships
Separation/Individuation /Autonomy	Connection/Bonds of Care Ideal of Impartiality (Fairness) Ideal of the Nurturing and Partial Caregiver (e.g., A Caring Mother).
Abstract/Formal	Concrete/Contextual/Narrative
Black/White Principled Thinking	Creative and Contextual Thinking

There is a great deal of debate about where the differences that Gilligan describes might originate. Some claim that they are biologically based; others see them as the result of cultural conditioning (perhaps, particularly the systematic oppression of women by men for millennia). And, regardless of where these differences originate, what we should do about them has also generated controversy. Should men and women try to become more like each other in their moral thinking? But the least that we can say about these differences is that women's moral voices deserve to be heard in the discipline of ethics. Hence, many of the papers that follow make use of the perspective of the Ethics of Care in order to try to understand our obligations with respect to family life.

The following excerpt from Gilligan's work describes some of her findings regarding the different ways that men and women typically think morally (especially as these differences actually occurred in some of the children Gilligan studied).

EXCERPT FROM *IN A DIFFERENT VOICE*[1] BY CAROL GILLIGAN

Over the past ten years, I have been listening to people talking about morality and about themselves. Halfway through that time, I began to hear a distinction in these voices, two ways of speaking about moral problems, two modes of describing the relationship between other and self. Differences represented in the psychological literature as steps in a developmental progression suddenly appeared instead as a contrapuntal theme, woven into the cycle of life and recurring in varying forms in people's judgments, fantasies, and thoughts. The occasion for this observation was the selection of a sample of women for a study of the relation between judgment and action in a situation of moral conflict and choice. Against the background of the psychological descriptions of identity and moral development which I had read and taught for a number of years, the women's voices sounded distinct. It was then that I began to notice the recurrent problems in interpreting women's development and to connect these problems to the repeated exclusion of women from the critical theory-building studies of psychology research. ...

The different voice I describe is characterized not by gender but theme. Its association with woman is an empirical observation, and it is primarily through women's voices that I trace its development. But this association is not absolute, and contrasts between male and female voices are presented here to highlight a distinction between two modes of thought and to focus a problem of interpretation rather than to represent a generalization about either sex. ...

The penchant of developmental theorists to project a masculine image, and one that appears frightening to women, goes back at least to Freud (1905), who built his theory of psychosexual development around the experiences of the male child that culminate in the Oedipus complex. In the 1920s, Freud struggled to resolve the contradictions posed for his theory by the differences in female anatomy and the different configuration of the young girl's early family relationships. After trying to

[1] Reprinted by permission of the publisher from IN A DIFFERENT VOICE: PSYCHOLOGICAL THEORY AND WOMEN'S DEVELOPMENT by Carol Gilligan, pp. 1-2, 6-7, 9-12, 14, 25-29, Cambridge, Mass.:Harvard University Press, Copyright © 1982, 1993 by Carol Gilligan

fit women into his masculine conception, seeing them as envying that which they missed, he came instead to acknowledge, in the strength and persistence of women's pre-Oedipal attachments to their mothers, a developmental difference. He considered this difference in women's development to be responsible for what he saw as women's developmental failure.

Having tied the formation of the superego or conscience to castration anxiety, Freud considered women to be deprived by nature of the impetus for a clear-cut Oedipal resolution. Consequently, women's superego - the heir to the Oedipus complex - was compromised: it was never "so inexorable, so impersonal, so independent of its emotional origins as we require it to be in men." From this observation of difference, that "for women the level of what is ethically normal is different from what it is in men," Freud concluded that women "show less sense of justice than men, that they an less ready to submit to the great exigencies of life, that they are more often influenced in their judgments by feelings of affection or hostility" (1925, pp. 257-258).

Thus a problem in theory became cast as a problem in women's development, and the problem in women's development was located in their experience of relationships. ...

Janet Lever (1976), considering the peer group to be the agent of socialization during the elementary school years and play to be a major activity of socialization at that time, set out to discover whether there are sex differences in the games that children play. Studying 181 fifth-grade, white, middle-class children, ages ten and eleven, she observed the organization and structure of their playtime activities. She watched the children as they played at school during recess and in physical education class, and in addition kept diaries of their accounts as to how they spent their out-of-school time. From this study, Lever reports sex differences: boys play out of doors more often than girls do; boys play more often in large and age-heterogeneous groups; they play competitive games more often, and their games last longer than girls' games. The last is in some ways the most interesting finding. Boys' games appeared to last longer not only because they required a higher level of skill and were thus less likely to become boring, but also because, when disputes arose in the course of a game, boys were able to resolve the disputes more effectively than girls: "During the course of this study, boys were seen quarrelling all the time, but not once was a game terminated because of a quarrel and no game was interrupted for more than seven minutes. In the gravest debates, the final word was always, to 'repeat the play,' generally followed by a chorus of 'cheaters proof' " (p. 482). In fact, it seemed that the boys enjoyed the legal debates as much as they did the game itself, and even marginal players of lesser skill participated equally in these recurrent squabbles. In contrast, the eruption of disputes among girls tended to end the game.

Thus Lever extends and corroborates the observations of Piaget in his study of the rules of the game, where he finds boys becoming through childhood increasingly fascinated with the legal elaboration of rules and the development of fair procedures for adjudicating conflicts, a fascination that, he notes, does not hold for girls. Girls, Piaget observes, have a more "pragmatic" attitude toward rules, "regarding a rule as good as long as the game repaid it" (p. 83). Girls are more tolerant in their attitudes toward rules, more willing to make exceptions, and more easily reconciled to innovations. As a result, the legal sense which Piaget considers essential to moral development, "is far less developed in little girls than in boys" (p.77).

The bias that leads Piaget to equate male development with child development also colors Lever's work. The assumption that shapes her discussion of results is that the male model is the better one since it fits the requirements for modern corporate success. In contrast, the sensitivity and care for the feelings of others that girls develop through their play have little market value and can even impede professional success. Lever implies that, given the realities of adult life, if a girl does not want to be left dependent on men, she will have to learn to play like a boy.

To Piaget's argument that children learn the respect for rules necessary for moral development by playing rule-bound games, Lawrence Kohlberg (1969) adds that these lessons are most effectively learned through the opportunities for role-taking that arise in the course of resolving disputes. Consequently, the moral lessons inherent in girls' play appear to be fewer than in boys'. Traditional girls' games like jump rope and hopscotch are turn-taking games, where competition is indirect since one person's success does not necessarily signify another's failure. Consequently, disputes requiring adjudication are less likely to occur. In fact, most of the girls whom Lever interviewed claimed that when a quarrel broke out, they ended the game. Rather than elaborating a system of rules for resolving disputes, girls subordinated the continuation of the game to the continuation of relationships.

Lever concludes that from the games they play, boys learn both the independence and the organizational skills necessary for coordinating the activities of large and diverse groups of people. By participating in controlled and socially approved competitive situations, they learn to deal with competition in a relatively forthright manner - to play with their enemies and to compete with their friends - all in accordance with the rules of the game. In contrast, girls' play tends to occur in smaller, more intimate groups, often the best-friend dyad, and in private places. This play replicates the social pattern of primary human relationships in that its organization is more cooperative. Thus, it points less, in Mead's terms, toward learning to take the role of "the generalized other," less toward the abstraction of human relationships. But it fosters the development of the empathy and sensitivity necessary for taking the role of "the particular other" and points more toward knowing the other as different from the self. ...

The problem that female adolescence presents for theorists of human development is apparent in Erikson's scheme. Erikson (1950) charts eight stages of psychosocial development, of which adolescence is the fifth. The task at this stage is to forge a coherent sense of self, to verify an identity that can span the discontinuity of puberty and make possible the adult capacity to love and work. The preparation for the successful resolution of the adolescent identity crisis is delineated in Erikson's description of the crises that characterize the preceding four stages. Although the initial crisis in infancy of "trust versus mistrust" anchors development in the experience of relationship, the task then clearly becomes one of individuation. Erikson's second stage centers on the crisis of "autonomy versus shame and doubt," which marks the walking child's emerging sense of separateness and agency. From there, development goes on through the crisis of "initiative versus guilt," successful resolution of which represents a further move in the direction of autonomy. Next, following the inevitable disappointment of the magical wishes of the Oedipal period, children realize that to compete with their parents, they must first join them and learn to do what they do so well. Thus in the middle childhood years, development turns on the crisis of "industry versus inferiority," as the demonstration of competence becomes critical to the child's developing self-esteem. This is the time when children strive to learn and master the technology of their culture, in order to recognize themselves and to be recognized by others as capable of becoming adults. Next comes adolescence, the celebration of the autonomous, initiating, industrious self through the forging of an identity based on an ideology that can support and justify adult commitments. But about whom is Erikson talking?

Once again it turns out to be the male child. For the female, Erikson (1968) says, the sequence is a bit different. She holds her identity in abeyance as she prepares to attract the man by whose name she will be known, by whose status she will be defined, the man who will rescue her from emptiness and loneliness by filling "the inner space." While for men, identity precedes intimacy and generatively in the optimal cycle of human separation and attachment, for women these tasks seem instead to be fused. Intimacy goes along with identity, as the female comes to know herself as she is known, through her relationships with others.

Yet despite Erikson's observation of sex differences, his chart of life-cycle stages remains unchanged: identity continues to precede intimacy as male experience continues to define his life-cycle conception. But in this male life cycle there is little preparation for the intimacy of the first adult stage. Only the initial stage of trust versus mistrust suggests the type of mutuality that Erikson means by intimacy and generatively and Freud means by genitality. The rest is separateness, with the result that development itself comes to be identified with separation, and attachments appear to be developmental impediments, as is repeatedly the case in the assessment of women. ...

These observations about sex differences support the conclusion reached by David McClelland (1975) that "sex role turns out to be one of the most important determinants of human behavior; psychologists have found sex differences in their studies from the moment they started doing empirical research." But since it is difficult to say "different" without saying "better" or "worse," since there is a tendency to construct a single scale of measurement, and since that scale has generally been derived from and standardized on the basis of men's interpretations of research data drawn predominantly or exclusively from studies of males, psychologists "have tended to regard male behavior as the 'norm' and female behavior as some kind of deviation from that norm" (p. 81). Thus, when women do not conform to the standards of psychological expectation, the conclusion has generally been that something is wrong with the women.

What Matina Horner (1972) found to be wrong with women was the anxiety they showed about competitive achievement. From the beginning, research on human motivation using the Thematic Apperception Test (TAT) was plagued by evidence of sex differences which appeared to confuse and complicate data analysis. The TAT presents for interpretation an ambiguous cue - a picture about which a story is to be written or a segment of a story that is to be completed. Such stories, in reflecting projective imagination, are considered by psychologists to reveal the ways in which people construe what they perceive, that is, the concepts and interpretations they bring to their experience and thus presumably the kind of sense that they make of their lives. Prior to Horner's work it was clear that women made a different kind of sense than men of situations of competitive achievement, that in some way they saw the situations differently or the situations aroused in them some different response...

The shift in imagery that creates the problem in interpreting women's development is elucidated by the moral judgments of two eleven-year-old children, a boy and a girl, who see, in the same dilemma, two very different moral problems. While current theory brightly illuminates the line and the logic of the boy's thought, it casts scant light on that of the girl. The choice of a girl whose moral judgments elude existing categories of developmental assessment is meant to highlight the issue of interpretation rather than to exemplify sex differences per se. Adding a new line of interpretation, based on the imagery of the girl's thought, makes it possible not only to see development where previously development was not discerned but also to consider differences in the understanding of relationships without scaling these differences from better to worse.

The two children were in the same sixth-grade class at school and were participants in the rights and responsibilities study, designed to explore different conceptions of morality and self. The sample selected for this study was chosen to focus the variables of gender and age while maximizing developmental potential by holding constant, at a high level, the factors of intelligence, education, and social class that have been associated with moral development, at least as measured by existing scales. The two children in question, Amy and Jake, were both bright articulate and, at least in their eleven-year-old aspirations, resisted easy categories of sex-role stereotyping, since Amy aspired to become a scientist while Jake preferred English to math. Yet their moral judgments seem initially to confirm familiar notions about differences between the sexes, suggesting that the edge girls have on moral development during the early school years gives way at puberty with the ascendance of formal logical thought in boys.

The dilemma that these eleven-year-olds were asked to resolve was one in the series devised by Kohlberg to measure moral development in adolescence by presenting a conflict between moral norms and exploring the logic of its resolution. In this particular dilemma, a man named Heinz considers whether or not to steal a drug which he cannot afford to buy in order to save the life of his wife. In the standard format of Kohlberg's interviewing procedure, the description of the dilemma itself - Heinz's predicament, the wife's disease, the druggist's refusal to lower his price – is followed by the question, "Should Heinz steal the drug?" The reasons for and against stealing are then explored through a series of questions that vary and extend the parameters of the dilemma in a way designed to reveal the underlying structure of moral thought.

Jake, at eleven, is clear from the outset that Heinz should steal the drug. Constructing the dilemma, as Kohlberg did, as a conflict between the values of property and life, he discerns the logical priority of life and uses, that logic to justify his choice:

> For one thing, a human life is worth more than money, and if the druggist only makes $1000, he is still going to live, but if Heinz doesn't steal the drug, his wife is going to die. (Why is life worth more than money?) Because the druggist can get a thousand dollars later from rich people with cancer, but Heinz can't get his wife again. (Why not?) Because people are all different and so you couldn't get Heinz's wife again.

Asked whether Heinz should steal the drug if he does not love his wife, Jake replies that he should, saying that not only is there "a difference between hating and killing," but also, if Heinz were caught, "the judge would probably think it was the right thing to do." Asked about the fact that, in stealing, Heinz would be breaking the law, he says that "the laws have mistakes, and you can't go writing up a law for everything that you can imagine."

Thus, while taking the law into account and recognizing its function in maintaining social order (the judge, Jake says, "should give Heinz the lightest possible sentence"), he also sees the law as man-made and therefore subject to error and change. Yet his judgment that Heinz should steal the drug, like his view of the law as having mistakes, rests on the assumption of agreement, a societal consensus around moral values that allows one to know and expect others to recognize what is "the right thing to do."

Fascinated by the power of logic, this eleven-year-old boy locates truth in math, which, he says, is "the only thing that is totally logical." Considering the moral dilemma to be "sort of like a math problem with humans," he sets it up as an equation and proceeds to work out the solution. Since his solution is rationally derived, he assumes that anyone following reason would arrive at the same conclusion and thus that a judge would also consider stealing to be the right thing for Heinz to do. Yet he is also aware of the limits of logic. Asked whether there is a right answer to moral problems, Jake replies that "there can only be right and wrong in judgment," since the parameters of action are variable and complex. Illustrating how actions undertaken with the best of intentions can eventuate in the most disastrous, of consequences, he says. "like if you give an old lady your seat on the trolley, if you are in a trolley crash and that seat goes through the window, it might be that reason that the old lady dies."

Theories of developmental psychology illuminate well the position of this child, standing at the juncture of childhood and adolescence, at what Piaget describes as the pinnacle of childhood intelligence, and beginning through thought to discover a wider universe of possibility. The moment of preadolescence is caught by the conjunction of formal operational thought with a description of self still anchored in the factual parameters of his childhood world - his age, his town, his father's occupation, the substance of his likes, dislikes, and beliefs. Yet as his self description radiates the self-confidence of a child who has arrived, in Erikson's terms, at a favorable balance of industry over inferiority - competent, sure of himself, and knowing well the rules of the game - so his emergent capacity for formal thought, his ability to think about thinking and to reason things out in a logical way, frees him from dependence on authority and allows him to find solutions to problems by himself.

This emergent autonomy follows the trajectory that Kohlberg's six stages of moral development trace, a three-level progression from an egocentric understanding of fairness based on individual, need (stages one and two), to a conceptions of fairness anchored in the shared conventions of societal agreement (stages three and four), and finally to a principled understanding of fairness that rests on the free-standing logic of equality and reciprocity (stages five and six). While this boy's judgments at eleven are scored as conventional on Kohlberg's scale, a mixture of stages three and four, his ability to bring deductive logic to bear on the solution of moral dilemmas, to differentiate morality from law, and to see how laws can be considered to have mistakes points toward the principled conception of justice that Kohlberg equates with moral maturity.

In contrast, Amy's response to the dilemma conveys a very different impression, an image of development stunted by a failure of logic, an inability to think for herself. Asked if Heinz should steal the drug, she replies in a way that seems evasive and unsure:

> Well, I don't think so. I think there might be other ways besides stealing it, like if he could borrow the money or make a loan or something, but he really shouldn't steal the drug - but his wife shouldn't die either.

Asked why he should not steal the drug, she considers neither property nor law but rather the effect that theft could have on the relationship between Heinz and his wife:

> If he stole the drug, he might save his wife then, but if he did, he might have to go to jail, and then his wife might get sicker again, and he couldn't

get more of the drug, and it might not be good. So, they should really just talk it out and find some other way to make the money.

Seeing in the dilemma not a math problem with humans but a narrative of relationships that extends over time, Amy envisions the wife's continuing need for her husband and the husband's continuing concern for his wife and seeks to respond to the druggist's need in a way that would sustain rather than sever connection. Just a she ties the wife's survival to the preservation of relationships, so she considers the value of the wife's life in a context of relationships, saying that it would be wrong to let her die because, "if she died, it hurts a lot of people and it hurts her." Since Amy's moral judgment is grounded in the belief that, "if somebody has something that would keep somebody alive, then its not right not to give it to them," she considers the problem in the dilemma to arise not from the druggist's assertion of rights but from his failure of response.

As the interviewer proceeds with the series of questions that follow from Kohlberg's construction of the dilemma, Amy's answers remain essentially unchanged, the various probes serving neither to elucidate nor to modify her initial response. Whether or not Heinz loves his wife, he still shouldn't steal or let her die; if it were a stranger dying instead, Amy says that "if the stranger didn't have anybody near or anyone she knew," then Heinz should try to save her life, but he should not steal the drug. But as the interviewer conveys through the repetition of questions that the answers she gave were not heard or not right, Amy's confidence begins to diminish, and her replies become more constrained and unsure." Asked again why Heinz should not steal the drug, she simply repeats, "Because, it's not right." Asked again to explain why, she states again that theft would not be a good solution, adding lamely, "if he took it, he might not know how to give it to his wife, and so his wife might still die." Failing to see the dilemma as a self-contained problem in moral logic, she does not discern the internal structure of its resolution; as she constructs the problem differently herself, Kohlberg's conception completely evades her.

Instead, seeing a world comprised of relationships rather than of people standing alone, a world that coheres through human connection rather than through systems of rules, she finds the puzzle in the dilemma to lie in the failure of the druggist to respond to the wife. Saying that "it is not right for someone to die when their life could be saved," she assumes that if the druggist were to see the consequences of his refusal to lower his price, he would realize that "he should just give it to the wife and then have the husband pay back the money later." Thus she considers the solution to the dilemma to lie in making the wife's condition more salient to the druggist or, that failing, in appealing to others who are in a position to help.

Just as Jake is confident the judge would agree that stealing is the right thing for Heinz to do, so Amy is confident that, "if Heinz and the druggist had talked it out long enough, they could reach something besides stealing." As he considers the law to "have mistakes," so she sees this drama as a mistake, believing that "the world should just share things more and then people wouldn't have to steal." Both children thus recognize the need for agreement but see it as mediated in different ways - he impersonally through systems of logic and law, she personally through communication in relationship. Just as he relies on the conventions of logic to deduce the solution to this dilemma, assuming there conventions to be shared, so she relies on a process of communication, assuming connection and believing that her voice will be heard. Yet while his assumptions about agreement are confirmed by the convergence in logic between his answers and the questions posed, her assumptions are belied by the failure of communication, the interviewer's inability to understand her response.

CHAPTER TWO

LOVE, SEX, AND MARRIAGE

INTRODUCTION

As noted in the introduction to this volume, the notions of marriage and family have always been somewhat in flux. Recent history in the West, however, has underscored just how fast they can change. Interracial marriage, homosexual marriage, polygamy, polyamory, and non-nuclear families have all moved from the taboo periphery of family life towards varying degrees of social acceptance. These changes do not come without ethical issues, however, and this chapter explores a cross-section of those issues.

Perhaps the most visible change to the family in the last twenty years has been the reinterpretation of marriage, both between same-sex couples and within heterosexual relationships. As more and different examples of marriages and their corresponding families emerge, questions about the nature of marriage and its associated ethical duties inevitably become a focal point of public debate. At the apex of this debate is the question of which kinds of arrangements should be recognized by the state as marriages and what kinds of benefits such recognitions should incur.

Traditionally, marriages are recognized by the state or a religious institution of some kind. However some couples see themselves as married even in absence of this recognition. In "Informalist Conceptions of Marriage and Some of Their Implications", Steven Weimer and Sangeeta Sangha carefully disentangle the legal aspects of marriage from its additional foundations in human relationships and lay out a conception of marriage entirely founded on the relationship between the people involved. In the second half of their paper, they draw out the implications of understanding marriage in such a way, presenting some surprising results about how such marriages might come to an end.

Seeing marriage as primarily an emotional relationship is by no means a new development. In Kathryn Norlock's "Teaching "Against Marriage," or, "But, Professor, marriage isn't a *contract*!", Norlock explores how prevalent this view is among college students in the US by describing her experiences teaching Claudia Card's famous article "Against Marriage". She identifies the opposing view as Kantian in nature and argues that educators have a duty to teach students the importance of recognizing marriage as a social and legal institution.

The benefits of legally recognized marriages have traditionally been denied to same-sex couples, but as Mark Strasser argues in "Marriage, Parenting, and Sexual Orientation", the harm also extends to their children. Citing recent state supreme court decisions that argue to the contrary, Strasser argues that the predicament of modern families requires the stability afforded by legally recognized marriage, especially when those families involve two parents of the same sex.

Whatever the nature of bonds of marriage, another central question is whether these bonds should be recognized between two people only (a requirement that marriages be "binary") or whether more than two people can responsibly undertake a marriage. Invoking John Rawls, Laura Osinski's paper "A Liberal Conception of Civil Marriage" defends the thesis that while traditional liberal defenses of marriage can accommodate same-sex marriages, the argument is much harder to make for marriages involving multiple sets of partners.

Multiple partners may create problems in another arrangement that is gaining popularity in some circles: polyamorous (or open) marriages. In her paper, "The Ethics of Polyamorous Marriage", Hallie Liberto draws parallels between Susan Moller Okin's account of women's vulnerability in traditional marriages and the cultural sexual norms that morally restrict men's access to partners in polyamorous marriages. According to her argument, Okin's reasoning would prevent polyandry from being a morally preferable alternative to adultery in traditional marriage.

In the final paper of the chapter, Stephen Scales explores what general moral obligations might accompany sexual behavior inside or outside of a marriage. "'Hooking Up': Moral Obligations and the Meaning of Sex" explores the differences between sex, love, and pleasure through a fictional dialogue between generations. After Scales settles on some relatively stable definitions, he asks what different moral perspectives might conclude from them about the old-fashioned idea that sex might indeed entail a moral obligation to love.

INFORMALIST CONCEPTIONS OF MARRIAGE AND SOME OF THEIR IMPLICATIONS

STEVEN WEIMER AND SANGEETA SANGHA

Introduction

The ongoing debate on same-sex marriage has prompted a reevaluation of our conception of marriage. One prominent position emerging from that reevaluation holds that we should abandon the idea that in order for a relationship to constitute a marriage, it must be recognized as such by some external, typically governmental or religious, authority. On this view, whether or not a relationship is a marriage should be taken to depend entirely on the nature of the relationship, and not at all on whether it has been acknowledged by an appropriate authority. We will call this the "informalist" understanding of marriage so as to distinguish it from the standard view, according to which marriage requires formal recognition by some authority. The informalist understanding is evident in both explicitly political and in more philosophical discussions of marriage. In the political arena, for example, the informalist understanding can be found underlying the attempts of those advocating same-sex marriage to frame the debate as a question about whether such unions should be *recognized* by the state as marriages – suggesting that the relationships in question already *are* marriages, and that whether the state acknowledges them as such is a separate question. The informalist understanding of marriage has also received philosophical support from Richard Taylor, who argues that:

> Marriage, if it is to have any significant meaning, is not a status that is conferred by the enunciation of vows and a pronouncement by a presiding official, and "getting married" does not, except in the most superficial sense mean having a wedding. ... People can become married without any

of those things happening, and, what is more surprising, every detail of that picture can be fulfilled *without any marriage having occurred.*[1]

On an informalist understanding of marriage, such as Taylor's, successful completion of the process customarily thought to result in a marriage – the wedding ceremony, certification of a marriage license, and the declaration that a couple is now married by some official in whom the state has vested the power to make such pronouncements – are therefore neither necessary nor sufficient for the existence of a *true* marriage. Whether or not a couple is truly married depends instead on the nature of their relationship. Hence, a loving and committed couple might be married despite never having gone through the legal and/or religious formalities, while a "green card marriage" entered into solely for citizenship purposes is not a *real* marriage at all, despite successful completion of those formalities.[2]

This informalist approach to marriage certainly has some appeal. Our aim in this paper is to examine it in closer detail, and to explore some of its implications. Development and defense of a complete informalist theory of marriage is not possible here. Our hope, rather, is merely to outline the general features a plausible informalist conception of marriage is likely to include, and then to highlight some of the more interesting implications such a conception would have for the practice and ethics of marriage. To this end, the first section of the paper introduces and evaluates one recently proposed informalist conception of marriage, namely Taylor's. Consideration of the ways in which Taylor's account is unsatisfying serves to point us in the direction of a more promising informalist understanding of marriage. We will argue that central to any plausible informalist conception of marriage will be the idea that marriages are committed, loving relationships between autonomous individuals. In Section Two, we discuss some of the implications that follow from such a conception.

---

[1] Taylor, Richard, *Understanding Marriage: Making it Work or Knowing When to Leave*, (Amherst, New York: Prometheus, 2004), p. 12. Italics in the original.

[2] We will frequently refer to married *couples*. We do so merely for simplicity's sake, and not to rule out the possibility that an informalist marriage might conceivably involve more than two people. Whether or not an informalist conception should allow for the possibility of "plural" marriages is an interesting question, but one we do not address here.

I

On the informalist understanding, whether or not a couple is married depends entirely on the nature of their relationship. The defining features of marriage might be specified in any number of ways, depending, for example, on whether heterosexuality, monogamy, and/or explicit vows are deemed necessary for a relationship to qualify as a marriage. We will take as our starting point the informalist conception recently proposed by Taylor. According to Taylor, "What is essential to being married is not anything readily seen, but rather a strong bond of love between its partners that is lasting and gives meaning to the idea of lifelong commitment."[3] He calls this bond "married love" and explains that it "rests upon, and in fact is one and the same, as the mutual fulfillment of needs. ... It is on this, and this alone, that genuine marriage rests."[4] On this account, a couple is truly married only if they have cultivated a "constant awareness" of, and attention to, one another's needs.[5] The relevant needs form a hierarchy. At the top are things such as the need for security and safety. At the bottom are the moment-to-moment needs to be paid attention to and appreciated by one's spouse, which, although trivial in themselves, are on Taylor's view essential to one's sense of self-worth. Awareness and attention to these needs, he explains, "convey the single, all-important message: *You count, you are important*."[6] In between the basic and trivial needs, "there is a whole continuum. Here should be placed such things as the need for cooperation, affection, intimacy, and so on—all the needs that we normally associate with deep love."[7] Somewhere included in that continuum are the needs created by sex. Although Taylor does not explicitly say so, it is presumably this that makes "married love" a form of romantic love rather than a deep friendship.

Taylor makes a strong case against the traditional, formalist understanding of marriage. He offers rather compelling examples of couples who have in one way or another failed to satisfy the conditions of formal marriage, but who certainly seem married in any meaningful sense of the word.[8] The informalist conception Taylor offers as an alternative,

---

[3] Taylor, p. 60.

[4] Taylor, pp. 68-69.

[5] Taylor, p. 8

[6] Taylor, p. 70.

[7] Taylor, p. 73.

[8] For instance, Taylor relays the story of a couple who, as they put it, "never got around to" being formally married: "we never even bothered to get a marriage license. This hasn't made any difference in our relationship; we certainly *feel*

however, is in several important respects unsatisfying. On Taylor's view the species of romantic love he calls "married love" is both necessary and sufficient for marriage – a relationship qualifies as a marriage if and only if it includes the constant awareness and mutual fulfillment of needs that are the defining features of married love. We will argue that this conception is problematic in three general ways: it employs a counterintuitive account of romantic love, it neglects the important role that commitment plays in distinguishing marriages from other romantic relationships, and finally, it fails to address the autonomy or authenticity of a relationship. Although we will not here specify a complete informalist conception of marriage, we will attempt to show that central to any plausible such conception will be 1) a psychological account of romantic love, 2) a commitment condition, and 3) a condition ensuring that this love and commitment are maintained in a minimally autonomous manner.

Addressing first romantic love: Taylor is correct to think that some form of romantic love is essential to marriage. The reason we want to say that a "green card marriage" isn't *really* a marriage, it seems, is that although the couple has fulfilled the relevant legal requirements, their motivation for doing so was entirely nonromantic. How exactly we should understand romantic love is a difficult question, and one we cannot hope to adequately answer here. We do, however, want to quickly address two related ways in which Taylor's account of "married love" is problematic. This brief critique will give us a better, though still quite rough, understanding of what it means to say that romantic love is essential to marriage.

First, Taylor places no requirement on the motivation behind the mutual fulfillment of needs that is on his account constitutive of married love. A pair of people might cultivate a constant awareness of each other's needs (or as close to this as Taylor could plausibly require)[9], and

---

married, and very happily so, and everyone thinks we are. ... We own all our property together, have joint wills, hold each other's health proxies, and we each have power of attorney for the other. ... And all this makes us wonder, what is marriage, anyway: would we be *more* married if we now looked up some justice of the peace?" (pp. 15-16)

[9] Although Taylor does not explain what he takes "constant awareness" to require, if our conception of marriage is to be of any practical relevance, "constant awareness" clearly cannot be taken literally. A couple can temporarily lose awareness of one another's needs by distancing themselves physically and/or cognitively, yet still be married. We set the question of how, if not literally,

might do their best to fulfill those needs, for purely instrumental reasons. The partners of a green card marriage might decide that the best way to prepare for examination by an Immigration Officer is to "play the part" of a truly married couple by living together and paying close attention to one another's personality and habits. This prolonged proximity and attentiveness may well cultivate the sort of awareness of each other's needs required by Taylor. If they also come to fulfill (many of) those needs – whether because they think this will prepare them even better, or simply out of courtesy – they would be in "married love" according to Taylor's definition. Admittedly, it is unlikely that any such couple would feel it necessary to get to know, and to satisfy, each other's sexual needs. The case could, though, be adjusted to include this class of needs as well. Imagine the same couple living in an invasive, totalitarian society like that in *1984*, where they are observed in the bedroom as well as the living room. In order to prove to the authorities that they are a *genuine* couple, they may have to cultivate the sort of mutual awareness and fulfillment of needs – including sexual needs – constitutive of love on Taylor's account. However, because they do so for purely instrumental reasons, it is difficult to accept theirs as a loving relationship. A loving couple, we want to say, pays attention to one another's needs not merely to achieve some end, but out of genuine concern for one another. As Frankfurt puts it, "love is, most centrally, a *disinterested* concern for the existence of what is loved, and for what is good for it."[10] Taylor would of course agree that romantic love must be distinguished from instrumentally advantageous companionship, but as it stands, nothing in his account enables us to make such a distinction.[11]

Second, and more importantly, the mutual awareness and fulfillment of needs Taylor identifies with love is in our view better understood as a consequence of love than as constitutive of love. It may be true that loving couples typically seek to satisfy one another's needs, but it strikes us as incorrect to say that their doing so *constitutes* love. We think it better to follow common parlance and say instead that they do so *out of*

"constant awareness" should be understood aside because, as is explained below, we believe that any such behavioral understanding of love will be counterintuitive.

[10] Frankfurt, Harry, *The Reasons of Love,* (Princeton: Princeton University Press: 2004), p. 42.

[11] He does at one point say that if you are "totally aware of [a person's sense self-worth], all the time, in someone you care deeply about, [then] you nourish the most powerful of human forces, which is love." (65) This suggests that it is intrinsically concerned couples Taylor has in mind, but the thought fails to make its way into his official definition of married love.

love. That is, romantic love should be identified with the emotion or
concern that regularly motivates lovers to pay attention to and fulfill each
other's needs, and not with the behavioral habits to which it leads. How
best to characterize this emotion and/or concern, we will not here attempt
to say. It may be that love is best understood as a special form of concern,
as an affirmation of value, or instead as an emotion or "emotional
complex." [12] We want merely to suggest that the romantic love essential
to marriage on the informalist conception should be defined as some such
motivational attitude, and not as the behaviors it motivates.

On Taylor's view, romantic, or more specifically "married," love is
not only necessary for marriage, but sufficient for it. We believe this to be
a mistake. Also essential to marriage is some form of commitment.
Taylor at times seems to acknowledge the important role that commitment
plays in marriage. As we have already seen, he at one point says that the
bond of love that is essential to marriage "gives meaning to the idea of
lifelong commitment." He also tells us that "when partners are united in
abiding love, then all the obligations of commitment are automatically
met." [13] This, though, appears to be a side-effect, rather than a condition,
of marriage on Taylor's view. While commitment may accompany
married love, it is on his account married love alone that is necessary for
marriage. That this is counterintuitive can be seen by examining Taylor's
comments on infidelity.

Taylor says that it is the bond of married love which "alone ... gives
rise to every moral consideration involving the behavior of its partners.
Infidelity, for example, is not merely the breach of some vow, but
behavior that destroys the bond of love uniting man and wife." [14] The
mention of vows is misleading here. Taylor makes clear that a married
couple need not have made any vows to one another. The presence of
"married love" is sufficient for a marriage, and such love, Taylor rightly
points out, "is not something that can be promised anyway." [15] That an
action breaches some vow is thus irrelevant on Taylor's account.
Infidelity is defined entirely in terms of its consequences: an action
constitutes infidelity if and only if it destroys the bond of married love. It

---

[12] For reviews of the various understandings of love see Badhar, Neera, "Love," in
Hugh LaFollette (ed.),*The Oxford Handbook of Practical Ethics* (Oxford: Oxford
University Press, 2003): 42-69; or Helm, Bennett, "Love", *The Stanford
Encyclopedia of Philosophy (Fall 2008 Edition)*, Edward N. Zalta (ed.), URL =
<http://plato.stanford.edu/archives/fall2008/entries/love/>
[13] Taylor, p. 63.
[14] Ibid, p. 60.
[15] Ibid, p. 62.

follows that if behavior typically taken to be an instance of infidelity – an extramarital affair, for example – does not have the effect of destroying the couple's bond of married love, then that behavior is not an infidelity after all.[16] This, though, seems wrong. We tend to think that in order to know whether a spouse's behavior constitutes an instance of infidelity, we do not need to know how things go with the couple *after* that behavior, but rather where things stood between them at the time of the behavior. That is, we tend to think that *if* an affair constitutes infidelity (as we shall explain, on the informalist conception it need not in every case), it does so not because of its consequences, but rather because it violates a commitment between the partners – namely, a commitment requiring sexual faithfulness. Taylor's account is unable to accommodate these thoughts. Because commitment is not essential to marriage on his view, the violation of commitment cannot on its own constitute a violation of the marriage – cannot, that is, constitute infidelity.

Now, we do not mean to suggest that a mutual commitment of sexual faithfulness is a necessary condition of informalist marriage. While such a commitment is certainly the norm, and while it thus may be appropriate to assume that a marriage includes such a commitment unless the partners have an explicit understanding to the contrary, the idea of an "open" marriage is in our view not a conceptual confusion. Our suggestion, rather, is that in order for a romantic relationship to constitute a marriage, there must be a mutual commitment to continue the relationship indefinitely, where continuation of the marriage is mutually understood to require certain things of each person – perhaps, but not necessarily, including sexual faithfulness. We will have more to say about these requirements shortly. The point we want to stress now is that this commitment to continue the relationship indefinitely, or as Brenda Almond has called it, the "quest for permanence," is as she says a "primary defining feature" of marriage.[17] It is this commitment to see the

---

[16] In fact, it may be that an affair actually *strengthens* a couple's bond of married love. Taylor notes that legal divorce can sometimes bring a couple closer, thereby making them "more" married, and there is no reason to think that an affair could not have the same effect. This possibility, though, does nothing to change the fact that, intuitively, the affair is an instance of infidelity – an infidelity with good consequences, but an infidelity nonetheless.

[17] Almond, Brenda, *The Fragmenting Family*, (Oxford: Oxford University Press, 2006), p. 23. On Almond's view, this "quest for permanence" is one of two primary defining features of marriage. The other is sexual exclusivity or faithfulness. As we have said, while it remains the norm, sexual faithfulness is not in our view necessary for marriage.

relationship through, in good times and in bad, that enables us to distinguish marriages from other romantic relationships. A relationship understood to be temporary – for instance, a wartime romance between a soldier stationed in enemy territory and a local woman, both of whom know that when the fighting ends, so too must their relationship – is for that reason not a *marriage* relationship.

There are of course several different senses of commitment. In this context, to say that a couple is mutually committed to continuing their relationship indefinitely might be to say that they have *promised* or *agreed* to continue the relationship, that they *intend* to do so,[18] or that they are deeply *invested* in doing so. While each of these understandings has some intuitive pull, we believe that on an informalist conception of marriage, the latter is the more appropriate. As we shall use the term, to say that someone is committed is not to report on something she does, as is the case with the "agreement" and "intention" senses of commitment, but rather to identify something she *is* – namely, invested or devoted.[19] This "investment" sense of commitment may often lead people to make explicit intentions, agreements, or promises, but it is not identical with these other

---

[18] Complicating things further is the fact that there are of course several different senses of "intention." We here assume a belief-desire model of intention, according to which to intend to A is to desire or will to A and to believe that this desire or willing will in fact lead one to A. See Grice, H.P, "Intentions and Uncertainty," *Proceedings of the British Academy,* vol. 57 (1971): 263-279. For a concise review of various theories of intention, see Bratman, Michael, "Intention," in Samuel Guttenplan (ed.), *A Companion to the Philosophy of Mind* (Oxford: Blackwell, 1995): 375-379.

[19] Here compare the "commitment conception" of marriage proposed by Eric Cave in his "Marital Pluralism: Making Marriage Safer for Love," *Journal of Social Philosophy,* vol. 34, no. 3 (2003): 331-347. Cave understands the commitment necessary for marriage as a form of rational intention. On his account, marriage involves the mutual adoption and rational nonreconsideration of rational intentions to be sexually faithful, to cooperate in maintaining a household, and to support one another (331-338). While in agreement with the general, informalist, thrust of Cave's account, we believe that the relevant sense of commitment is a form of volitional investment, rather than of intention. Our account differs from Cave's in two additional ways. First, whereas commitment is sufficient for marriage on Cave's account, we believe romantic love is also necessary. Lacking a love requirement, it is not clear that Cave's account is able to distinguish lovingly committed couples from those committed for purely instrumental reasons, such as the "green card" couples described above. Second, whereas Cave takes marriage to essentially involve sexual faithfulness, cooperation, *and* support, we will adopt a less demanding view, according to which only one of these is required.

forms of commitment.[20] That this is the more appropriate understanding of commitment in this context can be seen by considering the case of a new couple who, after a passionate weekend together, dramatically pledge to stay together forever, and who sincerely intend to do whatever this requires. Because such couples may be in love, according to some realistic, not overly-demanding conception thereof, if the commitment necessary for marriage were synonymous with intention or agreement, they would immediately qualify as married. However, we are reluctant to view such relationships (or at least the stereotypical, "head-over-heels," versions of them that immediately come to mind) as informalist marriages. The informalist will surely want to define marriage in such a way as to require a more substantive bond than the sort of intense, but as yet unsubstantial tie that typically binds such new couples. What this suggests is that the commitment necessary for informalist marriage is not something that can be willed, or performed, but something that must be developed. Our proposal, then, is that in the sense relevant to an informalist conception of marriage, for an individual to be committed to A is for her to be volitionally invested in A. It is for her to have a significant stake in A, and for her will to be organized *around* A as a result. This volitional investment reveals itself over time in the individual's deliberation and action. That is, and as Bratman explains, commitment in this sense involves both reasoning-oriented and action-oriented dispositions. The reasoning-oriented dispositions include the disposition to retain the commitment without reconsideration, to reason from the commitment to derivative commitments and intentions, and to constrain other intentions in light of the commitment.[21] When the time to act on an intention recommended by her commitment arrives, the committed individual will be disposed to do so. Applied to the specific commitment at issue here – the commitment to continue one's relationship indefinitely – the committed individual will be one who is not constantly second-guessing her commitment to the relationship, who regularly excludes from consideration actions that are not consistent with continuation of her

---

[20] It is because Taylor fails to distinguish between these two forms of commitment that he rejects the idea that commitment is necessary for marriage. Taylor treats "commitment" as a synonym for "contract," telling us that "Commitment and contract are basically concepts of finance, and what they presuppose is pure self-interest. When someone commits himself to certain terms, then it is presupposed that he does so for advantage; he expects to get something from it, in return for something that is given." (62)
[21] Bratman, Michael, *Intentions, Plans, and Practical Reason* (Cambridge: Harvard University Press, 1987), p. 17.

relationship, and who habitually recognizes and performs actions that are instead recommended or required by continuation of her relationship.

As we have said, a couple mutually committed in this sense will likely intend to stay together, and may formalize this intention by entering into an explicit agreement – perhaps doing so in the context of a public ceremony, i.e. a wedding. It is easy to understand why a couple might want to express their commitment to each other in such ways, and there may well be some benefit from doing so. On the informalist conception we are proposing, however, such intentions and agreements have no necessary connection with the relevant, volitional, sense of commitment. Vows and intentions may express or reflect a couple's volitional commitment, but they may not, for as we have said, couples sometimes make such pledges before volitional commitment exists. And it is possible for a couple to share a deep volitional commitment, yet never have expressed that commitment in the form of an explicit agreement or intention.

We have suggested that a plausible informalist conception of marriage will regard a relationship as a marriage only if it includes both mutual romantic love (on some plausible psychological account thereof) and a mutual commitment to continue the relationship indefinitely, where continuation of the relationship is mutually understood to require certain things of each person. Precisely what continuation of a relationship requires of its members will depend upon the parameters of that relationship. Because the partners to a marriage relationship have a good bit of leeway in defining the parameters of their relationship, requirements will vary from case to case. It is because most marriage relationships are understood to be sexually exclusive that extramarital sex typically constitutes infidelity. In a relationship understood by both spouses to allow for such behavior, it would not. We would suggest, though, that the partners to a marriage do not have complete freedom to define the parameters and requirements of their relationship in whatever way they please. Following Eric Cave, we can identify three requirements which, at least in modern western culture, marriages are commonly taken to include. [22] One of these is a requirement of sexual faithfulness. The others are, first, a requirement of cooperation – as Cave puts it, "to share in the tasks involved in maintaining a household together, although this obligation leaves them considerable latitude in apportioning these tasks" and second, a requirement of support, economic or otherwise, especially in times of

---

[22] Cave, 331. Cave puts these in terms of marital obligations, rather than requirements. For reasons explained below, we think it better to reserve the term "obligations" for the agreement sense of commitment.

need.[23] As a first stab at a minimal commitment condition for informalist marriage, it seems plausible to us to require that the partners to a relationship be mutually committed to continue their relationship indefinitely, where that commitment is mutually understood to include *at least one* of these three requirements. It is difficult to regard a relationship in which none of these things are required of its members – in which they are not expected to remain sexually faithful, to cooperate, *or* to support one another – as a marriage.[24]

Finally, we should add a condition ensuring that the romantic love and commitment necessary for marriage are maintained in a minimally autonomous manner, where this is taken to require merely that the couple possess (perhaps relatively modest) capacities for control over their mental lives (for instance, minimal rationality and self-awareness),[25] and that they are not prevented from applying those capacities to their pro-attitudes regarding the relationship by coercion, manipulation, or other such forms of interference. Taylor appears to have overlooked the need for such a condition,[26] but it seems clear that in order for mutual love and commitment to wed a couple, they must be authentic – must issue from the individuals involved in a meaningful way. An individual who is

---

[23] Cave, 331-332.

[24] Consider, for instance, the following excerpt from a letter to Bertrand Russell, from his first wife: "I am utterly devoted to thee, and have been for over 50 years … but my devotion makes no claim, and involves no burden on thy part, nor any obligation, not even to answer this letter." (Quoted in Almond, p. 26.) This acknowledgement of the fact that their relationship had changed such that nothing whatsoever was any longer required of Russell makes it patently clear that theirs is no longer a marriage relationship.

[25] Alfred Mele, *Autonomous Agents: From Self-Control to Autonomy,* (Oxford: Oxford University Press, 1995), 166-172. Mele's complete list of the self-control capacities relevant to autonomy includes the capacities to modify the strengths of one's desires in the service of one's evaluative judgment, to bring one's emotions into line with relevant judgments, to master motivation that threatens to produce or sustain beliefs in ways that would violate one's principles for belief acquisition and retention, to rationally assess and revise one's values and principles, to identify with one's values on the basis of informed, critical reflection, and to intentionally foster new values and pro-attitudes in oneself in accordance with one's considered evaluative judgments.

[26] Presumably, he did so for the same reason that he failed to say that married love necessarily involves *intrinsic* concern for one another – namely, that he seems to have been primarily concerned with the task of identifying what it is that the most intuitively compelling examples of informalist marriages have in common, and not with demarcating those core cases from other relationships that might share some of their features, e.g. instrumentally-motivated and non-autonomous couples.

volitionally committed to another, but who lacks the self-control capacities needed to assess and revise that commitment in a minimally rational way, is not *autonomously* committed, and on the account we are proposing, is therefore not married. Nor is an individual who is likewise committed and who possesses the necessary self-control capacities, but who is prevented from applying them to her love for and/or commitment to her spouse. This might be true of a person who has been systematically deceived about her spouse or her relationship, or who has been manipulated or abused in such as way as to make meaningful evaluation of her relationship impossible. That systematic deception precludes autonomous maintenance of love and commitment, and hence should prevent a relationship from qualifying as an informalist marriage, seems clear. A more interesting question is whether some extent of *true* information about one's partner and one's relationship is necessary for autonomy. It is possible for an informalist conception of marriage to hold that in order to be truly married, a couple must truly know one another. Whether this is a plausible condition of informalist marriage, and if so, how it might be spelled out, are questions we will not attempt to answer here.

Our proposal, then, is that a plausible informalist conception of marriage will include these three conditions: romantic love, commitment, and minimal autonomy. This is by no means a complete account of informalist marriage. We have provided only brief sketches of how we think the crucial concepts of romantic love, commitment, and autonomy should be understood on the informalist approach. We have also left unaddressed several more specific questions – such as whether marriage must be between a man and woman and whether it must be between only two people. Incomplete though it therefore is, the account we have sketched does give us a rough idea of what a plausible informalist conception of marriage might look like. In the next section, we will examine some of the implications that follow from such a conception.

II

One obvious implication of an informalist conception of marriage, and indeed a primary motivation for adopting such a conception, is that on an informalist approach, many legal "marriages" turn out not to be marriages after all. The necessary love and/or commitment will be lacking in some arranged "marriages," at least for a time, as well as in those "marriages" entered into for purposes of naturalization or personal wealth. It is unlikely that Anna Nicole Smith's relationship with oil billionaire J. Howard Marshall would have qualified as a marriage on the informalist approach. Perhaps, though, this could have changed if Marshall had lived longer – it is certainly possible for a merely legal marriage to become a "true" marriage as its members come to develop the necessary love and commitment.

The reverse is of course also possible. On an informalist conception, a true marriage can become a merely legal marriage, and can do so without any official divorce or annulment proceedings. The decrees of a legal or religious authority are no more relevant to the dissolution of an informalist marriage than to its creation. The existence of such marriages depends instead, and exclusively, on the nature of the relationship. Hence, if and when a relationship ceases to include the features necessary for marriage, it ceases to be a marriage relationship. This will be the case whenever the necessary love or commitment is no longer present in the relationship, or when they are no longer maintained in a minimally autonomous manner. Examples of the first form of dissolution are all too common. On the informalist conception of marriage, as soon as a spouse is no longer in love, or no longer committed in the relevant way, the marriage immediately ends. The formerly married couple may not realize that their marriage has ended, and hence may go on acting *as if* they were still married – may continue to live together, and change little in their day-to-day behavior – but on the informalist conception, this does not imply that they are in fact still married. In believing they are still truly married, such a couple is every bit as mistaken as are the partners to a sham "green card marriage." That they continue to act on the basis of that belief is likewise irrelevant. As we have argued, informalist marriage must be defined not in terms of a couple's behaviors, but rather the emotion and commitment underlying those behaviors. And as Taylor says, "When the bond of love [or, we should add, of commitment] is gone, then the marriage is dead, even though no steps have been taken to end it, and a dead marriage is not a marriage at all."[27]

If the couple does separate, official proceedings may then be necessary to divide up property and/or specify a custody arrangement, should children be involved. The point here is that on the informalist approach, no such proceedings are needed to dissolve the marriage. An interesting consequence of this is that some acts commonly regarded as infidelities would not in fact come in the context of an existing marriage, and hence not be infidelities after all. If the member of a marriage (or his or her spouse) ceases to have the necessary love or commitment prior to engaging in an affair, that affair is carried out by an unmarried person. For

---

[27] Taylor, p. 60.

instance, it may be the very fact that a spouse finds herself with a willingness to engage in an affair which makes her realize that she is no longer committed in the relevant way. Volitional commitment, recall, manifests itself in a disposition to exclude from consideration behaviors inconsistent with that commitment. This disposition need not be perfect – marriage is presumably consistent with some degree of temptation – but if an individual whose marriage is understood to require sexual faithfulness finds herself seriously considering an extramarital affair, this may be an indication that she is no longer committed in the necessary way. Were she still truly committed, a desire to pursue such an affair might not even occur to her, and if it did, would be quickly and firmly repudiated. The fact that her will is now not rebelling against the idea of "cheating," but going along with it, suggests that she is no longer volitionally committed to continuing the relationship. In a case like this, it is likely that her commitment has been waning, or lacking, for some time, but that she only realizes this in light of her willingness to have the affair.[28]

To say that by proceeding with an affair, such a person would not be committing an infidelity is not to say that she would be doing nothing wrong. It may be that the affair would eventually cause harm to her (former) spouse and/or her children, and that this provides her with a moral reason to refrain. In addition, there may be morally relevant promises involved. As we have said, while the sense of "commitment" relevant to the informalist conception of marriage is not that which is synonymous with "agreement" or "promise," it may often to lead a couple to enter into agreements and to make promises. A couple may have promised to remain sexually faithful until any necessary official proceedings are completed, or at the very least, to remain faithful until the nonexistence of the marriage is mutually recognized. Even apart from any such explicit agreement, there may be a reasonable and morally relevant expectation that the couple will remain sexually faithful until the ending of the marriage is mutually acknowledged.[29] We might think that if the marriage has ended, the other person has a right to be informed as soon as

---

[28] It is also possible for an affair to be an infidelity due to a loss of love, rather than of commitment. In this case, it would have to be that although their relationship no longer contains romantic love, the couple remains committed to continuing it indefinitely, and understand that commitment still requires that they not have sex with other people. An example of this might be a formerly romantic couple who are now friends, but who understand that, at least for the time being, their friendship precludes their moving on sexually – it may take some time before the friendship is capable of enduring that.

[29] We thank Eric Cave for pointing out this possibility in correspondence.

is possible. At the end of a long relationship, there may well be other
morally relevant considerations besides those we have mentioned. Our
point here is merely that infidelity is not among them, for in cases of this
sort, there is no longer a marriage to violate.

Indeed, on the account we have outlined, if the act *were* an infidelity,
that fact would not in itself make it a moral, i.e. interpersonal, wrong.
That is, unlike the agreement sense of commitment, on which a marital
commitment can be understood as binding the spouses *to* one another, on
an intention or investment sense of commitment, the committed individual
is bound not to her spouse, but in a sense, to herself. Commitment as
intention binds the agent's future plans and deliberations; commitment
as investment binds these by way of binding the agent's volitional make-up,
her will. On both of these latter approaches, the agent's commitment
places *demands* on her – it makes some actions unacceptable and others
mandatory – but it does not directly obligate her *to* her spouse. To violate
such a volitional commitment is thus not to wrong one's spouse, but rather
to violate something central to who one is; it is to betray *oneself*.[30] This
will strike some as counterintuitive, but it is worth emphasizing that for
the informalist conception of marriage to in this way imply that infidelity
is not itself a moral wrong is not for it to imply that infidelity is morally
benign. In virtually all cases, moral considerations of the sort described
above will have been generated by other aspects of the couple's
relationship, such as their capacity to deeply harm one another, the
promises they have made, and/or the reasonable expectations they have
come to form.

A second, perhaps more controversial, way in which an informalist
marriage might come to end is for the love and commitment to continue,
but for one of the married partners to lose the capacity to maintain them in
a minimally autonomous manner. A married spouse suffering from
advanced Alzheimer's disease, for instance, may come to lack the
rationality, self-awareness, or self-control necessary for even minimal
autonomy. In such circumstances, the relationship may, and hopefully
does, remain a loving one. But it no longer includes the sort of love
necessary for informalist marriage.

Violation of the "independence" half of the autonomy requirement can
also dissolve a marriage. That is, if both partners retain the self-control
capacities necessary for autonomy, but one or both of them is rendered
incapable of applying those capacities to their relationship, that

---

[30] For a discussion of this aspect of volitional investment, see Anderson, Joel,
"Autonomy and the Authority of Personal Commitments," *Philosophical
Explorations*, vol. 6, no. 2 (2003): 90-108.

relationship is no longer autonomously maintained. This will be the case when an initially autonomous marriage comes to include the sort of systematic deception, manipulation, or coercion described earlier. More interestingly, it may be that extreme cases of co-dependency remove the co-dependent's ability to maintain his or her love and commitment in an autonomous manner. If the co-dependent is dominated by the fear of abandonment to the point that he or she is incapable of realistically imagining breaking away from the relationship, then he or she would fail to satisfy the autonomy requirement.

In all of these cases, a marriage has ended despite neither spouse having intentionally ended it, and perhaps without either spouse knowing it has ended. This is a rather unsurprising implication of an informalist conception of marriage. A more interesting question is whether such a conception should allow for the opposite sort of case – that in which a marriage *begins* unintentionally and without the knowledge of the married couple. Nothing in the informalist conception we have outlined precludes this. On that account, two people are married if they autonomously share romantic love and a mutual commitment to continue the relationship indefinitely, where continuation of the relationship is mutually understood to require certain things of each person. As we have said, they need not be committed in the sense that they have performed some explicit, intentional act of commitment – making vows, for instance. Nor need they mutually understand their relationship to *be* a marriage; they need only understand what its continuation requires of them. A non-married couple could therefore "drift" into a marriage just as easily as married couples "drift" out of them. This may strike some as counterintuitive, and it is open to the informalist approach to avoid such an implication by including some condition requiring that in order to be married a couple must take themselves to be married. Since such a condition would require only that the couple *themselves* recognize their relationship as a marriage, and not that any *external* authority do so, it is consistent with the informalist approach to marriage.[31]

---

[31] Such a condition may not, however, be entirely consistent with what we have suggested is the core informalist idea – namely, that whether or not a couple is married depends entirely upon the nature of their relationship. To require for marriage that the couple takes themselves to be married is to add a condition which addresses the couple's understanding of their relationship, rather than the relationship itself, and as such is somewhat at odds with that core idea. To the extent that one is attracted to that core idea, one may wish, therefore, to resist inclusion of a "mutual recognition of marriage" condition. As we have said, though, an account including such a condition remains an informalist one.

Conclusion

Our aim here has been merely to outline what we take to be a plausible informalist conception of marriage, and to identify some of its implications. We leave open the question of whether these implications provide us with reasons to accept such a conception of marriage, or whether they instead amount to a *reduction*, of sorts, of such a conception.

Before concluding, we should point out that the question of whether the informalist conception is correct or appropriate is independent of the question of whether the state should "get out of marriage altogether." Although both questions have been brought to prominence by the same-sex marriage debate, and although some of those advocating governmental abandonment of marriage presumably assume an informalist understanding of marriage, there are two separate issues here. If the informalist conception is correct, that does imply that the state should cease to view its sanction as necessary for marriage. It does not, though, imply that the state should get out of marriage altogether. Even if the state no longer plays any role in determining whether a relationship is a marriage, there may be good reasons – reasons having to do with social stability, the rearing of children, etc. – for it to go on endorsing marriages, perhaps by granting the same sorts of benefits married couples now enjoy.[32] In this scenario, the state would merely be identifying and rewarding marriages, not creating and dissolving them. And conversely, if the informalist conception is not correct, that does not imply that the state's involvement in marriage should continue. Rejection of the informalist conception means only that recognition by some external authority is necessary for the existence of a marriage, that authority need not be affiliated with the state. It could be argued that marriage is an essentially religious concept, and that in order for a couple to be married they must therefore receive the sanction of a *religious* authority.

---

[32] We have in mind here things such as tax benefits, inheritance and death benefits, joint property rights, default surrogate decision-making, and spousal confidentiality.

TEACHING "AGAINST MARRIAGE," OR, "BUT, PROFESSOR, MARRIAGE ISN'T A *CONTRACT*!"[1]

KATHRYN NORLOCK

It is one of the ironies of my professional calling that I spend my days drumming the conception of marriage as a romantic relationship out of my students' heads, and my nights at home in one of the most harmonious marriages imaginable. By day, I teach classic philosophical texts containing arguments that marriage is a contract to which the state is an essential third party. I go home and think about the state's part in my marriage very little, if at all, preoccupied with conversation and sharing dinner, relaxed in the comforts that privilege provides in spades.

Certainly, when my students ask, I do not deny that one dimension of marriage may be the hoped-for romantic relationship that most of my students idealize. So how did I come to a point in my teaching wherein the two texts I use to discuss marriage are by Immanuel Kant, who asserts that sex degrades humanity and is only permissible (though still a bit degrading!) within a marriage contract, and Claudia Card, a radical lesbian feminist philosopher, who argues against entering marriage at all, and insists it is never required to legitimize one's behavior?[1] I didn't used to use these two pieces so exclusively, and in my earlier teaching days, attended more to texts which explored ethics within interpersonal and intimate dyadic relationships.

---

[1] My two primary sources for use in the classroom are Immanuel Kant's "Duties Toward the Body with Respect to Sexual Impulse," in *Lectures on Ethics,* trans. Louis Infield (London: Methuen and Co., 1963, 162-171), and Claudia Card's "Against Marriage," in *Same Sex,* ed. by John Corvino (Lanham, Md. Rowman & Littlefield, 1997, 317-330). In what follows, I more often explicate Kant's observations in the "Duties" by relying on his clearer, if drier, explanations of his view in "The Rights of the Family as a Domestic Society," from *The Science of Right* (Raleigh, N.C. Alex Catalogue, www.netlibrary.com), Chapter II., The Mode of Acquiring Anything External.

Yet I have come to the conclusion that students don't need to dwell any more than they already do on the intimate and romantic side of marriage, an aspect of which popular cultural depictions have already provided them abundant images. Even their direct, lived experiences with alternative possibilities, including their own family members' happy and unhappy heterosexual unions, inside or outside of marriage, divorces, nonheterosexual unions, or the single or multiple parenting arrangements under which many of them were raised, does not usually diminish the view among most of my optimistic 18- to 21-year old students that their own personal destinies include "the fairy tale." As I explain in more detail below, this turns out to be a deeply entrenched conception of a lifelong romantic relationship which is astoundingly isolated from any appreciation of the social or political context in which it would have to occur.[2]

The surpassing resistance I often meet to the idea of marriage as a contract has moved me to be all the more interested in teaching it, however. Students' very distaste for the contractual reality is fascinating to me. I gather from class discussions and student papers that their distaste reveals an attachment to a conception of marriage which is understandably personal, tied to images of oneself and one's longing for affection and intimacy, and often imagined as an escape from their previous or current social arrangements, which may have been unhappy, lacking affection, lonely, abusive, or economically distressed. The escapism of this image of marriage is borne out by the students' connection of their own tropes to examples drawn from date movies and reality television. I take this to be all the more reason to redouble my pedagogical and moral commitments to bring students around to a view of marriage as socially and politically forceful.

In what follows, I argue for encouraging greater awareness of students' interrelatedness and social surround, and I advocate diminishing the vision of marriage as an isolated and perfectly free choice between two individuals in love. To ignore the extent to which marriage is, among other things, a social contract, is ethically, personally, and politically obtuse. I see students who engage in such ignorance as undertaking personal risk, lacking full understanding of the particulars of the commitment, as politically inarticulate, undermining appreciation for why nonheterosexuals would want a share of the privileges of marriage, and as morally well-meaning but trading on status for an unequal share of social benefits. If nothing else, though, I find students at such an individualistic

---

[2] Non-heterosexual students are less likely to hold the fairy-tale view, but are not immune; just as privilege is not a guarantee of ignorance, so, too, minority status is not a guarantee of keen social awareness.

and self-creating point in their lives to be under-appreciative of what their public avowals mean to others, and marriage, in one sense, is indeed public.

Before I advance my pedagogical arguments, however, I will briefly sketch the philosophical arguments which have become such useful teaching tools for me, and against which my students dig in their heels, beginning with Immanuel Kant's.

Part One: Great Minds Think Alike

In teaching my students about the social and political valences of marriage, I choose to use essays by Immanuel Kant and Claudia Card because they are so different, but in one respect (and in this context, only one), Kant and Card are exactly alike. They both assert their conviction that the sociopolitical dimension of marriage is essential to understanding its full meaning and its value or disvalue.

Kant in brief

For Kant, marriage is an inviolable social contract, and not to be understood merely as long-term cohabitation within an intimate relationship "without a preceding contract."[3] On this understanding, people who live as though they are married in every sense but in "name" are not married at all. Kant grants that the contract alone is also not enough if done faithlessly between two with no intention of living it out, that is, marriage is more than marriage "in name only," but this is consistent with holding that the contract is socially and morally weighty. He means here simply that the contractual vow of marriage must be uttered with some meaningful intention, just as with any promise or contract.

Why does the contract matter so, to Kant? He gives several reasons, almost all of which are predicated upon the equal moral value of individuals, and the Categorical Imperative, which in one formulation, says that we must never use a human being as a mere means to our own ends, because each person is an end-in-himself, with his own goals, ends and projects.[4] We may use someone as a means with their consent, but even in these cases, Kant argues that one must have some sort of recourse

---

[3] Immanuel Kant, "Rights of the Family," from *The Science of Right*, 40.
[4] Kant, *Groundwork of the Metaphysics of Morals*, in Kant, *Practical Philosophy*, trans. Mary Gregor (Cambridge, Cambridge University Press, 1996), 73, 80.

if one is to have full moral rights against bad treatment. When rights are being denied, neglected or infringed, one must have "ground, in the circumstances, to complain of a lesion of his right," that is, standing to lay a public claim against another.[5] The parallel also holds; one must be "legally held to the fulfillment of their promise" when they would otherwise fail in their promises to an equal full adult; "the relation of the married persons to each other is a relation of equality as regards the mutual possession of their persons, as well as of their goods."[6]

Readers familiar with the sexism that Kant displays in other works may be pleased, or puzzled, to find such strong assertions of equality between men and women in Kant's conception of marriage. I grant that it is rare for Kant to assert such equality, and yet assert it he does; whatever his personal and cultural perceptions of men's and women's differences in talent and ability, their human worth is equal. This is never clearer than when he laments, in a line which always sends my students into vociferous objection, "Sexual love makes of the loved person an Object of appetite; as soon as that appetite has been stilled, the person is cast aside as one casts away a lemon that has been sucked dry."[7] Whether or not this is always an inevitable outcome of sexual behavior, the fact remains that Kant was concerned with the well-being of men *and* women when they are reduced to sex objects.

Note that Kant apparently held that sex always succeeds in reducing a whole person to a mere part, a sex object:

> The acquisition of a part of the human organism being, on account of its unity, at the same time the acquisition of the whole person, it follows that the surrender and acceptation of, or by, one sex in relation to the other, is not only permissible under the condition of marriage, but is further only really possible under that condition.[8]

In other words, you cannot possibly use someone sexually without using their whole body; bodies are not really divisible, despite the way sexual appetites can lend us to talk about a person's parts like so many cuts of beef. So Kant gives us two choices: Either (1) yield (or acquire) one's whole person with no promises at all and no standing to assert one's equal worth when one's rights are infringed, or (2) marry, that is, contract publicly with each other to yield (or acquire) each other for sexual purposes in the full presence of equal moral rights, and establish standing

---

[5] Kant, "Rights of the Family," from *Science of Right*, 39.
[6] Ibid.
[7] Kant, "Duties toward the Body," from *Lectures on Ethics*, 163.
[8] Kant, "Rights of the Family," from *Science of Right*, 39.

to assert those rights in a public and juridically enforceable way. Without equality in the contract, "it must be admitted by all that any one who might enter into it could not be legally held to the fulfillment of their promise if they wished to resile from it."[9] According to Kant, in satisfying one's sexual desires on another, one treats the other with less than the full respect he or she deserves.

Card in brief

Students who think Kant is almost entirely wrong would, one might think, then find much more friendly fare in the more modern sensibilities expressed by Claudia Card. In her widely reprinted essay, "Against Marriage," Card agrees with my 21st century, respect-filled and sexually active students that marriage is not required for the legitimization or the moral worth of their sexual behavior. She further agrees that marriage guarantees neither love nor respect, and that enduring, intimate relationships are valuable in the absence of marriage.[10]

Students cheer when they begin reading Card; her account could not be more different from Kant's. They are less enthused, however, when they reach the point at which Card suggests that, far from offering valuable legal protection to those who are violated, marriage actually may offer legal protection to spouses who are violators, that the state may take an interest in making marriage difficult to leave, and that divorce is costly and difficult. They often become completely disenchanted by the time Card criticizes "the legal rights of access that married partners have to each other's persons, property, and lives," which "make it all but impossible for a spouse to defend herself (or himself), or to be protected against torture, rape, battery, stalking, mayhem, or murder by the other spouse:

> Spousal murder accounts for a substantial number of murders each year. This factor is made worse by the presence of the second problem mentioned above (difficulties of divorce that lead many to remain married when they should not), which provides motives to violence within marriages. Legal marriage thus enlists state support for conditions conducive to murder and mayhem.[11]

---

[9] Ibid.
[10] Card, "Against Marriage," especially 317-320.
[11] Card, "Against Marriage," 323.

Card is certainly not outlining a fairy tale. There is nothing reassuring in the picture of the legal institution of marriage as she describes it. Finally, she completely loses the more liberal students who advocate gay marriage, and who expect to find an ally in her but instead encounter her opposition: "I believe that lesbians or gays should be reluctant to put our activist energy into attaining legal equity with heterosexuals in marriage— not because the existing discrimination against us is in any way justifiable but because this institution is so deeply flawed that it seems to me unworthy of emulation and reproduction."[12]

Given the above, she argues against entering into marriages even if a right to marriage is available. As my students argue vociferously against Kant, marriage is not necessary, right? "Let us not be eager to have the state regulate our unions," she urges, and to the objection that marriage often comes with external goods one might need, such as affordable health care, insurance, hospital visitation, social security benefits, and inheritance rights, she replies that these are reasons to fight for such goods to be available to all, and not to argue for entrance into marriage.[13] On the contrary, for the state to hold such goods out only to those who enter into the legal institution of marriage rather clearly reveals that for many, marriage is coerced:

> If marrying became an option that would legitimate behavior otherwise illegitimate and make available to us social securities that will no doubt become even more important to us as we age, [my partner and I] and many others like us might be pushed into marriage. Marrying under such conditions is not a totally free choice.[14]

Throughout, Card reiterates that she does not argue against loving, durable and intimate relationships. Rather, she argues against fighting for inclusion in a particular legal institution. As she says, in terms which my students reject as firmly as they ever rejected Kant, "I understand marriage as a relationship to which the state is an essential third party."[15] Their rejection, and my pedagogical strategies for undermining their rejection, inform the second half of this paper.

---

[12] Card, "Against Marriage," 318.
[13] Card, "Against Marriage," 321.
[14] Card, "Against Marriage," 322.
[15] Card, "Against Marriage," 320.

Part Two: Beyond the Fairy Tale

The first time that I ever taught about marriage in an introductory ethics course, I thought that in using Kant and Card, I was presenting my students the dutiful "two sides" minimally required of a professor, using wildly different arguments – Kant for, and Card against, marriage. When the same students expressed strong rejections of both, they often did so by advancing their own conceptions of marriage as more attractive alternatives. Understandably, their evidence relied upon their limited experiences, that is, the material provided by their experiences with dating, with sex and cohabitation, and their idealized examples of love and marriage from popular culture, frequently citing examples from movies and from television. No stranger to reality television myself, I marveled aloud at the number of women, in particular, who mentioned "the fairy tale" on such shows. My students didn't need to be told its contents, which they outlined for me with ease. It includes:

- Unsurpassed romantic love
- Exceptional sexual satisfaction
- Perfect, complete, and best friendship
- Social, economic and political security (usually assumed or implied rather than overtly explicated)
- At its best, in all respects *easy*, a finished end-point

Notably, almost all students specifically mention a proposal as either an easy end-point or a necessary step. And in not one year I've taught this do students include getting a license in the fairy tale. (Many do, however, including getting a ring or a house.)

When we discuss the idealized conception of marriage that the fairy tale informs, students recognize the depiction as idealized but argue for the value of those elements which, in their eyes, disprove Kant's and Card's accounts of marriage. Although students' accounts certainly include variations, there are a few elements on which they tend to agree: (1) Marriage is a romantic relationship, meaningful and loving. (2) The act of getting legally married makes no difference to two people in a truly committed long-term relationship. (3) Most of all, students express strong distaste for the idea that the state is an essential third party.

I find that when I teach these texts, my first job is to point out, regarding (1), that neither Kant nor Card ever deny the possibility that a marriage could include a meaningful or loving relationship. Kant describes an ideal and equal marriage as one in which "two persons become a unity of will. Whatever good or ill, joy or sorrow befalls either of them, the other will share in it. Thus sexuality leads to a union of human beings."[16] Card takes pains to clarify that she is not arguing against durable intimate relationships, homes or families, saying, "When the family is credited with being a bulwark against a hostile world, ...the bulwark that is meant often consists of a variety of deeply committed personal (as opposed to legal) relationships, and the stability of caring that they represent."[17] The arrangement of marriage, then, is compatible with intimacy and commitment, for both authors, though not required. This is a good juncture at which I introduce the idea of a *necessary* condition to students who have never encountered the concept before; my aim is to bring students around to an appreciation of complex concepts as having many dimensions, but at this point, I enjoy urging them to consider if they are ready to commit to saying that loving affection is the *sine qua non* of marriage. Their endorsement of love as necessary is reduced when I take them through a thought experiment. I ask them to imagine that they meet someone who really attracts them, physically and emotionally, and noting the presence of one or more rings on their fingers, that they ask, "Oh, are you married?" The person says no, but several months of intimacy later, reveals that they have a spouse for whom they have no warm feelings, "so I didn't lie to you, we're not really married." Students generally agree that the absence of love is insufficient to render their desired one unmarried, and quickly move on to (2), the argument that after extended togetherness, acts of marrying make no difference to two people in a truly committed long-term relationship.

When I ask my students to explain what (2) means, they tend to summarize it as follows: "Nothing changes—you don't feel any different." Here, I have excellent personal experience to draw upon; my own marriage occurred after over four years of happy cohabitation, and my memories of "before" and "after" remain fresh. Indeed, changes occurred, but not in the way my students imagined. Four years was enough time to establish our relationship firmly. It's not as though we woke up feeling differently *about each other*. However, as it turns out, we are not alone in the world. What changed were small and large interactions with everyone who was in a position to recognize our relationship. As I describe these to my students, I tend to keep a piece of chalk held to the blackboard in my classroom, and drop it an inch or two with every example that follows.

Some of our experiences were small. "Before," invitations were highly likely to be issued to only one of us, and not always with the

---

[16] Kant, "Duties toward the Body," from *Lectures on Ethics*, 167.
[17] Card, "Against Marriage," 320.

supplementary acknowledgement that the invitee might wish to bring a guest. My family members didn't always expect my partner at holidays and dinners, and were known to forget the partner's name, rough job description, and occasionally, existence. Expectations from coworkers and supervisors generally included the assumption of easy availability for last-minute and late-night duties. Car repair, home improvement, and most any service provider could often seem dissatisfied with relaying information for one to a "boyfriend" or "girlfriend." The experiences could be larger, too (and here, I start making longer drops with my chalk on the descending line on the board): Finances could be taken care of only on individual bases, even though our fortunes were thoroughly tied up in each other's past and future expenditures. Joint applications for anything related to our university's student benefits required robust signatures, proofs of identification, and often meetings to which we must both be present in person. Health care and insurance were available to one, not to both—though as young adults with uneventful lives, this seemed less consequential than it was. If my chalk isn't already at the baseboard by this time, I add the example of what my family's reaction would have been if I had become pregnant before marriage: "Oh, *no*, Kathryn." Then I draw that line straight down to the bottom of the board.

"After," social benefits flooded to us, and it wasn't the largest ones that had the greatest impact. We quietly added each other to health insurance and financial benefits, and then forgot about them, living the illness-free and nearly penniless lives of most young graduate students. The day-to-day differences were in the innumerable acts of recognition by every source imaginable, and in marveling at them to my students, I always manage to convey my surprise in a way which surprises and interests them too. I now start lifting the hand holding the chalk up the board, adding another segment with each successive example. I tell them about the transformation among distant family members who now expected each partner at every event, remembering names, jobs, and even minor life circumstances with ease. I tell of the invitations issued to both of us, by friends seemingly suddenly realizing that we wanted each other's company to an extent unnoticed for years prior. Coworkers and supervisors asked after new spouses, and seemed to presume my infinite availability less. Notably, every financial and trade service provider suddenly recognized our reliability and bonds of trust, granting each of us extraordinary amounts of information regarding the other's queries, to an extent which was bizarre. We had not fully realized that "husband" and "wife" were secret passwords to the world of recognition of our shared daily lives. If my chalk line is not as high as I can reach at this point, I add what my family's reaction would be if I had been able, at any point after marriage, to announce a pregnancy: "Hooray!" And I let the chalk shoot straight up the board.

When I elaborate on the extraordinary and daily impact of social recognition of our unitedness, my students laugh and exclaim at the giant √-shaped line on the chalk board, but they don't dispute my experience. Many of them have already had the limited experience of a romantic and intimate relationship which their parents do not recognize as permanent or likely to last, and most find it easy to imagine having commitments and relationships which go unacknowledged. As they become more engaged with the vision of marriage that I am outlining, they cease to concentrate on the clear image, previously dear to them, of two individuals making a free and unencumbered choice that affects only themselves. After my presentation, they take a new perspective, one which sees marriage as occurring in a thick relational context. And once I do this much to unseat assumption (2), I then find it a short step to discussing (3), their idea that the state is not an essential third party to marriage.

Of course, there are students who still hold out at this point, suggesting that if a couple managed to accomplish robust social recognition without the state-issued license, this would seem to satisfy most conceptions of marriage in everything but name. As a class, we usually tend to come to consensus at this point that very long-standing relationships sometimes get such recognition whether or not anyone actually "knows" if two are "really" married. And of course, the presentation of oneself as committed to and united with another should, ideally, get exactly the sort of rich social recognition I described as having been showered upon me and my husband within days of our exchange of vows.

Yet such social recognition is contingent upon the beneficence of others; to extend Kant's earlier point, a member of such a noncontractual relationship has no standing to lay claims to membership in an equal union if the social surround chooses to deny them. Some forms of social recognition are more basic to life than others. At this point in the classwide discussion of marriage, the demand for recognition of commitments, intertwined fortunes and personal needs is understandable to most everyone in the room, and it is not news to my students that the state is in a position to endow its citizens with benefits it would otherwise deny. In a country like the U.S., in which health is seen as a commodity available to employed and wealthy people, and access to affordable medical care is not something to which anyone has a right, my husband and I are annually offered the opportunity to add each other to our health insurance. This is an astounding benefit for an academic to acquire in a context in which I must be willing to live anywhere to work in my field, and my partner must be willing to quit his benefit-granting job if he is to join me. As long as we operate in a system in which access to "just" health care is predicated upon one's employment and marital status, the state is clearly a necessary third party to one's marriage; it is the arbiter of what rights marriage endows upon participants, and who counts as a participant, who is allowed "into the club."[18]

It is my final job in this unit of the semester to impress upon my students the difference between a descriptive and a prescriptive claim. Card, for example, argues that the state should not be in the position to legitimize only some unions, as married and therefore deserving of certain basic social benefits. Citizens should not live in unjust situations in which marriage is not a perfectly free choice. These are prescriptive claims ("should" claims), and it is up to my students whether or not to agree with the prescriptions either author advances. Yet the descriptive claims about marriage are those on which I attempt to focus my students' attention, and absent full appreciation of the following descriptive claims, I do not believe my students are best positioned to work out what prescriptive claims they ought to hold.

Descriptively, it is the case, whether it ought to be or not, that marriage is a multi-dimensional concept, and a legal institution, with massive cultural import. It is a formal recognition of the union of two people which endows a pair with rights and obligations that they are held to by each other, by the state, and by other people in their lives, and grants each standing to lay claim to rights, including rights against the state, corporations, and each other, which unmarried individuals do not have. Because of the intrinsic involvement of the state it is also costly to exit. And the public nature of the commitment, and the cultural understandings of the unit of a married couple, result in unquantifiably high varieties of social and personal recognition which does make one feel different—more trustworthy with information about the other, more interested in the well-being of another than previously assumed, and more likely to prioritize the role of another in one's life in making decisions, than previously expected, again, whether such recognition ought to be tied to marriage or not. One is seen as no longer isolated, as if one ever was.

Teaching an ethics class about marriage is pedagogically challenging. Although I think students ought to care a great deal about how they

---

[18] Jennifer Crossen, quoted by Merlene Davis, in "What if 52 percent voted not to let blacks drink at the fountain?" (Lexington Herald-Leader, Nov. 23, 2008). Available online at www.kentucky.com/181/story/602737.html. Accessed online 1/10/2009.

conceptualize marriage and how those denied access to marriage live, telling students what they ought to care about is rarely successful. Further, pointing out unequal shares of social benefits to a room full of people who stand to gain from them can yield defensiveness. And the attraction of the entrenched fairy-tale has personal importance to young adults, who hope for futures filled with happiness, affection and companionship with which reminders of divorce, state regulation and social injustices conflict. American students, in particular, operate in an exceedingly individualistic framework in which marriage is often described as an entirely private enterprise. This is what makes teaching the topic so exciting. It is my hope that by changing their perspective on marriage, I change my students' perceptions of their own selves as somehow isolated, and their choices as unaffected by social and legal institutions. With a more accurate apprehension of the multiple dimensions of marriage, every student is more likely to make informed and just decisions about their personal lives and the justice of their legal and social institutions.

MARRIAGE, PARENTING, AND SEXUAL ORIENTATION

MARK STRASSER

I. Introduction

Marriage provides a variety of symbolic and practical benefits both to individuals and to society as a whole. These advantages have been touted in the secondary literature recently, at least in part, out of a belief that the institution of marriage needs shoring up. What often is not stated by those writing in support of marriage is that most if not all of the benefits of marriage to society and to the individuals themselves accrue whether or not the marital couple is composed of individuals of the same sex or of different sexes.

Part II of this article discusses the benefits of marriage to individuals, their families, and to society, noting that as a general matter the symbolic and practical benefits of marriage are at least as important for same-sex couples as for different-sex couples. Part III of this article discusses the rationales offered in some of the recent state supreme court decisions upholding the constitutionality of the respective state's same-sex marriage bans. The article concludes that as a matter of law and public policy, the failure to recognize same-sex marriage harms the individuals themselves, society as a whole, and the very institution of marriage.

II. The Benefits of Marriage

State and federal law offer a variety of incentives for individuals to marry that run the gamut from tax benefits to evidentiary privileges. Federal law alone offers over 1,000 benefits based on marital status,[1] and

---

[1] Caleb W. Langston, Comment, "Fundamental Right, Fundamentally Wronged: Oregon's Unconstitutional Stand on Same-Sex Marriage," 84 Oregon Law Review 861, 867 n.22 (2005) ("In a report issued in January 2004, the United States

state law offers a variety of rights involving inheritance, insurance, and
tort among others.[2] Consider how some of these rights work. Two
unmarried individuals, Kim and Terry, are in a romantic relationship.
Both work outside the home. However, Terry is downsized because of the
bad economy. Were Kim and Terry married, Terry could be covered
under Kim's insurance policy. Because they are not, Terry may well be at
risk, especially if unable to find another job before her COBRA benefits
run out.[3] If Kim's place of work provides domestic partnership benefits
and Kim and Terry qualify, then Terry might be covered under Kim's
insurance. However, it might be noted, those benefits would be taxable,
whereas they would not be were Kim and Terry married.[4]

   Suppose that the picture is more complicated. Kim and Terry are
raising children, although the children are biologically related to only one
of them or, perhaps, to neither of them because the children have been
adopted. First, depending on the state, Kim and Terry may not each be
recognized as the legal parents of the children.[5] This means that if Terry is
the biological or adoptive parent and Kim is not recognized by the law as a
parent, Terry's being unemployed might have severe insurance
consequences for the children. Bracketing insurance benefits, a variety of
other privileges follow upon the recognition of parentage, including the
rights to authorize medical treatment, sign releases or, perhaps, the right to
visit a child in the hospital.[6] Whether or not Terry is employed, Kim might

---

General Accounting Office (GAO) identified 1138 federal statutory provisions that
confer benefits, rights, and privileges conditioned upon marital status.").
[2] See Baker v. State, 744 A.2d 864, 883-84 (Vt. 1999).
[3] John Sanchez, "2004-05 Survey of Florida Employment Law," 30 Nova Law
Review 123, 132 (2005) ("Under the Consolidated Omnibus Budget Reconciliation
Act of 1985 (COBRA), employers who already offer health benefits owe a duty to
offer continued coverage to most former employees and their dependents for
eighteen to thirty-six months or until coverage under another plan begins.").
[4] See Dominick Vetri, "The Gay Codes: Federal & State Laws Excluding Gay &
Lesbian Families," 41 Willamette Law Review 881, 903 (2005) ("An employee
with a domestic partner has the fair market value of employer-paid health benefits
included as additional taxable income to the employee.").
[5] See Benjamin G. Ledsham, "Means to Legitimate Ends: Same-Sex Marriage
through the Lens of Illegitimacy-Based Discrimination," 28 Cardozo L. Rev. 2373,
2375 n.17 (2007) ("Only one quarter of states recognize second-parent adoptions,
either by explicit legislation or by judicial decisions interpreting general adoption
statutes.").
[6] For example, in one Oklahoma case, the parents of a child requiring emergency
care were told that only one of the child's two same-sex parents could accompany
the child. See Finstuen v. Crutcher, 496 F.3d 1139, 1145 (10th Cir. 2007).

be precluded from exercising a variety of parental privileges to the detriment of all concerned.

Suppose that we change the picture. Terry is employed but would prefer to stop working to be home with the children or, perhaps, an elderly parent. Because of insurance difficulties, however, Terry is unable to do this, which might mean that elderly parents or young children would instead have to be taken care of in a less desirable setting.

While marriage affords various financial benefits, it affords other kinds of benefits as well. Commentators have noted that married individuals tend to invest more in their relationships than do comparable cohabiting couples[7] and, further, that married individuals tend to invest more in their children than do comparable cohabiting couples.[8] Yet, if the individuals themselves and their children are benefited because of the greater willingness to make individual sacrifices so that the family as a whole can benefit, then society as a whole benefits.

Notwithstanding the tangible and intangible benefits of marriage, the nation is witnessing a decline in the number of people who marry or remain married. Recent headlines trumpeted that more American households are headed by unmarried adults than by married couples, and marriage proponents immediately decried the breakdown of marriage and family. However, many of those extolling the virtues of marriage were at the same time arguing that marriage should nonetheless be denied to same-sex couples. Especially because many of the touted benefits are equally applicable regardless of the composition of the couple, such commentators are then put in the position of offering arguments to distinguish between same-sex and different-sex couples that either are nonsequiturs or actually undermine the value of marriage.

Some commentators contend that same-sex marriage makes no sense because it cannot serve the primary procreative purposes of marriage.[9] But

---

[7] See Robin Fretwell Wilson, "Evaluating Marriage: Does Marriage Matter to the Nurturing of Children?" 42 San Diego Law Review 847, 851 (2005) (suggesting that "the transformative power of marriage may lie first in the greater permanence of marital relationships and, secondarily, in the motivation of the parties to invest in their relationship").

[8] David D. Meyer, "A Privacy Right to Public Recognition of Family Relationships? The Cases of Marriage and Adoption," 51 Villanova Law Review 891, 908(2006) ("married parents appear to invest more in childrearing relationships than do cohabiting parents, even controlling for other factors such as education and income").

[9] See Lynn D. Wardle & Lincoln C. Oliphant, "In Praise of Loving: Reflections on the 'Loving Analogy' for Same-Sex Marriage," 51 Howard Law Journal 117, 161 (2007) ("the expansion of marriage to include same-sex couples would diminish

this kind of approach is wrongheaded for several reasons. First, while individuals may well marry because they want to have and raise children, this is a reason to recognize rather than ban same-sex marriage. Same-sex couples are having and raising children. While same-sex parents are not each biologically related to the children they are raising, the same might be said of many marital couples.

For a variety of reasons, it is much more common now for children to be raised by at least one parent to whom she is not biologically related. The child might be in a blended family where she was born of a previous relationship and brought into the marriage, or the child might have been adopted by one or both of the individuals raising her. If, indeed, one of the purposes of marriage is to provide a setting in which a child might prosper whether or not the child is biologically related to both of the individuals raising her, then same-sex marriage should be recognized.

Indeed, it may be even more important for same-sex couples than different-sex couples to be able to marry, precisely because both members of a same-sex couple raising a child will not be biologically related to the child. Because the ability to adopt a partner's child may be predicated on being married to that partner, and because the individual will not be biologically related to the would-be adopted child, it may be that the only way that the person would be able to protect his or her relationship with the child would be to marry his or her partner and then adopt the child.

It should not be thought that those states permitting a same-sex parent to establish a legal relationship with the child that he or she is helping to raise are primarily concerned about protecting the rights of the parent. On the contrary, these states are permitting these adoptions because doing so will promote the best interests of the child. An individual whose parent-child relationship is not legally recognized may be less willing to bond with the child or invest in the relationship in other ways. This means that the state's unwillingness to permit the same-sex couple to marry or to permit the non-biological partner to adopt may result in the child's missing benefits that she otherwise might have had.

It goes without saying that people who cannot or will not have children nonetheless marry, and that they are not undermining marriage by doing so. People legitimately marry for all sorts of reasons. There is no *one* purpose to marry, and even were that purpose to provide a setting in which children might prosper, that would militate in favor of recognizing same-sex marriage.

---

the meaning and message of marriage about procreative responsibility of parents, and would undermine the primary, procreative social purposes of and interests in marriage").

Other commentators explain that same-sex marriage should not be recognized lest the appropriate roles of men and women be undermined. Yet, one of the reasons that some women are reluctant to marry or remain married is that they reject the kind of roles that traditionalists assert that women should have in marriage.[10]

The state has an interest in helping adults and their children to flourish, and it is for this reason among others that the state should permit same-sex couples to marry. It is of course true, however, that same-sex couples, like different-sex couples, may for whatever reason decide to divorce. Yet, the state has an interest in assuring an *organized* breakdown in relationships, for example, in dividing property or in establishing child custody, visitation and support. Here, too, it would be helpful for the state and the individuals themselves for same-sex couples to come under marriage laws so that property interests can be established and custody and visitation can be decided in a way that would promote the best interests of the child.

Different-sex couples who divorce are sometimes so angry or hurt that they consciously or unconsciously prefer to punish their ex-partners than promote the best interests of their children. Same-sex couples whose relationships are ending might be similarly tempted. Yet, the potential costs to the child are even greater where the adult partner is neither the adoptive or biological parent of the child. Absent legal recognition of the relationship between the child and the ex-partner, the custodial parent might be able to preclude the child from ever again seeing the ex-partner, harm to the child notwithstanding.

Both same-sex and different-sex partners can benefit from the stability and investment afforded by marriage. Further, other family members of both types of couples also stand to benefit. Society, itself, can benefit both from the increased productivity and satisfaction of the marital partners and from the benefits afforded to other family members such as children or aging parents. As a matter of public policy, states should afford this option to same-sex couples.

The claim here is not that there is something wrong with those couples who choose not to marry. Nor is the claim that couples who do not choose to marry are rightly denied any or all of the myriad benefits currently reserved for those who marry. Rather, the claim is that the kinds of state and individual interests that are promoted by marriage do not depend on the sexes of the would-be married individuals.

---

[10] See Linda C. McClain, *The Place of Families: Fostering Capacity, Equality and Responsibility* 143 (Cambridge: Harvard University Press, 2006) (suggesting that the gap between expectations of gender equality and the reality of marriage has led many women to divorce).

III. Some Recent State Decisions Regarding Marriage

Recently, several state supreme courts have addressed whether their respective state's same-sex marriage ban violates state constitutional guarantees. Each case involved an interpretation of that state's constitution. Because the language of the respective constitutions differ and because the case law interpreting those provisions differ, one might well expect different analyses. The focus here is on a few of the policy arguments that were offered in some of the opinions upholding the marriage bans.

In *Conaway v. Deane*, the Maryland Supreme Court upheld that state's ban because "the State has a legitimate interest in encouraging marriage between two members of the opposite sex, a union that is uniquely capable of producing offspring within the marital unit."[11] The court understood that children are born into same-sex relationships, and that some different-sex couples either cannot or will not have children.[12] However, the court reasoned that "the fundamental right to marriage and its ensuing benefits are conferred on opposite-sex couples not because of a distinction between whether various opposite-sex couples actually procreate, but rather because of the *possibility* of procreation."[13]

Yet, the court's rationale was unpersuasive for a few reasons. First, it is no more possible for sterile different-sex couples to procreate than it is for same-sex couples to procreate. To suggest that sterile couples have the possibility of procreating by making use of assisted reproductive technologies may imply that same-sex couples also have that possibility. Second, consider why the state's interest allegedly is in helping not only those who actually procreate but those who have the possibility of procreating. Basically, those who currently say that they will not have children may change their minds or, perhaps, may have a child accidentally. Or, they may decide to adopt. But those in same-sex relationships may adopt or may change their minds and decide to make use of assisted reproductive techniques.

The state's interest in providing a stable home for children that might be born into the relationship is *promoted* by recognizing same-sex unions. Were the state only interested in helping those children who are the biological offspring of both of their parents, the state would not try to promote adoption as much as it does.

---

[11] See Conaway v. Deane, 932 A.2d 571, 630 (Md. 2007).
[12] See id.
[13] Id. at 633.

There is something quite troubling in a court's upholding a ban on same-sex marriage in the name of procreation when this means that couples who cannot have children are afforded the benefits of marriage *but that couples who can and do have children are not.* Precisely because such a policy hurts those it is allegedly designed to help, namely, children, the most plausible explanation is that this rationale is not doing any work but is being offered instead of the real reason that such a ban is being maintained.

There was no analysis in the Maryland opinion regarding how reserving marriage for different-sex couples would somehow promote their marrying or their having children. Instead, the court simply chose not to discuss the connection between denying marriage rights to same-sex couples and promoting marriage among different-sex couples. Thus, the court upheld the ban, notwithstanding that (1) no reason was offered to think that the marriage ban would in fact do what it was allegedly designed to do, namely, encourage different-sex couples to marry, and (2) the ban would have a real adverse effect on couples who were in fact raising children.

Other courts have tried to legitimate their state's same-sex marriage bans, although they were no more successful than was the Maryland Supreme Court. In *Hernandez v. Robles*, the New York Court of Appeals suggested that the "critical question is whether a rational legislature could decide that these benefits should be given to opposite-sex couples, but not same-sex couples."[14] The court pointed out that the Legislature could have believed that different-sex relationships "are all too often casual or temporary,"[15] that an "important function of marriage is to create more stability and permanence in the relationships that cause children to be born,"[16] and that the Legislature might therefore decide to "offer an inducement—in the form of marriage and its attendant benefits—to opposite-sex couples who make a solemn long-term commitment to each other."[17]

A number of points might be made about the *Hernandez* analysis. Traditionally, one of the reasons that same-sex couples were thought unsuitable for marriage was their alleged difficulty in maintaining long-term relationships.[18] The *Hernandez* court is turning that charge on its

---

[14] See Hernandez v. Robles, 855 N.E.2d 1, 7 (N.Y. 2006).

[15] Id.

[16] Id.

[17] Id.

[18] See Yvonne A. Tamayo, "'I Just Can't Handle It': The Case of Hernandez v. Robles," 28 *Women's Rights Law Reporter* 61, 63 n.30 (2007) ("opponents of

head, implicitly suggesting that same-sex couples with children have less difficulty remaining together and thus are less in need of the inducements of marriage.[19]

Even were there more of a need for different-sex couples to have that inducement, it is not as if the Legislature had to choose between the two groups—*both* same-sex and different-sex couples could be given the benefits to induce them to either get married or remain married. No reason was offered to believe that affording these benefits to same-sex couples would somehow make those benefits less attractive to different-sex couples.[20] Further, there is every reason to think that providing these inducements to same-sex couples would have some of the beneficial effects that will allegedly accrue by offering these benefits to different-sex couples.

The court offered another rationale to support the same-sex marriage ban, namely, that the Legislature could rationally decide that it would be better, all else equal, for a child to have parents of different sexes rather than parents of the same-sex.[21] Yet, same-sex couples are having and raising children whether or not they can marry. Denying same-sex couples the right to marry would not result in children being raised by different-sex parents rather than same-sex parents; instead, it would simply mean that those children who are being raised by same-sex parents would be denied all of the benefits that might have accrued were their parents able and willing to marry.

Perhaps the court was thinking that were same-sex couples able to marry, the increased emotional and financial stability and security that marriage might bring would induce even more same-sex couples to have children. For example, more same-sex couples might adopt children in need. Yet, such couples would not be taking children out of their happy homes where they were thriving while being raised by their different-sex

---

same-sex marriage often allege that the duration of same-sex couples' relationships, as well as their level of commitment, "propensity" towards promiscuity and rate of domestic violence render homosexuals incapable of providing stable homes for their children").

[19] Compare Morrison v. Sadler 821 N.E.2d 15, 26 (Ind. App. 2005)

Members of a same-sex couple who wish to have a child, on the other hand, have already demonstrated their commitment to child-rearing, by virtue of the difficulty of obtaining a child through adoption or assisted reproduction, without the State necessarily having to encourage that commitment through the institution of marriage.

[20] See Hernandez, 855 N.E.2d at 30 (Kaye, C.J., dissenting).

[21] Id. at 7.

parents. Instead, the children would be taken out of foster homes or some other insecure placement, which would presumably be viewed by the state as a benefit rather than a drawback.[22]

Or, it might be that such couples would feel more secure and thus would be more likely to take advantage of assisted reproductive techniques to produce a child. But for such children, the question is not whether they will be raised by same-sex parents rather than different-sex parents. Rather, the question for these children is whether the state will provide same-sex couples the option to marry, thereby making it more likely that these children will be brought into the world at all.

Indeed, the *Hernandez* court's analysis was especially surprising because New York is one of those states permitting each member of a same-sex couple to be the legal parent of the same child.[23] If the state of New York really believed that it was bad for children to be raised by same-sex couples, one would not expect the state to afford such recognition. Apparently, New York's highest court believes it rational for the Legislature to permit same-sex couples to have parenting rights but to deny them the marital benefits that might make their relationships more stable and secure and that would also benefit their children, all in the name of promoting the interests of children.

In *Andersen v. King County*,[24] the Washington Supreme Court also offered some surprising rationales to uphold that state's same-sex marriage ban. For example, the *Andersen* court suggested that the Washington Legislature might have believed that "encouraging marriage for opposite-sex couples who may have relationships that result in children is preferable to having children raised by unmarried parents."[25] Such a suggestion would be unremarkable were the court trying to justify a decision to accord rights to different-sex couples. But no one was challenging doing that. Rather what was being challenged was the failure to accord such rights to same-sex couples, and no reason was offered to believe that it would be preferable for children to live with unmarried rather than married same-sex parents. Indeed, in what was one of the more surprising aspects of the Washington opinion, the *Andersen* court

---

[22] See Margaret F. Brinig & Steven L. Nock, "How Much Does Legal Status Matter? Adoptions By Kin Caregivers," 36 *Family Law Quarterly* 449, 469 n.67 (2002) (citing with approval House Committee report stating, "There seems to be almost universal agreement that adoption is preferable to foster care and that the nation's children would be well served by a policy that increases adoption rates.").

[23] See In re Jacob, 660 N.E.2d 397 (N.Y. 1995).

[24] 138 P.3d 963 (Wash. 2006).

[25] Id. at 982.

recognized "the need to resolve the sometimes conflicting rights and obligations of the same-sex couple and the necessary third party in relation to a child,"[26] but then implied that this "provides a rational basis for limiting traditional marriage to opposite-sex couples."[27] But this is exactly wrong.

Basically, the court recognized that when same-sex couples are raising a child, a third party often is or was involved. It may be someone who provided eggs or sperm; it may be a gestational surrogate who carried the child to term; or, it may be someone who produced a child but had his or her parental rights terminated voluntarily or involuntarily. Yet, precisely because of the involvement of a third party, it may be more rather than less important for same-sex couples to marry and to be able to create a zone of privacy for themselves and their children.

Ironically, the concern mentioned by the Washington court, namely, that it would be important to establish the rights and obligations (if any) of any third party who had assisted the same-sex couple in becoming parents, is less of a concern in the state of Washington, because it is one of the states whose adoptions laws have been interpreted to permit second-parent adoption by same-sex couples.[28] Thus, the same-sex couple can make clear that they are the only ones with parental rights and obligations with respect to their child by having the partner adopt the child.

Suppose, however, that the current partner of the biological parent cannot adopt the child because the child has another parent with rights and responsibilities, for example, the ex-partner of the biological parent. In that event, the current partner would not be able to adopt the child even were the state of Washington to recognize same-sex marriage. Thus, the reason cited by the Washington court to limit marriage to different-sex couples is either irrelevant, because same-sex couples can make use of second-parent adoption to make clear who has parental rights and responsibilities, or a reason to permit same-sex marriage, precisely because it is preferable to have children raised by married rather than unmarried parents.

---

[26] Andersen, 138 P.3d at 982.

[27] Id.

[28] See Adam K. Ake, Note, "Unequal Rights: The Fourteenth Amendment And De Facto Parentage," 81 *Washington Law Review* 787, 788 n.4 (2006) ("Washington is among the states with adoption statutes interpreted to permit same-sex, second-parent adoptions. See Washington Revised Code § 26.33.140 (2004); State ex rel. D.R.M. v. Wood, 34 P.3d 887 (Wash. App. 2001).").

IV. Conclusion

Marriage confers a number of benefits on individuals, their families, and society as a whole. Almost all, if not all, of those benefits would accrue regardless of whether the couple is composed of individuals of the same sex or of different sexes.

Recent decisions by state supreme courts upholding their respective state's same-sex marriage ban illustrate the irrationality of current refusals to recognize such unions. None of the proffered reasons supported withholding marital benefits from same-sex couples; instead, the reasons were either irrelevant, because they involved a misunderstanding of the state's legitimate goals, or they in reality supported the extension of those benefits. That specious reasons are offered to support a policy that harms individuals and society as a whole suggests that marriage itself is being used to reinforce traditional sex roles and to impose an undeserved burden on a disfavored minority, which can only tarnish an institution that marriage proponents claim to be protecting. The failure to recognize same-sex unions is a public policy disaster—it harms individuals, society, and the institution of marriage, itself.

A LIBERAL CONCEPTION OF CIVIL MARRIAGE[1]

LAURA OSINSKI

The debate over the definition of civil marriage raises two separate questions. Should the state regulate marriage at all, or should it simply let persons enter into a marriage contract on any terms they wish? Answering yes to the first question raises the second: What justification can be offered to support the state's terms for civil marriage, which will necessarily exclude or not recognize certain forms of union not fitting the definition of civil marriage? I argue that on both practical and theoretical grounds, the state must set out terms—a definition—of civil marriage which will regulate (restrict) who may or may not be recognized as having a civil marriage and at least some terms of the civil marriage contract.

In this paper, I develop a conception of marriage based on a Rawlsian understanding of political justification, that is, a conception of civil marriage that could be agreed to (or at least not rejected) by reasonable persons who view each other as free and equal. I argue that by appealing to public reasons—the liberal principles of autonomy and of equality—there is justification all reasonable comprehensive doctrines can accept that civil marriage must be binary. Plural marriage fails to respect the equality of persons and thus is not defensible on a liberal conception of civil marriage, though it could be permitted, that is, not criminalized, provided it respects the autonomy of persons. Same-sex marriage, by contrast, is compatible with both liberal principles of autonomy and equality, and therefore is defensible on a liberal conception of civil marriage.

---

[1] A portion of this paper was initially presented at the 10th International Conference on Ethics Across the Curriculum sponsored by Towson University in the fall of 2008. I received many helpful comments and suggestions by audience members at this conference. I would also like to thank Andrew Levine for a number of useful suggestions and important criticisms of an earlier draft of this paper.

Why Should the State Regulate Civil Marriage at All?

By civil marriage I mean marriage sanctioned by the state. This is distinct, of course, from marriage as defined and recognized by various religions and/or associations. Given the religious and moral connotations of marriage, perhaps a liberal state committed to secularism should not involve itself in recognizing certain forms of social union as marriage. Perhaps, instead, the state should take a more libertarian view regarding marriage and simply leave it up to consenting adults to decide what kind of marriage they wish to enter into, with whomever they choose, and on terms the parties agree to. Marriage, then, will mean whatever consenting parties agree to—more than two people, people of the same sex, for a length of time of one's choosing, say one year or five years or for a lifetime.

Notice, however, that already a certain assumption is being made— marriage, civil or religious, ought not to involve children, nor should it involve coercion of adults. In other words, even if the state wishes to leave marriage arrangements to individuals to decide, it is nonetheless the case that the state must not only refuse to recognize or enforce marriage arrangements involving minors, but that it ought to prohibit such arrangements by assigning criminal penalties to adults engaging in such practices, regardless of the religious or moral view that might condone it. The political ideal that best expresses the apprehension of liberal society to sanction arranged marriages—marriages that are entered into usually at the behest of one or both parents without the meaningful consent of either party (usually the future wife)—is the principle of autonomy. In very basic terms, the principle of autonomy explains the value of living one's life according to a plan of one's own choosing. We express the moral equality of persons in terms that reflect equal respect for each person's autonomy. Without consent we are reduced to a mere thing, to be used for someone else's ends. In the context of marriage, this is most tragic in the plight of young women, often girls, in parts of the world where their marriages are arranged by their fathers (or other guardian) as debt payment, to purchase livestock, crops, or simply to mediate in some way the family's wrenching poverty.[2]

In principle then, the state ought not to recognize marriages that involve coercion. Those who wish to enter into marriages of this sort, usually through an arranged marriage contract, will be denied an opportunity to do so. In other words, a liberal state may reject this

---

[2] *Chicago Tribune*, Tribune Special Report, December 12, 2004, Section 1, page 1.

particular conception of marriage, even if a particular religion or culture accepts it.

At a minimum, then, the state must define civil marriage as respecting the autonomy of persons, broadly understood. Are there any other requirements? Consider two adults who consent to a marriage contract through their church which does not permit divorce for any reason. In the event one spouse wishes to exit the marriage, they will receive nothing— no custody rights to children, no property, nothing. Suppose after five years of marriage, the wife decides to seek a divorce through civil court that will allow her custody (or visitation) rights to her children. But the husband objects, explaining that they both consented to a marriage contract which does not permit divorce. Should the state enforce any contract that consenting adults sign? If we take a libertarian view of marriage and let individuals decide the terms of marriage, it is conceivable (likely) that persons will sign agreements that fail to treat persons equally. The state must then decide—it cannot remain neutral—whether to enforce these contracts. If the state grants the wife a divorce, over the objections of her husband, then the state has assumed that marriage arrangements which prohibit divorce will not be enforced, i.e., such marriages are not considered civil marriages in the event of disagreement between the parties, much like in the earlier example, arranged marriages of minors are indefensible, and therefore do not meet the standard for civil marriage in a liberal state.

We can begin to see the basic need for a definition of civil marriage. If the state is going to defend its decision to enforce or not enforce marriage contracts, as it must to prevent violations to autonomy and equality of citizens, it can only do so if it has a working definition that it can appeal to in denying some arrangements while enforcing others.

There are, of course, a host of practical problems that arise in defending a conception of civil marriage. Some one thousand federal benefits are tied to marriage status, including child custody, joint property, insurance, etc. The point I wish to make here is that it is conceivable (possible?) that the state could remove itself from granting these benefits on the basis of marital status—simply remove marriage as a preferred status. But even if it could, that would not change the fact that the state still needs to restrict enforceable marriage contracts to those that in some sense respect the autonomy and equality of persons. So this is our point to begin assessing a variety of different marital arrangements: 1) How can we articulate these liberal ideals of autonomy and equality of persons; and 2) Which marriage arrangements demonstrate or embody these ideals sufficiently well, which do not, and are some in-between? We might consider traditional monogamy, plural marriage, same-sex marriage, limited term marriage, and group marriage.

Let us add a further dimension. There are many areas of life where the state awards certain benefits or restricts access to citizens on the basis of some normative conclusion about the value or worth of citizens' endeavors—ways of life. The state is neutral with respect to certain conceptions of the good (provided these conceptions do not involve what we typically consider harmful or criminal activity toward others), even though the state relies on normative considerations in awarding various sorts of benefits. So, for example, the state rewards homeowners with the benefit of a tax deduction that is not available to renters. The state is neutral with respect to whether citizens decide to rent or own a home because the state allows either choice (neither choice is prohibited). Yet at the same time, the state provides a benefit to those who own homes that is not available to those who rent. Similarly, those who create pornographic images are not eligible for National Endowment for the Art funding, while another photographer who chooses a more socially valuable subject will be.

So, for example, if the requirements for a conception of civil marriage include that no more than two people can be married to each other at the same time (the binary requirement), it would not follow from that requirement that groups of persons wishing to be married to one another (or a polygamist wishing to be married to more than one wife at the same time) should be prohibited from doing so; only that their arrangement, possibly recognized by a religion or other association as a marriage, does not meet the requirements of civil marriage. There would be nothing illegal about these alternative arrangements (an example of J.S. Mill's experiments in living), except that the state denies them recognition by the state. This is an important difference. Being denied state approval for one's living arrangements or religious marriage does not prevent or prohibit you from being married in your church, for example. Your day to day living arrangements can function very similarly to those who do meet the requirements of civil marriage.

Still, being denied the opportunity for civil marriage carries significant costs, such that those requirements, which necessarily will exclude some kinds of arrangements between consenting adults, must be defensible on the basis of liberal legitimacy. These costs include many financial implications, end of life issues, in some cases child custody concerns, just to name a few. All these areas will leave persons who wish to have a civil marriage but do not meet the requirements, with fewer options and less money than they would otherwise have if the state recognized their marriage. In addition, there is the issue of respect. When one's preferences for who to live with and on what terms becomes the basis for state recognition or lack of recognition of any sort, this requires an explanation in terms of public reasons.

Public Reasons in Support of a Binary Requirement for Civil Marriage

We begin this discussion with public reasons and whether civil marriage ought to be regarded as a constitutional essential—a matter of basic justice to which public reasons ought to apply. While Rawls is not specific on whether the right to marry the persons of one's own choosing is a constitutional essential, he does include freedom of movement and free choice of occupation. If these are included, it is hard to imagine how the freedom to choose whom to marry is not also in that category. At any rate, it seems clear that choice in whom to marry reflects a conception of the good that citizens, characterized as free and equal, would want the state to protect.

Certainly in cases where the marriage involves a minor, or is non-consensual, the marriage in question rises to this level, since there is a violation of the liberal principle of autonomy—the marriage does not treat one of the parties as free in the sense that they are being used for someone else's end and not their own. Or consider a decision to deny civil marriage to interracial couples. This is obviously a violation of the state's obligation to treat persons equally and not on the basis of an arbitrary difference and rises to the level of a constitutional essential.

Rawls states, "The point of the ideal of public reason is that citizens are to conduct their fundamental discussions within the framework of what each regards as a political conception of justice based on values that the others can reasonably be expected to endorse and each is, in good faith, prepared to defend that conception so understood. This means that each of us must have, and be ready to explain, a criterion of what principles and guidelines we think other citizens (who are free and equal) may reasonably be expected to endorse along with us."[3] Comprehensive doctrines are of two kinds—reasonable and unreasonable. Those that are reasonable recognize that state power cannot be used to decide constitutional essentials based on that comprehensive doctrine. Those who do not share the belief in that comprehensive doctrine, yet are equal citizens, could not

---

[3] Rawls, John, *Political Liberalism* (New York: Cambridge University Press, 1993), p. 226.

reasonably be expected to accept the use of state power in this way. Democratic legitimacy arises out of the recognition of the need for public reasons.

But in the context of civil marriage, what kind of political values constitute public reasons in favor of who may or may not be married and under what terms? Since the concept of marriage seems inextricably tied to religious views and dogma, what values can the state assert that do not rely on comprehensive religious doctrines? I suggest the two that form the basis of our understanding of persons as citizens—liberal autonomy and equality. The question is, what regulations on marriage respect the autonomy and equality of citizens?

A liberal principle of autonomy will ensure that persons cannot be used to advance another's ends, unless the person shares in those ends.[4] Does this principle support a binary requirement for civil marriage? I do not think so. Rawls describes his understanding of citizens as free meaning, "viewing themselves as self-authenticating sources of valid claims—they regard themselves as being entitled to make claims on their institutions so as to advance their conceptions of the good (provided these conception fall within the range permitted by the public conception of justice)."[5] How can marriage arrangements violate a liberal principle of autonomy? Whether there are two or more than two within a marriage, the rights afforded to each marriage partner will have much to do with whether the persons within the marriage have a guarantee of autonomy. Within a binary marriage, if one spouse (the woman, for example) can do nothing without the consent of her husband, she is a mere means. She is not, on this scenario, a self-authenticating source of valid claims. Rather, her husband is the source of these claims, and in that sense, his ends are pursued, and she is a means to those ends. No one could in principle consent to this arrangement. But if we understand civil marriage as guaranteeing roughly reciprocal rights to the parties, then a binary marriage arrangement does not in principle violate autonomy.

But would plural marriage violate autonomy of persons? One might argue that polygamy necessarily represents coercion of one party by the other. The first wife is not really in a position to consent to her husband's decision to marry additional wives. In this sense, the husband is enlisting her (as his spouse) in a relationship—plural marriage—that represents his

---

[4] I am adapting Arthur Ripstein's discussion of coercion in his recent article "Authority and Coercion" to my understanding of political autonomy. See *Philosophy and Public Affairs*, vol.32, no.1, p.18.

[5] Rawls, John, *Political Liberalism* (New York: Columbia University Press, 1993), p. 32.

ends, not hers. Assuming the woman has a meaningful choice in whether to enter into a polygamous marriage, it seems to me that she may choose such an arrangement. In other words, polygamy is not in principle a violation of autonomy because it could be an end that she sets for herself, perhaps because she believes it is part of her religious duty, for example. In addition, it seems entirely plausible that some women may find polygamy advantageous to their own ends. At least one woman defending polygamy has argued that it affords her better childcare opportunities, since her children consider her husband's other wives as close family.[6]

There is, however, a different concern regarding plural marriage from the point of view of liberalism. I will argue shortly that plural marriage, while not in principle a violation of autonomy, is a violation of the moral equality of persons. My point here is not that a woman ought never to choose polygamy. Only that, in so choosing, she elevates her concern for other values, a perceived benefit in childcare, for example, over an equal marriage. And while the state ought to respect her liberty to set such priorities as ends in her life, the state ought not to recognize or benefit such relationships because they do not respect the equality of persons. In other words, persons must be free to pursue ends, even when those ends subject themselves to unequal status (at least to a point), but these decisions need not be, indeed ought not to be, endorsed, condoned, or rewarded by the state.

What I am proposing is three categories for state action: 1) marriage arrangements and marriage contracts that are prohibited, that is, illegal, and perhaps even criminal; 2) marriage arrangements that are permissible, that is legal, but not recognized as civil marriage with the attendant benefits and status; and 3) marriage arrangements that are encouraged and rewarded by being given the name civil marriage with the accompanying benefits.

So far, we can see the difference between 1 and 2. Marriage arrangements that violate autonomy of persons ought to be prohibited. But what about the distinction between 2 and 3? We should see that persons enter into contracts that are enforceable but that are not strictly equal. An employer/employee contract, for example, is not a contract between equals, and sometimes it may be quite unfair if the employee is desperate enough for work. However, at a certain point, the contract becomes unenforceable, so unequal that it becomes a slave contract. There is much disagreement of course about what that point is, but the key here is that

---

[6] Joseph, Elizabeth "Polygamy is Good Feminism", *Morality and Moral Controversies*, 7th ed. by John Arthur, Pearson Prentice Hall, New Jersey, 2005.

some amount of inequality is permissible, morally and legally. I propose a similar distinction between marriage arrangements. Those, such as binary unions that are in principle (though not always in practice) equal (as well as respecting autonomy of the parties) are to be rewarded with the designation by the state of civil marriage, category 3 in the above list. Those unions which are not in principle equal, such as polygamy (the reason for this will be explained below), are to be tolerated, provided they do not violate autonomy, but do not receive the designation of civil marriage. Plural marriages fall in category number 2.

Public reasons, on a Rawlsian framework, are reasons that no persons, understood as free and equal, could reasonably reject. Coercion by the state in the form of civil or criminal sanctions against different marriage arrangements on the grounds that the arrangements constitute unequal social relationships, could reasonably be rejected by those (adults) who wish to pursue this way of life, for example because of religious reasons. At the same time, it cannot be reasonably rejected that the state should wish to promote, by awarding specific benefits, those relationships that embody the liberal ideals of autonomy and equality, assuming the conception of persons as free and equal.

Why think that plural marriage is unequal? To begin, it is helpful to think of marriage as it is frequently understood—as a union. How many ought to comprise this union, under what conditions, and so forth remain to be determined. But the basic notion of a union (more than one) is central to any understanding of marriage. (The common phrase for monogamous marriage is "two as one.") If we begin with this notion of a union, we can represent marriage as a pie-shaped diagram, with husband and wife each comprising half of the union. (See figure 1.)

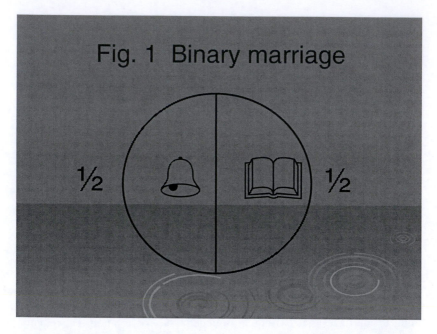

Fig. 1 Binary marriage

Each half of the union represents the interests of the corresponding spouse, with each allocated 50% of the union. Historically, this traditional form of marriage was not at all equal in this respect. The husband's interests/wishes/desires might have been the sole determinant of what the marriage union would be and the decisions that were made. My point is merely that this binary form of marriage allows in principle for the possibility of an equal distribution of interests/needs/desires within a union. So that, if the parties should wish to, their interests, etc., can be equally respected, in virtue of the husband and wife each having an equal share of their union.

It is this feature that gives some marriages or unions the quality of being a relationship between rough equals, a necessary condition of state-sanctioned civil marriage on my account. How would a plural marriage or union be represented? There are several possibilities, none of which can, in principle, provide for an equal distribution of interests. The interests at stake are most often reciprocal in nature. The couples physical relationship, their decisions regarding children—whether to have them and how many, property arrangements and other financial entanglements allow one spouse greater opportunities than the other, in principle. Thus, the inequality in a plural marriage follows from this lack of reciprocity.

Suppose, for example, a husband has four wives. We can represent this arrangement as shown in figure 2.

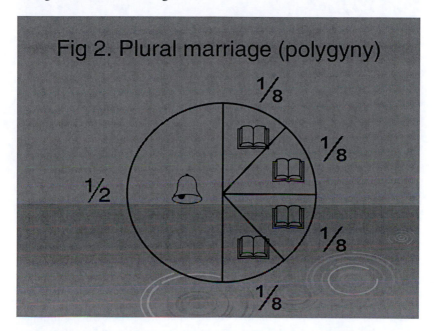

Fig 2. Plural marriage (polygyny)

The husband's share of the union is 50%, as it would be under monogamy, but the four wives must split the remaining 50% share, leaving them each with 1/8 of the union, compared with the husbands ½. This four to one ratio, in favor of the husband's interests cannot in principle be made equal to each wife's smaller share, no matter how kind and loving the husband.

Perhaps there is a more favorable way to represent this union. Since the husband is married four times, each wife does have a 50% or equal share of her union. It's just that the husband has four separate pie-shaped unions, with 50% of each. (See figure 3.)

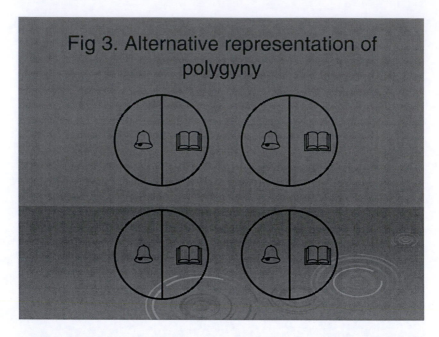

He can, in principle, then, be in a roughly equal union with each of his four wives. The problem with this view is that, in virtue of his additional unions, his interests as a husband are multiplied four times the interests of any individual wife. His total of 2 compares with her .5, so again we have an inherently unequal relationship between husband and wife.

Finally, we might represent his union with four wives on a single pie-shape, but instead of affording the husband 50%, simple divide the pie 5 ways, one fifth of the pie for each of the five people so connected, as shown in figure 4.

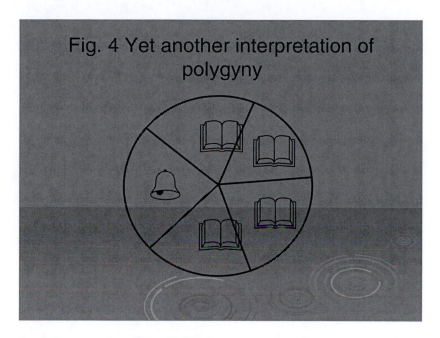

Fig. 4 Yet another interpretation of polygyny

In this way, the union would represent each party's interests equally—as 20% of the union. This description might represent a group marriage perhaps, where all of the partners are married to one another. But it does not represent a polygamous arrangement. The husband has greater legal and moral standing over all four marriages than any one of the four wives would have in the say over conditions in the other marriages. In other words, each individual wife has a stake in one marriage union only, whereas the husband has a similar stake in four. His interests as a husband are represented four times as much as the interests of any of the four wives. Unless the wives also had four husbands, their interests as members of a union, cannot in principle be equally represented.

I would like to address two objections at this point. First, with respect to figure 2, why see the husband's marriage interests as additive? That is, why not use the four separate pies as four distinct, but equal unions? In other words, why should it matter to each wife that her spouse has additional marriages? The reason the number of marriages matter is because of the reciprocal nature of the rights and/or interests of spouses. For example, a couple's decision about whether to have children will not rest with each of them equally. In other words, whether or not husband and wife become parents will not be determined by each spouse equally. If the wife chooses not to, the husband has three other opportunities. If the husband and one wife differ regarding property arrangements, he may, by enlisting the consent of a second wife, affect his financial condition such that the financial condition of the other wives will also be affected, without their consent. In contrast to a binary marriage, where each spouse has full veto power over the decision of the other, the women in a polygamous marriage must form a coalition, in a sense, to exert that same veto power over the husband's decisions, while the husband in a polygamous marriage has no such additional requirement.

The second objection is to offer this analogy to plural marriage. Marrying additional spouses is no different than having additional children. Just because couples have more than one child does not entail that the first child is loved any less or that his or her interests are somehow compromised by the additional siblings. Comparing a marriage union to a couple's decision to have children fundamentally misunderstands the marriage relationship. Children have a fundamentally different standing in relationship to their parents than they do between themselves. So while it is reasonable to say that a husband with multiple wives could in principle treat all his wives equally, he cannot in principle treat each wife equal to himself. In fact, the willingness to have children and how many is one of the interests that each party in a marriage will have represented. And it provides a useful illustration of how plural marriage dilutes the interests of the wife (in this case) compared with the husband. His decision or interests regarding fatherhood will necessarily take into account fatherhood with all his wives. The desire for companionship, even for material matters of inheritance and so forth will require on the husband's part, some accommodation of all his wives' interests/needs and so forth. Each wife cannot in principle stand in relation to him as his equal, but rather as one of a group of four (in this example) who must share in some sense the "wife's share."

The previous discussion is meant to be a defense of the binary requirement of civil marriage. Plural marriage whether in the form of polygyny or polyandry is inherently unequal to whichever spouse is left with the smaller share of the union. On this liberal conception of civil marriage, there would be no grounds for excluding from civil marriage same-sex couples, since in principle a same-sex monogamous marriage can represent rough equality as much as a heterosexual one.

But are these criticisms of polygyny applicable to all forms of group marriage? Might there be equality between spouses in a plural marriage where there are equal numbers of men and women, as in figure 5, or in a same-sex marriage with three or more spouses of the same sex (see figures 6 and 7)?[7]

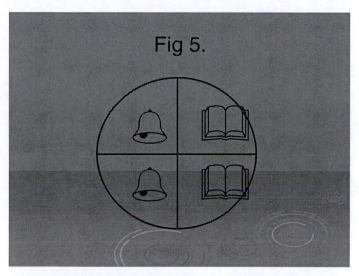

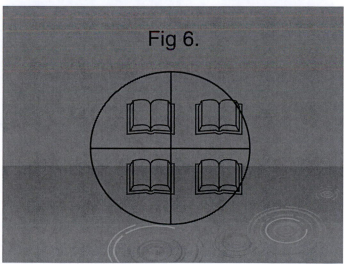

[7] I am grateful to Adam Potthast for raising this question, and especially grateful to Michael McFall for providing helpful feedback to me as I tried to develop an adequate response to this question.

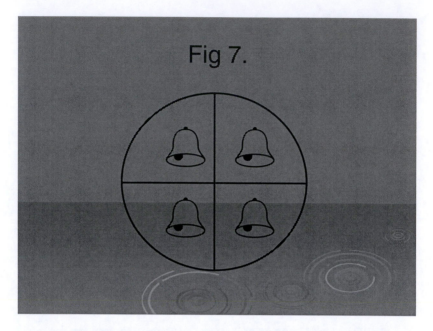

Fig 7.

At first glance, it looks like a group marriage with equal numbers of males and/or females would solve the inequality that is represented in polygyny (and polyandry). But I think it is important to ask what the equality is relative to. Certainly a group marriage could model equality relative to a voting procedure, for deciding a household budget or chores, for example. This would be something like the equality present in a communal living arrangement. But if we ask whether an individual is equal relative to another individual in matters concerning relationships, I think the answer is no.

Consider two couples: John and Mary are a couple in a group marriage with another couple, Bob and Jane. Each man is married to each woman; each woman is married to each man. Whenever there is a binary relationship in this group marriage, whenever one person's time, attention or affection is given to one other person, then equality between the four is not maintained. If John and Jane enjoy some kind of time and affection with each other, then it will exclude Mary and Bob. Just considering Mary's situation for a moment, she will enjoy no part of this binary relationship between John and Jane. Perhaps she does not mind this, but it is nonetheless the case that were Jane not in this marriage, Mary would reasonably expect to receive the attention from John that is now being shared with Jane. She has an unequal share of the binary relationship between John and Jane. Notice that it changes nothing to say that Mary could make up her unequal share by having a binary relationship with Bob. Because people are not interchangeable, she cannot make up her unequal relationship relative to John and Jane by having a binary relationship with Bob.

The fact that each of the spouses in a group marriage are all subject to the same (equal) possibility of these unequal binary intragroup relationships does not help. The problem is that as long as marriage is understood to be fundamentally about relationships and maintaining them, the work (or enjoyment) of this is done frequently through binary interaction, and that's the source of the inequality that they all share. The same set of difficulties arise in a group marriage comprising more than two same sex spouses.

There is, however, another difficulty with my insistence that civil marriage should model the equality of persons. By arguing for a binary union, I've not explained why, in the area of marriage only, equality requires a 50% share, so to speak. When we consider all the projects we involve ourselves in—volunteer organizations, businesses (as when we buy stock), professional organizations, and even the state itself—nowhere do we assume we must have a 50% stake with only one other partner (where each has veto power) in order to model the equality of persons. Why think we need such a model of equality for civil marriage?[8] In other words, if I'm willing to accept a 1% stake in a company, through a stock purchase, we do not conclude that my equality has been undermined. Or when we contribute to a cause that is important to us, we do not feel that our equality is undermined simply because our contribution in time and effort is a small fraction of the total contributed to the charitable or political organization. How then can I argue that our equality is undermined when we enter a marital arrangement that reflects less than a 50% share with only one other partner?

The answer to this question I think turns on the goal or purpose of these different enterprises. In all of the cases other than marriage, there is a goal or purpose outside of the relationship between the participants. In the case of business, the goals have to do with producing a useful product or service at a profitable price. For philanthropic organizations, the goals generally have to do with achieving some improvement in the lives of those who would otherwise suffer, and so on. But the goals or purpose of marriage are not generally understood to be expressed in these terms. Marriage is an accomplishment if there is a certain relationship obtained

---

[8] I thank Robert Muhlnickel for raising this important question.

between the spouses. There isn't any external standard for assessing its goals other than—are the spouses in a mutually rewarding relationship? It is because marriage is so firmly connected to relationships, not external goals, that the equality of persons takes on a different requirement—as an ideal—in this endeavor compared with the other goal-driven examples where equality does not require binary relationship. This is perhaps another way of saying that the conception of civil marriage I have been developing implicitly relies on a normative understanding of marriage that draws on a distinction between a companionate model verses a business model of marriage.[9]

In addition to these concerns, there are a number of objections that arise to my general thesis that a liberal conception of marriage will be a binary conception, resting on the equality and autonomy of persons. I list several of these below and my responses to them.

Objections

1) The argument for polygamy on the basis of religious liberty. Historically, polygamists in the US have argued in court for the right to have polygamous marriages recognized by the state on the grounds of religious liberty. Notice, however, that in these cases, the state not only did not permit civil marriage for polygamists, it also criminalized their activity. The question here should be not whether polygamy ought to be illegal. Provided it takes place between consenting adults, there seems to be no reason to criminalize these experiments in living. Instead, the question should be whether the state must recognize polygamy as entitled to the status of civil marriage.

Obviously, religious liberty does not afford persons unlimited rights. Religious injunctions and requirements must comport with the fundamental liberal conception of persons as free and equal. It seems defensible, then, for the state to require civil marriages to respect both autonomy and the equality of persons, even if (especially if) particular religions or cultures do not.

In summary, as long as the practice of marriage is decriminalized, persons have religious liberty to pursue any lifestyle they choose, provided they are consenting adults. But the state need not recognize and condone

---

[9] I am referring here to Richard Posner's discussion of companionate marriage—a marriage between approximate equals built on love and trust of the spouses—in contrast to a business model that serves purposes external to the relationship of the spouses. See his book, *Sex and Reason* (1992).

every legal activity. Selfishness is not a crime, but the state will afford benefits (in the way of tax deductions) to those who give to charity while denying those benefits to persons who do not.

2). The liberal conception of marriage I've outlined doesn't take into account the interests of children. Consider the prohibition against marrying someone too closely related. Siblings, for example, may not marry. A parent may not marry a child, even if the child meets the minimum age requirement and consents. What is the concern in each of these cases that justifies the state's prohibition against these marriages? Primarily, the concern would be for the welfare of the children of related parents. In general, the more related the parents, the more likely the chance that recessive traits will be expressed, and those that are harmful can seriously damage the physical and mental wellbeing of the offspring. In many states, first cousins are permitted to marry, because the increase in background birth defects, compared with non-related spouses, is thought to be quite small (an increase from 4% to 6%).

But this concern for the welfare of children does not, apparently, extend to the children of non-related couples who are aware that they have a very high chance of passing on a severe genetic disease to their children, should they have any. States permit non-related persons to marry regardless of their genetic makeup. There are other examples where it would seem that the welfare of children, while important, is certainly not a sufficient condition for determining who should be permitted to marry, according to the state. Divorce, for example, is generally understood to be detrimental to children, but it is permissible presumably because the state must consider the autonomy and welfare of the spouses as well as the children.

The welfare of children, then, plays some role in developing a standard for what constitutes the essential characteristics of civil marriage, but it is not determinative. In general terms, the most it could show would be that a conception of civil marriage ought to promote stable, long-term relationships. That requirement will not, however, rule out much. It will not support a binary requirement for civil marriage, nor the fidelity requirement, both defended by the Massachusetts High Court. And it would not justify a prohibition against same-sex marriages, barring any new information regarding the welfare of children raised by same-sex couples.

However, if we add to this liberal conception of civil marriage an interest in promoting stable, long-term relationships, then it seems reasonable to conclude that group marriages and limited term marriages (that would otherwise meet the requirements of autonomy and equality that I've outlined above), would not meet the criteria for civil marriage. They would be permissible (not illegal), but participants in them would not receive the state sanctioned benefits of a civil marriage.

3) Denying consenting adults civil marriage status is paternalistic. This objection states that even though men in a polygamist relationship have more than each wife (if the wife dies, for example, he does not have to split any inheritance or benefits with other husbands), what ought to matter from the point of view of the state is consent. If adults give meaningful consent (in that they have alternatives available to them), yet still choose polygamy, then there is no basis for the state to deny them civil marriage status. To do so is paternalistic. This is a good objection. Here the state's rationale cannot be based on concern for third parties (which is often the case when defending other paternalistic state prohibitions—drug use, seat belts and helmet laws, for example) because we've already explained that concern for children, while a necessary condition of a conception of civil marriage, is not sufficient. And it may turn out that polygamy is no better or worse for children than any other form of marriage currently accepted.

Here is where I again invoke the distinction between the state promoting certain ways of living and tolerating or permitting alternative ways of living. As long as the parties give meaningful consent, there is indeed no basis for criminalizing these alternative marriage arrangements. But since people can and do give meaningful consent (under non-ideal conditions) to inherently unfair and unequal contracts and relationships, it is not the case that simply because people consent to polygamy that it must be fair. It is not fair in the sense that behind a veil of ignorance, the men who practice it would likely never endorse it if they knew there was the equal possibility that they would be one of many husbands with one wife. The fact that it is inherently unequal (though consented to) is grounds for the state to not promote or sanction this marriage arrangement, though at the same time protecting its legality.

4.) Why think marriage has to be for life? Why can't consenting persons take vows for a limited term marriage? My response to this objection is to propose the idea that civil marriage is an institution that represents an ideal—it's not for everyone. But it means something to a society to recognize an ideal social form of organization that represents the hope of something many people consider an intrinsic good—long term relationships. Imagine how much less of a celebration marriage would be if the couple—at the outset—agreed to be married only for 1 year, or 5 years. Even though divorce allows for an early exit, it is understood generally as a kind of failure, probably because of this ideal of a union based on an understanding of reciprocity—to promise to sacrifice one's personal interests for the other. As unrealistic as this ideal seems to be, given the divorce rate, society is better for having an institution that offers every person an opportunity for making and keeping such a promise because it promotes long-term, (ideally) stable and caring relationships which are good for adults and children. Adults are free to choose alternate kinds of relationships, but the state can, without discriminating, offer greater recognition (and benefits) to those who choose to try this ideal.

5) On this liberal conception of civil marriage, the state would have to permit adult incest and sibs marrying, particularly if one or both parties agreed to be sterilized so there would be no concern for harm to their offspring. While this objection has force, there seems to be no disagreement that states ought to enforce some limit on the degree of relatedness between spouses, and that this is not an arbitrary requirement, nor one that unduly limits the autonomy of persons. Perhaps this agreement simply reflects a social taboo, but from the perspective of a liberal conception of marriage, marriage between closely related persons, assuming consent, would perhaps fall into the second category—permitted, that is not criminal, but not recognized as a civil marriage, with none of the attendant benefits.

Conclusion

In summary, the previous discussion is meant to answer the first question I started with—Should the state regulate civil marriage at all?—with a yes. In the absence of some definition of civil marriage, the state will be unable to fairly adjudicate the many disputes that will arise from ad hoc marriage contracts based on religious, cultural, or other commitments that will continue regardless of whether the state defines civil marriage. In light of this need, the basis for such a definition will have to be acceptable to persons from many different religious and cultural perspectives. Some of these perspectives may not honor the liberal values of autonomy and equality, and so at a minimum, I have argued that a liberal conception of marriage based on autonomy and equality of persons will rule out some conceptions of marriage. My suggestion of a three tier system acknowledges the differences that consenting adults may have with respect to living arrangements. But by privileging those marital arrangements, namely a binary arrangement, that have the possibility of embodying the

liberal values of equality as well as autonomy, the state respects the moral
equality of persons.

THE ETHICS OF POLYAMOROUS MARRIAGE

HALLIE LIBERTO

Many philosophers argue that the moral problem with adultery is the breaking of a promise, and the deception of a loved one. Accordingly, these same philosophers point to open, or polyamorous marriages as a form of marriage in which adultery is not morally wrong.[1] In what follows, I discuss the special sorts of moral issues that might be contentious in a polyamorous marriage, and point out the inequalities that might arise that are particular to such marriages. These inequalities, I argue, are the foundation for some moral hazards of the type that Susan Moller Okin describes in her work on *traditional* marriage, "The Vulnerability of Women in Marriage." Okin shows that women in traditional marriages face cultural expectations that land them in gender roles with limited opportunities to enrich their lives outside the home and, ultimately, less than equal exiting power within their marriages. I will illustrate an analogous inequality of opportunity to enrich one's life, and an inequality of exiting power that arises in open marriages. I conclude that: if one accepts the vulnerability of women in marriage, as Okin describes it, as a circumstance riddled with moral problems, then one must also admit that open marriage is not a morally unproblematic alternative to adultery within a traditional marriage.

---

[1] In distinguishing polyamorous marriage from monogamous marriage, I am only referring to the number of extramarital romantic partners permitted to members of the couple (one or more for a polyamourous marriage, zero for monogamous marriage). When I refer to *traditional* marriages, I mean not only that the marriage is monogamous, but also that the couple is heterosexual, and that the spouses conform to fairly traditional gender roles, as is described in Okin's *Justice, Gender, and the Family*. That is, the woman in the marriage is more likely to take off time from her career to be a primary care-giver; the man of the couple is more likely to have a career and prioritize it in a way that eventually yields him more earning power.

Adultery and Polyamory

While other sexual norms of the Western world that were largely accepted until the second half of the 20th century have diminished (e.g. social prohibitions on premarital sex, varieties of sexual activities, and varieties of sexual partners) the sexual norm of marital monogamy, that is, a social prohibition on adultery, has remained. Modern philosophers have determined that the moral problem with adultery, the reason why this particular segment of old-fashioned marital ideals has remained a part of our public morality, is because adultery involves the breaking of an important promise and, typically, involves deception.   Don Marquis believes that the promise of sexual fidelity is only as important as the other promises made in a marriage contract, and as marriage involves promises conditional on a partner's fulfillment of the contract (and not a set of unconditional, or covenantal promises), adultery is morally permissible in cases in which an adulterer's spouse has not fulfilled other aspects of the marriage contract (like promoting the other's happiness, etc.).[2] Marquis' acceptance of adultery in certain contexts still adjoins adultery with morally problematic marriages. Whether it is the adultery that first breaks a marriage contract, or whether it is some other failure of contractual fulfillment, there is promise breaking involved in the said marriage. However, Wasserstrom insists that we need not think of adultery as a sign of a broken marriage contract. After all, contracts do not need to include promises of fidelity. Though an open, or polyamorous marriage would involve adultery, adultery in polyamorous marriages should not be wrong, since adultery is only wrong in virtue of promise breaking.[3]

Moral Obligations of Polyamory

We are all quite familiar with what is commonly thought to be the moral requirements of traditional, monogamous marriages.   However, there are some questions that need to be fleshed out in order to determine the moral requirements of a polyamorous marriage. To start, let us assume that all of the non-sexual aspects of a polyamorous marriage contract remain similar to the non-sexual aspects on a monogamous marriage

---

[2] Marquis, Don.   "What's Wrong With Adultery?" in *What's Wrong: Applied Ethicists and Their Critics*, ed. David Boonin and Graham Oddie. Pp. 231-238. (New York, N.Y.: Oxford Unversity Press, 2005).
[3] Wasserstrom, Richard.   "Is Adultery Immoral." in *Philosophy and Sex*, ed. Robert Baker and Frederick Elliston, pp. 207-21 (Buffalo, N.Y.: Prometheus Books, 1975).

contract. For some couples, sexual inclusivity will come with demands on open sexual communication, for others, as Wasserstrom points out, it will function only under a "don't ask, don't tell" policy. However, I would like to examine the moral requirements that are shared more generally for polyamorous couples, and these will relate to the moral guidelines followed for interactions with extramarital partners, and the guidelines followed for the distribution of time spent on the upkeep of the marital relationship, the *primary partnership*.

Let us imagine a married couple, we'll call them Anne and Bob. Bob meets another woman, Christine. Now, what are Bob's responsibilities to Christine before he attempts to have an affair with her? If Anne and Bob are in a monogamous marriage, and Bob does not inform Christine of this marriage before initiating the affair, we would all probably agree that Bob has acted wrongly. We would certainly say that Bob has wronged Anne, for the reasons mentioned by Wasserstrom: promise breaking and, possibly, deception. However, we would also say that Bob has wronged Christine. Why? Well, there are a couple of candidate explanations for why it is that Bob has wronged Christine in this scenario. (1) He has involved her in an activity that morally wrongs Anne, and (2) He has, in some way, deceived Christine as to the potential outcomes of their affair.

Let's first consider (1). Christine has wronged Anne in the situation described above only if (and not necessarily if) she has harmed her intentionally, or through carelessness or omission. Now, since Bob did not inform Christine of his marriage to Anne, it cannot be said that Christine intentionally harmed Anne. Since we do not think that sexual partners have the moral obligation to inquire about the marital status of their partners before engaging in sex, we cannot say that Christine has harmed Anne in virtue of carelessness or omission. Hence, Christine has not wronged Anne. Since Christine has not wronged Anne in the situation described above, we cannot say that Bob's failure to disclose his marital status is wrong in virtue of his involving Christine in wronging Anne.

Explanation (2) for why Bob has wronged Christine holds more potential. There are few contexts in which Bob can *assume* that Christine is not interested in a relationship with future marital possibilities. In fact, whether or not Bob wrongs Christine by deceiving her as to the potential outcomes of their affair will depend entirely on the context in which he meets and becomes intimate with Christine, and upon the nature of their affair. Imagine that in case (A) Bob meets Christine at a bar, both are slightly drunk, and little information is exchanged between Bob and Christine before they become intimate, and the intimacy develops to the point of sex in the course of a single night. In case (B) Bob meets

Christine at a local conference, library, or party of a friend. The two correspond over the internet for some weeks afterward, before meeting on a couple of occasions, and finally grow sexually intimate. Obviously, there will be a lot of gray area between the two poles I've just described, but that is appropriate as there will be a corresponding gray area in the moral requirements to which Bob is subject with respect to Christine.

In case (A), it is likely that Bob has no duty to Christine to disclose his marriage to Anne. In case (B), Bob certainly has a duty to Christine to disclose his marriage to Anne. If Bob met Christine in a circumstance somewhere in between (A) and (B), it is likely he would have a duty to Christine to disclose, as the moral requirement probably leans affirmative in cases of uncertainty. How might these requirements change if Anne and Bob were in a polyamorous marriage? To begin with, Bob would not necessarily be wronging Anne by his affair with Christine. However, given that Christine's expectations for a possible future with Bob are unaltered, it seems that Bob has the same set of moral responsibilities toward Christine as he did before. The only difference is that now, in situations of type (B), Bob probably is required to disclose not just that he is married, but that his marriage is polyamorous. Otherwise, Christine might justifiably think that Bob's marriage might be problematic and ending, and that the affair might, indeed, contain some future potential.

So, it seems that only in cases of type (A) may Bob conceal his marriage status to an extramarital partner. However, in cases like type (A), Bob might have more stringent duties to Anne. A sexual partner met at a bar, of which little is known, is also a more dangerous sexual addition to a marriage, for health reasons. Considerations like this might reduce Bob's extramarital affairs to ones more like type (B), which would come with the accompanying responsibility of the disclosure of marital status.

Responsibilities of maintaining a marriage, or a primary partnership, are also intrinsic to the morality of polyamorous marriage. Extramarital affairs (especially of type (B)) are time-consuming. It stands to reason that a polyamorous marriage would involve constraints on how much time could be spent with partners outside of the marriage. Depending on the length and nature of the affair, Bob is likely to wind up with relationship responsibilities to both Anne and Christine that will involve a tension. If Bob is not careful about the responsibilities he accrues to Christine, this tension could turn into a conflict of moral responsibilities.

Potential Inequalities

As in any marriage, there are certain inequalities that can be expected to arise in most polyamorous marriages. There will be times at which one partner is putting more time into household labor than is the other. There will be decisions that have to be made, such as, where to move for the benefit of whose career, that could benefit one partner in a marriage much more than, and perhaps at the expense of, the other partner. One partner in a marriage might have the enjoyment that accompanies being a spendthrift, while both suffer the financial consequences. One might have his or her welfare greatly improved by living close to family and old friends, in a native country, while the other's welfare is diminished by the effects of distance on familial relationships and old friendships. So, there is nothing particular to polyamory about inequality, per se. However, there are some inequalities that are particular to polyamory.

For instance, in a polyamorous relationship, one partner might have greater access to a pool of willing extramarital partners. If a couple has chosen a polyamorous marriage then, presumably, a variety of sexual partners is an important element of each spouse's perceived well-being. An inequality of this access could carry the same weight as an inequality of meaningful work outside the home, or an inequality of valuable friendships and familial support.   Once partners of a polyamorous marriage are involved in extramarital relationships, there are potential inequalities that could occur with respect to the time spent nurturing the marriage, the time spent with extramarital partners, and time spent developing and fulfilling extra-marital commitments.   Compare the following two situations.   In situation (1), Bob asks Anne to move to Omaha with him so that he might accept a promotion in his company. Anne knows she will not be able to find work in her career line in Omaha that is as rewarding or lucrative as her work in New Jersey.   However, Anne realizes that Bob will never be satisfied in his career if he gives up this opportunity, and she doesn't want him to resent her for preventing a move that could have brought him this satisfaction. The couple arrives in Omaha and, sure enough, Bob makes friends at work, Anne struggles to meet people and struggles to find a good job. In situation (2), Donna asks Eli for a polyamorous marriage.   Eli agrees, because he is not sure that Donna will marry him otherwise, and doesn't believe he has any deep seated objections to polyamory. However, Donna finds it easy to have affairs with willing, extramarital partners, and spends a fair amount of time in extramarital relationships. Eli (perhaps being less sexy than Donna in a conventional sense) has a harder time. It seems that the inequalities involved in situations (1) and (2) are similar in kind. In both cases there is one partner who has a greater amount of life-goods than the other due to an agreement made by both, combined with factors that were evident to all parties about the state of the world (that is, Anne's poor job prospects in Omaha and Eli's unattractiveness).

One might ask, what is the significance of the inequalities that are particular to polyamorous marriages if they are so similar in kind to the sort of inequalities we see regularly in traditional marriages? After all, we don't think that marriages in which one partner makes sacrifices for another partner's job prospects are morally problematic. Or do we? Susan Moller Okin argues that the sorts of inequalities that arise in marriage from these sorts of sacrifices *are* sometimes morally problematic.[4] She points out that society systematically generates conditions under which women make sacrifices that can leave them powerless, or relatively so, within a marriage.

Traditional Marriage, Well-being, and Exit

Okin thinks that traditional marriage (heterosexual, monogamous marriage), the way it is situated in our society, generates a serious social injustice, rife with moral problems. Okin focuses on three stages: the period of anticipation of marriage, marriage itself, and separation or divorce. Before marriage, young girls and young women are brought up to anticipate marriage, and to anticipate having families. Women are encouraged to choose careers that will allow them the flexibility to raise a family. Women are, to some extent, mentally prepared for a shift from employed labor to household labor. Okin argues, that even if there are natural differences between men and women that are partially responsible for a woman's set of familial expectations, they are, at the very least, supported and promoted by society.

During marriage and child-rearing, even many feminist couples decide that the man should continue paid labor while the woman opts for full-time child rearing. Often the husband is slightly older than the wife, has been in his career path a bit longer, and makes slightly more money. For these reasons, a traditional division of labor makes economic *sense* for the couple. Of course, after a few years in which he has been working and she has been raising children, the difference in the couple's earning power is more dramatic. A woman's career options, at this point, are more limited.

---

[4] Okin, Susan Moller. *Justice, Gender, and the Family*. New York, Basic Books: 1989. p. 134-169.

If financially feasible, the women might continue to stay home because she feels more important in her role at home than she would feel at work after such a long absence. Due to this, her husband's earning power will creep higher and higher, while her own plummets (or, at best, remains the same). In addition to his earning power, the man has a career that may offer him more respect, rewards, and responsibility over time, whereas the woman has household work and childcare that will involve less responsibility (and possibly less respect and rewards) over time.

Even if the couple never gets divorced, the fact that the husband can bring his earning power into a single life, and the wife cannot, generates a difference in *exit power*. Just as in the market, the party with more exit power also has more voice. This creates a power imbalance within the marriage. So, for Okin, there are two important inequalities in traditional marriages. An inequality of valuable life-pursuits, and an inequality of exit power that renders an inequality of voice within the marriage.

Okin thinks that our society is, at least, partially responsible for generating the inequality of power and voice between men and women in marriage, due to society's promotion of traditional gender roles. Further, these gendered inequalities make women worse off than they would otherwise be. Since women are worse off due to a system that is, at least, partially socially generated, the inequality is an injustice.

Polyamorous Marriages, Well-Being, and Exit

In the case of polyamorous marriages, the inequality of access to extramarital partners amounts to inequality of access to important life-goods. However, does the inequality of access to extramarital partners *also* render an inequality in exit power? Okin claims that the knowledge that a husband will have monetary security if he is single (and the wife will not) generates more exit power for the husband. If this is correct then surely the presence of extramarital partners, perhaps partners who are already embroiled in affairs with a polyamorous spouse, will generate more exit power for this spouse. After all, the attention of extramarital partners and the support they provide in relationships provides an immediate emotional recourse to which spouses can turn in the event of a separation. This suggests that a member in a polyamorous marriage who has more access to extramarital partners, is also more likely to have greater exit power.

Before we examine whether or not such an inequality could be an injustice, it is important to point out that, even if it is not an injustice, the correspondence between the inequality of access to extramarital partners and the inequality of exit power still generates moral problems, namely, unfairness. One question that Okin does not ask is: how much moral blame can we assign to a person who recognizes the inequality in his marriage, benefits from it, recognizes that the inequality reduces the welfare of the other spouse, and does not act to make the marriage more equal? It seems fair to say that this person is, at least, involved in a morally problematic situation. So, no matter how the inequalities of exit power and access to meaningful life-goods caused by the particular circumstances of polyamorous marriages are generated, a member of a polyamorous marriage might find him or herself in a moral pickle. For instance, if Anne has a greater variety of partners and more access to partners outside of marriage then does Bob, she might recognize the inequality of exit power this renders her, and be in the same moral predicament as the man benefiting from more exit power in a marriage like Okin describes. If a man in an Okin-style traditional marriage is in a morally problematic situation, then a person with the advantages of exit power resulting from greater access to (and involvement in) extra-marital relationships is *also* in a morally problematic situation. The situation might not be morally irredeemable. However, it seems that both Anne and the man in the traditional marriage that Okin describes are morally responsible for doing *something* to correct the inequality of power that is harming their partners.

Polyamory and Injustice

Okin claims that the reason why the unfairness she describes in traditional marriage is actually a social injustice has to do with the unfairness being socially caused, especially since society could cease causing the unfairness. Similarly, if the inequality of partner-access, and the differential in exiting power produced by this unfairness, were generated by society, it would constitute an injustice. According to Okin, conventional gender norms are the social influence responsible for turning the inequalities of earning power, access to rewarding careers, and exit power into social injustices.

Could it be possible that the access to willing extramarital partners could also depend on conventional gender norms?[5] Recall what we earlier established pertaining to the morality of polyamory. In most cases, it is the moral responsibility of the polyamorous marriage partner to disclose

---

[5] In what follows, what I argue will pertain only to heterosexual, polyamorous couples.

his marital status to extramarital partners before intimacy commences. That means that, if a man is fulfilling his ethical duties, the pool of people that a heterosexual, polyamorous husband might access for extramarital affairs is the group of women that are interested in entering an affair with a polyamorously married man. On the other hand, the pool of people that a heterosexual, polyamorous wife might access for extramarital affairs is the group of men that are interested in entering an affair with a polyamorously married woman. I'd like to attempt to make an educated hypothesis that the first pool of people described is smaller than the second. That is, the group of women interested in relationships with polyamorously married men is smaller than the group of men interested in relationships with polyamorously married women. We would have good reason for believing this only if the stereotype was true that said that men are less likely, in any given relationship, to care about commitment and future marriage prospects for their relationships.

Is it really true that men are less concerned about marriage prospects when they enter into relationships? Judith E. Owen Blakemore, Carol A. Lawton, and Lesa Rae Vartanian completed research in 2005 testing approximately four hundred college students. Students were asked a series of questions that together rated their "desire to marry." Women respondents reported looking forward to marriage with more excitement and import than did male respondents. More women than men expect to gain social status (among family and peers) from being married. Of those men who do expect to gain status through marriage, the amount of status they expect marriage to provide is not as high. Women are more likely to consider marriage to be the accomplishment of an important life goal.[6] Additionally, given that the average age of a first marriage is almost two years older for men than it is for women,[7] it might be reasonable to assume that women envision their marriages occurring earlier then men envision for their own lives. These pieces of empirical data do not give us direct information about the pools of partners available to spouses in polyamorous marriages. However, if, as of 2005, American women are more interested in marriage and rank it higher on their priority lists than do men, then it seems likely that women would be less interested than men in spending time and energy in relationships with people who are already married (and whose extramarital affairs do not signal relationship problems, as they would for members of monogamous marriages). If this

---

[6] Blakemore, Judith E. O., Carol A. Lawton, and Lesa Rae Vartanian. "I Cant's Wait to Get Married: Gender Differences in Drive to Marry." *Sex Roles, Vol. 53, Nos. 5/6, September 2005 (©2005).*
[7] U.S. Census Bureau, Marriage Age Rankings, *http://factfinder.census.gov*

turns out to be true, then women in polyamorous marriages will have a wider array of extramarital partner options, resulting in greater exit power and access to valued life-goods. Since the inequality of import men and women place on marriage is, at least partially, socially generated, the resulting inequalities of exit power and life-goods are injustices for the same reasons that these inequalities are injustices when they result from the causes Okin describes.

Conclusions

In this paper I have attempted to show that polyamory is not a state of marriage that renders adultery morally unproblematic. I have suggested that the inequality of access to extramarital partners that will arise in polyamorous marriages is as serious a moral problem as inequalities of opportunity to pursue chosen careers, or inequalities of earning power. In fact, I've argued that, like the inequality of earning power, the inequality of access to extramarital partners might yield unequal power of exit and, hence, unequal voice within marriage. I have also suggested that, in addition to the inequality within polyamory being morally problematic, it might also constitute a social injustice if it turns out that society has generated a larger pool of potential extramarital partners for one sex than another. I have cited some empirical data that grounds my hypothesis that, in general, women in polyamorous marriages will have larger pools of extramarital partner options then will men. As extramarital partners serves as important life goods for members polyamorous couples, and as extramarital partners increase exiting power (and, hence, voice within marriage) for members of polyamorous couples, a smaller pool of potential extramarital partners amounts to a *vulnerability* for men in polyamorous marriages.

Of course, all things considered, these men *still* might have more exit power, rewarding life goods, and voice within marriage due to the other inequalities in marriage discussed by Okin. After all, a polyamorous couple might conform to otherwise very traditional gender roles when it comes to the prioritization of careers and the division of childcare. So, I am not arguing that men in polyamorous marriages are, all things considered, worse off than women in polyamorous marriages. I am simply arguing that the inequality of access to extra-marital partners is one more potential source of injustice within marriage for us to keep in mind.

"HOOKING UP" MORAL OBLIGATIONS AND THE MEANING OF SEX[1]

STEPHEN SCALES

When I try to explain the meaning of the term, "Hooking up" to Granny, she gets very upset. "The kids these days" she says, "have no respect for the moral obligations attached to sex. Sexual activity carries with it more than an obligation to physically pleasure another person. Sex carries with it the moral obligation to love." Of course I nod and tell her that she must be right, *but I find myself unable to support her view with any good argument.*

1) What is Sexual Activity?

In order to discover which moral obligations attach to sexual activity, we need first to understand what sexual activity consists in. Sexual interaction may be the most intimate and meaningful activity most of us will ever engage in, and yet it is very difficult to say exactly what it is. It may not be possible to give a list of necessary and sufficient conditions that will accurately discriminate between what we want to call "sexual activity" and what we want to call something else. We could start with a pair of lists: one of activities which seem to us to be clearly sexual activities, and one of activities which seem to us to be clearly nonsexual. For instance, we could compose the following table:

[1] An earlier version of this paper was presented at the Towson University College of Liberal Arts Colloquium on "The Meaning of Sex" in November 1999. My thanks to the participants for their helpful comments and suggestions. I would also like to thank Carol Caraway (President of The Society for the Philosophy of Sex and Love), Wolfgang (Walt) Fuchs, Wing-Chun Wong, and the students in my 1997-2003 Phil: 253 and Phil: 341 classes (most especially Sankari Muralidharan and John Bova) for their very useful comments on earlier versions of the paper. My apologies to Jerry Fodor for so blatantly stealing his dramatic device (cf. Fodor, Jerry, "Observation Reconsidered", *Philosophy of Science*, 51 (1984) pp. 23-43.)

Sexual activities	Non-Sexual Activities
Consensual Heterosexual intercourse	An Ordinary Handshake
Consensual Oral sex	Sharing a Meal
Consensual Anal sex	Playing Basketball
Consensual Mutual Masturbation/	
Petting	Exchanging Ideas with a Friend
Consensual Voyeurism	Watching a Play on Broadway
Consensual Exhibitionism	Showing My Son My New Car
Consensual Sado-Masochism	Going to the Dentist
Consensual Phone-Sex	Calling My Mother on Mother's Day
Consensual Cyber-Sex	Doing research on the W.W.W.
Rape (Non-consensual sex: Oral,	
Anal, etc.).	Punching my Boss in the Nose
Bestiality	Walking My Dog
Pedophilic Sex	Hugging My Son
Masturbation	Talking to Myself

But perhaps this will not quite do. Let me explain why not. In Granny's considered view, any activity can be a sexual activity. Whether it is a sexual activity depends entirely on the physiological/psychological state of the agent. In "Plain Sex", Alan Goldman presents a definition of 'sexual activity'. He says:

> ...sexual desire is desire for contact with another person's body and for the pleasure which such contact produces; sexual activity is activity which tends to fulfill such desire of the agent...The desire for physical contact with another person is a minimal criterion for (normal) sexual desire, but it is both necessary and sufficient to qualify normal desire as sexual[2]

This definition does not seem to us to be entirely satisfactory. First of all, it restricts sexual activity to activity aimed at the satisfaction of desire for *contact* with the body of another person. There seem to us to be many forms of sexual activity which do not aim (strictly) at contact with the body of another. For example, masturbation, voyeurism and exhibitionism might all be described as sexual activities, but none of them aim at the satisfaction of desire for contact with the body of another. Goldman is aware of this deficiency and he points out that:

> Voyeurism or viewing a pornographic movie qualifies as a sexual activity, but only as an imaginative substitute for the real thing (otherwise a

---

[2] Goldman, Alan, "Plain Sex", *Philosophy and Public Affairs* Vol. 6, No. 3 (Spring 1977), reprinted in Olen, Jeffrey and Barry, V., *Applying Ethics: A Text with Readings (fifth edition),* (Belmont, CA, Wadsworth, 1999), p. 92.

deviation from the norm as expressed in our definition). The same is true
of masturbation as a sexual activity without a partner[3]

Granny and I think, however, that in order to be more exact, the
definition of sex ought to include this fact explicitly, rather than relying on
an unexplained distinction between "normal" and "abnormal" desires.

Furthermore, this definition restricts sexual activity to activity aimed at
the satisfaction of desire for contact with the body of another *person*.
Clearly, unless we are to adopt an extremely wide definition of "persons"
(one which includes non-human animals) this definition will exclude
bestial activities from the category of sex. But Granny is fairly certain that
bestiality is sexual activity.

Finally, and most importantly, this definition may be not only too
narrow (excluding some activities which ought not to be excluded) but
also too broad (including some activities which should not be categorized
as sexual). Consider, for example, my hugging my son. When my 8-year-
old son, Duncan wakes up in the morning, he is very warm (relative to the
ambient temperature of his room). Indeed, he feels like a hot potato. On
occasion he crawls into bed with me and I like to hug him when he feels so
warm. Thus, I have a desire for contact with his body and for the pleasure
which such contact produces. But I don't at all want to call that desire
"sexual." Unless I were a pedophile, that is, unless I became aroused from
touching my son, unless I aimed at the satisfaction of a desire for a very
particular *kind* of pleasure (accompanied by a core of the typical
physiological symptoms of arousal and reproductive functioning in our
species) it would be a definitional stretch (at least) to call my hugging my
son sexual.

In place of Goldman's definition, Granny and I suggest the following
definitions:

1) "Sexual activity" is activity which is primarily aimed at the satisfaction
of sexual desire.
2) "Sexual desire" is desire for contact (real or imagined) with the body of
another being and for the sexual pleasure produced by such contact.
3) "Sexual pleasure" is pleasure which is typically accompanied by (at
least some of) a set of certain physiological reactions in organisms which
are primarily associated with the reproductive functions of those

---

[3] Goldman, Alan, "Plain Sex", *Philosophy and Public Affairs* Vol. 6, No. 3 (Spring
1977), reprinted in Olen, Jeffrey and Barry, Vincent, *Applying Ethics: A Text with
Readings (fifth edition),* (Belmont, CA, Wadsworth, 1999), p. 94.

organisms (e.g., in humans, genital engorgement, increased heart rate, shallow breathing, flush, pupil dilation, genital mucous secretion in females, etc.).

Any of the activities described as "non-sexual" in the lists above could turn out to be sexual activities according to this definition; whether my hugging my son is a sexual activity depends entirely on my physiological/psychological state at the time that I am doing the hugging. If the aim of my hug were to satisfy a desire for sexual pleasure, then the hugging would count as a sexual activity. Thus, if our definition is correct, then the attempt to delineate activities as sexual or non-sexual on the basis of behavior alone (abstracted from physiological/psychological states) is misguided.[4]

2) Sex and Moral Obligations

For the sake of argument, let us assume (with Granny) that Kantian moral theorists have got things mostly right. Let us assume that all rational beings have a moral obligation to respect the dignity of other persons. Let us further assume that this respect is primarily evidenced in an abstaining from interference with the autonomous actions of other persons. That is, as long as persons are not violating the autonomy of other persons, they should be allowed to choose their own lives for themselves.

What kinds of obligations would follow with regard to sexual activity? Well, we can assert the following moral minimum requirements with regard to sexual activity or any other activity: In our dealings with other persons, we are morally obligated to respect the autonomous choices of those persons. This requirement follows from the necessity of seeing myself as guided by principles which are binding on all rational beings (in order to be able to see myself as an autonomous rational agent at all). Kant's argument that all rational beings, to the extent that they are

---

[4] In what follows, I use the expressions 'sex' and 'sexual activity' interchangeably. I must admit that some of my students don't agree with this identification. A friend of mine once told me that she had only had sex with three people. Since I knew she usually had more (physically intimate) boyfriends than that in one month, I asked her what she could mean. She said "Oh, yeah. I fooled around with all of those boys, but we never had *sex*." By 'fooled around', she meant that she had engaged in oral sex, mutual masturbation, phone sex, even anal sex. Thus, for her, the meaning of the word 'sex' was restricted to vaginal intercourse only. Since I can't square this particular usage with the rest of my (our) own talk about sex, I prefer to simply equate 'sex' with what I have defined as 'sexual activity'.

autonomous, are guided by the Categorical Imperative is well known and we will merely rely on it (and on Granny's good sense) here. The outcome of this is that one clearly has an obligation to obtain informed consent from other persons before engaging in (interactive) sexual activities with them. It is for this reason that rape is wrong: rape violates the autonomous personhood of the other; it treats the other as a thing (an object whose goodness is merely instrumental in the satisfaction of my own desires), rather than as a person (an intrinsically valuable self-conscious subject of experiences capable of and entitled to her own autonomous choices).

As children are not able to give informed consent with regard to sexual activities (one cannot be adequately informed about sex until one has some clearer conceptual understanding of it than children typically possess), this requirement cannot ordinarily be fulfilled with regard to them. Granny wants to define a "person" as a being that is self-conscious[5] and has the potential to be a rational being (rationality being defined by us as the ability to solve complex conceptual problems along with the ability to guide one's life according to the Moral Law which binds all rational beings). Thus, children clearly are (potentially autonomous) persons with rights and we have moral obligations to them which preclude engaging in sexual activity with them.

Non-human animals are (Granny presumes) not rational beings. Thus, our obligations with respect to them may be different. We here use the term "obligations *with respect to* them" rather than "obligations *to* them". Even on the Kantian assumption that we can only have *obligations to* other persons, we may still have *obligations about* beings which are non-persons (e.g., dogs, trees, the earth, etc.). We believe that it is from this type of source that a prohibition against bestiality might be grounded. But we will not pursue that subject here. Instead we want to examine the question of the proper relationship between consensual sexual interaction between adult humans and love. Is the moral minimum of eliciting informed consent all that is required in order to have morally acceptable sex? What about Granny's suggestion that moral sex requires love?

---

[5] Following Michael Tooley in "Abortion and Infanticide", *Philosophy and Public Affairs*, vol. 2, no. 1 (Fall 1972), excerpted in Velasquez, M. and Rostenkowski C. (eds.) *Ethics: Theory and Practice* (Englewood Cliffs, NJ, Prentice-Hall, 1985), pp. 243-249. The self-consciousness requirement for personhood claims that in order to have a serious right to life (be a full-fledged person), a being must possess the concept of a self as a continuing subject of experiences and believe that it is itself such a subject.

3) What is Love?

It may seem that we are getting murkier and murkier. After all, we've offered a rather vague definition of sex and now we want to investigate the concept of love, perhaps the most vague and mysterious concept in our language. But maybe we can talk about love in a limited way. We can simply specify the boundaries of the concept ("draw a line" as Wittgenstein would say), and then analyze the connection between this narrowly defined concept of love and sexual activity as we have defined it. With that strategy in mind, we offer the following definition: X's loving Y consists in X's taking an affectionate, sincere, and (intentionally, at least) life-long interest in the interests of Y and actively seeking to promote those interests. Of course, this is all a matter of degree. I mean, to some degree or other, I take an interest in the interests of everyone I meet. But if I love everyone I meet, then any requirement to love the people I have sex with will be meaningless. Here we want to restrict the domain of possible objects of my love. Love is not merely caring, but caring deeply; it is not merely taking an interest in the interests of another, but placing those interests at the heart of my own interests. X's loving Y, then, consists in X's taking so great an active interest in the interests of Y that the interests of Y assume a central position in X's interests and gain a status of equal or nearly equal importance to the most important ends in X's life. I cannot have that kind of attitude toward everyone I meet simply because the human mind is too feeble to remember all of the interests of all of the people I meet, much less to actively seek the satisfaction of all of those interests.[6]

I can, however, love some people. Indeed, I do. There are some humans (both adults and children) who I know and care about much more deeply than others. These people share relationships of caring with me that they don't share with any other people. And it is from these relationships that love blossoms. Knowledge of the heart of the other commonly elicits a response of care and nurture; familiarity breeds not contempt, but love (Granny beams at me approvingly when I say this). The deep affection of a loving relationship is ordinarily based on a deep admiration of the other; this is usually the *ground* of love, and it can be

---

[6] Of course, affection (cathecting) is also required in order to correctly describe a relationship as a 'loving' one. We don't want to say that a court-appointed guardian of a child "loves the child" simply because she takes the promotion of the interests of the child as central to her completion of her duties as a lawyer (and hence, as central to her life).

deepened by the profound knowledge of the other which can develop in intimate relationships.

Now that we have some working definitions of the concepts of 'sex' and 'love', we can, perhaps, more fruitfully approach the question: "Is sex without love wrong?"

4) The Argument from Practical Consequences

"If people have loveless sex, bad things will happen," says Granny. She lists: "Unwanted Pregnancies, an increase in sexually transmitted diseases, and many, many broken hearts." Although I sympathize with her intuitions here, I tactfully suggest that sex without love does not *necessarily* (I stress this word for Granny's benefit) lead to these things. People can engage in loveless "safe sex" (i.e., sexual activity in which the participants attempts to minimize the chances of pregnancy and STD transmission) just as well as they can engage in loving safe sex. As for Granny's suggestion that loveless sex is wrong because it results in more "broken hearts", I point out that if two people have an agreement to engage in loveless sex, the chances of one of them having his dreams dashed would actually seem to be decreased rather than increased. I take up this possibility more directly in Section Six.

5) The Argument from a Duty to Care for Oneself: Sex as Sharing Bodily Autonomy

Another way in which we might attempt to ground the claim that love is required for moral sexual activity is by thinking not in terms of obligations to the other, but rather in terms of obligations to the self. I have a duty to treat myself as a person, that is, as an (at least potentially) autonomous rational being. Kant says that I have a perfect duty to treat "humanity, whether in [my] own person or in the person of another, always at the same time as an end [in itself], and never simply as a means."[7] Again, Granny relies on Kant's arguments for this claim without investigating it further.

But what does that have to do with loveless sex? Well, in order to successfully engage in sexual activity, I must let down my defenses to a certain extent. That is, sex necessarily involves a "being taken over" by my bodily sensations. I have to enter into a more primal-animalistic state

---

[7] Kant, Immanuel, *Grounding for the Metaphysics of Morals* (translated by James W. Ellington (Indianapolis, Hackett Publishing Company, 1981), p. 36.

than that in which I ordinarily exist. If I don't find myself more and more
embodied in sex, more and more subject to the sensations produced in me
by the other, then somebody is not doing it right. We might want to claim
that what is involved here is a sharing of my bodily autonomy. I have to
allow another person a certain degree of control over my bodily sensations
and responses. I have to share what is (in Kantian terms) the most
valuable aspect of my being, my autonomy. But if this is the case, then
perhaps we can ground an obligation of love in a duty to treat myself as an
end in myself rather than merely as a means (to the satisfaction of my
desire for physical pleasure). If sexual activity between Tom and Mary
requires an opening up and sharing of the self,[8] then Tom has a duty to
make sure that he has good reason to believe that the person with whom he
is sharing himself will care for his self. That is, Tom has a duty to make
sure that he has good reason to believe that Mary loves him.

This argument seems promising, but we should not be pulled in too
quickly. Notice first that what is required here is not that Tom love Mary
but that Tom have good reason to believe that Mary loves him. But
secondly, the argument will not even work that far. I put my life in the
hands of my surgeon. I might be said to "share my autonomy" with the
person whom I authorize to cut into me while I am unconscious (even
more so than with the person with whom I engage in sexual interaction).
And perhaps this fact imposes upon me a moral responsibility to make
sure that I have good reason to believe that my surgeon will take an
interest in my interests while I am on the operating table (e.g., I should
check into her qualifications, certification, temperament with regard to her
patients' wishes, etc.). But there is no requirement that I have good
evidence for the claim that my surgeon *loves* me (i.e., takes an active and
affectionate interest in the satisfaction of my interests indefinitely into the
future). Thus, the Kantian perfect duty to the self can only ground a claim
that I ought to insure that those with whom I engage in sexual activity take
an interest in my interests while I am "in their care" (i.e., while we are
having sex). I should only have sex with persons whom I have good
reason to believe are not dangerous sociopaths, etc. But this is surely less
than we were looking for. After all, the same sort of restrictions can be
applied to activities like sharing a car ride to Buffalo, or walking to the
store together. This argument gives us no *special* requirements about
insuring that I have good reason to believe that my *sexual* partners care for
me.

---

[8] Indeed, in most sexual interactions (e.g., either homosexual or heterosexual
intercourse, etc.), one person actually invites another person inside his/her own
body; there may be no more emotionally vulnerable position to be in

6) Sex as a Language and Lying with One's Body

In "Sex and Perversion", Robert Solomon says:

Whatever else sexuality might be and for whatever purposes it might be used or abused, it is first of all language…It can be enjoyable, not just on account of its phonetics, which are neither enjoyable nor meaningful in themselves, but because of *what* is said. One enjoys not just the tender caress but the message it carries; and one welcomes a painful thrust or bite not because of masochism but because of the meaning, in context, that it conveys.[9]

In "Between Consenting Adults", Onora O'Neill extends this interpretation of sex as a meaningful language into the ethical realm. She says:

Deception is a pervasive possibility in sexual encounters and relationships. Not only are there well-known deceptions, such as seduction and breach of promise, but varied further possibilities. Many of these reflect the peculiarly implicit nature of sexual communication. Commercial and various distanced sexual encounters standardly use the very means of expression which deeper and longer lasting attachments use. But when the endearments and gestures of intimacy are not used to convey what they standardly convey, miscommunication is peculiarly likely. Endearments standardly express not just momentary enthusiasm but affection; the contact of eyes, lips, skin conveys some openness, acceptance, and trust (often enough much more); embrace conveys a commitment which goes beyond a momentary clinging. These are potent gestures of human emotional life. If insufficient trust and commitment are present to warrant such expression, then those who use these endearments and gestures risk giving false messages about feelings, desires, and even commitments…If the expressions are taken at face value, yet what they would standardly express is lacking, each is likely to deceive the other.[10]

Granny is impressed with this line of thinking "The kids today" says

[9] Solomon, Robert, "Sex and Perversion" in Baker, R. and Elliston, F. (eds.) *Philosophy and Sex* (Buffalo, NY, Prometheus Books, 1975), pp. 279-86. Reprinted in Velasquez, M. and Rostenkowski C. (eds.) *Ethics: Theory and Practice* (Englewood Cliffs, NJ, Prentice-Hall, 1985), p. 319.
[10] O'Niell, Onora, "Between Consenting Adults" *Philosophy and Public Affairs* v. 14 (Summer 1985) pp. 252-77. Reprinted in Jeffrey Olen and Vincent Barry (eds.), *Applying Ethics: A Text with Readings (fifth edition),* (Belmont, CA, Wadsworth, 1999), p. 100.

Granny "lie with their bodies. Kisses and caresses typically convey feelings of love and caring which are not conveyed in a handshake. So if Tom engages in sexual activity with Mary without feeling any of the love which such activity normally expresses, then Tom is lying to Mary with his body. As lying is a violation of the requirement to respect the personhood of the other, such activity would fall below the moral minimum requirement set out by Kant; it would be wrong. Since sexual gestures mean "I love you", then sex in the absence of love is a fraud. And this fraud will exist whether or not Tom believes that Mary is deceived about his feelings and intentions. That is, Tom's thinking that what they are doing is merely exchanging physical pleasure does not change the fact that sex has a certain specific meaning; it typically expresses love."

Again, I am sympathetic to Granny's intuitions here, but I don't think this argument will work quite as strongly as she needs it to work. First of all, it seems that Tom and Mary could explicitly agree that what they are doing does not mean what Granny assumes it means? They could make a contract like the following:

A Contract for Meaningless Sex

We, the undersigned, do agree on this twenty-first day of October, 2007 to engage in meaningless sexual activity with one another. More specifically, we agree:

1)   That for the next two hours, all of the physical touching which occurs between us will not convey any emotional content; that the conventional meaning of sexual activity notwithstanding, we intend to express no love or commitment by any of the physical activity in which we will engage.

2)   That each one of us has fully informed the other about his/her health status; that we will use all reasonable precaution to avoid injury to one another, pregnancy, and the transmission of diseases; that in the event of an unwanted pregnancy, we will both accept full responsibility for the care of a child (if Mary chooses to carry the baby to term); and that we will each do our best to satisfy the sexual desires of the other (be a "good lover").

Tom _____
Mary_____

It seems that even if sexual gestures usually mean what Granny thinks they mean, Tom and Mary could avoid lying with their bodies by entering into such an explicit contract. But Granny's argument is even worse off than this. Even in cases where there is no explicit agreement about the meaning of sexual activity, the argument will fail if sex simply means something different than what Granny thinks it means.

7) Meaning and Subcultures

The meaning of a physical gesture, like the meaning of a word, is determined (at least in part) by its place in a social-semantic field, by its connections and contrasts with other words and gestures in a language or form of life. We are said to understand a word if we grasp its connections to other words such that we are able to use the word to communicate in the language. Briefly, meaning is use and occurs in social context.

But what do sexual acts mean? Well, how are they used around here? Although it may be the case that there was a time in which sexual acts were used to convey the sorts of things that Granny says they convey, are they always used that way in America in 2007? Of course, the answer is no. The meaning of sexual acts will change as we move from one subculture to another. Among a group of porn stars, for example, sexual activity may mean nothing more than "good morning" means to you and I.

And time, as well, may bring changes in the meaning of sexual activities. If meaning is use, then as people come to use a gesture differently, it will come to mean something different. This, it seems to me, is happening in our own culture. The meaning of sex is dwindling. Why? Well, as the semioticians would say, it is a victim of the overdetermination of the signifier. Sex means everything from power to pleasure to love to money to death. It sells cars and soap; it's part of every sitcom on TV; it even headed our political news during several recent years; it is everywhere and everything. But of course, if sex means everything, then sex means nothing. As I said earlier, meaning is determined by connections *and contrasts* in a semantic field. But if a word or a gesture points to nearly everything in the field, its meaning dwindles.

8) An Explanation of Granny's Intuition:
The Influence of the Body on the Meaning of Sex

I've been wondering why it is that I'm so attracted to Granny's intuitions about the meaning of sex despite the fact that meaning can change across subcultures and across time. And I think I have a bit of an answer. In our culture, the meaning of sex is dwindling, but sex is not meaningless for us today. Despite what MTV implies about the meaning of sexual activity, it is not simply an exchange of pleasure. For women especially, it has profound emotional significance. And there is good evolutionary reason for the fact that women generally attach greater meaning to sex than men do.

In "Sex Without Emotional Involvement: An Evolutionary Interpretation of Sex Differences", John Townsend points to several studies (both within our own culture and across several cultures) which support the claims that men are more willing than women to engage in sexual relations in the absence of emotional involvement and marital potential and are more likely to seek sexual relations with a variety of partners for the sake of variety...Men are more readily aroused sexually than women by visual stimuli (e.g., by the sight of a potential sex partner); consequently, evaluation of acceptability for coitus can be virtually instantaneous for men but tends to take longer for women. Men place more emphasis then women on physical attractiveness in choosing partners for sex or marriage, and women place more emphasis than men do on socioeconomic status.[11]

Researchers explain these differences as an evolutionary result of differences between the sexes in minimal parental investment. Townsend says:

> What might be a simple act of copulation for the male can result for the female in the medical risks of pregnancy and delivery and the lifelong investment of motherhood...because their reproductive risks and opportunities differed, male and female evolved complex dimorphic, emotional-motivational mechanisms...Males evolved the tendency to become sexually aroused by visual stimuli, and to spread investment among several females when circumstances permitted, because natural selection favored males who were attracted to a great variety of partners, and who assessed these partners' acceptability for intercourse largely on the basis of physical attributes that serve as cues to fertility, e.g., muscle tone, complexion, facial and bodily proportions, absence of wrinkles, etc...[Females evolved] a more selective process of mate evaluation...with more emphasis on partners' potential for parental investment - social dominance, prowess, nurturance - and less emphasis on physical attributes that serve as cues to fertility...Women do [cognitively] evaluate... potential for [parental] investment as part of their evaluation of mate attractiveness...But an emotional mechanism that was only tied to a cognitive appraisal of investment could be maladaptive because it could fail to function when, in fact, female reproductive risks and opportunities were involved. To be maximally effective, this mechanism must be closer

---

[11] Townsend, John Marshall, ""Sex Without Emotional Involvement: An Evolutionary Interpretation of Sex Differences", *Archives of Sexual Behavior* vol. 24 # 2 (April 1995), p. 174.

to the genes, and hence, more directly tied to the act that produces female reproductive risks and opportunities... engaging in vaginal intercourse, in and of itself, [may activate] feelings of closeness and vulnerability in women.[12]

But men too, if they remain in relationships long enough, connect sex and emotional commitment. Why? Although some would say that both men and women have merely been socialized to accept a culturally constructed romantic norm which connects sex and love, it seems to me that there is something about the impact of sex on our bodies which restricts the ordinary meaning of sexual gestures.

Although the meaning of a gesture, like the meaning of a word, is extremely plastic, there are some facts about the bodies we inhabit which restrict the plasticity of the meaning of gestures which physically impact on our bodies. The act of punching a person in the nose, although it can mean many things, will not ordinarily be used to mean "good morning". Because of the kinds of bodies we have, being punched in the nose every morning would just cause us too much pain. I want to say that I suspect the same sort of thing to be true of sexual gestures. Although they can mean many things, there are some facts about the way these gestures impact upon our bodies which restrict the field of their meaning. Sex won't ordinarily stand for nothing more than physical pleasure; its meaning will ordinarily or naturally be connected to emotional-motivational mechanisms we have inherited along with our bodies. Thus, there are some natural reasons for my attraction to Granny's intuitions.

9) Loveless Sex and Moral Danger

Beaming at me, Granny declares, "Well, perhaps sexual gestures don't always mean one and only one thing, but, because of the ways in which sexual interaction impacts upon our bodies (engaging motivational/emotional mechanisms which we have inherited along with our blood), loveless sex is morally dangerous!" "Morally dangerous? What does that mean?", I ask her. Granny responds: "Oh come now, don't be so slow! You and I both know that some things we do are morally dangerous. And some of them are so morally dangerous as to be wrong. For instance, consider a gun enthusiast taking target practice by aiming at a bush in his backyard.

---

[12] Townsend, John Marshall, "Sex Without Emotional Involvement: An Evolutionary Interpretation of Sex Differences", *Archives of Sexual Behavior* vol. 24 # 2 (April 1995), pp. 175-6.

Of course, it's always theoretically possible, no matter how much he tries to check, that he will fail to see a young child hiding in his bushes. But if he doesn't even bother to look, and just shoots into the bush wily-nily, then he's failing to be safe (and hence risking doing something wrong). Now it makes some difference whether the gun-enthusiast lives several miles from his nearest neighbor (and hence has little reason to think that a small child might be hiding in his bushes), or whether he lives next door to an unfenced daycare center and frequently sights young kids playing in his bushes. In the latter case, he seems required to take greater care to insure that there aren't any children in the path of the bullets. To shoot without checking in that case would be taking such a *risk* of doing something wrong, that it *would be* doing something wrong." "Hmmm...moral danger, eh? ", I say, "Well, I'm not sure if I'm following you there, but let's see how this relates to loveless sex." Granny, clearly exasperated with my obtuseness, continues: "Can't you see? Because of the ways in which sexual interaction impacts upon our bodies (engaging inherited motivational/emotional mechanisms), loveless sex runs the moral danger of being a lie; it is so morally dangerous as to be wrong. Even if there is no one meaning to sexual gestures, since there is a danger (some likelihood) that they will be taken to communicate love and commitment (and to bring about such reactions in the other), if Tom employs them in the absence of any such intentions, he risks misleading the other (Mary) so much that he is essentially lying to her." I can hear in her voice that Granny is attached to this argument and she frowns deeply when I point out to her that the possibility of misleading the other occurs in every communicative exchange, and that the duty to clarify communication exists on both sides of the communicative encounter. Every communicative act is "morally dangerous" in that one risks misleading the other.

10) The Argument from Sexual Virtue

"Well what about Aristotle?" Granny counters, "Doesn't he tell us that engaging in certain activities tends to produce dispositions to engage in those activities (that virtue and vice are the children of habit)?" "Yes" I respond. OK, well people who engage in sex without love are divorcing their personalities from their sexual activities. If we follow Aristotle, (or our contemporary, Roger Scruton)[13], we can see that such people are likely

---

[13] Roger Scruton provides this argument for Granny in *Sexual Desire* (The Free Press, 1986), excerpted by permission in Jeffrey Olen and Vincent Barry (eds.),

to fall into a habit of divorcing love and sex; eventually, they develop a disposition, a vice. They become the kind of people who habitually divorce love from sex; such people have a very difficult time reuniting their sexual activities and their personalities (just think of the difficulty prostitutes and strippers have in trying to maintain long-term monogamous relationships)." "So, how does it follow that loveless sex is wrong?" I ask. "Well, since erotic love (the union of sexual desire and love) is a part of the full human good, and since loveless sex tends to make us less able to experience that erotic love, loveless sex is vicious." "Hmm, that sounds promising, but I have a few questions for you: first, why should we believe that erotic love (the union of sexual desire and love) is a part of the full human good? After all, your hero, Dr. Scruton allows that those who practice complete sexual abstinence or chastity are to be admired. Presumably, these people love others without sexually desiring them (or without fulfilling their sexual desires). Why are they allowed to divorce sex from love and be praised for it, while those who engage in loveless sex are condemned as vicious? And secondly, even if we did believe that the union of sex and love was part of the full human good, how would it follow that every act of loveless sex is wrong? After all, we don't have sex with every person we love, and nobody would claim that that is wrong. Why should we be required to love everyone we have sex with? It may even be the case that engaging in loveless sex allows many people to become better able to achieve erotic love; if the evidence we discussed earlier is correct, having sex may actually (physiologically) *cause* attachment and love in many cases. If we chastely wait for an attachment (or devotion) to the other to develop on its own, we may miss out on an opportunity to *create* such a bond through sexual union." Flustered but not defeated, Granny furrows her brow and begins to try to come up with some other justificatory scheme that will allow her to hang on to her gut feelings about sex and love. Once she gets attached to an intuition, it's nearly impossible to shake her free.

11) Conclusion

In sex, we reconnect with our physicality, our animality. Sexual interaction allows us to explore with another the mystery of ourselves as

---

Applying Ethics: A Text with Readings (fifth edition), (Belmont, CA, Wadsworth, 1999), pp. 85-91.

embodied consciousness.[14] Sex has often been morally connected to love; for Granny it remains so (and perhaps because of understandable evolutionary causes). But it has become the custom in some parts of our society to engage in sex strictly in pursuit of the physical pleasure which we derive from it. Is that O.K.? Is it morally permissible to have sex without feelings or commitment? Granny insists that sexual activity carries with it the moral obligation to love. I sit and commiserate with Granny when she is upset like this, but I'm not at all sure I could stand up for her views as my own. As the Spring dawns and she croaks on about "what it was like in my day", a young man's fancy turns to thoughts of...well...not exactly love.

---

[14] The body of the other is vulnerability, the fragility and incompleteness of her project, her ignorance and finitude manifest in flesh (not as meat, but as lived-body). Thus, the expression, "I've got your back" manifests care as such; to care is to care for the other's back (both figuratively and literally). Each of us is blind to her own blind spots, yet each stands in relation to the other as the only sighted person in a world full of blind people. This is why Jose Saramago's novel, "Blindness" presents such an apt description of our ethical relations to one another.

CHAPTER THREE

PARENTS AND CHILDREN

INTRODUCTION

What ethical obligations exist between parents and children, and what grounds those obligations? Do we have a right to procreate? Do we have a right to parent the children we create? Because what it means to be a parent has splintered in recent years (e.g., into genetic parent, social parent, birth parent, etc.), these questions have opened up into new territory. How should we understand the moral rights and duties of parents to their children? And what about the children? What sort of moral expectations should we have with respect to the actions of adult children toward their parents? Can we find some helpful guidelines or norms to allow us to sort out our obligations as children? All of these questions (and more) are examined in this chapter.

Is there a right to procreate? Is there a right to parent? Should we limit who may be accorded parental rights? In "Making Parents: Conventions, Intentions, and Biological Connections", Yvette Pearson investigates the question of what it is that creates an ethical obligation to act as parent to a particular child. Since the widespread use of assisted reproductive technologies (ART's) has complicated this question immensely, Pearson examines the ground of parental obligations in relation to the question of whether we each have a right to procreate. She argues that these questions are better considered in terms of our obligations to children, rather than in terms of the rights and desires of adults.

In "The Foundations of Licensing Parents", Michael McFall examines some of the personal and social harms caused by severely abusive and neglectful parenting, and argues that both ethical reasoning and political philosophy support the claim that we ought to license people before they are allowed to be parents. McFall considers, but ultimately rejects, objections to this proposal based on a right to procreate or on the illegitimacy of prior restraint.

In "Intergenerational Justice and Care in Parenting", Stephen Scales also supports the claim that people should need a license in order to be accorded the social rights of a parent. Attacking the idea that parental rights spring from a biological connection, Scales argues that both a Rawlsian contractarianism and a focus on the responsibility to care ought to shape our understanding of our duties as parents.

How ought we to understand the duties that parents have toward their children? What sort of model of childrearing might help us in answering this question?   In "Ho, Ho, Hoax: Santa Claus and Parental Deception", Ernani Magalhaes uses the example of the Santa Claus myth to investigate a teleological perspective on the principles that ought to guide parents' childrearing decisions. He argues that there is no justification for parents deceiving their children about Santa Claus, and that such deception is not consistent with a concern for all the facets of a child's well-being.

In "Moral Children", Wade Robison argues that even small children are capable of giving and understanding moral reasons, and that we ought to engage them in this process throughout the course of their development. Moving from findings about the moral capacity of chimpanzees and bonobos to anecdotal playground behaviors, Robison spells out a case for a model of childrearing which takes seriously the moral capacities of children, and which ought to lead to the end of the parental pseudojustification, "because I said so."

And finally, what about the responsibilities of children?   In "Filial Responsibility for Aging Parents", Charles Zola takes up the question of whether adult children have duties to care for their aging parents based upon a sense of gratitude. Drawing upon both a feminist ethics of care, and an analysis of Aquinas' comments on the virtue of prudence, Zola offers concrete and practical advice about how the adult children of aging parents can navigate the difficult path of caring for their parents without losing themselves in the process.

Rather than leading to a stultifying relativism, the multiplicity of norms governing family life across cultures may instead become a source of cross-fertilization and inspiration for our thinking about the ethics of family life.   In "A Reflection on Confucian Ethics of the Family", Suk Choi explores the extent to which, despite the traditional understanding of Confucian ethics as an authoritarian system, the Confucian ideal of filial piety can be extended as a universal moral value. Choi investigates how a Western (enlightenment) ethics of the family may be enlarged and enriched by cultural resources springing from an Eastern tradition.

Although there are many more ethical questions regarding the bonds between parents and children than could be addressed in any (finite) set of papers, the work of these authors profitably opens up many of these questions. Not only do they outline theoretical perspectives that may prove useful, they also offer concrete practical guidance with regard to how we may best carry out our obligations as parents and as children within the family.

MAKING PARENTS: CONVENTIONS, INTENTIONS, AND BIOLOGICAL CONNECTIONS

YVETTE PEARSON

Weaving a Tangled Web?

First, I will explore apparent inconsistencies surrounding the importance attached to intentions and genetic connections in determining who has parental rights or obligations and how attitudes regarding the relative importance of these elements have influenced various conventions/social practices. Both intentions and genetic connections carry significant weight to the extent that taking them into account serves the interests of those who are either attempting to procreate or have succeeded. In some cases intentions carry more weight than genetic connections, and vice versa. I will also discuss another relevant biological connection—the gestational connection between women and offspring—but it is worth noting that this has almost always been viewed (and valued) to the extent that it indicates a genetic connection with the child. Regardless of whether primacy is given to intentions or biological connections, especially genetic connections, the main focus is on the desires of those attempting to procreate rather than the ability of prospective parents to fulfill obligations toward offspring. Instead of focusing on likely impact of emphasizing one or the other on the welfare of offspring, whether intentions or genetic connections are regarded as significant is usually determined by the goals or desires of the procreators.

Intention

Though many people spend a fair amount of time and money trying to avoid procreation, some people do intend to procreate. And in many cases they succeed. However, when sexual interaction does not or cannot result in progeny, creating or acquiring children requires intentional acts aimed specifically at bringing children into the world or into the home of those who wish to rear them. Aside from these circumstances, however, the relationship between intention and procreation can be difficult to establish. There may be no identifiable intentions at all—either *to* procreate or to avoid it—or the precise content of the intention might be difficult to determine. Even when intentions are clearly stated (e.g., in surrogacy agreements or gamete vendor consent forms) or when they are implied by the mere act of going to a fertility clinic and asking for assistance, it remains unclear what weight those intentions should carry. Even if a clear intention regarding procreation can be identified, it can still be challenging to figure out whether intentions have changed over time or which intentions actually "count". It is possible that a person might intend at T1 to procreate and rear a child but intend otherwise at T2. Intentions don't have expiration dates attached to them. It is unclear, for example, whether the intention at T1 should take precedence over that at T2 or vice versa, or the extent to which the context in which either intention is formed ought to be considered morally relevant.

In the absence of explicit contracts, which are rarely present in the context of procreation, it can be difficult to determine a person's intentions with respect to procreation. Furthermore, even if there is something as clear as a written document or some other evidence of the person's intentions (e.g., embryos created with gametes that the person had voluntarily left at a fertility clinic), there remains the possibility that her intentions may be altered by various factors. For example, a couple may agree to use their gametes to create fertilized eggs via IVF with the initial intention of transferring them to the woman's uterus but decide later that they do not want to attempt to create a child in this manner. Chan and Quigley have argued for the contentious claim that once a person has agreed to "engage in IVF for purposes of having a child…[he/she] has ceded any right…not to become a genetic [parent] of the child that the embryo would become."[1] This means that once this first step has been taken, neither party should be permitted to stop the other from moving forward and transferring the fertilized egg in an attempt to create a child. But this is problematic, insofar as it assumes the irreversibility of an intention to procreate and suggests that merely *willing* to create, bear, and rear a child carries with it the same obligations as following through with these actions. There is no turning back after that point; one is held accountable for intending to bring into existence a child to whom one

---

[1] Sarah Chan and Muireann Quigley, "Frozen Embryos, Genetic Information, and Reproductive Rights," *Bioethics* 22, no. 8 (2007): 447.

would have moral obligations. The problem with Chan and Quigley's position is an apparent failure to distinguish carefully between rights and obligations toward children and those we might have toward zygotes or early embryos. Moreover, if we consider more typical cases where people intend to procreate, this view proves to have problematic implications. For example, consider the case of a couple expressing an intention to procreate, attempting to do so via intercourse, but ultimately failing to achieve pregnancy or losing the pregnancy due to miscarriage. The couple may subsequently decide to wait for months or years before attempting to procreate, or they might decide against becoming parents. Chan and Quigley's view suggests that the couple should follow through with their original intention despite their reasons for having changed their minds, given their view that one's intention to procreate, expressed by creating IVF embryos or agreeing with one's partner to do so, is irrevocable.

Despite the presence of explicit agreements in contexts in which third parties are involved in the procreative process, such as gestational surrogates or gamete vendors, questions arise about the moral relevance and relative weight of the intentions of the various parties involved. Although people often follow through with their first intentions, there have been some well-publicized cases of surrogate mothers or "intended parents" changing their minds either during the pregnancy or once the child is born. Additionally, there are gamete donors/vendors who desire to connect with their progeny or come to regret their previous decision. Likewise, some children created using donor/vendor gametes develop a desire to find their genetic parents. Such problems arise despite the seemingly clear beginnings of certain types of procreative endeavors, so it is little wonder that things remain unclear in cases where procreation is *not* well thought out.

One of the most flagrant mixed messages related to the relevance of intention in the procreative process involves the clear intention on the part of a gamete vendor/donor that his/her gametes be used in attempts to create children. While there are no guarantees that their gametes will lead to the creation of a take-home baby, the intention on the part of the gamete vendor is clear. In such cases, however, the gamete vendor, who participates (intentionally) in procreation this way, is not held accountable for the resultant offspring. Intent to procreate in this manner does not entail in our society an obligation to rear the offspring. In fact the vendor consent forms usually state explicitly that the vendors have neither rights nor responsibilities toward the offspring. More problematically, and unlike cases of adoption, the vendors in the U.S. are not given any kind of assurance that their progeny will be properly cared for and are given no means of following up to make sure. This purely contractual view of parental obligation has struck some as a strange arrangement. For example, Daniel Callahan made the following observation regarding the practice of anonymous sperm donation: "It is as if everyone argued: Look males have always been fathering children anonymously and irresponsibly; why not put this otherwise noxious trait to good use?"[2]

Juxtaposed to this state of affairs is the social convention that the creation of a child when there is no intention to do so, or perhaps even a clear intention to avoid doing so, may entail obligations toward the child. For example, if a sexual interlude between two virtual strangers results in a child, the biological father of the child is often required to provide financial support. He cannot be compelled to participate otherwise in the child's upbringing, but he is held accountable to some degree regardless of whether he intended to procreate. For obvious reasons, e.g., self-interest or feeling betrayed by the child's mother, several nonvoluntary/involuntary fathers disagree with the notion that they ought to be held accountable for their progeny. And while the view of the involuntary father is more often backed by emotion, e.g., feelings of resentment rather than principled opposition to supporting offspring created unintentionally, others have argued that the practice of forcing men to pay child support is morally suspect. For example, Brake,[3] Fuscaldo,[4] and Weinberg,[5] among others, have questioned the implicit assumption that being causally responsible for the existence of a child entails moral responsibility.[6] Brake argues that while a man may be obligated to "share certain costs *immediately* incurred as a result of sex, his responsibility comes to an end when [the woman] gives birth."[7] She argues that the obligation is owed to the woman not the resultant child. However, this seems to rest on a confusion about to whom obligations are owed. Arguably, neither men nor women are obligated to embryos qua embryos (e.g., there is no obligation to bring all embryos to term), but we do have obligations toward *children*. Thus, I agree with Weinberg's assertion that we are responsible for what happens to gametes that develop into beings with moral status if we choose to take risks with

---

[2] Daniel Callahan, "Bioethics and Fatherhood, *Utah Law Review* 3 (1992): 741.

[3] Elizabeth Brake, "Fatherhood and Child Support: Do Men Have a Right to Choose?" *Journal of Applied Philosophy* 22, no. 1 (2005): 55-73.

[4] Guiliana Fuscaldo, "Genetic Ties: Are They Morally Binding? *Bioethics* 20, no. 2 (2006): 64-76.

[5] Rivka Weinberg, "The Moral Complexity of Sperm Donation," *Bioethics* 22, no. 3 (2008): 166-78.

[6] Brake, "Fatherhood and Child Support, 61.

[7] Brake, "Fatherhood and Child Support," 63.

our gametes *qua* hazardous materials.[8] Though obligations toward children
can later be transferred through various mechanisms, e.g., adoption, the
fact that transfer is required implies that the person doing the transferring
possesses the obligations (or rights) that they are transferring. This view
does not require that we subscribe to the view that parenthood is grounded
solely in genetics; instead, the relevant feature is that the creation of a
child was a reasonably foreseeable consequence of our actions.

In today's world, a gamete vendor who claims that he/she never
intended to help rear the children that result from the use of his/her
gametes is off the hook, and can probably point to a consent form or
agreement that says just that. On the other hand, a man who finds out that
he has inadvertently contributed to the existence of a child but claims that
he never intended to either create a child or rear one will find his request
to bow out of parental responsibility readily rejected. Hence, in
contemporary society, intended procreation need not come with social
enforcement of obligations, while unintended procreation usually does.
This state of affairs is just one indication of our wildly inconsistent
attitudes toward the relative importance of the presence (or absence) of
procreative intentions.

Even though the intention of an involuntary father—i.e., to avoid
procreation—is distinct from that of the gamete donor who *does* intend to
procreate, there is no distinction in these cases in terms of reasonable
foreseeability. So, even if either the gamete donor or the participant in the
one night stand claims to be surprised by the outcome or retracts what
seemed to be the obvious intention at the time of the action in question—
i.e., the gamete sale or sexual interaction—that this was a reasonably
foreseeable outcome of presumably voluntary actions is not a matter of
dispute. Any informed, rational evaluator given the facts of either case
would concede that the creation of a child was a reasonably foreseeable
outcome in either case.

Conventions/Biological Connections

Genetic connections

Without providing an exhaustive list of conventions that have shaped
our views of parenthood and corresponding social and legal practices, I
want to point to a few that seem to have had a significant impact. One
thread that runs through many prevailing conventions is the emphasis on

---

[8] Weinberg, "Moral Complexity of Sperm Donation," 171.

genetic connections between parents and offspring, as captured in the saying "blood is thicker than water". The idea is that genetic connections trump other kinds of relationships among people. One consequence of this is that becoming a parent through traditional adoption arrangements is viewed as a last resort—something one does only if they are infertile and unsuccessful with attempts to circumvent their fertility problems. Another consequence of this emphasis on the importance of genetic connections is that in many legal disputes genetic connections have often carried greater weight in determining custody and child support than other factors, such as (a) an established social relationship between a child and a particular adult; (b) a gestational connection between a woman (genetically related or not) and a newborn; or (c) the intentions of genetically unrelated adults to rear the offspring.

In the previous section I discussed the convention that requires men to provide economic support to genetically related children who were created through voluntary sexual intercourse that led to the child's existence. Here, however, I will elaborate on the associated practice of using DNA testing to absolve one of responsibility toward children. As Bartholet puts it, men claim that "if a DNA match alone can be used to force [men] into parenthood, then the absence of a DNA match should enable them to escape parenthood."[9] In some cases men are relieved of legal obligations toward children with whom they have no genetic connection, despite their having been the only father a child has known for its entire life. For example, in *Doran v. Doran* (2003), a man who had been rearing a child for 10 years was granted permission by the Pennsylvania Superior Court to remove himself entirely from the child's life.[10] Regardless of whether a man is genetically connected to the child, a decision can be made at an early stage by the man that he would participate in rearing the child(ren). The ability to rescind this decision once a relationship has been established with child(ren) over the course of a year or more, regardless of the presence or absence of a genetic connection, is to neglect the interests of both the child and the man in continuing the relationship. If a man makes a clear decision to help rear particular children, he should not walk away from that commitment, even if it turns out that he is not genetically connected to the children. If we reject the idea that gamete vendors should be permitted to participate in the lives of their progeny because allowing it

---

[9] Elizabeth Bartholet, "Guiding Principles for Picking Parents," in *Genetic Ties and the Family*, ed. Marth A. Rothstein, Thomas H. Murray, Gregory Kaebnick, and Mary Anderlik Majumder (Baltimore: Johns Hopkins University Press, 2005), 146.

[10] Bartholet, "Guiding Principles," 133.

would disrupt children's lives, we should also acknowledge that permitting a father to dissolve an established parent-child relationship is likely to be at least as disruptive and injurious to both the child and the father as the introduction of an additional family member.

In the preceding discussion about the confusion surrounding the significance of intentions, I discussed the relatively recent convention that stipulates that individuals who donate or sell their gametes to fertility clinics for the purpose of assisting others in procreation have no obligations or rights toward progeny created via assisted reproductive technology (ART). The genetic connection between gamete vendors or donors and their progeny is trumped by the intentions and desires of those who seek assistance in procreation. This is not to suggest that the gamete donors/vendors find this problematic (in most cases); instead, the point is that although the genetic connection has most frequently been the trump card, there is this exception to that general rule.

The use of donor/vendor gametes is aimed primarily at ensuring that at least one member of the infertile couple will have a genetic connection to the offspring, presumably because genetic connections between parents and children are highly valued. However, as Bartholet points out the use of donor/vendor gametes amounts to disregarding the *child's* "need for generational continuity [by which she means a connection to forebears or descendants] while at the same time asserting their own."[11] Andrews also notes that it is a peculiar state of affairs when many divorced fathers are doing genetic tests to determine whether they are "really" fathers to their children while men whose wives use "donor" sperm consider themselves fathers of the resultant offspring.[12]   These practices illustrate an inconsistent attitude toward genetic connections—they are treated as both important and unimportant at once.

Additionally, the fact that the child's genetic origins are often a closely guarded secret, even to the child, suggests an even more mysterious state of affairs wherein the *appearance* of genetic connections rather than actual genetic connections is desired. Granted, the creation of genetically related children is the primary goal of most attempts to procreate via assisted reproductive technology, but once it is established that this goal is not achievable, except in cases where attempts to adopt a child have failed, it is unclear why the prospective parents would opt to create a child that

---

[11] Bartholet, *Family Bonds*, 228.
[12] Lori B. Andrews, "Assisted Reproductive Technologies and the Challenge for Paternity Laws," in *Genetic Ties and the Family*, ed. Marth A. Rothstein, Thomas H. Murray, Gregory Kaebnick, and Mary Anderlik Majumder (Baltimore: Johns Hopkins University Press, 2005), 187-88.

lacks a genetic connection to them rather than adopt an existing child who would have no less of a genetic connection to them.

Gestational connections

While the main biological connection of interest has been the genetic connection between fathers and offspring, the separation of gestational connections from genetics or intent to rear raises additional questions about who counts as the "real" parent. Surrogates have been around for centuries, but the traditional way of becoming a surrogate was through insemination with the intended father's sperm. In today's world, however, a donor/vendor egg may be used by either a gestational surrogate or the intended mother. Hence, while the fact of giving birth used to be evidence of a woman's genetic connection to a child, this is no longer necessarily so. Moreover, even when the gestational and genetic connections to the child are both found in the same woman, disputes have arisen about whether these ties trump pre-conception intentions to transfer parental rights to, e.g., the genetic father and his partner, once the child is born. Probably the most infamous case was the 1988 *Baby M* case, where the first court ruled that the intended father, Mr. Stern, and his wife were the child's legal parents and that Ms. Whitehead, the surrogate—the genetic and gestational mother—had no legal claim to the child due to her pre-conception agreement with the Sterns. In this case, the genetic connection between Mr. Stern and the child, coupled with his and Ms. Stern's intention to rear the child, took precedence over the genetic and gestational connections between the child and Ms. Whitehead. This initial ruling, which was a first move toward allowing intentions to carry greater weight, was eventually overturned and Ms. Whitehead was given visitation rights. In a 1993 case, *Johnson v. Calvert*, Ms. Johnson agreed with the Calverts to gestate an embryo created with the Calverts' gametes and relinquish the child at birth. Ms. Johnson, who claimed to have bonded with the child during gestation, sued for custody. The court ruled in favor of honoring the initial intentions of the parties but also appealed to the significance of genetic connections between the Calverts and the child in the decision. It was not until the 1998 *Buzzanca* case that we see intent to rear as the *sole* basis for deciding legal parentage, but since then *intention* has continued to play a significant role in some decisions regarding legal parentage. For example, in the case of *K.M. v. E.G.,*[13] it was decided that the birth mother was the only legal mother because her partner, the genetic mother, had

---

[13] 13 Cal. Rptr. 3d 136, 146 (Cal. App. 1 Dist. 2004)

relinquished rights to the child through the egg donation process.[14] The court used the donor consent form signed by the egg donor/intended mother and as evidence of having the usual intention of gamete vendors. This decision, however, was reversed by the California Supreme Court on the ground that the genetic connection, combined with the egg donor's intention to rear the children with her partner, was enough to establish parentage. Her intention put her on a different footing from an anonymous sperm/egg donor, who would not be held accountable with regard to the child.[15]

A further development—or twist—in cases involving gestational surrogates was the 2003 Maryland case, *In re Roberto d. B.*, both the gestational surrogate and the intended father, who was also the genetic father, were petitioning jointly to keep the birth mother's name off the twins' birth certificate. They argued that since she was neither the genetic mother nor the intended mother that she should not be on the birth certificate. Furthermore, it was pointed out that if the lack of a genetic connection between a man and a child can be used to escape legal parentage—something usually done because an intent to rear is *already* absent—the lack of a genetic connection between a woman and a child, coupled with the lack of intent to rear on the part of the gestational surrogate, should mean that she is not the legal mother of the child.

The following scenario, however, illustrates a problematic implication of this rationale. Imagine a woman who agrees to gestate an embryo created from her husband's sperm and a donor/vendor egg and join him in rearing a child created in this manner. Suppose that she changes her mind during pregnancy, because he has cheated on her or because they have decided to divorce. In any case, she no longer intends to rear the child once it is born and claims that since she is not genetically connected to the child, she is not its "real" mother and therefore has no legal (or moral) obligations toward it. Again, we confront the problem of shifting intentions and how they are to be incorporated into determinations about the relationship between particular adults and children in a world where such significance is attached to genetic connections. It is also reasonably clear that the offspring in such cases are probably the ones with the most to lose, even if they are not the only losers in such cases.

---

[14] Sherry F. Colb, *When Sex Counts: Making Babies and Making Law* (New York: Rowman and Littlefield Publishers, Inc, 2007), 70-71.
[15] Colb, *When Sex Counts*.

The Root of the Confusion

There are at least two primary contributors to inconsistent attitudes regarding the relative importance of genetic connections and intentions discussed above. Other deeply entrenched beliefs may also contribute to inconsistent attitudes, but the emphasis on individual autonomy, which manifests in the claim that there is a right to procreate, and the widespread acceptance of genetic determinism appear to be dominant forces driving us into the whirlwind of inconsistencies.

There is a widespread assumption that individuals have a right to procreate—i.e., a right to create genetically related offspring. This assumption has been incorporated into documents such the 1948 Universal Declaration of Human Rights, which states that "men and women of full age, without any limitation due to race, nationality, or religion have the right to marry and found a family" (Article 16). Although some argue that a right to procreate is a fundamental right,[16] others ground this right in other more basic rights, e.g., the right of self-determination or a right to privacy. Arguably, a right to privacy is itself grounded in a right of self-determination, so I will focus mainly on the notion of a right to procreate that is grounded in individual autonomy. For example, John Robertson, one of the few people who argues for a right to procreate, instead of merely assuming there is such a right, defines "procreative liberty" as "a right to reproduce or not *in the genetic sense*, which includes rearing or not, as intended by the parents…includ[ing] female gestation, whether or not there is a genetic connection to the child."[17] He also describes procreation as central to "personal identity, meaning and dignity."[18] Hence, Robertson's account of "procreative liberty" is grounded in individual autonomy.

People's reluctance to question whether individuals have a right to procreate is unsurprising, given our scandalous history of morally bankrupt efforts to regulate people's procreative activities (e.g., 20th century eugenics programs in the United States, Germany, and the United Kingdom). Many, including Robertson, view the right to procreate as a prima facie right and assert that the burden of proof is on those who would

---

[16] See, e.g., John Lawrence Hill, "What Does it Mean to Be a Parent? The Claims of Biology as the Basis for Parental Rights," *New York University Law* Review 66 (1991): 353-420.

[17] John A. Robertson, *Children of Choice* (New Jersey: Princeton University Press, 1994), 23.

[18] Robertson, *Children of Choice*, 30.

deny that there is a right to procreate.[19]   However, despite the fact that societies have gone horribly wrong in past attempts to regulate procreation, the contemporary view that the primary consideration in the context of procreation should be the interests or desires of those who are attempting to procreate, fails to consider adequately the interests of those who are brought into existence by such actions.

Those who defend a right to procreate seem to confuse a right to engage in consensual sexual intercourse or collaborative attempts to procreate with a right to achieve certain results. Though individuals may have a right to cooperate with others in various ways, it does not follow from such a right that those individuals have a right to any particular consequences of those actions or a right to impact those who are not voluntary participants in the collaboration. The fact that there may be a right to *attempt* to procreate, which amounts to a right to have consensual sex or to collaborate with other willing parties in an attempt to procreate using assisted reproductive technologies without the interference of others, does not imply a right to bring another person into existence. To use Millum's barbershop quartet analogy,[20] one's right to form such a group with others does not entail a right to inflict our talent on an unwilling third party, much less bring a child into existence so that we will have an audience.

Whether there is a genuine right to procreate remains controversial, and whether a coherent account of a right to procreate can be developed remains to be seen. In addition to the general problems related to asserting a right to procreate, there is also the problem of asserting a right to something that might be impossible to obtain. Onora O'Neill, for example, has noted this problem with asserting a right to health, which is distinct from claiming that there is a right to an environment that provides the *opportunity* for normal health (e.g., right to clean water, basic

---

[19] I have argued elsewhere that Robertson's account of procreative liberty is defective and so do not provide a detailed analysis of his position here. See Yvette Pearson, "Storks, Cabbage Patches, and the Right to Procreate," *Journal of Bioethical Inquiry* 4, no. 2 (2007): p. 105-115.

[20] In response to an earlier version of this paper, wherein I denied the existence of a negative right to procreate, Joseph Millum pointed out that a person has a (negative) right to form a barber shop quartet with other willing parties and implied that there was no distinction between the negative right of two or more consenting parties to procreate and the right of four consenting individuals to form a barbershop quartet. While I agree that individuals have a right to engage in consensual sex or attempt to procreate through the use of assisted reproductive technologies, I do not think it follows that they have a right to the possible outcome of such actions—i.e., a genetically related child.

nourishment, etc.).[21] There are many unfortunate cases where providing health-maximizing conditions will fail to result in a healthy individual. As O'Neill puts it, "since it will never be possible to guarantee health for all, there can be no obligation so to do...there can therefore be no right to health."[22] Likewise it is problematic to assert that there is a right to create genetically related offspring or to acquire a child through adoption, goals that might be out of reach for some, even in the absence of morally problematic barriers such as the eugenic sterilization laws of the past.

In addition to the deeply entrenched assumption of a right to procreate, another pervasive assumption that contributes to the confused state of affairs regarding the relative importance of genetic connections and intentions in the context of procreation, is the assumption of genetic determinism (or genetic essentialism), which is the view that everything about us—our physical traits, personality, career choices, hobbies, etc—is reducible to our genotype. James Watson, for example, claimed that "we used to think our fate was in the stars. Now we know, in large measure, our fate is in our genes."[23] Many others have echoed this sentiment in their discussions of genetic testing, cloning, genetic engineering, preimplantation genetic diagnosis (PGD), or other issues related to procreation. On one level people seem to understand that procreation is a gamble and that the outcome of rearing a child is no less a mystery, but the overwhelming preference to procreate with one's own genetic material, even when strenuous effort is required, suggests that individuals believe that there is something more valuable or more predictable about using their own genetic material and rearing genetic progeny than, say, adopting an existing child.

This widespread embrace of genetic determinism has contributed to the importance placed on ensuring that there is a genetic connection to the children with whom one has established, or intends to establish, a parent-child relationship. The commitment to creating genetically related offspring has fostered the growth of a profitable assisted reproductive technology industry that has helped many circumvent their infertility and realize the goal of bringing genetically related children into the world. Ironically, however, this has led to the creation of children whose "generational continuity" is compromised (i.e., by the use of gametes from

[21] Onora O'Neill, *Autonomy and Trust in Bioethics* (New York: Cambridge University Press, 2002).
[22] Onora O'Neill, *Autonomy and Trust in Bioethics*, 79.
[23] Robert N. Proctor, "Resisting Reductionism from the Human Genome Project," in *Classic Works in Medical Ethics,* ed. Gregory Pence (New York: McGraw-Hill, 1998), 342.

anonymous donors/vendors) by the procreators' quest to guarantee the same "generational continuity" for at least one of the prospective parents. Here we see a tension between the emphasis on individual autonomy and the embrace of genetic determinism. Moreover, we see a shift from valuing actual genetic connections between parents and offspring to valuing the mere *appearance* of genetic connections. We know only *that* people value genetic connections, not *why*, and people's reasons for valuing the veneer of genetic connections are even more mysterious.

As the preceding discussion suggests, the emphasis on individual autonomy eclipses other relevant considerations, such as the welfare or other interests (e.g., in "generational continuity") of the offspring. The focus on rights—or supposed rights—and interests or desires of adults dominates not only reproductive decision making but also decisions about who has parental obligations or entitlements toward children. How a particular adult values genetic connections to others will impact whether she will attempt to create a genetically related child, pursue a relationship with genetic progeny (e.g., created through anonymous gamete donation/sale or unintentionally), or continue or break off an established parent-child relationship. The interests of children, particularly when decisions whether to procreate are being made, are viewed as secondary, if they are considered at all.

Ultimately, it appears that the focus on the rights and interests of adults has obscured our view of obligations toward offspring. As a hedge against this, the focus of procreative decisions, as well as discussions about procreation, should shift to emphasize obligations toward offspring rather than the rights and interests of procreators. In addition this shift in perspective, it is likely that continuing advances in the field of genetics, coupled with an expanded effort to educate the public, will alter some of the beliefs and attitudes toward procreation and offspring that are currently influenced by the prevailing assumption of genetic determinism.

THE FOUNDATIONS OF LICENSING PARENTS[1]

MICHAEL MCFALL

The positive influence that parental love has in the lives of humans cannot be overemphasized. Unfortunately, this is also true of the negative influence of child maltreatment. Hugh LaFollette's "Licensing Parents"[2] provides an invitation to examine both parental love and child maltreatment. In this essay, I examine why we should seek to eliminate child abuse and neglect in the first place, and I do so by appealing to political philosophy in addition to ethics. I then evaluate assumptions that seem to ground opposition to licensing parents. I focus on issues that best speak to our understanding of justice and the family, so I set aside issues of implementation which usually detract from the more fundamental philosophical issues. If my analysis is correct, then this essay will make the argument for licensing parents more powerful.

1. Parenting and Political Theory

Adeimantus tells Socrates, "[W]e've been waiting all this time supposing you would surely mention the begetting of children – how they'll be begotten and, once born, how they'll be reared – and that whole community of women and children of which you speak. We think it makes a big difference, or rather, the whole difference in a regime's being right or not."[3] There are many reasons why Adeimantus is correct about the importance of childrearing, but the foremost is captured by Laurence Thomas, "Parental love, then, provides the grounding for the sense of worth bestowed by moral equality – such love provides the soil, if you will, in which the sense of worth afforded by moral equality may take root…parental love paves the way for having the proper appreciation of

---

[1] This essay is a condensed version of my forthcoming *Licensing Parents: Family, State, and Child Maltreatment* (Lanham, MD: Lexington Books).

[2] *Philosophy and Public Affairs* 9 (1980).

[3] Plato, *The Republic*, trans. and ed. Allan Bloom (New York: Basic Books, 1991), Bk. V, 449d.

one's moral worth."[4] A proper appreciation of one's moral worth is integral to appreciating the moral worth of others. Consequently, the love bestowed by parents serves as a foundation for how children will relate to peers and fellow citizens. If children are raised properly, parental love will be expressed deeply and frequently to them. This deeply rooted experience of constant love will then be foundational for children as they mature and experience life's vicissitudes.

An ideal society generates its own support by having citizens who are primarily motivated to do good from knowing it is the right thing to do rather than from fear of punishment from the state. Families play an important role in determining this because human character is largely contingent upon nurturance received as a child. The family is the most powerful source of inequality in society because there is great disparity in the quality of nurturance provided to children by their parents. The chasm between maltreated and non-maltreated children is particularly wide. Yet families should not be abolished because alternative structures cannot provide the same kind and level of love and nurturance that decent parents provide. By claiming that a vast difference in childrearing is the most profound inequality, I do not take, say, economic or racial inequalities as non-existent. Rather, I simply ask what one would prefer: being a racial minority today raised by loving and competent parents or being part of a racial majority but having severely neglectful parents. Likewise, would one rather be raised in an economically poor family by loving and competent parents or be raised by wealthy but severely abusive parents?

Child maltreatment is a threat to egalitarian theories because of the vast inequality that it produces. Adults can often be compensated for brute bad luck, and this allows for some inequalities to exist in an egalitarian society because such inequalities can be compensated for later. However, no amount of compensation can fully compensate a child when he suffers from being severely abused or neglected because the moral and developmental psychology of children is not yet mature. A truly egalitarian society should thus ensure that the most important fair share that citizens receive is decent parenting. Universal decent parenting will allow for other inequalities, but it will eliminate the most profound inequality. Child maltreatment also poses a challenge to libertarianism. An ideal libertarian state requires decent citizens with fellow-feeling to minimize the need for the state to use resources to punish lawbreakers. Yet the formal system of a libertarian state does not mold the character of its

---

[4] *The Family and the Political Self* (Cambridge: Cambridge University Press, 2006), 36.

citizens. Rather, informal organizations such as the family form character. A libertarian society presupposes decent parenting.

Earlier I mentioned that child maltreatment is a non-compensable harm, and I will now justify that claim while showing why, in addition to being ethically important, child maltreatment has grand implications for political philosophy and policy. Studies show that child maltreatment has a negative effect on human biology, especially adverse influences on brain development.[5] This manifests in various ways. A decreased hippocampal size is common in adults who have experienced post-traumatic stress syndrome due to severe childhood maltreatment; this helps explain the memory loss experiences by many victims.[6] Increased electrophysiological abnormalities, especially in the left side of the frontal, temporal, and anterior regions of the brain have also been found in maltreated children. This helps support the thesis that early childhood development can alter brain development, especially the limbic structures. Improper development can lead to affective instability and poor control over anger, impulse, and stress.[7] Lastly, childhood trauma may be more harmful than trauma experienced as an adult due to the combination of trauma, psychology, and neurodevelopment.[8] Because the human brain is formed in early childhood, harms to its development are often irreparable.

---

[5] See Charles A. Nelson and Floyd E. Bloom, "Child Development and Neuroscience," *Child Development* 68 (1997); Sandra J. Kaplan, David Pelcovitz, and Victor Labruna, "Child and Adolescent Abuse and Neglect Research: a Review of the Past 10 Years. Part I: Physical and Emotional Abuse and Neglect," *Journal of the American Academy of Child and Adolescent Psychiatry* 38 (1999); Sue Gerhardt, *Why Love Matters: How Affection Shapes a Baby's Brain* (New York: Brunner-Routledge, 2004).

[6] J.D. Bremer, P. Randall, T.M. Scott, S. Capelli, R. Delaney, G. McCarthy, and D.S. Charney, "Deficits in Short-Term Memory in Survivors of Childhood Abuse," *Psychiatry Research* 59 (1995); J.D. Bremer, P. Randall, E. Vermetten, L. Staib, R.A. Bronen, C. Mazure, S. Capelli, G. MaCarthy, R.B. Innis, and D.S. Charney, "Magnetic Resonance Imaging-Based Measurement of Hippocampal Volume in Posttraumatic Stress Disorder Related to Childhood Physical and Sexual Abuse: A Preliminary Report," *Biological Psychiatry* 41 (1999).

[7] See Yutaka Ito, Martin H. Teicher, Carol A. Glod, David Harper, Eleanor Magnus, and Harris A. Gelbard, "Increased Prevalence of Electrophysiological Abnormalities in Children with Psychological, Physical, and Sexual Abuse," *Journal of Neuropsychiatry and Clinical Neurosciences* 5 (1993); Yutaka Ito, Carol A. Glod, and Erika Ackerman, "Preliminary Evidence for Aberrant Cortical Development in Abused Children: A Qualitative EEG Study," The *Journal of Neuropsychiatry and Clinical Neurosciences* 10 (1998).

[8] M.D. De Bellis and F.W. Putnam, "The Psychobiology of Childhood Maltreatment," *Child and Adolescent Psychiatric Clinics of North America* 3

Society as a whole suffers immensely from child maltreatment. Though relatively few children in the United States are abused, with most estimates not exceeding 5%, over 80% of incarcerated criminals were abused by their parents when children, 66% of institutionalized delinquents had child maltreatment histories, and one-half of maltreated children died at an early age, become alcoholic or mentally ill, or have been convicted of a serious crime.[9] It does not seem that maltreated children have a significantly different perspective about what is just. Rather, there often seems to be a gap between maltreated children's abstract knowledge of what is right and their performing right actions. One of the best studies on this reports, "[C]hildren who have been maltreated do not internalize different standards of behavior...[yet] abused and neglected children are more aggressive than their nonmaltreated counterparts. Thus, the findings reveal an apparent discrepancy between children's moral valuations and their aggressive behavior."[10] Maltreated children are not necessarily any less knowledgeable than their non-maltreated peers about what actions are just, but maltreatment often precludes the requisite desire to be formed in order to make moral knowledge efficacious. The above statistics are particularly troubling because about 30% of those who are maltreated will maltreat their own children, and this rate is five to six times higher than the rate of abuse in the general population.[11] Focusing on the elimination of child maltreatment would greatly benefit individuals and society.

Three things are likely to be felt by children who have been severely abused or neglected: betrayal, a sense of powerlessness, and stigmatization.[12]

(1994); M.D. De Bellis, M. Keshavan, D.B. Clark, B.J. Casey, J. Giedd, A.M. Boring, K. Frustaci, and N.D. Ryan, "A.E. Bennett Research Award. Developmental Traumatology Part II: Brain Development," *Biological Psychiatry* 45 (1999).

[9] See LaFollette, 185 n.4 and Joan McCord, "A Forty Year Perspective on Child Abuse and Neglect," *Child Abuse and Neglect* 7 (1983).

[10] Judith G. Smetana and Mario Kelly, "Social Cognition in Maltreated Children," in *Child Maltreatment: Theory and Research on the Causes and Consequences of Child Abuse and Neglect*, eds. Dante Cichetti and Vicki Carlson (Cambridge: Cambridge University Press, 1989), 636. This observation takes into account that children are more likely to judge hypothetical than actual transgressions as wrong, regardless of maltreatment status.

[11] Joan Kaufman and Edward Zigler, "The intergenerational Transmission of Child Abuse," in Cicchetti and Carlson (1989), 135.

[12] These are nicely captured in David Finkelhor and Angela Browne, "Assessing the Long-Term Impact of Child Sexual Abuse: A Review and Conceptualization," in *Family Abuse and Its Consequences: New Directions in Research*, eds. Gerald

Betrayal, particularly by close authority figures such as one's parents, precludes the healthy developmental roots of reciprocity. Betrayal also short-circuits the likelihood of positively reciprocating with fellow-feeling with one's peers and fellow citizens. In addition to being directly harmed by particular acts of betrayal, children are likely to be negatively affected by the effects of witnessing a poor behavioral model. Not only is one harmed immediately by the direct particular harm of experiencing maltreatment and by a more general harm of being less likely to respect and trust authority figures, but a child is also at increased risk to imitate abusive behavior itself. A sense of *powerlessness* can stultify the will to act properly when coupled with betrayal because reciprocation has not developed properly. A sense of powerlessness can also work directly insofar as even if one wished to act positively he may choose otherwise because he feels his worth is so little that he does not possess the ability to be efficacious. *Stigmatization* can be harmful because healthy citizens should have self-respect and recognize themselves as having equal social standing. However, it is extremely difficult to maintain self-respect if one's formative developmental stages are strongly connected with feelings of badness, shame, and guilt.

2. Licensing Parents

Now that the importance of the family and the harms of child maltreatment have been sketched, I will outline Hugh LaFollette's argument for licensing parents. LaFollette begins by arguing that society can and should regulate an activity if it meets the following conditions: (i) the activity is potentially harmful, (ii) safe performance of the activity requires a certain competence, and (iii) we have a moderately reliable way to determine competence. Parenting can clearly be harmful to others, and it takes a certain competence to parent decently. The most controversial of these conditions in relation to licensing parents is (iii), but LaFollette cites studies which he deems moderately reliable. Furthermore, many such tests have been developed in the last thirty years.[13] LaFollette notes that we

---

Hotaling, David Finkelhor, John T. Kirkpatrick, and Murray A. Straus (London: Sage Publications, 1980).

[13] For example, the Child Abuse Potential Inventory had a sensitivity rate (ability to identify abusers correctly of 85% with 15% false negatives and a specificity rate (ability to identify non-abusers correctly) of 89% with 11% false positives. See M.A. Disbrow, H. Doerr, and C. Caulfield, "Measuring the Components of Parents' Potential for Child Abuse and Neglect," Child Abuse and Neglect 1 (1977). Articles on the Child Abuse Potential Inventory have since been published

accept licensing drivers, doctors, and lawyers by these conditions. He is also careful to note that we deem it acceptable to deny licenses even if this causes serious inconvenience to those denied a license, and we deny licenses even if the licensing procedure is not 100% accurate.

LaFollette notes three major theoretical objections to licensing parents, and I provide his response in brackets: (i) people have a right to rear children [but some rights must be limited by other rights or rights of others and parental rights are conditional], (ii) licensing parents would entail too much intrusion into people's lives [but only those who were actually denied licenses would encounter a high degree of intrusion], and (iii) licensing parents employs prior restraint insofar as it restricts action before harm occurs [but the very nature of most kinds of licensing is to restrain action before harm occurs; therefore, most licensing procedures that we accept presuppose prior restraint].

LaFollette considers five practical objections: (i) it is difficult to agree upon adequate criteria for what it means to be a good parent [but licensing parents only seeks to exclude very bad parents], (ii) there is no reliable way to predict who will maltreat children [but he cites early predictive tests], (iii) administrators of the licensing test will make mistakes [but this also occurs in other licensing programs], (iv) administrators of the test will sometimes abuse the procedure [but this also occurs in other licensing programs], and (v) it is impossible to implement a system of licensing parents [LaFollette wavers here but suggests that we might remove children from parents who failed the test and put them up for adoption]. Finally, LaFollette demonstrates that we already license parents insofar as we license adoptive parents and consistency entails that we should license all parents.

LaFollette seeks only to prevent the very worst parents from parenting. In terms of this essay, this means preventing those who will maltreat their children. In addition to appealing to the aforementioned tests, it may also be helpful to prevent those who have been convicted of rape, murder, or sexual assault from parenting. Due to higher rates of maltreatment, it may

---

in the *Journal of Clinical Psychology* and the *Journal of Consulting and Clinical Psychology*. Likewise, the Family Stress checklist yielded a sensitivity rate of 80% with 20% false positives and a specificity rate of 90% with 10% false positives. See Solbritt Murphy, Bonnie Orkow, and Ray M. Nicola, "Prenatal Prediction of Child Abuse and Neglect: A Prospective Study," *Child Abuse and Neglect* 9 (1985). Articles on the Family Stress Checklist have since been published in *Child Abuse and Neglect*. A third test has been developed recently: Kym L. Kirkpatrick, "The Parental Empathy Measure: A New Approach to Assessing Child Maltreatment Risk," *American Journal of Orthopsychiatry* 75 (2005).

also be prudent to require parents to be 18 years-old and married.[14] It must also be noted that licensing parents, however formulated, is not arbitrary: being permitted to rear is based on the likelihood of maltreating one's children. This is illuminating because the status quo system of parenting *is* completely arbitrary insofar as anyone can parent, including thirteen year-olds, drug-dealers, and child abusers. Finally, some may oppose licensing parents based on stories about child services failing to protect children or some adoptive parents maltreating their children. Yet the rate of maltreatment is higher in non-adoptive families than in adoptive families.[15] If one opposes licensing parents based on accounts of maltreatment in adoptive families, then one should be more opposed to the practice of allowing people to rear their own biological children freely because the latter practice is more dangerous for children.

3. Rights and Prior Restraint

The two foundational objections against licensing parents are that all people have a right to rear children and that licensing parents punishes some people before they have been proven guilty. I wish to make sense of these claims and show why they are not powerful objections to licensing parents. To aid in this, I employ three thought projects to determine the underlying intuitions involved with regards to rights, prior restraint, and licensing parents.

There are many ways to interpret the rights-objection to licensing parents. One way to interpret it is that all people have a right to rear children, but this is too strong because it would yield infertile people a

[14] My necessary conditions for licensing parents largely overlap LaFollette's: (i) licensing parents must be a compelling interest of the state, (ii) a test must exist to predict with reasonable precision which potential parents will likely maltreat their children, (iii) there must be no less invasive solutions that will yield the similar desired effects of licensing parents, (iv) the policy of licensing parents must be able to be implemented effectively, (v) it must be demonstrated that prospective parents do not have an indefeasible right to parent, and (vi) the kind of intimacy and privacy that is important within the family cannot be violated.

[15] See LaFollette, 194 n.9. For more recent statistics, in 2004 only 0.6% of parental perpetrators of child abuse were adoptive parents. *Child Maltreatment: U.S. Department of Health and Human Resources, Administration on Children, Youth, and Families* (Washington, D.C.: U.S. Government Printing Office, 2006), 78. However, according to the 2000 U.S. Census, 2.4% of children were adopted. *United States Census. Adopted Children and Stepchildren – Census 2000 Special Report* (U.S. Department of Commerce, 2004), 2. These statistics are from different sources, but it is clear that the rate of abuse is lower in adoptive families.

right to rear children. Securing this right would sometimes be problematic because it would require transferring the children of fertile parents to infertile people who sought to be parents. This would be impermissible to one who thought that all have a right to children because the rights of some fertile parents would be usurped. Another way to interpret the rights-objection is that government cannot intervene in the family because the family is a natural and pre-political institution. Yet there are at least three reasons why this is a bad argument. First, it is unclear why something that occurs before society forms should be given privileged status. Many things existed before society (murder, human sacrifice, etc.) but it is unclear why these should be given privileged status. Second, perhaps what is meant is that society was formed to protect families. Yet this objection only has power if society were created to protect families that were formed in ways that did not violate the rights of any family members. If society were formed to protect a family structure that oppressed the rights of one or more of its members, as those that allow child maltreatment do, then society is founded on oppression and it is unclear why this should be perpetuated. Third, if one believes that society cannot intervene in the family because the family is a pre-political institution, then one is committed to believing that the state cannot set age limits to marry, forbid relatives from marrying, or ban polygamy. Most importantly, it would commit one to opposing state removal of abused or neglected children from their parents. Another interpretation of the rights-objection is that parents have rights to parent because they have natural love and affection for their children. Most people do naturally love their children, which is why most people should be permitted to parent, but not all parents love their children. Child maltreatment occurs, and maltreatment does not seem compatible with love. It may be objected that all parents do love their children but that some are not competent enough to raise children in a minimally decent way. Though I believe it false that *all* parents love their children, I concede this for the sake of argument but point out that neither love nor competence are sufficient conditions for decent parenting. Love and competence are each necessary conditions, but independently they are insufficient. In any case, not all people have the competence and love requisite to be decent parents, and this objection fails.

I have noted bad rights-objections that are often used when thinking about the parent-child relationship, but the best way to understand parental rights comes from one of the greatest natural rights theorists, John Locke. Locke writes, "Adam and Eve, and after them all *Parents* were, by Law of Nature, under an obligation to preserve, nourish, and educate Children, they had begotten, not as their own Workmanship, but the Workmanship of their own Maker, the Almighty, to whom they were to be accountable for them."[16] More importantly, Locke writes,

> Nay, this *power* so little belongs to the *Father* by any peculiar right of Nature, but only as he is Guardian of his Children, that when he quits his Care of them, he loses his power over them, which goes along with their Nourishment and Education, to which it is inseparably annexed, and it belongs as much to the *Foster-Father* of an exposed Child, as to the Natural Father of another: So little power does the bare *act of begetting* give a Man over his Issue, if all his Care ends there, and this be all the Title he hath to the Name and Authority of a Father.[17]

More succinctly, James Kent writes, "The rights of parents result from their duties."[18]

Even if one concedes that not all families and parents are equal and that mere biological relation does not necessarily yield parental rights, complications remain. After all, parents and children have rights. A system that only recognizes the rights of children is as unjust as a system that only recognizes the rights of adults. Thinking about the rights of both children and adults would greatly help progressing towards a more just society. Yet to think about child maltreatment only in terms of competing rights claims misses the most important point. This point follows from what Locke writes above, but the ramifications of this are rarely made clear: *some* people do not have a right to parent, and *some* people never had a right to parent. It is not that the state is justified in taking away their right to parent for some greater good in a system of licensing parents. Rather, because no right existed in the first place, or the right was lost somewhere along the way when one became incapable of caring or loving a child decently, the state simply forbids such people from seeking to exercise a right that they do not have.

Most potential parents will not have a problem fulfilling their most basic duties to any children that they might have because the natural affection of love will motivate them to know how their children should be

---

[16] *Two Treatises of Government* (Cambridge: Cambridge University Press, 1996), 305

[17] Locke, 310. Locke also writes, "*Paternal* or *Parental Power* is nothing but that, which Parents have over their Children, to govern them for the Children's good," and "The *Power*, then *that Parents have* over their Children, arises from that Duty which is incumbent on them, to take care of their Off-spring, during the imperfect state of Childhood," 381 and 306.

[18] *Commentaries on American Law* (New York: O. Halstead, 1832), Vol. II, Part IV, Lecture XXIX, Section II, "Of the Rights of Parents," 203.

treated and behave accordingly. For most parents bearing a child entails an implicit contract to fulfill certain duties to that child, or at least ensure that these duties are fulfilled by others. This is at least true when the parental role is undertaken voluntarily, as it is in our society where contraception is readily available, abortion is legal, and adoption is a socially acceptable practice. Yet some people are unable to love or care for children and are thus unable to have a duty to love or care for them. Parents who are unable to fulfill duties to children cannot have duties to children if ought implies can. Some severely mentally retarded people, for example, cannot have a duty to love or care for children because they cannot love or care for children in a way necessary for children to develop properly. They should not be allowed to rear children if the nature of children creates a duty for others to love them. Likewise, some otherwise normally-functioning people are unable to love, or at least love in a healthy way. Such people cannot have a duty to love any potential children that they might bear. The vulnerability of children, as well as their moral and legal rights as citizens, should entail that they only be raised by individuals who have a duty to love and care for them.

Licensing parents allows those who will fulfill their duties broad discretion in how their duties will be fulfilled yet precludes those without duties to children from rearing children. An overarching objection to licensing parents is that it is paternalistic. The charge is thought to be devastating because it implicitly refers to being paternalistic to *adults* and in this sense paternalism is usually and justifiably a pejorative term. However, licensing parents is not limited to adults; it is also about children. By definition, paternalism (and maternalism) is what children need to develop properly. In our current system, the state will *eventually* "protect" many of the children of individuals who disregard (or lack) the most basic duties to children. Unfortunately, state intervention *after* children have been maltreated does not protect them in any meaningful way, as the harm is often irreparable.

Some may concede that parental rights are defeasible, but by 'defeasible' they mean only something that can be taken away after harm has occurred. This is too narrow because a defeasible right is simply a right that is subject to forfeiture – nothing about defeasibility requires forfeiture *after some act*. The objection is that parental rights are defeasible but the state cannot take that right away before one has been shown unfit to exercise that right. However, that presumes that the *state takes away* the right. Yet that does not accurately describe what mostly happens in licensing parents. Rather, the state merely acts in accordance with the recognition that some individuals are incapable of fulfilling a duty and because they are incapable of fulfilling a duty then they cannot have parental rights. The state does not cause this right to be lost or take it away; the state simply recognizes that some people do not have the right in the first place, or they lost it along the way, and the state ensures that those without such rights do not parent.

3.1 Mill's Bridge

The thesis that the desires of adults should trump the well-being of children demonstrates an unhealthy overvaluing of adult liberty and freedom. Mill saw this clearly,

> A person should be free to do as he likes in his own concerns, but he ought not to be free to do as he likes in acting for another, under the pretext that the affairs of the other are his own affairs. The State, while it respects the liberty of each in what specifically regards himself, is bound to maintain a vigilant control over his exercise of any power which it allows him to possess over others. This obligation is almost entirely disregarded in the case of family relations, a case in its direct influence on human happiness, more important than all other taken together.[19]

Many cite this passage because of its relevance to women, but it is also relevant to children:

> It is in the case of children that misapplied notions of liberty are a real obstacle to the fulfillment by the State of its duties. One would almost think that a man's children were supposed to be literally, and not metaphorically, a part of himself, so jealous is opinion of the smallest interference of law with his absolute and exclusive control over them.[20]

Finally, Mill writes about prior restraint and liberty explicitly,

> If either a public officer or anyone else saw a person attempting to cross a bridge which had been ascertained to be unsafe, and there were no time to warn him of his danger, they might seize him and turn him back, without any real infringement of his liberty...Nonetheless, when there is not a certainty, but only a danger of mischief, no one but the person himself can judge of the sufficiency of the motive which may prompt him to incur the risk; in this case, therefore (unless he is a child, or delirious, or in some state of excitement or absorption incompatible with the full use of the

---

[19] John Stuart Mill, *On Liberty* (London: Penguin Books, 1985), 175.
[20] Mill, 175.

reflecting faculty), he ought I conceive, to be only warned of the danger;
not forcibly prevented from exposing himself to it.[21]

This example can be taken to argue that the prior restraint of licensing
parents is unjustified because there is no certainty of harm, only a danger
of it; therefore, prospectively bad parents should only be warned that they
pose a danger to any children that they might rear. However, Mill would
reject that conclusion because the harm posed is only to the bridge-walker
"himself." If the bridge-walker only poses harm to himself, then Mill and I
would in most cases allow him to cross the bridge, even if it would almost
certainly entail his death.

To better capture the prior restraint involved in licensing parents,
consider a modified bridge case. A man approaches a bridge that
authorities have estimated has a 90% chance of collapsing and killing
those who walk on it. This man, unlike the one in Mill's example, seeks to
cross the bridge with two of his young children in his arms. His actions
now also affect his two children. His children cannot act for themselves;
their father must act for them. Considering what Mill says about one's
actions when they harm others, the state is justified in restraining the
father from crossing the bridge and almost surely killing himself and his
children. *Certainty* no longer matters; the *likelihood* for danger gains
importance. It does not suffice merely to warn the man that he will be
killing his children if he crosses a bridge. His epistemic foundation does
not matter; he may believe that there really is not a 90% chance that the
bridge will collapse, despite what the experts say. Or he may believe that a
risk does exist but that the risk does not apply to him. The modified bridge
case captures something importantly different from the unmodified bridge
case. If one accepts prior restraint in the modified bridge case, then one
should accept the prior restraint of licensing parents.

3.2 Going to the Doctor

Presume that a couple wishes to bear a physically healthy child. The
couple consults with a doctor who informs them that if they bear a child
there is a 90% chance that the child will have a serious physical disability.
If the parents take physical health to be a necessary condition for their
child, then it would be irrational for them to bear a child with the
knowledge that they are so unlikely to have a healthy child. Now suppose
that a couple wishes to rear a child only if they have good reason to
believe that they will rear their child in at least a minimally decent way.

---

[21] Mill, 166.

Suppose that the couple makes clear their belief that abusing or neglecting a child is not minimally decent. Suppose further that this couple consults with an expert who informs them that there is a 90% chance that they will abuse or neglect their child. If they choose to rear a child, they are no longer acting in their rational interests (while simultaneously being unjust to that potential child and society). It is one thing to desire to rear children, but it is another thing entirely to actualize this desire with the knowledge that one is almost certain to abuse or neglect a child. Conceding that the desire to raise a child trumps the desire to raise a child in the manner that a child deserves fails to recognize or protect children in any meaningful way.

People in the above cases should not bear or rear children. One way to justify this is to argue, as David Velleman does, "people should not deliberately create children who they already know will be disadvantaged."[22] However, this position is too strong. Most children, in some way or another, will be disadvantaged. Some children will have more than their share of advantages, and some will have more than their share of disadvantages. Yet it is unacceptable to procreate deliberately when the resulting children will be disadvantaged below the threshold of decency – being abused or neglected. When asked if they would rear a child knowing with 90% accuracy that they would maltreat their child, very few people maintain that they would. Some object, "But *I* know that the test is wrong because *I* know that *I* would parent decently." This simply denies the predictive power that has already been assumed. But when asked if we should tolerate others parenting in such a situation, considerably more are accepting. What changes? We might think that some *other* people's desires, unlike ours, do not change after knowing that they are likely to maltreat their child. As such, it is wrong to prevent the desire of adults to be fulfilled, especially if this hinders them from coming closer to fulfilling their lifeplan. Ignoring the fact that rearing in such cases will, nine times out of ten, not fulfill their lifeplan and make life hard for themselves and their children, it remains the case that "human beings do not simply accept passively a set of aims or a lifeplan. Rather, values, aims and plans are all subjects for deliberation and choice."[23] People are able to control their

---

[22] J. David Velleman, "Family History," *Philosophical Papers* 34 (2005), 364.

[23] David Gauthier, "Political Contractarianism," *The Journal of Political Philosophy* 5 (1997), 138. It is for this reason that Gauthier also writes, "If, as seems psychologically plausible, the social growth of a child is significantly enhanced by being raised in an emotionally warm and stable environment in which the child develops strong affective ties with an adult of each sex, and especially its natural parents, then persons who want children will need to commit themselves,

desires with varying degrees of success, but what are we to say of the person who *still* wishes to rear while knowing that he will likely maltreat his children? The person who chooses to rear in such a scenario likely reveals that the 90% probability that he will maltreat his child is probably too low for him in the sense that his lack of adequately valuing his potential child's well-being demonstrates that he will almost surely maltreat his child. If one has good reasons for not seeking to rear a child when told by a expert that one has a 90% chance of maltreating his children, then one also has good reasons for why others should not seek to parent in the same situation.

3.3 Capturing Wives

Children cannot claim rights for themselves, unlike many other minority or oppressed groups. This is pertinent when recognizing that we only recently allowed the state to intervene in the family to protect women from abusive husbands. However, the case is more severe for children, especially very young ones, who cannot seek the police or flee from the family to evade abuse, as adult women can do. Children can be severely maltreated for years without anybody outside the family knowing. Some women may choose not to report their abuse to the police, but young children do not even have this choice. Furthermore, unlike the case of the battered or raped wife, children do not consent to their relationship. Consenting to marry does not justify spousal abuse, but children do not have *any* power concerning who their parents will be. Discussing married couples is particularly relevant if we imagine treating adult women as we treat children. Suppose that women could be claimed as wives by men who capture them (this captures the analogy of entering a relationship with no consent), and suppose that the state respects this practice as legal. Suppose further that a small population of men could be identified, with 90% accuracy, as likely to be extremely abusive to their wives. Overlooking the injustice of women having to marry whomever they are captured by, assuming it is just for the sake of argument (as it is a fact that children never give consent to the families into which they are born), our society would find it morally repugnant if the men identified as 90% likely to maltreat their spouses were able to marry women. Furthermore, our

---

so far as possible, to create and maintain such an environment. That some will not want, or even be able, to do this is in no way to condemn them, but rather to indicate the sort of constraints imposed on acceptable life-plans, insofar as these plans involve children, by the demand for effective upbringing, which must be part of any set of interaction acceptable to all," 147.

society would likely forbid such men from marrying in the first place (assuming that they only marry non-consensually by capturing women). We would not argue, as we sometimes do with regards to parenting and child maltreatment, "Well, marriage is important to people and a right that all people have. Besides, there is no guarantee that all such men will abuse the wives with whom they entered into a non-consensual relationship because there is a 10% chance that everything will work out just fine. It is best to let the men abuse the women and then remedy things after the abuse. That is, if such maltreated women came forward. And if such men allowed them to leave the house. And if..." The situation of children is worse than that of women in this scenario. Adult women can survive without spouses, but young children cannot survive without parents. Adult women do not need spouses to develop psychologically (at least not for the most basic stages of development), but parents are essential for child development. Adult women are psychologically developed, they have some belief system of right and wrong, and spousal abuse need not entirely form their moral psychology. However, children are largely shaped by their early experiences in life, and being abused as young children is likely to cause them to develop in an unhealthy way.

Citizens entered into relationships where consent is *completely* absent, when such citizens are *completely* vulnerable, deserve extra protection from the state – a kind of protection that is not and should not be given to those who are not *completely* vulnerable and do not *completely* lack consent. This should be clear from the story about captured wives, and such women were not even completely vulnerable and did not completely lack consent. They did not completely lack consent because they could have emigrated, committed suicide, killed their spouse, etc. to avoid their almost inevitable maltreatment. If we could only choose to be ensured that we would not be maltreated by our parents (which would also largely ensure that we would not maltreat our own children if we were to parent later) or to be ensured that we would be completely free to parent later (while accepting that we could be maltreated by our parents and, furthermore, if such maltreatment occurred then we would be at high risk to maltreat our own children) then I take it that most would choose the former. This lends some credence to the former being a more basic right, if merely comparing rights.

These three scenarios shed much light on deep intuitions related to licensing parents. First, rights function quite differently once third-parties, especially children, are involved. Second, sometimes the sufficient likelihood of an event, not certainty, is sufficient to restrain others justifiably when the danger posed is sufficiently harmful. Third, noncoercively addressing a problem caused by a set of indecent people is sometimes unlikely to succeed if those involved are truly indecent. Forth, even if the argument for licensing parents were somehow denied as inconsistent with other licensing practices, then this need not invalidate the justification of licensing parents. It has been shown that children are so vulnerable that it may be justifiable to provide them with more protection than what most laws today provide.

4. Alternatives

Because this essay seeks to capture the deeper philosophical objections to licensing parents, I do not here consider particular pragmatic objections concerning implementation or alternatives to licensing parents. It is unjustified to implement licensing parents if it cannot be implemented effectively, and alternatives should be embraced if they are less invasive and as effective as licensing parents. Rather than examining various alternatives, I will articulate pertinent points about child maltreatment which show why most alternatives to licensing parents are less effective or more invasive than licensing parents.

One alternative is to address child maltreatment as an economic problem. Maltreatment and poverty are often correlated, but decent parenting should be the primary focus even when children are in poverty because decent parenting is sufficient to yield psychologically and morally healthy children. However, not living in poverty is insufficient to yield such children. Poverty itself is not harmful; although the residual effects of being poor can be harmful. Yet child maltreatment itself is harmful, as are the residual effects of maltreatment. Likewise, living in poverty with good parents is unlikely to yield harm; however, maltreated children are likely to be harmed deeply regardless of their family's economic status. Merely having resources, without considering *which* resources are the most valuable or *who* ought to provide them, can be insufficient for healthy child development. This is well-illustrated in studies of children of affluent parents.[24] These studies are important because they provide a case where

---

[24] See S. Luthar, "The Culture of Affluence: Psychological Costs of Material Wealth," *Child Development*, 74 (2003); S.S. Luthar and B.E. Becker, "Privileged but Pressured: A Study of Affluent Youth," *Child Development*, 73 (2002); S.S. Luthar and K. D'Avanzo, "Contextual Factors in Substance Abuse: A Study of Suburban and Inner-City Adolescents," *Development and Psychopathology*, 11 (1999); S.S. Luthar and Shawn J. Latendresse, "Comparable 'Risks' at the Socioeconomic Status Extremes: Preadolescents' Perception of Parenting," *Development and Psychopathology*, 17 (2005).

one variable in question, resources, is non-constant, and another variable in question, incompetent parents, remains constant. This is further illustrated in a comparative study of high socioeconomic status (SES) suburban students and their low SES inner-city counterparts; the high SES suburban youth had increased levels of anxiety and elevated use of cigarettes, alcohol, marijuana, and hard drugs.[25] The affluent children perceived their parents as physically and emotionally unavailable to the same degree that children in poverty did.[26] In the case of the suburban youth, perceived isolation from one's parents, particularly low perceived closeness to mothers, was identified as highly problematic.[27] One might think that having greater wealth would permit greater familial closeness because reduced economic hardship reduces stressors. The opposite was found. Feelings of isolation probably resulted from little family time together due to their numerous after-school activities for children and their parents' demanding career obligations.[28] Greater resources do not necessarily translate into healthy child development. Furthermore, good parenting is a necessary condition for healthy child development across sociodemographic groups and perceived closeness to parents promotes healthy child development.[29]

Another alternative is to address child maltreatment through various rehabilitative or educational programs. Rehabilitation programs do exist with various success rates, but they are insufficient for several reasons. First, child maltreatment is not usually a mere cognitive error. Most people know, for example, that raping one's daughter or bludgeoning one's son until he cannot walk is wrong. Rather, some people's moral knowledge is insufficient to preclude their actions. If we happen upon individuals who

---

[25] Luthar and D'Avanzo, 1999.

[26] Luthar and Latendresse, 2005.

[27] Luthar and Becker, 2002.

[28] Luthar and D'Avanzo, 1999; R.B. Shafran, "Children of Affluent Parents," in John D. O'Brien, Daniel J. Pilowsky, and Owen W. Lewis, eds. *Psychotherapists with Children and Adolescents: Adapting the Psychodynamic Process* (Washington, D.C.: American Psychiatric Association, 1992).

[29] See M.A. Zimmerman, D.A. Salem, K.I. Maton, "Family Structure and Psychosocial Correlates Among Urban African-American Adolescent Males," *Child Development*, 66 (1995); E.L. Cowen, P.A. Wyman, W.C. Work, J.Y. Kim, D.B. Fagen, and K.B. Magnus, "Follow-Up Study of Young Stress-Affected and Stress-Resilient Urban Children," *Development and Psychopathology*, 9 (1997); P.A. Wyman, E.L. Cowen, W.C. Work, L. Hoyt-Meyers, K.B. Magnus, and D.B. Fagan, "Caregiving and Developmental Factors Differentiating Young – At-Risk Urban Children Showing Resilient Versus Stress-Affected Outcomes: A Replication and Extension," *Child Development*, 70 (1999).

genuinely do not know that the above cases are wrong, then one should take serious pause about whether they should ever parent. A similar kind of alternative is to try to rehabilitate parents after they have maltreated children. Yet even if a program could be designed to have a 100% success rate without any recidivism, this would still mostly evade the problem. First, while these parents would no longer *continue* to maltreat their children, they would have *already* maltreated their children. Consequently, devastating developmental harm would probably have *already* occurred in their children. Secondly, reaching those at the highest risk would often be impossible due to high degrees of social isolation and disregulatory behaviors that exist among some who maltreat; such programs would likely be unsuccessful even if they could be found but did not participate. For example, group sessions for one study involving home-visitation and parent group sessions had to be cancelled because so few of the parents had actually attended.[30] Another kind of rehabilitation argument puts forth various means of frequently monitoring families, but this is problematic because intimacy requires privacy. Healthy families need privacy to flourish, but constant monitoring precludes this. Licensing parents can protect this privacy because it would allow all who were permitted to parent to parent with the same freedom that parents enjoy in our current system.

Conclusion

If children are not reared decently, then we can expect that those who have been maltreated, as well as their society, will suffer serious harm. Preventing child maltreatment does have a price, but it is unclear that we cannot afford it. Furthermore, it is unclear that licensing parents is as costly as we think. It has neither the costs of Plato's communal childrearing and eugenics nor the vast invasion of privacy and elimination of love and the family depicted in twentieth-century dystopian novels. People would still be free to marry and have sex with whomever they wanted. Licensing parents does involve bureaucracy, but asking people to show that they seek to have children, in addition to proving that they are capable of parenting decently, is not asking too much, especially if this process alone would be sufficient to deter those who really do not wish to

---

[30] W.J. van Doornick, P. Dawson, P.M. Butterfield, and H.I. Alexander, Parent-Infant Support Through Lay Health Visitors," Final Report Submitted to the Bureau of Community Health Service, National Institute of Health, Department of Health, Education, and Welfare, 1980.

rear children from bearing children. Besides, decent prospective parents would want to know whether they would likely maltreat their children, and they would voluntarily refrain from doing so if told that they would.

Some people are unable to love or care for children in a minimally decent way. If ought implies can, then some people cannot have a duty to rear children. If parental rights result from duties, then some people do not have rights to rear children. Trusting *all* people with the responsibility of rearing children is imprudent and immoral. We acknowledge this in our adoption policies. Furthermore, this is evident when we are careful about who we allow to babysit our children. If we do not know the intentions, character, or competence of a person, then granting that person trust is imprudent. It is sometimes reasonable to grant trust in situations where the stakes are small. Trusting another in a matter of high stakes may be only imprudent, not immoral, if the only harm posed by the trust is to oneself. Yet granting trust when trust is unjustified and may negatively affect others seriously, as is the case of allowing another responsibility to care for a child, is imprudent *and* immoral. Licensing parents promotes healthy trust. Parental love is one of the most powerful gifts that can be given, and when this gift is given by a competent parent then his child has the most secure foundation to be a decent human being and citizen. Licensing parents does not eliminate the family, love, intimacy, or privacy needed for humans to flourish; it helps secure the possibility of their fruition.

INTERGENERATIONAL JUSTICE AND CARE IN PARENTING[1]

STEPHEN SCALES

1) Introduction

Since Carol Gilligan's exploration of the distinctive moral development of women[2], there has been a great deal of debate over the proper response to her findings. Surely, the ethics of care deserves a voice in the philosophical canon, but what should be our attitude towards it as a moral theory and with regard to our actual development as moral persons? Is an ethics of care superior to an ethics of justice, or is it a sign of stunted moral development (as Kohlberg's scale would have it)? Or ought we somehow to integrate these two ways of moral thinking, and if so, how? Although I can't claim to answer any of these questions in any general and definitive way, I think I do have an answer to the possible integration or complementarity of these views with regard to the moral task of parenting. I will argue that there are requirements of justice that parents care for their children. I claim that the rights, privileges, and obligations of parenthood spring not from a biological blood tie, but from a social agreement (between a prospective parent and the moral community) that designates the adult as parent. Since this agreement requires consent on both sides (the community and the prospective parent), and since state disruption of family life after an initial social authorization of a parent can be extremely damaging to children, we have both an obligation and a serious interest in insuring that adults who seek the status of parent are at least minimally psychologically healthy, rational, and willing and able to provide continuous care for a child *before* we grant such a person the status of parent. I will refer to such minimally competent, willing, and able care

---

[1] Reprinted with permission from "Intergenerational Justice and Care in Parenting" in *Social Theory and Practice* , Volume 28, Number 4 (October 2002), pp. 667-677.
[2] Gilligan, Carol, *In a Different Voice: Psychological Theory and Women's Development* (Cambridge, MA, Harvard University Press, 1982).

providers as "good enough" parents. In essence, I am arguing for a right of the moral community (in the person of a legitimate state[3]) to license or certify adults as "good enough" parents. In the final section of my paper, I will look into the force that a particular loving parent-child relationship exerts on the desire for social justice.

2) The Myth of Blood-Rights: The Ownership Model and Parental Rights

We are beginning to awaken from a sort of moral nightmare with regard to our conception of the source of parental rights and obligations. For the great majority of the history of humankind, parenthood has been seen as a biological relationship which establishes the ownership of one human being (the biological parent) over another (taken to be) quasi-human being (the child). But this is surely an evil and morally hideous view.   Children, although they are not-yet-fully-autonomous rational beings, are certainly fully human persons. They are self-conscious beings with the potential for full rational autonomy. And I believe that if we can take anything as a fundamental moral truth, it is the idea that one person cannot "belong to" another in the sense of ownership. Although many people believe that there is a natural right of all persons to raise their biological children as they see fit, I see no justification for such a right. The phrase "Because I made it" may be able to justify a right to dispose of property, but it cannot do so for persons.

U.S. Courts and Legislatures demonstrate that our own society is seriously conflicted about the relationship between biological reproduction and parental rights. At least five states[4] have passed some sort of parental rights legislation in the past 10 years. And a Parental Rights Amendment has been introduced in more than half of the United States.[5]

---

[3] Although it seems to me that the legitimacy of a state might be grounded in the protection of "human rights", and/or political liberties, and/or in the consent of the governed (as evidenced in the institutions of democratic government), an attempt to spell out exact criteria for determining the legitimacy of a state is beyond the scope of this essay.

[4] Kansas, Michigan, Ohio, Oklahoma, and Utah all passed such legislation between 1994 and 1996. See Mack, D. (1997) *The Assault on Parenthood: How Our Culture Undermines the Family* (New York, NY, Simon and Schuster).

[5] It states quite simply (and rather ominously to my way of thinking), "The right of parents to direct the upbringing and education of their children shall not be infringed". It has been defeated in Kansas, North Dakota, Virginia, and Colorado with the help of child welfare advocates, educators (The NEA and PTA), children's

With Regard to the courts, consider the case of baby Richard in Illinois in 1995. His biological mother Daniella Janikova put him up for adoption four days after his birth and told his biological father, Otakar Kirchner that he had died. Although Otakar believed that the boy was alive, he did nothing to verify this belief until Daniella told him about her lie two months later. As Baby Richard had already been living with adoptive parents for almost fourteen months before the case got to trial, the best interests of the child came into apparent conflict with the rule of the myth of blood-rights. The court decisions in this case illustrate the internal conflict in the judicial system regarding the myth of blood-rights. After the lower court ruled that the adoption could proceed, Otakar appealed. In the appellate court, Justice Rizzi said:

> Fortunately, the time has long past when children in our society were considered the property of their parents. Slowly, but finally, when it comes to children even the law has rid itself of the Dred Scott mentality that a human being can be considered a piece of property "belonging" to another human being. To hold that a child is the property of his parents is to deny the humanity of the child. Thus, in the present case we start with the premise that Richard is not a piece of property with property rights belonging to either his biological or adoptive parents. Richard "belongs" to no one but himself....It is his best interest and corollary rights that come before anything else, including the interests and rights of biological and adoptive parents....The fact that we have the Adoption Act in Illinois is a recognition in the law that it takes more to being a parent than being one of the sexual partners to the physiological formation of a child.[6]

The Illinois Supreme Court, in its reversal, took a more conservative stand with regard to blood. Justice Heiple wrote:

> The adoption laws of Illinois are neither complex nor difficult of application. Those laws intentionally place the burden of proof on the adoptive parents in establishing both the relinquishment and/or unfitness of the natural parents and, coincidentally, the fitness and the right to adopt of the adoptive parents...These laws are designed to protect natural

---

rights groups (The ACLU), and health providers (AAPediatricics). See Mack, D. (1997) *The Assault on Parenthood: How Our Culture Undermines the Family* (New York, NY, Simon and Schuster).
[6] Goldstein, J., Solnit, A., Goldstein, S., and the late Anna Freud (1996) *The Best Interests of the Child: The Least Detrimental Alternative* (New York, NY, The Free Press), pp. 53-54.

parents in their preemptive rights to their own children wholly apart from any consideration of the so-called best interests of the child. [7]

There is no natural right to be a parent. I do not possess the right in abstraction from a social contract in which I am obliged to act as a "good enough" parent. This is the fundamental mistake of the myth of blood-rights: it implies that there is a right to parent that is founded upon, emanates from, or originates in biological reproduction. I recognize no such right. If the myth of blood-rights were really true, if it were really the case that all children which I sire "belong to me" and that I have the right to raise them "as I see fit", then all of our moral intuitions about the proper treatment of children would have to be rejected as mere sentimental or liberal claptrap. The fact that the acceptance of a principle like the myth of blood-rights would require us to abandon our most deeply held moral intuitions concerning children seems to me to be the strongest possible argument which could be made against any moral claim; it's as close as we get in ethics to a slam-dunk refutation.

Although I want to urge that biological relationship cannot by itself establish parental rights, we ought not to treat what is ordinarily an important human tie too lightly. For biological parents, the fact of having biologically produced a child usually produces an understandable sense of possessiveness and moral connection. But however understandable this is, it does not by itself justify a claim to parental rights over the child. It seems that *children* may understand the ground of functional/moral parenthood better than most adults do. They have no conception of biological relationships of blood. What they do know is that "Dad is the one who takes care of me"; that is, parents are identified as the adults who are authorized to care for the child on a day-to-day basis and to whom the child is attached. The designation of an adult as a parent need not be tied to blood at all. I take it that our positive moral appraisal of adoption by caring nonbiological parents and of the termination of the parental rights of unfit biological parents displays that biological reproduction is neither necessary nor sufficient for morally legitimate parenthood.

---

[7] Goldstein, J., Solnit, A., Goldstein, S., and the late Anna Freud (1996) *The Best Interests of the Child: The Least Detrimental Alternative* (New York, NY, The Free Press), pp. 59.

3) The Myth of the Autonomous Child: The Miniature Adult Model and Children's Rights

It cannot be the case that we ought to treat our children as fully autonomous beings. Indeed, it seems to me that it would be clearly wrong to do so. If my seven year-old son, Duncan chooses to eat a large bag of caramel candies for dinner and stay up past midnight, I would be failing in my duties as a parent if I simply accord to his wishes because he is a member of a species whose adult members are typically capable of guiding their lives according to the dictates of reason. Although children are persons, they are not merely miniature adults. They are not fully autonomous rational beings and it is wrong to treat them as if they are. It displays a lack of care (which is required by the social role of parent). Until my son is an adult (or until he displays the capacity to guide his life according to principles which are binding on all rational beings), my duty is to care for him and look out for his interests despite what he says he wants; paternalism is not necessarily a bad trait in parents.

As children become more and more able to function as rational agents, parents ought to allow them to become more and more free to participate in the development of the rules and decisions that govern family life. Part of shaping a person with the capacity for self-government is to allow him (in relatively safe situations) to make choices for himself. [8] These two (paternalism and limited and safe autonomy) do not necessarily conflict in the concrete practice of parenting. [9]

In *Equal Rights for Children*, Howard Cohen says,

---

[8] Actually, I think that parents sometimes overestimate their influence in shaping the lives of their children. In the context of the other influences on the child's future as a person (genetic inheritance, peer-influence, media-influence, etc.), parents have much less of an impact than they think. Judith Rich Harris attacks parents' inflated sense of their own power in her book (1998) *The Nurture Assumption: Why Children Turn Out the Way They Do* (New York, NY, The Free Press). Although I agree with her point that parents don't create their children in social isolation, I would stress that parents have special power over children due to the child's love and due to the law, and that they also have special responsibilities which peers, or educators do not have.

[9] I am bound by duties of justice to care for my son as a reasonable, well-informed caregiver: continuously providing resources, nutrition, shelter, education, and love, facilitating the achievement of a life-plan which has not yet taken shape. This requires that I take care to keep his options open, to foster an appreciation for what John Rawls calls the principles of rational choice, and, eventually, helping him to imaginatively realize various possible futures for himself, so that he can choose his own way in life.

Unless relevant differences can be demonstrated, it is not right to treat people differently; it is unjust. In my view the differences between adults and children have been overstated...Children are presumed to be weak, passive, mindless and unthinking; adults are presumed to be rational, highly motivated and efficient.[10]

Now I do not want to argue with Cohen's claims here. I think that it is true that children are underestimated to a great extent. Some individual children may display a greater sense of responsibility and rational control than I and most adults I know. But I don't think that we ought therefore to make the assumption that children are fully autonomous and rational beings from the moment of birth onwards. The law makes a strong distinction between adults and children. Adults are presumed to be responsible and capable of autonomously deciding what is in their own best interests, while children are presumed to be not-yet-competent, dependent and in need of continuous care by adults who are personally committed to assume such responsibility. And I think that these are the right presumptions to make. There are certainly cases in later childhood where persons who are legally children may legitimately want to exert their rights to control their own lives against their parents or others. But we don't want to be in a situation where children are presumed to be capable of deciding everything for themselves from the word go. Children process information, mark time, and experience separation very differently than adults. They need to be protected, provided for, and cared for. We don't want to move into a world of child-labor, child-marriage, and child-contracts. I hope these remarks give some indication of why and how I think it is appropriate that the community requires that parents *care for* their children as children (rather than merely treat them justly as miniature adults)

4) Pushed and Pulled: Parental Care as a Duty of Justice

So how does parenthood bind me? It binds me as a contract or promise to adopt any other role binds me. We require that parents care for their children much more than we require that they care for anonymous strangers, and this results from the fact that they have chosen to play and

---

[10] Cohen, H. (1980) "Children's Rights and Borrowed Capacities", excerpted from (1980) *Equal Rights for Children* (Totowa, NJ, Littlefield Adams), 56-61, reprinted in Houlgate, L. (ed.) (1999) *Morals, Marriage, and Parenthood: An Introduction to Family Ethics* (Belmont, CA, Wadsworth), pp. 217-219.

been accepted to play the social role of parent.[11] Interestingly enough for the inquiry into the relationship between justice and care, this role requires care.

In thinking about what it is we are bound to require of adults in order to certify them as "good enough" parents, we ought first to think about some of the requirements of care. These will include the ability to satisfy basic nutritional needs, provide shelter, protection, education, and to love the child. Love must be required because the modeling of love forms an essential part of the moral (or social) development of the individual. Displaying love in one's interactions with a child does not merely mean that I feel some sentimental affection for the little tike. By 'love' here, I mean a certain structure of relationship in which one takes an active and (intentionally, at least) life-long interest in the interests of the other, making the development (and happiness) of the other one of the central (as opposed to trivial) goals of one's life.

We might think of the obligations of parenthood as arising out of an intergenerational Rawlsian original position (IROP) in which rational deliberators are deprived of knowledge not only of their class, social status, natural characteristics, etc., but are also ignorant regarding to which generation they belong. It seems to me that questions of intergenerational justice can be very fruitfully pursued from such a standpoint.[12] What sort of rules about reproduction and parenting would rational deliberators choose in such a situation, given that they have a clear understanding of our best current scholarship on the needs of developing humans? Well, given that deliberators in an IROP would be deprived of knowledge of

---

[11] I want to point out that, although I claim that parental rights and duties arise from an agreement between "the moral community" (in the person of the state) and the prospective parent, the parental duty to care for a child (owed by a parent to the moral community (state)) is *not* merely a duty to reproduce a mindless follower of whatever the state policies happen to be.   Care cannot aim at producing good citizen-robots; its focus must necessarily be the real interests of the cared-for child as a person. Since the development of critical reasoning skills is required for the fulfillment of the potential autonomous personhood of any child, no parent who fails to aid her child in developing such skills can be said to be caring (well) for the child. I think it is helpful to keep in mind the difference between the *ground* of the parental duty to care (an agreement) and the *object* of such care (the child)

[12] I first encountered the idea of an IROP in David Richards' "Contractarian Theory, Intergenerational Justice, and Energy Policy", reprinted with permission in Michael D. Bayles and Kenneth Henley (eds.), *Right Conduct: Theories and Applications (Second Edition)* (New York, Random House, 1989), pp. 358-367; originally published in Douglas MacLean and Peter G. Brown (eds.), *Energy and the Future* (Totowa, NJ, Rowman and Littlefield, 1983), pp. 131-150.

their generation, they would not sanction a principle which allowed just anybody to become a parent with no demonstration of competence, rationality, information, resources, or, in general the ability to care. Surely, with even a tiny amount of information regarding human physiology and psychology, they would recognize the profound vulnerability of children, their complete dependence on adult caregivers for their protection. And they would also clearly see the damage that can result from bad, uncaring, or incompetent parenting. Given their mutual disinterest and their desire to guarantee for themselves an assured minimum of life-prospects, they would choose to protect themselves from bad parents. They would demand what we might want to call "good enough" parents. These are not perfect parents, but they demonstrate the minimal psychological health, competence, knowledge, resources, and capacity to care which would shield children from the most heinous acts of bad parenting.[13]

Persons do not have to demonstrate that they are perfect parents in order to be accorded the status of parent. Such a principle would not be adopted from within the framework of the IROP which I described. As any student of the human species can tell, humans usually derive a great deal of fulfillment from the process of parenting children; some find in it their greatest challenge and their greatest psychic rewards. Since rational deliberators in the original position would have access to this general knowledge about human psychology, they would recognize parenthood as a general good. Not wanting to forever deprive themselves of this good, they would surely reject any requirement that persons demonstrate that they would be perfect nurturers in order to be accorded the role of parent within society. As we all have our good and bad days, our strengths and our weaknesses, they could be absolutely certain to fall outside of the extension of the class of perfect parents. There are no such "perfect" creatures on the earth.

Humans, despite their vulnerability during childhood, are extremely adaptive creatures. As long as care and love are connected with reason

---

[13] Although I have adopted a Rawlsian standpoint from which to advance the claim that the moral community may legitimately restrict the class of persons who are allowed to act as parents, others have worked to offer alternative ethical-theoretical foundations for it. In "Do We Have an Unqualified Right to Parent?", a paper she delivered at the Pace University Center for Applied Ethics conference on *The Ethics of Parenting* in February, 1999, Bridget Newell offers a utilitarian argument for the legitimacy of the social restriction of parental rights to those who are "fit" parents. Although Newell utilizes a completely alien theoretical framework, she arrives at nearly the same policy conclusions as myself.

and information in parents, they will count as "good enough". Actually, it seems to me that what the moral community is bound to require is not the current possession of these capacities, but rather a demonstrated willingness to work to acquire them. If the moral community gets into the process of certifying persons as parents, we never want a person denied certification to be sincerely able to say to her estranged offspring something like, "They took you away from me and I had no choice in the matter". Rather we ought to construct requirements that would only allow one sincerely to say, "I failed to enter into or follow through on commitments to acquire parenting skills which rational deliberators would choose to require of any prospective parent".[14]

Our preference for maintaining the privacy of family life would be sanctioned by rational deliberators in an IROP. As Goldstein, Solnit and Freud recognize *in The Best Interests of the Child,*

> To safeguard the right of parents to raise their children...free of government intrusion, except in cases of neglect and abandonment, is to safeguard each child's need for continuity..[Our preference for minimal state intervention is reinforced by our recognition that] the law is

---

[14] Several colleagues have asked me about one possible consequence of taking my view seriously; I refer to this worry as "The supply and demand problem". Suppose that some persons biologically produce children that they have no ability, desire, or plan to parent. Wouldn't we then end up with billions of children without parents? That is, wouldn't the implementation of this view result in a severe rise in parentless children (an oversupply of children relative to the supply of "good enough parents")? In response, I would point to the social mechanisms we have already set up to insure that people procreate more responsibly; we require that persons who procreate but do not adopt (or are not allowed to adopt) the social role of parent pay child-support money to those who do stand in the role of parent to such children. Now, it's true that this has not been an ideal solution; many people do not pay these funds on time or at all. But that seems to me to be a result of weak and diffuse (decentralized) enforcement mechanisms rather than an indictment of the policy as such. I would advocate stricter and more centralized enforcement of child-support orders and penalties as a mechanism to provide a disincentive to the production of children toward which one has no intention of acting as parent. Although I believe that parental rights and duties flow from an agreement between a prospective parent and the moral community, people who voluntarily reproduce, but then refuse to (or are unable to, or are not certified to) act as parents still have duties to their offspring, *just not the duties of a parent.*

incapable of effectively managing, except in a very gross sense, so delicate and complex a relationship as that between parent and child. [15]

Rational deliberators in an IROP would recognize this fact and it would strengthen their insistence on taking steps to avoid the necessity of later state intervention by certifying the competence of prospective parents *before* they are designated as parents. They would also be aware of the fact that biological parents are typically emotionally tied to their biological children, and would take account of this fact by granting a sort of right of first refusal to biological parents. That is, they would sanction a rule which looks first to license biological parents, and only resorts to other competent caregivers when biological parents show inability *and* unwillingness to become certified as "good enough" parents.

In "Licensing Parents", Hugh Lafolette argues that just as we legitimately regulate other activities (like driving and practicing medicine), so we ought to regulate parenting. Our certification of competent doctors and lawyers and drivers is appropriate with regard to activities which are potentially harmful to others, require a certain level of competence to be done safely, and for which we have moderately reliable procedures for determining that competence.[16] Parenting badly is certainly potentially harmful to children. And we can identify at least some of the capacities and skills which "good enough" parents display. The only remaining question is whether we can reliably test for such skills and competencies.

Since I am not a psychologist, I don't feel qualified to (precisely) identify the kinds of qualities for which we ought to test in certifying parents. I have been more concerned to argue for the principle that parental rights are conferred by the moral community rather than by biological happenstance. But since the question arises about the sorts of things for which we ought to be testing prospective parents, I would say that what we are looking for includes minimal psychological health (the capacity to love and to work), legal competence, rationality, and either full relevant information regarding our most successful current scientific views about human development, education, and nurture, or (more realistically) a willingness to learn some such skills and information (as evidenced, e.g.,

---

[15] Goldstein, J., Solnit, A., Goldstein, S., and the late Anna Freud (1996) *The Best Interests of the Child: The Least Detrimental Alternative* (New York, NY, The Free Press), p. 7.

[16] Lafolette, H. (1980) "Licensing Parents", *Philosophy and Public Affairs* 9, 2 (1980): 183-197 Reprinted by permission of Princeton University Press in Houlgate, L. (ed.) (1999) *Morals, Marriage, and Parenthood: An Introduction to Family Ethics* (Belmont, CA, Wadsworth).

by participation in parenting-skills classes). I'm sure that adult and child psychologists, working from both ends can give us a much fuller picture of the properties for which we ought to be testing prospective parents. And if we do not already possess such specific knowledge, it would not be unrealistically difficult to construct a longitudinal study of many thousands of parents in order to determine which parental traits are correlated with children becoming psychologically healthy, well-adapted, socially integrated adults.

As Lafollette points out, we already do this sort of testing for prospective adoptive parents. Before we authorize their adoption of a child, we conduct extensive psychological testing, interviews, home visits, etc.. Could it be that this certification of minimal parental competence in adoption cases has anything to do with the fact that biological parents abuse their children at a rate approximately five times that of adoptive parents?![17] The law must make the child's needs paramount. It is in society's best interests to do so. Each time the cycle of grossly inadequate parent - child relationships is broken, society stands to gain a person more likely to be capable of becoming a "good enough" parent for children of the future. Thus, we very likely avoid a whole chain of abusive and unhealthy parent-child relationships that would lead to a socially dysfunctional future.[18]

---

[17] Lafolette, H. (1980) "Licensing Parents", *Philosophy and Public Affairs* 9, 2 (1980): 183-197 Reprinted by permission of Princeton University Press in Houlgate, L. (ed.) (1999) *Morals, Marriage, and Parenthood: An Introduction to Family Ethics* (Belmont, CA, Wadsworth), p. 205.

[18] One anonymous reviewer worried about the possibility that people who were certified but then later turned out to be very bad parents, could use the fact of their certification as protection from scrutiny of their bad parenting practices. I want to say here that we shouldn't make the perfect the enemy of the good. Because of the privacy of the family, it's already true that it's very difficult to reliably recognize report, and respond to the ongoing abuse and neglect of children by their parents. I want to present the certification of parents before they are granted parental rights as an *addition to (not a replacement of)* our existing laws about abuse and neglect. Would such a system result in the complete elimination of bad parenting (i.e., by people who have been certified)? Certainly not! But it might help to reduce the incidence of bad parenting. And, as a lucky accident, it might turn out that an explicit recognition of the moral status of parents (as deriving their only legitimate parental powers from the moral community in the first place) would make other people more willing to report cases of what appears to them to be abuse and/or neglect.

5) It Takes a Village: The Reciprocal Demands of Justice and Care

The bonds of love impact us in ways that extend far beyond the nursery. Not only is it the case that the abstract roles I adopt as a person determine my obligations to care for my child, but the concrete and specific relationship of care which develops between me and my child determines, (to some extent) my responsibility to demand and work toward social (especially intergenerational) justice. The force of my love for another specific person necessarily demands that I take steps to insure that the society of which I am a member foster a future in which my son can thrive. This follows from my definition of love as including taking an active and intentionally life-long central interest in the interests of the other. Since in order to love my son, I have to care about his future, I also have to care about intergenerational justice. If, through a political process, I participate in the use of resources which are borrowed from his generation in order to give my own generation a bigger piece of the intergenerational pie than he will ever get, then I cannot be said to be loving him. Thus, the lines of moral force work both ways. The parent as moral person is bound by justice to care for the child and the parent as parent is bound by love to work towards intergenerational social justice.

The demand for intergenerational social justice, which ought to be generated in us by the love of our children (as well as by other factors), should extend to intragenerational justice as well: we are all social creatures, and no family can live in a social or political vacuum. So if love requires that I take an active and intentionally life-long central interest in the interests of the other, then my love for my son imposes a responsibility on me to take an interest in the kind of society in which my son will one day live. But that society can only be made up of individuals, Duncan's future colleagues, friends, fellow citizens, etc.. Loving Duncan requires that I take an interest in their future selves. But that requires that I care about the influences that are shaping them today into the persons they will be tomorrow. And of course, this includes their parenting. I am required to take care that they are being parented by "good enough" parents and that those parents have the resources and assistance to give their children an environment in which they will develop into healthy, productive, and morally upstanding people. [19] If I really love my son, in other words, I must care about the socialization of his future fellows.

---

[19] Our duties regarding children stem from the fact that we have been recognized in the adoption of certain roles which give us duties beyond those we would

Finally, let me return to the question of the interrelation of the ethics of justice and the ethics of care. Of course, even childless people who love nobody have abstract duties to work towards intergenerational and intragenerational social justice. But for me these duties are brought home by my love for my real bodily son, Duncan. Love, it is true, is an abstract project. It involves a conscious attention to the objective life-long interests of the other. But love is also something into which I am drawn. The bonds of love tie me almost against my will. And it is the day-to-day interaction with another particular person named Duncan that strengthens those bonds. For me and for those with similar bonds, love is not abstract at all. It is a force that calls to us and calls us forward towards justice. [20]

---

ordinarily have toward such beings. Certainly, I have duties not to destroy or injure children for whom other adults have been designated as parent, but I have no perfect Kantian duties qua rational being, to be a parent to them. If I have special perfect duties regarding children, they must arise from the various roles I adopt beyond the fact of my autonomous agency (e.g., my roles as citizen, as neighbor, as teacher, as father, and so on).

[20] Originally presented at the Pace University Center for Applied Ethics conference on *The Ethics of Parenting*, February 1999 under the title, "The Parent as Person and as Parent". I am grateful to the conference participants for their helpful comments and questions. I would also like to thank Walt Fuchs, Wing-Chun Wong, Jo-Ann Pilardi, Rose Ann Christian, Gary Backhaus, John Bova, Elaine Scales, and two anonymous reviewers from *Social Theory and Practice* for their helpful suggestions and encouragement.

HO, HO, HOAX:
SANTA CLAUS AND PARENTAL DECEPTION

ERNANI MAGALHAES

1. A Tempting Argument

A simple argument seems to show that a central component of one of the most cherished and widespread family traditions is morally wrong.
(1)   Lying is wrong.
(2)   A parent's telling her child there is a Santa Claus is a lie.
(3)   Therefore, a parent's telling her child there is a Santa Claus is wrong.
The fact that the modern incarnation of the Christmas tradition involves deception has long troubled both critics and participants. Along with cold weather, each December brings with it spirited criticisms and equally strenuous defenses of Santa in major publications. It seems to many at odds with plain human morality to deceive a child about the existence of a being the child is intended to love. It seems to many especially at odds with the specific duties of parents to lie to their children in this way. What is more important to being a good parent than maintaining the trust of one's children? And what can be more likely to undermine this trust than lying to them?

But the simple argument is not successful as it stands. One problem is that (1) is ambiguous. (3) follows from (1) and (2) if (1) asserts that lying is *always* wrong. But lying is not always wrong. *Pace* Immanuel Kant (1978), it is permissible to lie to a murderer seeking my mother about her whereabouts. Nor does it help to think of (1) as asserting that lying is usually wrong. Even if most lies are wrong, it at best follows that the Santa Claus lie is likely one of the wrong ones.

What is involved in the wrongness of lying, anyway? The wrongness of lying can be understood in a number of different ways. From a consequentialist perspective, one might think that lying is wrong because it tends to bring about such bad effects as undermining trust, alienation, and a sense of grievance in the deceived. From a Kantian perspective less rigid than Kant's, one might hold that lying is wrong because it violates the autonomy of the person deceived. The deceived is manipulated into believing something in a way that violates her capacity to decide for herself what to believe. And there are many other options. The basic claim of the paper—that parents ought not to lie to their children about Santa—does not depend on adopting any one of these conceptions. That said, it will be helpful to work within the framework of a specific account which captures well our ordinary sense of the wrongness of lying. We have, according to W. D. Ross, a *prima facie* duty to act (or not act) in certain ways. We have, for example, a *prima facie* duty to keep our promises and not to hurt others. S has a *prima facie* duty to do K when, other things being equal, S ought to do K.[1] In other words, a *prima facie* duty to do K has a tendency to make a K action morally right. According to Ross, we have the *prima facie* duty not to lie (1988: 19). Since there are other *prima facie* duties—including the duty of beneficence to promote overall happiness and the duty of non-maleficence not to harm others—the *prima facie* obligation not to lie may be overcome by these other duties. There is a presumption that lying is wrong, which does not entail that lying is always or even usually wrong. To see how this theory works, notice that any particular action is of a number of different kinds. Consider a mother's telling her child that Santa is bringing the child gifts. That specific act is an instance of lots of different kinds of acts. It seems to be an instance of a lie, because the mother encourages the child to believe something the mother does not believe. It may be an instance of a promise kept, because the mother has promised her husband to tell the child about Santa's gift-giving. It may be an instance of someone's well-being being promoted, because the child will enjoy the prospect of Santa coming with gifts. According to Ross, since lying is *prima facie* wrong, there is a *prima facie* reason not to tell a child about Santa. But this *prima facie* strike against Santa may be overcome by other morally significant considerations—other types that the action falls under, such as promoting the child's well-being and keeping a promise.

So I take (1) to claim
  (1*) Lying is *prima facie* wrong.

This handles one problem with the argument. But the argument is still invalid. To get from the *prima facie* wrongness of lying to the wrongness of a parent's lie to her child about Santa, it must be the case that other

---

[1] This is also now often called a *"pro tanto"* duty.

moral considerations do not outweigh the presumption against lying. The other moral considerations mainly involve the duties specific to being a child's parent. The moral question raised by the Santa Claus tradition involves not just anyone's lying to children but *parents'*[2] lying to *their* children.[3] It often happens that whether it is permissible to do a certain thing to someone depends on who the agent is and who the patient is. Whether it is permissible to do a certain thing to a child surely depends in many cases on whether the agent is the child's parent. It is not permissible (generally) for a stranger to compel a certain young child to go to school. It is permissible for that child's parents to compel the child to go to school. Thus the question of whether it is appropriate for parents to lie to their children about Santa will depend on an understanding of how parents ought to relate to their children. I will shortly sketch a model of parental duties and show that these duties are not served by, and indeed often conflict with, lying to children about Santa. Thus I will show that there are no other morally significant benefits that wipe away the moral stain of the fact that telling children about Santa is a lie.

But is telling children about Santa really a lie? I must pause here to consider this objection.

2. Lying and Pretending

It might seem not only false but question-begging to characterize the Santa Claus story as a lie. The word has a negative moral connotation that suggests if something is a lie then it must be wrong. I admit it would be question-begging to describe the Santa story as a lie if it were an analytic truth that lying is wrong.[4] Then to say that the story is a lie would analytically imply that it is wrong. And I would be implicitly claiming that telling children there is a Santa is wrong in describing doing so as lying. But even though lying is *prima facie* wrong, it is not a conceptual truth that lying is wrong. To see this, note that the concept of a white lie is perfectly intelligible. (Indeed, there are white lies.) Contrast in this respect lying and murder. There are no "white" murders. Part of the concept of a murderous act is that it is wrong. It would be incoherent to suppose

---

[2] Although I continue to write of parents, I really have in mind caregivers in general, rather than biological parents specifically.
[3] I assume it is frequently morally appropriate for a child's caregiver or parent to exert authority in order for the child to acquire certain traits. I also assume that the domain of this authority is not unlimited: there are significant restrictions on how a parent or caregiver may morally rear her child.
[4] That is, roughly, the meaning of "is a lie" includes "is wrong."

something was a permissible murder. Describing an act as a lie, therefore, unlike describing it as murder, does not by itself entail that the act is wrong.

But even if it does not beg the question, it may still be false to claim that telling children about Santa is lying. Tales from fiction, admittedly, are not lies. Adults do not lie in telling children about Red Riding Hood or Snow White. But descriptions of Santa Claus are not fiction in the sense that typical descriptions of Red Riding Hood are. The difference between a fictional story and a lie is in the intention of the speaker. A fictional story involves pretending that something is the case (see Walton 1990): imagining that Red Riding Hood is walking through the forest or making believe that Snow White is meeting the prince. If the intention is successfully recognized, the audience does not believe but only imagines that Red Riding Hood is walking through a forest. The intention of a person who lies is not to get the hearer's imagination to work, but to get her beliefs to work. The assertion of P is a lie when the person who asserts P intends for her audience to believe P even though the person does not believe P herself. The parent who tells her child about Red Riding Hood does not believe Red Riding Hood is walking through the forest. But the parent does not lie since she has no intention that the child will come to believe this either. The parent who tells her child about Santa Claus also does not believe in Santa. But in the case of Santa the parent does intend that the child will believe he is real. Since the parent does not believe what she says yet intends for the child to believe, the parent lies.[5] In fact, psychological research confirms that the different intentions are recognized by children, who typically still think Santa Claus is real after they recognize that such fictional characters as Red Riding Hood are not (Sharon and Wooley 2004).

There are stages in a child's development when, although she is able to believe and disbelieve various propositions, she is unable to distinguish fact and fiction. There are points in the child's development when she simply lacks a concept of fiction or pretense. Presumably, a child who is unable to adopt the pretense attitude involved in fiction, and who is told about Red Riding Hood, will believe what she is told no matter what the parent's intention. Does a parent who tells this child about Red Riding

---

[5] Nathan Schluetter objects that the Santa tale is not a lie because "its intention is not deception, or to lead children into error" (2005: 12). Schluetter is right that perhaps the ultimate or main aim is not to deceive or lead the child into error. As I discuss below, parents believe worthwhile goals are promoted by the tradition. But deception and error are clearly among the aims of the tale, since, again, the parent intends to get the child to believe something the parent does not.

Hood lie? More significantly, does a parent who tells this child about Santa lie? It is not easy to say, but fortunately for my purposes I don't need to say. I propose we restrict our consideration to cases of children who clearly are able to distinguish fact and fiction. In very many cases, the child who is told about Santa is at an age that she is able to distinguish reality and make-believe. At that stage, there is clearly an option available to the parent. She can tell stories about Santa in a way that does not encourage the child to believe that he exists.

3. Parental Duties

The question I'm interested in is whether parents do the right thing when they lie to their children about Santa Claus. The way I propose to get at this question is to consider what parents ought, and ought not, to do in relation to their children. I will not be concerned with the more frequently discussed question about what rights children have. One reason for this is that the issue of children's rights is most immediately relevant to the issue of the circumstances in which it is legitimate for the government to interfere with a parent's childrearing choices. But my concern is not with the government at all. It is only with whether it is morally permissible to tell children about Santa Claus. The issue of the permissibility of the Santa lie is neither here nor there with respect to the issue of whether the government may legitimately prevent parents from telling their kids about Santa. (Although, I should say I believe that it would be a clear abuse of power for the government to forbid parents from telling their kids about Santa.) The question of children's rights is only relevant insofar as a child's right to such and such might imply a duty on the parent's part to ensure that a child has such and such. Since the ultimate aim is to understand what parents ought to do, I will focus on the duties of parents—those obligations that account for why parents ought to treat their children in certain ways.

Accounts of parental duties may be either minimalist or maximalist. According to a maximalist account, which I will endorse here, the parent has a duty to ensure the child's flourishing in a number of different domains, physical, emotional, psychological, and moral. According to the maximalist, the duty of the parent is to both take care of the child's basic needs and encourage the child's acquisition of many of the various qualities that are desirable for a human being to have. The minimalist holds that the main duty of the parent—beyond providing for the child's basic physical needs—is to ensure that the child has the rational capacities necessary for making autonomous decisions. On this account, the parent's main job is not to steer the child in any particular direction, but simply to give her the tools to decide for herself the direction in which she would like to go. The parent's main job, in other words, is to ensure that the child will have as many options as possible open to her when she is an adult.[6] On the more robust conception, autonomy is but one of a number of valuable psychological traits a parent ought to promote in her child. Maximalism concedes that the capacity to choose rationally among alternatives is an important skill. But it insists that more important than having many options open to one is making the right choice among those options. Note that the substance of my argument would not be altered by adopting the more minimal account of parental duties. There is no reason to suppose that telling children about Santa Claus tends to promote a child's autonomy. A child who is told about Santa is not thereby one who will have more life options open to her. Indeed, one reason why I adopt the maximalist view is that this conception provides an intelligible framework for understanding the motivation behind many of the pro-Santa arguments.

At the most general level, a child may flourish[7] either physically or psychologically.[8] A parent has an obligation to ensure that her child is at least provided with the basic physical necessities of food, shelter, and medical care. A parent also has an obligation, within reason, to promote the child's health and physical abilities beyond this minimal level. A parent's duty to promote her child's psychological well-being includes the duties to promote the child's emotional, intellectual, and moral flourishing. A parent ought to ensure that the child is emotionally healthy, intellectually competent, and morally virtuous. That different parents are bound to have different ideas about what is involved in having these traits in no way detracts from the parent's duty to promote them. Similarly, that there are

---

[6] See the literature on Feinberg's notion of a "right to an open future" (Feinberg 1980): Morgan (2005), Hasman and Holm (2004), and Mills (2004).

[7] "Flourish" is sufficiently flexible to capture the different sorts of goods whose possession by the child it is plausible to suppose the parent has a duty to promote. The parent ought to rear a child in such a way as to increase the likelihood that the child will behave morally. The parent also ought to rear a child in such a way as to increase the likelihood that the child will have a good life. The goodness involved in a good life is not obviously the same as that involved in doing what is right.

[8] Arguably, in addition to inducing the child to acquire certain physical and psychological characteristics, a good parent is also one who has some affection toward her child. A parent who (somehow) succeeded in producing a virtuous, healthy, intelligent child but who felt completely indifferent toward her well-being would seem to be a bad parent. I will not consider this requirement further because it is farfetched to suppose one cannot feel affection for one's child without encouraging the Santa Claus deception.

different ideas about just what the virtue of honesty requires in no way detracts from an individual's obligation to be honest.

It is almost a tautology to say that the most important of the psychological domains is moral flourishing. Indeed, the goal of promoting a child's moral capacities constrains the pursuit of the other two psychological goals. The good parent does not aim to promote just any emotion in the child, or even some wide range of emotions. Not all emotions are equally important for a child's flourishing. A good parent need not promote jealousy in the child at all, for example. And while it is clearly good to encourage the child to be sympathetic, it is good mainly because of the role of sympathy in a virtuous human being's life. Sympathy is worth developing to a large extent because it is conducive to leading a morally upright life.

The same is not entirely true of intellectual flourishing. Becoming more intelligent seems to be intrinsically beneficial, even though obviously intelligence may not always be used for just ends. A child flourishes intellectually when she has a fairly accurate conception of the world, has judicious reasoning abilities, and is able to reflect to some extent independently of the influence of others. Analytical reasoning and assimilating facts are conducive to these aspects of intellectual flourishing. Reasoning well, arguably, is not only beneficial as a means to leading a more moral or good life, but is also intrinsically valuable.

Where does the Santa Claus deception fit into these parental goals? Lying is *prima facie* wrong. So there is a *prima facie* case against the permissibility of telling one's child about Santa. The practice could be justified, nonetheless, if it could be shown to be conducive to fulfilling some of these parental duties. And this is in fact the spirit in which the Santa tradition is generally defended. It is said to help keep kids "nice" rather than "naughty", enhance their imagination or sense of magic, and so forth. But there is a general argument that parental lying has little or no place in the pursuit of these goals. The pursuit of the child's flourishing in any of these domains requires a trusting relationship between the parent and child. It is difficult if not impossible to acquire this relationship if the child does not have confidence in her parent. The confidence must rest ultimately on a track record of reliability. It is a mere platitude that lying undermines trust. The child who is lied to about Santa Claus is less likely to trust her parent. Indeed, the child who is lied to about Santa is a bit more likely to lie herself. [9] As John Locke wisely recommended to parents,

[9] Although the influence of Santa deception has not been tested specifically, psychologists conclude on the basis of some correlations between parental and child honesty or dishonesty that "[i]t seems quite likely that children repeatedly

Chapter Three

"[y]ou must do nothing before [the child], which you would not have him imitate" (Locke 1989). [10] These consequences of lying about Santa show that in order for the practice to be justified, it must be not only beneficial; it must be sufficiently beneficial to redeem the harm of undermining filial trust and encouraging a child to deceive.

If Santa deceit is justified it must be because of its tendency to promote one or more of these parental goals. Evidently, the goal of promoting physical flourishing is not relevant. If Santa deceit has a place in good parenting it must be as a means to promoting the child's psychological flourishing. But how is the Santa fib supposed to promote either intellectual, moral, or emotional flourishing in the child?

4. Intellectual and Emotional Flourishing

It might seem the deck is unfairly stacked against justifying Santa. Psychological flourishing has been identified in terms of emotional, moral, and intellectual flourishing. And these, in turn, may seem to essentially involve the promotion of a set of adult aptitudes in the child. On this interpretation, the goal of parenting is to make good adults out of children. But, the objection goes, there is more to proper childrearing than making children into good adults. The parent should also promote attitudes, tendencies, and experiences that are appropriate to the child that need not assist the child in becoming a good adult. A good parent should encourage a child to play, for example. The parent should encourage the child to play even if playing weren't conducive to the child's acquiring the possession of valuable adult traits. The moral value of the Santa Claus tradition, the objection continues, is to be found precisely in this realm of childhood-specific virtues. Cynthia Clark (1995: 44), for example, suggests that Santa deceit promotes the age-appropriate cognitive virtue of faith. According to Clark, belief in the absence of evidence, such as is supposedly found in the child's attitude toward Santa, is beneficial for a child even if it is not a virtue for an adult. In his famous "Yes, Virginia, There Is a Santa Claus" editorial, Francis Church identifies the relevant cognitive virtue promoted by Santa deceit as "childlike faith." By ignoring

---

exposed to parental honesty or dishonesty will imitate the behavior their parents model" (Eisenberg and Valiente 2002: 120).

[10] As psychologists Diana Baumrind and Ross Thompson note, "Truth telling is such a difficult discipline to acquire, and the principle of veracity has such utility in social life that parents need to act as models especially when it is awkward or uncomfortable to tell their child the truth" (2002: 13).

this realm of childhood-specific virtues, the objection concludes, my conception ignores the most plausible justification of Santa deceit.

No doubt a good parent is not necessarily one who does her utmost to accelerate the process of producing a good adult out of her child. There are tendencies that are mainly beneficial only for children, and which ought to be promoted even if they are unlikely to bring about any aptitudes that are valuable for adults. Indeed, one part of being a good parent is encouraging the child to have no-strings-attached fun. And it is undeniable that young children enjoy the fruits of believing in Santa. But this aspect of good parenting is encompassed by my conception, which speaks of flourishing in general, not just of that flourishing which is likely to bring about a good adult. Playing should be promoted because it is conducive to a child's emotional flourishing, even if it is not conducive to the future adult's flourishing.

In addition to faith, Clark sees wonder and awe as among the psychological benefits of the Santa experience. The child finds Santa Claus' existence and activities fantastic and remarkable. Faith, wonder, and awe are attitudes often associated with the experience of the divine. It has been rightly noted (e.g., Breen 2004) that children often associate Santa with God—Santa knows all, he is completely benevolent, and works in mysterious ways. Many agree with Clark that this sort of quasi-religious experience is beneficial for children. Since these traits straddle the boundary between the intellectual and emotional, perhaps Santa deception is justified because it promotes the child's age-appropriate intellectual *cum* emotional flourishing.

Let's first consider faith. Faith involves believing something for which one lacks evidence, or even something that conflicts with one's evidence. Whether faith is beneficial for a child or not, it is clear that the child's attitude toward Santa is not a case of faith. What could be more reasonable than believing something that is attested by the entire adult world—weathermen, teachers, neighbors—and confirmed by such hard facts as the missing cookies and empty glasses of milk found on Christmas morning? Nor is it necessary for the child to "suspend disbelief", as Breen claims (2004: 456), in order to think of Santa as performing his extraordinary feats. Suspending disbelief about something means not believing but rather imagining that the something is occurring. Although suspension of disbelief is clearly essential to a child's flourishing, there is no hint of it in the child's attitude toward Santa. The suspension of disbelief is something that happens within the context of pretense. Pretense involves imagining something one does not believe is real. But the child does not pretend there is a Santa Claus—she believes. It is the parent who would need to suspend disbelief to imagine Santa Claus traveling to every child in one night. The child believes this is both possible and actual.

Concerning awe and wonder, the association between God and Santa in children's minds makes Santa deceit especially problematic for religious believers. Stipulate that religious parents believe wonder and awe to be worthwhile attitudes for children. The religious parent has an appropriate object for wonder and awe: God, or whatever divine entity or entities she worships. If the parent intends for the child ultimately to feel wonder and awe toward God, why not encourage the child to experience wonder and awe toward God? Indeed, encouraging them to feel wonder toward Santa is problematic since children who discover the truth about Santa often come to question God as well.

Non-religious parents do not experience wonder and awe toward any supernatural entity. They may, nonetheless, consistently believe that wonder and awe are elements of a child's intellectual *cum* emotional flourishing. On this view, wonder and awe toward the supernatural is an appropriate attitude for a child but not for an adult. The popularity of this view seems like an appealing anthropological explanation for the ubiquity of the Santa Claus tradition even among secular parents. Although they do not find themselves able to adopt the attitude of wonder and awe (toward the supernatural), secular parents understand the appeal of such an experience. Indeed, perhaps *because* their intellectual milieu makes it untenable for secular parents to adopt these attitudes, it is all the more tempting to experience the attitudes vicariously by encouraging them in their children.

But this is armchair explanation, not moral justification. A careful consideration of the child's actual attitude toward Santa shows that there is no element of it that is specifically intellectually beneficial. Wonder and awe are reactions toward a being that is perceived to be remarkable, majestic, or unusually powerful. Consider just the sense that Santa Claus is magical. The magical *per se* is that which defies ordinary explanation. Something can be conceived to be magical and good, magical and neutral, or magical and bad. If believing that magical things are afoot is good, there must be an element of goodness in thinking something is magical and neutral or magical and bad. But no one will seriously argue that it is beneficial for the child to believe that there is an evil magical structure to the world. In fact, rather than mitigating its apparent threat, believing that an evil is magical has a tendency to increase the threat. So what is really believed to be beneficial in the child's attitude toward Santa is the fact that Santa is thought to be magical and *good*. It is not Santa's magic that is appealing, but his goodness. Is believing there is an extraordinarily good being in the world conducive to the child's emotional or intellectual flourishing—age-appropriate or otherwise? It is no doubt pleasant for the child to believe there is this benevolent force. Of course it is beneficial, even necessary, for the child to have confidence that she is loved and will be cared for, but it is doubtful whether there is any deep intellectual *cum* emotional benefit in believing in an extraordinary benevolent force such as Santa.

But perhaps the belief in Santa's benevolent force has beneficial effects for the child's moral development. I now turn to effects of Santa belief on the child's moral development.

5. Moral Flourishing

The justification of the Santa Claus deception that most frequently comes up in conversation appeals to the supposedly beneficial moral influence of the experience on the child. The experience is supposed to make the child more virtuous in various ways. Santa is said to watch children to see whether they are naughty or nice and parents sometimes cajole their children to be nice by warning that Santa will not bring them gifts otherwise. But it is doubtful whether Santa belief has a salutary moral influence in this way. In addition to the fact that parents do not generally follow through on their Santa-related threats, outsourcing reward and punishment to Santa seems to be a bad idea, anyway. Psychologists have found that in order to be effective, punishment should closely follow the inappropriate behavior and be accompanied by an explanation of why the behavior is inappropriate (Parke 2002: 597). Santa's punishment satisfies neither of these conditions. Moreover, part of the point of punishment and reward is to foster a certain kind of mutually respectful relationship between human beings (Bugental and Grusec 2006: 402); the child will recognize that other human beings have boundaries that should not be crossed. Deferring moral authority to Santa in no way fosters such relationships.

Santa Claus is also a gift-giver, and it may seem that the tradition is justified by the beneficial moral effects of this trait. The thought is that since children admire Santa Claus they will mimic his generosity. Wonder and awe are relevant here, since having these feelings toward Santa may be thought to be beneficial because they make it more likely that children will strive to mimic Santa's generous behavior. But empirical research has failed to uncover any correlation between participation in the Santa Claus tradition and increased generosity among children (Dixon and Hom 1984).

And it stands to reason that there would be no impact. Children are not encouraged to be generous during the tradition. The tradition may even encourage a certain misplaced confidence in children that they need not worry about others, since Santa Claus will take care of them.

In sum, Santa Claus deceit is not conducive to any of the goals of good parenting. But this leaves the parent convinced by my argument with a difficult problem. Even if it is wrong to lie about Santa, the practice is extremely widespread, and parents who choose not to must decide what to tell their children. If children are told there is no Santa, it may seem difficult to prevent their spoiling the fun for other children. I believe this problem, though delicate, is overstated. It is fundamentally the problem of minority families: children of non-religious families or families whose religion differs from that of the majority face the similar problem of determining how to prepare the child for a world that does not share her beliefs. The key to solving the problem in all these cases is a virtue often thought to be encouraged by Santa deceit. Children must be encouraged to be tolerant of others' beliefs and values, even when those beliefs are not their own.[11]

[11] Many thanks to Danny Shapiro, Matt Talbert, an audience at the "Ethics in the Family" conference, and especially Lisa Wellinghoff for challenging and illuminating discussions. I owe a special debt of gratitude to my (then future) mother-in-law Judy Wellinghoff, whose skepticism about the kind of person who would be Scroogish enough to question telling kids about Santa inspired me to write this paper.

Moral Children

Wade L. Robison

I begin with a story:

I was shopping when I heard, "You're a witch! You're a witch!" I looked around the corner and saw two children in a shopping cart. In the seat was a pretty little girl, 18 months to 2 years, dressed in a frilly dress, tears just starting to form. Sitting in the cart itself was a little boy, perhaps 3 or a little older, well-dressed as well. He was looking up at his sister, saying over and over, in a soft voice, "You're a witch! You're a witch!"

The mother suddenly appeared around the corner of the aisle and said, "Stop it! Stop it! I told you not to do that to your sister!" The little boy looked stunned. "But they're only words! They're only words!" The mother looked exasperated. "I don't care! Stop it! You're making your sister cry." She gave him one last look as he looked up, all innocence. Then she turned and went back down the aisle. I could count the beats: A one, a two, a three, and the little boy began to sing, "You're a witch, you're a witch, you're a witch!" The little girl burst out crying. The mother burst around the corner. "Stop it!! I told you to stop it!!" The little boy looked hurt. "I'm singing!! I'm just singing!" What a clever little boy! A budding Attila the Hun. It is easy to see the nature of his moves:

Move #1: "Sticks and stone can break my bones, but words can never hurt me." If he is just talking, what is the harm?

Move #2: And who can object to a child singing a song? Songs bring joy to life! And he was singing. How could any parent object?

These are both moral moves—diabolical, to be sure, and very clever, but, still, excuses that, were they the whole truth, would parry his mother's moral criticism. He is purposefully causing his sister to cry and then, caught out, responds by noting how really harmless his talking is and how beneficial his singing is. He is saying, "You complained when I was just talking. So I'm going to do something good, something you can't complain about at all but ought to compliment"—in response to your complaint—"and sing." What is a mother to do with a son like that?!

If we pay attention, we shall find small children constantly making moral moves—sympathetic responses to the crying of other children, a tearful insistence that "It's not fair!" There is even moral correction. Another little girl in a cart in a grocery store apparently could not think of the name of what she wanted to be for Halloween. Her mother was going through possibilities as the little girl got more and more frustrated. Finally the mother said, "Oh! I know! You want to be a fireman!" The little girl said, "Not a fireman! A fire woman!!"

I think we should take these moves for what they could be. I do not say "what they are" because I am not appealing to empirical research here. My evidence is generally anecdotal, but I think its power is that it will resonate with any parent, anywhere. What parent has not been met with a child's insistent "That's not fair!" as the parent tried, or not, to be even-handed with the children.

I have three theses to hawk:

Children, even small children, are perfectly capable of giving moral reasons for what they do. Whatever we may think of the reasons that young boy gave, they are the right kind of reason. They would exonerate him if he were only doing what he says he is doing.

We should encourage them to give reasons for what they do, or fail to do, and to give the proper kinds of reasons.

We should continue to do this throughout their childhood and through their school years.

These theses look simple, but they are not. There is a theory of child-rearing buried in the first, a theory about the developmental stages of children in the second, and a theory of education in the third.

The theory of child-rearing presupposes that, as has been said, children are like experimental scientists, trying out things to learn their limits and the limits of the world, both natural and social. They are not necessarily doing this intentionally, but they are doing it, they are learning, and their pushing on the limits of their world includes the moral limits. We should begin, however, with the assumption that they are not learning everything, but come to the world as young children with moral sensibilities at least as highly developed as young chimpanzees and bonobos—with the capacity for a sympathetic response to the plight of others, for instance.

We should take advantage of this experimental mode by providing them with reasons for the behavior we wish them to engage in and the behavior we wish them to avoid, with reasons, that is, both for why they are being chastised and for how they are being asked to behave. It is a tonal matter as much as anything else. Giving reasons and letting reasons rule your life requires a reasoned manner, a reasoned tone of voice, among other things, not "Stop it!! Stop it!!" or "Because I say so." Neither is the appropriate kind of reason to provide a child if we are to engage them in the process of creating an ethical life. Our aim ought not to be just to have children stop behaving badly. Our aim ought to be that they learn why the limits of morality are what they are with the aim of internalizing moral norms and, more importantly, internalizing the concept that moral behavior can be reasoned. We ought to model and to teach by the manner in which we respond to their moral experimentation.

This sort of response on our part ought to continue throughout their education so that they will, we hope, continue throughout their lives to reason. We ought to be concerned with teaching students how to reason and solve problems. We should want them to learn a methodology that allows them to think through problems to the truth and forces them to provide reasons for their results. The aim thus ought to be to develop just those categories for reasoning illustrated by that little boy in the cart, but to encourage their development to help a potential Attila the Hun become, if not a Gandhi, at least an essentially moral person.

I will concentrate here only on the first claim I have made, that children have the capacity for moral behavior and briefly argue that they also have the capacity to give moral reasons for what they do. I will begin by comparing the behavior of children with that of chimpanzees and bonobos. The underlying argument will be that if members of our extended family can evince moral behavior, children can too.

§1. Bonobos and Chimpanzees

Frans de Waal has written extensively about the social, political and, yes, moral lives of chimpanzees and bonobos. It may seem strange to think that such animals have social, political, and moral lives, but one cannot help but be struck, in reading Chimpanzee Politics, by how close to our political lives the chimpanzees' political lives seem and by how the criteria for a successful leader is what we would hope for in one of ours—the capacity to end disputes before they escalate into potentially harmful confrontations and the capacity to do so with an even hand, without playing favorites.[1]

---

[1] Frans de Waal, *Our Inner Ape* (New York: Riverhead Books, 2005), pp. 54 & 82. See also Frans de Waal, *Chimpanzee Politics*, revised edition (Baltimore: Johns Hopkins Press, 1982), esp. p. 118.

What is perhaps more compelling are the anecdotes de Waal provides of what for all the world we would call moral behavior. To give the moral status of these anecdotes their due, we should think of what we are doing here as gathering observational material for later theoretical work. John Rawls speaks of creating a theory of justice through working out a reflective equilibrium. On my understanding of this view, we start with our initial judgments about what is just and then work out a theory that explains and justifies those judgments, modifying the theory and rejecting some judgments and accepting others we originally had not noted. As we reflect on our original judgments and our original theory to explain and justify them, we modify the one and the other until we reach an equilibrium. Obtaining equilibrium will not guarantee truth. It will ensure a coherent view, but that is all. The theory will have to be supported on other grounds than that it makes sense of our judgments or, rather, of those we have culled.

Just so, here we should consider ourselves starting with our judgments about what appears to be moral behavior. Those judgments may be mistaken, but if so, there is time enough later, when we construct a moral theory, to correct our initial mistakes. Those mistakes may come about because, for instance, our judgments may simply be social constructs so deeply embedded and internalized that we have difficulty imagining that they might be mistaken.

De Waal provides some stunning anecdotes. Here is his description of a young male chimpanzee helping an older female:

> The Arnheim chimpanzees spend the winters indoors. Each morning, after cleaning the hall and before releasing the colony, the keeper hoses out all the rubber tires in the enclosure and hangs them one by one on a horizontal log extending from the climbing frame. One day Krom was interested in a tire in which the water had been retained. Unfortunately, this particular tire was at the end of the row, with six or more heavy tires hanging in front of it. Krom pulled and pulled at the one she wanted but could not move it off the log. She pushed the tire backward, but there it hit the climbing frame and could not be removed either. Krom worked in vain on this problem for over ten minutes, ignored by everyone except Otto Adang, my successor in Arnhem, and Jakie, a seven-year-old male chimpanzee to whom Krom used to be the "aunt" (a caretaker other than the mother) when he was younger.

> Immediately after Krom gave up and walked away from the scene, Jakie approached. Without hesitation he pushed the tires off the log one by one, as any sensible chimpanzee would, beginning with the front one, followed by the second in the row, and so on. When he reached the last tire, he

carefully removed it so that no water was lost and carried the tire straight
to his aunt, where he placed it upright in front of her. Krom accepted his
present without any special acknowledgment and was already scooping
water with her hand when Jakie left.[2]

As de Waal says, "It is hard to account for Jakie's behavior without
assuming that he understood what Krom was after and wished to help her
by fetching the tire."[3]

Jakie's feat is all the more startling when we describe more fully what
he did. First, he recognized that Krom had a problem, and he recognized
that the problem was not simple, but complex. To help Krom, Jakie would
need to remove all the tires in front of the tire with the water and then very
carefully, so as not to spill the water, do all the following: remove the tire,
carry it over to Krom, and stand it up in front of her, making sure she had
it before he left. Jakie not only noticed that Krom had a problem,
displaying a sensitivity to the concerns of others that we should admire in
anyone, but figured out what the problem was and worked out the complex
set of steps that he needed to do to help her. And he did not just shrug his
shoulders and go on, but stopped and helped Krom—an act of compassion
that, again, we should admire in anyone.

A second example concerns Kakowet, "the old male bonobo" at the
San Diego Zoo. The moat around the enclosure is two meters deep and
needs periodic cleaning. It had been drained and scrubbed, and the keepers
had gone to the "valve to refill [the moat] with water when... Kakowet,
...came to their window screaming and frantically waving his arms so as to
catch their attention." It turned out that "several young bonobos had
entered the dry moat but were unable to get out. The keepers provided a
ladder,...", and Kakowet pulled out the smallest one, who was unable to
climb out on his own.[4]

De Waal points out that Kakowet was familiar with the routine at the
zoo and so knew that once the moat had been cleaned, the keepers would
refill it. Kakowet not only knew that, but realized that the young bonobos
would drown unless he did something. What he did was not try to save the
youngsters himself, but stop the keepers from filling the moat, a much
more intelligent choice. Kakowet gave a paradigmatic performance of
what we would teach keepers to do in such a situation: do not try to save
the youngsters yourself, but give yourself and others time by getting the

---

[2] Frans de Waal, *Good Natured: The Origins of Right and Wrong in Humans and
Other Animals* (Cambridge, MA: Harvard University Press, 1996), p. 83.
[3] Ibid.
[4] *Our Inner Ape*, pp. 190-91.

water turned off. Indeed, we would not find anything amiss in the description were we to discover that Kakowet were a person instead of a bonobo.

One of de Waal's favorite examples concerns Kuni, a female bonobo, who saw a starling hit the glass of her enclosure...[and] went to comfort it. Picking up the stunned bird, Kuni gently set it on its feet. When it failed to move, she threw it a little, but the bird just fluttered. With the starling in hand, Kuni then climbed to the top of the tallest tree, wrapping her legs around the trunk so that she had both hands free to hold the bird. She carefully unfolded its wings and spread them wide, holding one wing between the fingers of each hand, before sending the bird like a little toy airplane out towards the barrier of her enclosure. But the bird fell short of freedom and landed on the bank of the moat. Kuni climbed down and stood watch over the starling for a long time, protecting it against a curious juvenile. By the end of the day, the recovered bird had flown off safely.[5]

Kuni, as de Waal says, put herself in the bird's place, understanding "the circumstances of another"—an essential feature of moral behavior. Jakie displayed that capacity for empathy when he saw that Krum wanted the water in the tire and could not get it. What is remarkable about Kuni is that she understood the circumstances of not just another bonobo, but a different kind of animal entirely.

So we have Jakie and Kakowet and Kuni. They each displayed a capacity for causal reasoning and for good behavior that we would laud a child for. They each saw that another being had a problem that caused or would cause harm unless they helped: Krum could not get the water; the youngsters would drown in the moat; the starling needed help flying. They each solved the problem at hand—Jakie almost nonchalantly, Kakowet very wisely, Kuni carefully and with great care. And they each did what an individual ought to do after seeing that another needs help and figuring out how to provide it.

These are not simple capacities. Seeing that another being has a problem requires, for instance, that we differentiate ourselves from others, see ourselves as one being and others as other beings. It also requires that we recognize that the other being is the kind of being that can have problems and can be helped. The other being is not like a stone or a stump, but a living being with concerns and interests—just like oneself. Recognizing a kinship with others and especially, as with Kuni, different kinds of others is to make a crucial move into the moral world.

---

[5] Ibid., p. 2; see also p. 178.

To feel empathy for the plight of others is yet another crucial step. We can recognize others as distinct from ourselves and see that they, like us, have concerns and interests, but feel no concern ourselves about their concerns. Sociopaths are paradigmatic examples of human beings who fit into this category. Jakie and Kakowet and Kuni, on the other hand, acted as though they felt empathy for those they helped.[6] Indeed, for all the world, if we did not know that they were not human beings, we would have not hesitated at all to describe them as feeling empathy.

Yet we can feel empathy for someone's plight without doing anything to help. Helping others can be a difficult matter. It requires putting one's own immediate concerns and interests to one side and may require subordinating those concerns and interests to those of others. We do not know what Jakie was about to do when he happened upon Krom, but whatever it was, it took second place to helping Krom. In addition, Kuni and Kakowet clearly went out of their way to help those they saw in need.

All three also understood enough of the situations they were in to figure out how to help those in need. Kakowet had to know that the youngsters would die if they were left in the moat and so had to know that water is dangerous. He had to know what "the usual operating procedure" was to understand the danger the youngsters were in and how best to help them. Jakie had to realize how the tires were positioned in order to know how to remove them one by one. Little children work with stacking rings to learn to recognize such a configuration and learn that to get at the bottom ring, they must remove the ones on top one by one.

Were we to imagine that Jakie, Kakowet, and Kuni were human beings, we would give them moral credit for what they did and for the way in which they went about doing what they did. Were the human beings children, we would be astonished at their precocity, and surely any parent would be rightly proud of a child who acted the way Jakie, Kakowet, and Kuni acted.

---

[6] I hesitate to put the matter this way if only because, as I go on to say, if Jakie, Kakowet, and Kuni were human beings, we would not hesitate at all to attribute empathy to them. To say that they "acted as though they felt empathy" would be to raise a red flag and make the reader wonder if they writer thought they had ulterior motives. It is difficult to imagine what ulterior motives the three could have, and, indeed, if we were to attribute ulterior motives to them, we would be attributing an even more developed capacity -- the capacity to do good for some perhaps nefarious purpose. It seems less problematic to say they felt empathy, but I have put the matter as I have to draw attention to the issues involved in describing their behavior.

§2. Non-Kantian Apes

Whether the three acted morally is, however, quite another matter. Two different issues need to be addressed before we can make that judgment, one about what we think is necessary for morality and one about what we think Jakie, Kalowet, and Kuni were thinking when they behaved as they did. We are all familiar with someone doing something that appears to be just the right thing to do, but doing it for purely selfish reasons. So it matters for judging that the apes' behavior is moral what was going on in their heads. In short, we need to ask:

• What is required for morality?
• Do Jakie, Kalowet, and Kuni have what it takes to be moral?

Some moral theorists argue that despite the apparent sophistication of Jakie, Kakowet, and Kuni, none behaved morally. Jakie may look like a Good Samaritan, for instance, but in the eyes of some moral theorists, he failed to do the one thing he needed to do in order to be moral. He failed to consider what it would be like if everyone just walked by Krom and failed to help her. On this view, he did what a moral being ought to do, help someone in need, but he failed to do it for the right reason, because, that is, it was the right thing to do. And that failure means that his behavior failed to be moral.

Christine Korsgaard hawks this view in responding to de Waal's views about how morality evolved. There is, she claims, a sharp divide—a "deep discontinuity"—between the animal kingdom and us,[7] and the difference is that unlike animals, we are conscious "of the grounds of our beliefs and actions."[8] We are self-conscious, Korsgaard argues, with Kant, in a way in which no animal seems to be. We are conscious that we are moved to act in this way or that and so come to have "a certain reflective distance from the motive"—a distance which allows us to ask, as animals do not ask, "Should I be moved in this way?"[9] We can then consider the moral question, "Ought I to do what I am moved to do or something different?"[10]

It is an empirical question, Korsgaard says, how extensive is the capacity for this sort of self-governance. Korsgaard is careful to leave the

---

[7] Christine M. Korsgaard, "Morality and the Distinctiveness of Human Action," in Frans de Waal, *Primates and Philosophers: How Morality Evolved* (Princeton: Princeton University Press, 2007), p. 103.
[8] Ibid., p. 113.
[9] Ibid.
[10] Ibid.

question open, but refers to Kant's view that "the form of self-consciousness that underlies our autonomy may also play a role in the explanation of some of the other distinctively human attributes…" and to other philosophers noting "the connection of self-consciousness of this sort with the capacity for language."

If that is right, then the capacity for normative self-government and the deeper level of intentional control that goes with it is probably unique to human beings. And it is in the proper use of this capacity—the ability to form and act on judgments of what we ought to do—that the essence of morality lies,…[11]

So she has answered both questions with which we began this section:

What is required for morality?
Normative self-governance, Korsgaard claims.

Do Jakie, Kalowet, and Kuni have what it takes to be moral?
No, not likely, she thinks. They may well have had beliefs and even arrived "at those beliefs under the influence of evidence"[12]—though what may seem like an odd phrase, "under the influence," makes it clear that just as a drunkard does things without the use of reason, but under the influence of alcohol, so animals may be influenced by evidence although, apparently, they do not think through in any way whether the beliefs they have arrived at under the influence of evidence are in any way appropriate.

Korsgaard does recognize that animals may act intentionally. A dog may see a bone and run to it, intending to pick it up. Just so, a human may see some fudge and reach for it, intending to pick it up. Yet neither intention is reasoned—though each intention and the beliefs associated with it are certainly influenced by the evidence of the senses. I see some fudge and reach for it because, among all the relevant beliefs I have, I believe that fudge tastes good and that a piece of it is there, in front of me, for the taking (and is not, say, a mirage). If I hesitate because fudge gives me a sugar high and is fattening besides, then I have become self-conscious about my desire to eat the fudge and what I do may then be determined by my reason, not by my desire. I am asking, when I hesitate, "Should I be moved to eat this fudge?" Animals have no such capacity for self-conscious correction of desires and beliefs, Korsgaard is claiming. So they act as they are inclined to act, not as reason would tell them they ought to act, and for that reason they cannot be moral, cannot act morally.

---

[11] Ibid., p. 116.
[12] Ibid., p. 114.

The difference between humans and animals is not a matter of degree, but of kind:

> A form of life governed by principles and values is a very different thing from a form of life governed by instinct, desire, and emotion—even a very intelligent and sociable form of life governed by instinct, desire, and emotion....Even if apes are sometimes courteous, responsible, and brave, it is not because they think they should be.[13]

So, according to Korsgaard, though Jakie may have been responsible and courteous in helping Krom get the water from the tire, he fails the test for being moral: he lacks the capacity to decide whether he ought to be responsible and courteous.

§3. The evolution of morality

Korsgaard refers to Darwin's claim that the rise of human self-consciousness may be due to the conflict between "our social instincts and our appetites." The latter are episodic and insistent, and so we are "under frequent temptations to violate [our] social instincts for the sake of [our] appetites." Yet "once a social animal's mental faculties develop to the point where she can remember giving way to such temptations" and realizing that it was "not worth it," she "will eventually learn to control such impulses." We see this development in individuals, that is, and that recapitulates the development of the capacity in human beings to control our impulses.[14]

It is an integral part of this explanation that an animal—a human being, say—first has an appetite and then acts on that appetite, only later learning to back off to so as to have "a certain reflective distance from the motive" sufficient to ask, "Should I be doing what my appetite tells me to do?"[15]

It would be a real problem for human beings if we were all, as a matter of our nature, moved to do our fellow human beings grievous harm

---

[13] Ibid., p. 117.

[14] Ibid., pp. 115-16.

[15] Korsgaard notes at one point "the connection of self-consciousness of this sort with the capacity for language." We know that apes have quite sophisticated linguistic abilities and that they are conscious of themselves, recognizing themselves in mirrors, for instance. As we become more adept at figuring out how to communicate with animals in languages that are mutually accessible, perhaps we can get more leverage on settling the empirical question whether some animals, at least, do possess self-consciousness of the sort Korsgaard thinks essential to morality.

whenever we could, without cause and without warning. Teaching a child in that sort of world to think about what he or she is naturally moved to do—slam playmates with bricks or whatever else is handy, kick and kill a sibling—would be an imperative of high urgency for us. The mother with the budding Attila the Hun could scarcely risk leaving him alone with his little sister, and we would all walk with a great deal more caution around our fellow human beings, not knowing for sure when one would act on impulse and not exercise the kind of self-control that would be absolutely necessary for us to have social lives.

Darwin's story of the evolution of the self-control Korsgaard thinks essential to our being moral would be far less likely a possibility were we so constituted. That we trust our children to play together and trust their inevitable conflicts not to rise to the level of grievous harm is evidence enough that whatever our "nature," we are not always compelled to a self-conscious examination of what we are moved to do in order to avoid the horrible lives we would otherwise lead. Indeed, what we know is that human beings often act on impulse to help others. If we were to become self-conscious about what we then do, we would only confirm that what we desire to do is what we ought to do.

De Waal is concerned about the evolution of morality, and the strength of his research on our nearest relatives is that he finds in their behavior just the sort of behavior we would want to find among humans. Would that we had leaders who were able to settle disputes before they escalated into armed conflict and were able to settle them with an even hand! And would that our children would stop whatever they are doing to help an older female in need!

On this understanding of what de Waal is doing, Korsgaard's criticism rather misses the point. Perhaps she is right, with Kant, that Jakie cannot act morally because he lacks the capacity to decide whether he ought to be responsible and courteous and right that he did not act morally because he did not decide to be responsible and courteous. If so, many human beings fail to be moral: the bar for moral behavior is set very high by Kant and Korsgaard. But even if we assume that Kant and Korsgaard are correct in setting the bar that high, that does not cut into the essential point de Waal is making.

We find in the behavior of chimpanzees and bonobos just the kind of behavior we would want to find if we are to come to have a moral world—even in the Kantian sense. De Waal's point is that the social character of apes and human beings has created the conditions for a ready movement into a fully moral world. Whether Jakie thought through what he was doing for Krom, or even thought about what he was doing—other than in the sense of seeing a problem, figuring out how to solve it, and solving it—what he did was praiseworthy. How much easier it would be to fashion a moral world from a world in which individuals were more naturally inclined to do good than from a world in which they were more naturally inclined to do harm.

Even if there were a difference in kind between what apes are capable of doing and what we are capable of doing, we can more readily understand how what we are capable of doing could evolve from what apes are capable of doing than how it could evolve were we incapable of anything resembling morally praiseworthy behavior in our more primitive state. De Waal's point is that we have already begun to move into morally acceptable behavior—if not Kantian perfect behavior—in a social state like those of the apes.

§4. Moral children

We can now return to our original query about whether children, even small children, are perfectly capable of giving moral reasons for what they do. We start on a playground, as it were, already far removed from the world of an eye-for-an-eye that we mistakenly thinks mars the behavior of animals. We know that children, even small children, are capable of sympathetic responses to the plight of others. Any parent can tell you a charming story about when so-and-so was a baby and was so nice to a little friend. We also know, from anecdotes like that of the little boy in the cart and others from our own experiences as children and our children's experiences, that little children are capable of giving reasons for their behavior.

That they generally give reasons for behavior that strikes us as inappropriate is not unexpected. We rarely ask children to provide reasons for doing what we consider good. We do ask them to explain why they do something bad, and so they become adept at providing reasons for bad behavior: "He hit me first!" or "It was an accident!" or "I was only teasing!" But giving reasons for bad behavior, even bad reasons, is giving reasons and so is evidence that children are capable of providing reasons for their behavior.

We should encourage this—not just by asking them why they behaved as they did when they did something bad, but by rewarding them with kudos when they do something good and providing for them the proper reasons for that good behavior. "That's a very nice way to play with your little brother, sharing your toys like that" or "Instead of hitting him back, you should tell him it's not nice to hit people" or "It's O.K. to tease people, but you should be careful to tease them nicely."

Children seem particularly adept at noting differences in treatment that strike them as unjust. As all parents know, "But that's not fair!" is a common refrain with children, and we can no doubt all remember instances from our childhood where we thought we were being treated unfairly. I remember complaining to my mother that my brother, six years older than I, was getting a far greater allowance than I. She explained that he was older. I remember arguing that we were getting an allowance for doing the jobs around the house—taking out the garage, cleaning up after the dog—and that I did exactly what he did and so therefore deserved exactly what he was getting. I remember thinking that age ought not to make a difference if we did the same work. "Equal pay for equal work!" was the principle I was arguing under though I could not have expressed it in that way at the time. This all occurred before I was five. Far from encouraging me in this argument, or praising me for at least giving an argument, my mother said, "That's just the way it is." I did not think it a good response then, and I do not now think it a good response. It amounted to her saying, "Because I say so." She would have done far better to have said something like, "Well, I can see your point, but your father and I think that your brother deserves more because he goes to school and has more expenses than you."

That move would have taught me that there can be different grounds for different treatment. "Equal pay for equal work!" does not always apply. Children are, I suggest, capable of quite sophisticated forms of argument. Here is an instance that strikes me as much more sophisticated than any I ever gave as a child and certainly sophisticated enough to make us marvel at how this child could think.

I was driving a little girl, all of five, home from day care, when she said, out of the blue, "It must be terrible to be ugly." I hesitated to respond, not knowing what had prompted this remark, but asked, "Why do you say that?" She proceeded to give a number of reasons: they do not have any friends, they sit in the corner by themselves, they are always the last person chosen for a game. I said something noncommittal, like "Yes, that is terrible." She then said, "It's not fair!" I agreed, and she was silent for a long time. Then she said, "And besides, it's not their fault. They were just born that way, and it's not their fault they were born that way." I agreed, and she was quiet until we were driving into her mother's driveway. She then said, "And you know what else?" "No, what?" "They're still ugly."[16]

---

[16] I have told this same story in "In the moral zone," Teaching Ethics, forthcoming.

I took her to be saying that even though they were being treated unfairly for something they were not responsible for, we still looked upon them in an unfair way: "They're still ugly." We cannot readily get out from under our social norms.

John Rawls would find this child a kindred spirit. She is arguing, after all, just as he argues in A Theory of Justice, that in distributing social goods we should ignore such morally arbitrary natural contingencies as race, sex, and, yes, a person's appearance. We can only wish that all adults were as sophisticated in their moral reasoning.

§5. Concluding remarks

I suggested that we start with our initial judgments about what is moral and what is not, leaving to later the question whether we can provide a theory to explain and justify them or, rather, those which survive the determination of a theory. We have examined briefly one moral theory on the basis of which all the examples from the primates and, indeed, all the examples from children are to be rejected as nonmoral. But even if we were to adopt that theory, those examples have a place. The acts described are just the sort of things that we ought to do—provided only that we consider first whether we ought to do them and base our decision that we should on principle. Indeed, if we wonder how it is that humans have evolved to have, as Korsgaard argues, a distinctive form of life, we need such examples to make the evolutionary story plausible. As noted above, it is far easier to move into what Korsgaard and Kant would consider a fully moral world if we move from a world in which individuals are naturally inclined to do good.

That children are capable of doing good and of providing even quite sophisticated explanations of why they ought to do good is, I think, beyond doubt. The judgments they make about what is right and what is wrong—it is right to treat ugly children the way more attractive ones are treated and wrong to treat them differently just because they look different—is evidence we need to take into account in developing a moral theory. It is also evidence we need to take into account when we consider how best to rear our children. We should treat them as being at least as sophisticated as the primates, perfectly capable of behavior we judge moral, and, more than that, we should treat them as perfectly capable of providing reasons for their behavior.

Given those capacities, we, as adults, have an obligation to encourage them in exercising those capacities. That means encouraging their judgments about the world when they are right and encouraging them to give reasons for their judgments. It also means that we ourselves must behave as we think they ought to learn to behave. "Because I say so" has no place in child-rearing any more than it has a place in a moral theory. If we want children to learn how to behave morally, we need to provide a model of how to behave.

FILIAL RESPONSIBILITY FOR AGING PARENTS AS PRUDENTIAL CARE

CHARLES ZOLA

Introduction

There has been growing interest in filial responsibility as well as ethical care of the aged.[1] For example, at the national level the President's Council on Bioethics has recently issued the text *Taking Care; Ethical Caregiving in our Aging Society*, a work that addresses issues arising in the care of the elderly, especially those with Alzheimer's and those at the end of life.[2] At the local level, area agencies on aging provide resources for the elderly and their caregivers, and they vigorously investigate reports of elder neglect and abuse. Also, elder abuse task forces comprised of social service agencies and community leaders sponsor programs designed to raise public awareness about elder victimization.

Yet, despite the great work of government agencies, much care for the elderly is delivered by family caregivers. Most people contend that adult children should have some sense of gratitude toward their parents on account of their parents' past efforts and sacrifices in raising them to maturity. This obligation usually translates into caring for parents as they

---

[1] See: Nancy Jecker, *Aging and Ethics* (Clifton N.Y.: Humana Press, 1991); Jane English, "What Do Grown Children Owe Their Parents?" *Philosophical Perspectives on Sex and Love*, ed. Robert M. Stewart (New York: OUP, 1995)300-303; Jeffery Blustein, "The Duties of Grown Children." *Philosophical Perspectives on Sex and Love*. ed. Robert M. Stewart (New York: OUP, 1995) 304-312; Norman Daniels, "Am I My Parents' Keeper?," *Midwestern Studies in Philosophy* 7 (1982): 517-540; Mark Wicclair, "Caring for Frail Elderly Parents: Past Parental Sacrifices and the Obligations of Adult Children," *Social Theory and Practice* 16.2 (1990): 163-189; Michael Collingridge and Seumas Miller, "Filial Responsibility and the Care of the Aged," *Journal of Applied Philosophy* 14. 2 (1997): 119-128;

[2] President's Council on Bioethics. Taking Care; Ethical Caregiving in our Aging Society 1 August 2008 <http://www.bioethics.gov/>.

age and 41% of caregivers for persons over 65 are children.[3] The obligation is fulfilled in various ways, depending upon the circumstances of the particular relationship. However, parental need for care gradually increases, sometimes to the point where they become totally dependent upon others for help and sustenance. This places incredible demands upon adult children. Despite the best intentions, it can be an overwhelming and seemingly insurmountable challenge.

I suggest that two different schools of ethical thought can aid adult children in their efforts. Virtue ethics stresses the essential role that prudence plays in making and executing moral decisions; while feminist care ethics emphasizes the relational moral dynamics of the care-giver/cared-for relationship. In this paper I draw from both moral perspectives and identify salient, common features that can provide guidance for adult children who practice filial responsibility for elderly parents.

The Care of Elder Care Ethics

Elder care ethics is usually understood as a specific area of applied ethics that falls under the broader scope of medical ethics. In the late 70s and early 80s when applied medical ethics came into its own, the buzz words that anchored the discussion were autonomy, beneficence, non-maleficence, and distributive justice. No doubt, such principles have a place in the discussion; however, as Moody has pointed out, these terms have limited applicability in dealing with the reality of caring for the elderly, especially those who suffer from Alzheimer's disease.[4]

One remedy to the situation is the important moral insights of care ethics which provides a needed corrective to the abstract, principle oriented approach. In my estimation, care ethics affords a better moral framework by which elder care can be understood and practiced. Nel Noddings has provided an invaluable analysis of the moral dimensions of the care-giving experience.[5] As she sees it, the care-giver relationship is characterized as an "un-equal meeting" of persons, where the care-giver addresses the cared-for not as a "case" but as a person. The moral

---

[3] "Selected Caregiver Statistics." Family Caregiver Alliance. 12 October 2008 http://www.caregiver.org/caregiver/jsp/content_node.jsp?nodeid=439.

[4] Harry Moody, *Ethics on an Aging Society* (Baltimore: Johns Hopkins University Press, 1992) 46-54.

[5] Nel Noddings, "The Cared-For," *Caregiving; Readings in Knowledge, Practice, Ethics, and Politics*, ed. Suzanne Gordon, Patricia Benner, and Nel Noddings (Pennsylvania: University of Pennsylvania Press, 1996) 21-39.

relationship demands reciprocity of "warm acceptance and trust." For Noddings, the parent/child and teacher/student relationship are paradigmatic examples of the care-giver/cared-for relationship.

Noddings insights are easily applicable to the typical adult child/elder parent relationship, and her analysis offers a lucid clarification for understanding its moral dimensions. In this relationship the usual parental superiority over children is incrementally reversed as adult children gradually take more control over their aging parents' affairs. Parents become more dependent upon their adult children to manage mundane tasks, setting up an unequal relationship that can be quite unsettling for both the parent and the adult child.

The reciprocity of which Noddings speaks can only be accomplished if adult children care for their aging parents in a way that does not objectify them but respects them as unique persons, having their own personal history and values. Elderly parents, on the other hand, will be more receptive to the care extended to them when they feel secure that their adult children have their best interests in mind. In this sense, the adult children must exercise their care giving role in such a way that it generates a responsive attitude on part of the cared-for parent. While no one doubts that most adult children desire that their elderly parents enjoy a certain quality of life, the problem is how such a good moral end can be achieved. An answer to this question is found in Aquinas' analysis of the virtue of prudence.

A Prudential Elder Care Ethics

Virtue is defined as an excellence and virtue theory classifies two types of virtues: intellectual and moral.[6] The former refers to the excellence of understanding truth and goodness; the latter refer to practice of good habits, commonly called the moral virtues. Prudence, however, is a virtue occupying a middle ground in this classification. Prudence must both know the good and devise the means or habits by which that good end is to be realized. In this sense, good intentions are not good enough. They must be accomplished in concrete acts that make the good real, not a mere ideal. Pivoting between knowledge and action, prudence is often defined as "right practical reason."

Prudential actions require the interplay of several other virtues that are called the integral parts of prudence. The best analysis of these integral parts is given by Thomas Aquinas in the Second Part of his *Summa*

---

[6] Aristotle. *The Nichomachean Ethics*, Book 2.

Theologiae. He explains that although a house is a single structure, it is comprised of several individual and integral parts: the roof, foundation and the walls. Similarly, prudence is understood as a single virtue that entails several other virtues: memory, docility, shrewdness, understanding, caution, foresight, circumspection, and caution. Each has an integral role to play in the exercise of moral virtue. Prudence's primary role is to find the exact means by which the moral virtue is practiced. As such, prudential decisions arise from and respond to the particularity of the situation.

Aquinas points out that "the whole process of prudence must needs have its source in understanding."[7] There is a distinction between two types of understanding. On one hand, there is understanding as an intellectual virtue that is cognizant of universal, practical principles such as, 'do good and avoid evil' or 'a child should give what is due to his parents'. On the other, there is the understanding of some particular, singular matter: 'Performing X *is giving due* to my parents'. While moral action demands knowledge of abstract precepts, there is an empty formalism about them. Such principles lack the knowledge of the particulars of exactly what actions will constitute respect and care for one's parents. The focus of prudence is not the general; rather, it is rooted in the understanding of the particulars.

Aquinas' insight is echoed by Patricia Benner and Suzanne Gordon: "The trust needed between providers and patients [adult children/elderly parents] illustrates another characteristic of practice—it is always socially situated and must relate to the particular person and situation as they evolve through time."[8] Personal, lived experience can render better practical principles because they are drawn from the actual personal circumstances of the situation. This practical understanding is known only by "discovery through experience, or through teaching."[9] It is here we are able to appreciate the integral parts of memory and docility.

Aquinas defines memory as a type of knowledge that is a recollection of past experiences. He points out that "memory of the past is necessary to take good consul for the future."[10] Adult children do well, then, to recall

---

[7] Thomas Aquinas. *Summa Theologiae* trans. Fathers of the English Dominican Province (New York: Benzinger Brothers, 1947) II.II. 49.2. All quotations are taken from this translation.

[8] Patricia Benner and Suzanne Gordon, "Caring Practice," *Caregiving; Readings in Knowledge, Practices, Ethics, and Politics*, ed. Suzanne Gordon, Patricia Benner, and Nel Noddings (Pennsylvania: University of Pennsylvania Press, 1996) 45.

[9] Aquinas, II. II. 47.15.

[10] Aquinas, II. II. 49. Reply Obj.3.

their past experiences with their parents when deliberating about how to care for them in their advanced years.

Memory serves as a powerful tool that reminds children of the all the past efforts and sacrifices that their parents made to nurture them to maturity and serves to engender in them a sense of moral obligation toward parents. But memory can't simply be understood as a means to inspire care, it must function primarily as a 'knowing' of what to do in the practice of the moral virtue itself; therefore, we must see memory's practical value.

Memory helps one understand what the course of care giving will be. Recollection of the past enables the adult child to understand the demands and requirements of the care giving experience because it has somehow already been imparted through the example given by one's own parents. Many of the obligations which once fell upon the shoulders of parents as they cared for their children now fall upon the shoulders of their adult children as they return this care. Kupfer observes: "Taking care of our parents returns us to our origins by mirroring their nurturance of us. In this return to our origins we return to our parents as only *we* can: returning their unconditional love with our gratitude-love."[11]

The aspects of care giving are not mere generalities; they must be done in ways that respect the person to whom they are directed. In caring for elderly parents, children need to recall the quality of life that their parents once enjoyed in order to assure that their parents' familiar lifestyle can be maintained to the best degree possible. Children have an irreplaceable role to play in the type of care extended to their parents because they are intimately connected to their parents' personal history and lived experience. Who can know what a parent's favorite foods, holidays, clothes, and sports teams are, or know those things that annoy a parent better than a child? Memory is an invaluable cognitive resource for adult children who seek to maintain a certain quality of life for their aging parents, but it has practical implications as well.

If elderly parents suffering from dementia have not made any formal, legal declarations concerning end of life decisions, adult children can often find themselves in a very uncomfortable situation. This discomfort can be exacerbated if several siblings propose competing views concerning the course of action that should or should not be taken. Here, memory provides an invaluable resource, since children can recall the values that their parents had expressed when they were mentally sound. Based upon

---

[11] Joseph Kupfer ,"Can Parents and Children be Friends?" *American Philosophical Quarterly* 27.1 (1990):23.

these previously disclosed values, children can exercise surrogacy confident that that their decisions are in agreement with their parents' own moral values.

However, not all knowledge is derived from our own experiences; often it must be gained from sources beyond us. The integral part of docility regards the acquisition of knowledge though the experience of others. In caring for their elderly parents children enter into a new stage of the relationship, and this experience spawns many questions. Although the relationship with one's parent is unique and can be traveled by no one else, adult children can learn much about what this journey might hold from others who have gone down that road. Gerontology has become one of the fastest growing areas of interest in health care and social work. Adult children do well to tap into the resources of these fields of study to better understand the aging process. Through consulting self-help manuals, web sites, and local government agencies, adult children can learn about the aging process and the needs of their elderly parents.[12]

Sometimes adult children dismiss the suggestion to seek advice from others, feeling that to seek help is a sign of weakness or intellectual inaptitude. But here one needs to avoid one of the vices associated with docility. Aquinas points out one can easily miss the mark of docility through pride by thinking that one has nothing to learn from others. He warns that "no man is altogether self-sufficient in matters of prudence."[13]

Perhaps one of the best resources for adult children is the parent himself. Adult children profit much by listening and learning from their own elderly parents about their expectations and hopes. They should consult parents about how they would like to be cared for. Even when such wishes can not be fulfilled for practical reasons, children can still make the effort to learn the values that their parents hold. When one does not consult parents, then parents become mere passive recipients of the choices and actions of their adult children, and they are thereby essentially reduced to objects of interest. Such a disposition is grossly contrary to the reciprocity underlying an ethics of care.

As Nodding points out, caring requires a type of "sharing."[14] When parents share their thoughts and ideas with their children, it presents a

---

[12] See: www.aarp.org/internetresources for an incredible online directory of websites dealing with aging; the Administration on Aging has its own website: www.aoa.org which can help in financial planning as well as the Social Security Administration's website: www.ssa.gov. Another helpful resource for caregivers is www.caregivers.org. These are only a few of the hundreds of resources available.

[13] Aquinas, II. II. 49. 3.

[14] Noddings, "The Cared-For" 33.

wonderful occasion for children to learn about how their care giving should be exercised. Elderly parents should feel that they are, in fact, being listened to by their children because it affirms their own personhood and respects their dignity as integral parts of the care giving experience.

In an investigation of those factors indicative of a caring relationship, Tarlow identified the importance of talking in the care giving relationship, since it is a primary means by which concern is expressed and received: "Talking in caring relationships was therefore both a sign that all was well and a process used to generate and maintain caring relationships. Talking could be both a means and an end."[15] It might be awkward for adult children to discuss certain matters with their parents, such as hygiene habits or financial issues, but adult children will not be able to be effective caregivers unless they do so. They must discover ways to open lines of communication with their elderly parents in order to learn how to maximize the quality of their parent's life.

Understanding may be had through memory and docility, but Aquinas also argues that knowledge may be gained from one's own ability. This refers to the integral part of shrewdness, which refers to a person's ability to make a ready and clear assessment of the particulars of the matters at hand.[16]

One of the biggest challenges that adult children have when caring for elderly parents is to recognize that the dynamics of the relationship have changed. The power nexus of the adult child/elderly parent relationship is radically reversed from earlier days. As children we are cared for by parents and think of them as towering authority figures to whom we must submit. This image of parenthood is engrained in one's consciousness and is not easily given up. In some way, one's sense of self-understanding is inextricably related to it and the dynamic shapes the way that the parent and child relate to each other. But as parents age and become less independent, they have a gradually decreasing ability to exercise authority over their personal affairs. Because of the influence of the earlier paradigm, many adult children fail to appreciate this reversed dynamic until some type of financial or health problem arises. Adult children can be caught off guard as they are catapulted into having to take care of the crisis. Such an unfortunate circumstance can be prevented through shrewdness.

---

[15] Barbara Tarlow, "Caring: A Negotiated Practice that Varies," *Caregiving; Readings in Knowledge, Practices, Ethics, and Politics*, ed. Suzanne Gordon, Patricia Benner, and Nel Noddings (Pennsylvania: University of Pennsylvania Press, 1996) 64.

[16] Aquinas, II. II. 49.4.

Prudence does not escape reality by pretending that all the difficulties of the aging process will magically be corrected or stop. Shrewdness enables the adult child to "size-up" the reality of the parent's life situation. Effective care giving requires that adult children see their parents for who they are, not who and what they wish them to be. But since this assessment is of contingent, particular matters of action, of all the integral parts, shrewdness is the most susceptible to error.[17]

In order to avoid an inaccurate assessment of the matters at hand, adult children must be vigilant in reviewing their elderly parents' physical, mental, and financial situation. As such, the adult child cannot care from a distance; the caregiver must be present to the cared-for. As Noddings points out, an ethics of care is characterized by "involvement, inclusion, engagement, and engrossment."[18]   Effective elder care requires an active participation with one's parents and the issues relative to their lives. Tarlow observes: "Being there seemed to be a special case of caring; it signaled commitment, especially in the family."[19]

Care giving relates not only to the dimension of space through 'being present', but it also refers to the dimension of time. Foresight addresses the temporal aspect of the elder care giving experience. The experience is not a onetime event; it has duration that will be contextualized by many unknowns and multiple possibilities. Because of this, foresight is necessary, since it is concerned with directing "future contingencies, in so far as they can be directed" so that the good end of one's moral actions may be attained.[20] Adult children must think and act in ways that can "see down the road" of life. Perhaps one of the most difficult aspects of caring over time is that adult children have to act in a way that takes account of the fact that relationship will eventually end in death.

In exercising foresight, adult children recognize the special urgency and gravity of the elder care situation. A parent might make mistakes in caring for her children, but there is still time to correct them. In the case of elderly parents, one realizes that time is running out. The means employed now can add or subtract quality and even quantity to the years which are left. The deliberation about the means of care requires that a child "see down the road" and make plans about end of life issues concerning health care, financial planning, and funeral arrangements when the time arises. Foresight, as related to care giving, anticipates and prepares for future

---

[17] Aquinas, II. II. 47. 3 Reply Obj.2
[18] Noddings, "The Cared-For" 31-35.
[19] Tarlow, 61.
[20] Aquinas, II. II. 49. 6.

events. Even the best formulated plans are subject to future contingencies, and this spirit of preparedness is essential for effective care giving.

However, anticipating and planning for future contingencies occurs contemporaneously with present circumstances, since the direction of a future plan of action hinges—to some degree—on the current circumstances. One cannot plan future action unless one first reckons with the present, and this calls for circumspection. Circumspection "compares means with the circumstances."[21] Tarlow's observation is similar to Aquinas's definition: "Those caring wanted to understand what needed to be done in the present in order to achieve some desired end that would assure the future well-being or happiness of the person cared about."[22] In this sense, children must recognize what means are presently available to help in the care giving experience.

Adult children act circumspectly when they utilize the resources that are at their disposal at the right time and in the right way. It is rare that a caregiver can provide everything which is necessary for those for whom he cares. Sometimes it is necessary to enlist the help of others, since often they might be more qualified to deal with a situation than the child can. If there are other siblings, their input needs to be taken into account, and their help should be enlisted. Sharing the obligations associated with elder care does not necessarily indicate an abdication of filial piety or diminish a child's commitment; rather, it affirms it.

Even in cases where an elderly parent lives in a skilled care or nursing facility, adult children can not take a laid back attitude and assume that such facilities alone are sufficient. Statistics show that 27% of victims of elder abuse in the Commonwealth of Pennsylvania live in state licensed facilities. Unfortunately, 66% live in their own homes or the homes of the care givers.[23] Such statistics appeal for more active involvement by adult children so that professionals or even their siblings don't abuse their parents. Institutions are never an adequate substitute for the personal involvement of children in terms of assuring a certain quality of life. However much a benefit they provide, such facilities only stand in the place of adult children and should never be viewed as the primary care giver. The adult child is always the primary caregiver who needs to exercise due circumspection over any personal or material resource that will be employed in the care giving process.

---

[21] Aquinas, II. II. 49.7.

[22] Tarlow, 68-9.

[23] "Elder Abuse 101, Statistics." Temple University Harrisburg Institute on Protective Services. 10 October 2008. http://www. temple.edu/harrisburg/Institute-on-Protective-Services/Elder-Abuse-Statistics.asp

An essential characteristic of circumspection is a keen sense of self-awareness. If adult children don't take proper inventory about what can realistically be done given their own talents and capacity, then their care giving can eventually turn into a burden. This might lead to the parent being neglected or marginalized. Without proper self-evaluation much can be lost and so adult children need to exercise caution as well.

Aquinas holds that caution is primarily concerned with those things which prevent one from exercising a virtue; therefore, we must view caution as relating primarily to the caregiver's own acting, that is, what are those things that prevent the caregiver from being effective? One of the greatest dangers in care giving is the amount of stress it can cause for the caregiver. Even in optimal care giving situations, there is always the possibility that the amount of effort required will cause the care giver to burn out, become depressed, or over wrought with anxiety that they are not doing enough.

Adult children exercise caution by paying attention to their own health and well being. If they personally care for their parents, they might consider getting away from the situation or placing their parents in respite care while they take some time off. Having someone come into the house a few hours a day to do some chores might also be a practical option. Like all other aspects of prudence, the shape which caution takes in a particular person's life will vary according to persons and circumstances.

On a related note, adult children need to guard against becoming too aggressive in their role as care givers. When adult children do too much, too soon for their failing parents, it can accelerate their parents' growing dependency. Effective elder care strives to maintain the elderly person's independence and effective capacities. Adult children must recognize that their parents have their own personal dignity and should be allowed as much autonomy as possible for as long they are able.

Parents must be granted their own rightful place in the relationship according to their capacities. Elderly parents should not be treated as pawns. Although she might have power over her parents' affairs, the adult daughter should see herself as a leader, not a boss. In relating caring to the parent child relationship, Noddings points out that parents allow the child to "take hold of what he can do. She does not keep him in a subservient position…".[24] Noddings insight reminds us that care giving is primarily about ameliorating the quality of life for the cared-for, not the self-aggrandizement of the care-giver.

---

[24] Noddings, "The Cared-For" 24.

Applying Aquinas' thoughts on prudence and its integral parts to the situation of caring for elderly parents reveals how nuanced the adult child's decision making is. Many factors have to be considered that relate to material and immaterial resources, as well as make accommodations for the temporal aspects of care giving. This analysis has shown how contemporary analysis of the care giving experience coincides with several key areas of Aquinas's thoughts concerning prudential moral action: reciprocal, active engagement between the caregiver with the cared-for; the need for the care giver to learn more about how best to provide care; and, most importantly, the observation that care giving is not an abstract activity, but one that is deeply personal and grounded in everyday experience.

Conclusion

In caring for one's elderly parents, the adult child walks down a road that no one else can. There are no maps about how that journey will exactly unfold or what direction children are specifically to take. Each caregiving encounter is unique and is shaped by the personalities of those involved; the experience is quite particular. At best, only general ideas can be offered. Ultimately, each child must determine how best to care for her parent given the circumstances within which she finds herself. Adult children often struggle to provide care for their own children as well as their elderly parents. This is a tough balancing act, especially when faced with the everyday challenges of work and personal commitments.

Aquinas' theory of prudence offers practical, general directions for adult children as they navigate their way down the path. Many views espoused by contemporary feminist care ethicists echo the insights of Aquinas. When these two seemingly divergent schools of thought are compared, a wonderful synthesis of ideas concerning elder care emerges. By drawing from these insights, adult children can take comfort in knowing that they are making an earnest effort to understand the aging process, the particular circumstances of their situation, and are vigilantly committed to seeing that the means are executed. It is my hope that the suggestions offered here can provide some guidance for those who are fortunate enough to have the opportunity to do so.

A REFLECTION ON CONFUCIAN ETHICS OF THE FAMILY

SUK CHOI

Confucianism has been facing many challenges, competing with Taoism, Mohism, Legalism, and Buddhism in the East Asian tradition in order to warrant its value and legitimacy as a philosophy, moral/political code, and religion. Since in the late 19th century Western civilization was introduced to the East Asian countries, Confucianism has been challenged not only by Western ideologies which attempted to prove their superiority in many ways, but also by people inside, that is, both Confucians and anti-Confucians, who have been hurt, or who thought that they have been hurt by the Confucian tradition.[1]

---

[1] Let me introduce some typical examples of such serious criticisms: 1) In 1965 Joseph Levenson, in one of the 3 volumes of his book, *Confucian China and Its Modern Fate*, had already evaluated Confucianism as "a historical monument, eliciting (instead of inculcating) a piety towards the past." (Routledge, 1965. P. 100) 2) Needless to say, the Cultural Revolution that happened in China in the 1960s and 1970s, was an unforgettable and tragic disaster for Confucianism. 3) In Korea, around the end of the previous millennium, a book, *Confucius Should Die in order for Our Country to Survive* was published and has become a best seller. The author is a scholar in the field of Chinese Linguistics, and thus, we assume, has a thorough understanding of Confucian texts, East Asian history/culture/philosophy, current economic/social/political situations in East Asian countries, etc.. He claims that Confucius must re-die now, more than 2000 years after Confucius actually died, based on his claim that Confucian ideology has negatively impacted the political, social, economic, and educational fields in Korea. His contention is that the available period of Confucianism as a valuable ideology has expired. 4) In 1997, when the Asian Financial Crisis, (often referred as the IMF (International Monetary Foundation) Crisis) occured, many scholars and journalists, hurried to blame the Confucian style of management in business, and most of them concluded that it is the time for Asian countries to abandon any aspect of the Confucian tradition and to incorporate western styles of government, business, and education. They named this movement "Globalization". The question of whether systems of business and management influenced by Confucianism

Many elements of the Confucian philosophical system, especially Confucian ideas of family, family love, and filial piety, have been attacked because these ideas have often been evaluated as the main reasons for the social corruption of the East Asian countries. In this paper, concerning the theme of this volume, *Ethics and the Family*, I will examine Confucian ethics of the family, focusing especially on the Confucian idea of filial piety and some critiques of it, and then introduce a new Confucian vision based on the Confucian idea of filial piety.

One of the common and negative evaluations of Confucianism is that it is simply an authoritarian and totalitarian ideology. Although Confucianism emphasized the value of the family, its social and political realization has turned out to be harmful to human societies in many ways such that even some defenders of Confucianism have criticized Confucian ethics of the family as a type of parochialism and nepotism to be overcome. Indeed, these are strong and serious claims. I would agree with them, on the one hand, that, since the economic, political, and social formats of the communities which maintained Confucian culture have changed and the world has experienced mixed diverse cultural heritage, we need to reevaluate how Confucianism has had, should, or can make an impact on human lives. On the other hand, however, we must recognize that there is a distinction between philosophy (theory and ideology) and its practical realization in political, social, and economic fields. In addition, even if it is claimed that Confucianism is responsible for all of the undesirable realizations, the question of whether or not the claim is justified, still remains. In this sense, in the first section I will deal with an example of such criticisms in order to show that some critiques are drawn from misunderstandings of the Confucian texts. Such misunderstanding or fixed images of Confucianism based on those misunderstandings are often supported by some empirical and historical data.[2]

---

should be blamed for the economic crisis is an interesting and serious issue to be reexamined. There are diverse perspectives regarding questions such as "What does globalization mean?', "How should globalization proceed (if it should)?", and so on, but what I want to point out here is that Confucianism has always been a major target whenever those who want to establish a mentality of globalization offer criticisms and negative diagnoses of the traditions of Asian countries. For a further reading on the problems of Confucianism and the issue of the survival of Confucianism, see William Theodore de Bary, *The Trouble with Confucianism* (Harvard University Press, 1996) and Gilbert Rozeman, ed., by, *The East Asian Region: Confucian Heritage and Its Modern Adaptation* (Princeton University Press, 1991).

[2] A typical example of such a case is found in the article, "Psychocultural Dynamics within the Confucian Family," written by Walter H. Slote in Walter H.

Many scholars in the field of Asian philosophy, history, religious studies, and Asian studies have been attempting to look for a proper understanding of the Confucian texts and for their constructive critiques of the old but still invaluable tradition. They have been trying to develop a new and grand Confucian vision under the names of such philosophical, social, and cultural movements as 'New Confucianism,' 'Boston Confucianism,' or 'Post-Confucianism,' with which we are now familiar. As a student of Confucianism, I strongly support the goals of these diverse attempts, but, as a student of philosophy, my support is more critical. Although we ought to appreciate that these strenuous attempts are on-going, it seems to me that, at least up to now, these attempts have not succeeded in motivating contemporary philosophers to pay serious attention to Confucianism as anything more than a historical artifact (rather than a living philosophy). In the second section, I will critically examine a recent claim by Tu Wei-ming, who is one of the contemporary leading Confucian scholars. And then, in the final section, I will suggest some points of Confucianism to be extended, hoping that they will possibly be helpful for motivating contemporary philosophers to re-consider Confucianism.

1

Serious critiques of the Confucian tradition have been looking for textual evidence to support the claim that Confucian ideology unavoidably leads to undesirable realizations.[3] Oftentimes such attempts have been too much oriented by the critics' established intentions, and thus they have overlooked essential meanings of some passages, chapters, and/or the whole context.

One of the most important claims of Confucian ethics of the family can be read in the first chapter of the book, the *Analects*;

Slote and George A. DeVos, ed., by, *Confucianism and the Family* (Albany: State University of New York Press, 1998).

[3] It should also be pointed out that most criticisms of Confucianism have been drawn from the texts of Classical (ancient) Confucianism. This is not simply because all of the criticisms have assumed that the essence of Confucianism can be found in the four core classics, *Analects, Mencius, Ta Hsueh,* and *Chung Yung*. There can be different views on this issue, but it should be noted that there is a period of more than one millennium of so called neo-Confucianism. In this paper I will focus my discussion on examples from the four core classics, because the main targets of the major critiques can be found in them.

Filial piety and brotherly respect are the root of humanity (*jen*). (*Analects* 1:2)[4]

Filial piety is one of the most significant virtues in the community Confucius pursues. Thus, Confucius' instructions are often very concrete and cautious. For example;

> Young men should be filial when at home and respectful to their elders when away from home. They should be earnest and faithful. They should love all extensively and be intimate with men of humanity. (*Analects* 1:6)

Confucius says, "When a man's father is alive, look at the bent of his will. When his father is dead, look at his conduct. If for three years [of mourning] he does not change from the way of his father, he may be called filial. (*Analects* 1:11)

Mencius also mentions such implications regarding the relation between filial piety and brotherly respect, and four Confucian core virtues;

> The actuality of humanity consists in serving of one's parents. The actuality of righteousness consists in obeying one's elder brother. The actuality of wisdom consists in knowing these two things and not departing from them. The actuality of propriety consists in regulating and adorning these two things. (*Mencius*, 4A:27)[5]

The emphasized points become stronger especially when we read the parts where Confucius mentions the relation between filial piety and the concrete forms of propriety and behaviors toward one's parents in terms of how to realize filial piety. For example,

> Meng I Tzu asked about filial piety. Confucius said, "Never disobey." [Later] when Fan Ch'ih was driving him, Confucius told him, "Meng-sun asked me about filial piety, and I answered him, "Never disobey."" Fan Ch'ih said, "What does that mean?" Confucius said, "When parents are alive, serve them according to the rules of propriety. When they die, bury them according to the rules of propriety and sacrifice to them according to the rules of propriety." (*Analects* 2:5)

---

[4] Translations from the *Analects* are adapted from Wing-tsit Chan, trans., *A Source Book in Chinese Philosophy* (Princeton: Princeton University Press, 1969), unless otherwise indicated.

[5] Translations from *Mencius* are adapted from Wing-tsit Chan, trans., *A Source Book in Chinese Philosophy* (Princeton: Princeton University Press, 1969) or D.C. Lau, trans., *Mencius* (Penguin Books, 1970). *Source Book*, p.76.

As many commentators have already pointed out, "Never disobey" does not mean blind obedience to one's parents. Even when a son's opinion is different from that of his father,[6] according to Confucius' teaching, "in serving his parents, a son may remonstrate with them. When he sees that they are not inclined to listen to him, he should resume an attitude of reverence and not abandon his effort to serve them. He may feel worried, but does not complain." (*Analects* 4:18)

We should not read 'the rules of propriety' only as the rules and customs in Confucius' time. Furthermore, it is not fair to criticize the different contents of propriety from our current standpoint. Although Confucians always deal with propriety as a primary condition for being genuine humans and thus emphasize the significance of tradition, they never exclude the flexibility and context of different situations. Rather, a deeper concern with more fundamental aspects of filial piety should be understood beyond strict observance of propriety and any form of serving parents:

> Tzu-yu asked about filial piety. Confucius said, "Filial piety nowadays means to be able to support one's parents. But we support even dogs and horses. If there is no feeling of reverence, wherein lies the difference?" (*Analects* 2:7)

> Confucius said, "If a man is not humane (*jen*), what has he to do with propriety (*li*)?" (*Analects*, 3:3)

Paul Woodruff correctly interprets that "Genuine filial piety does not bend a child's mind, but provides a structure for the expression of its natural feelings towards its parents."[7] In this sense, "filial piety must be sincere and reverent"[8] and thus Confucians teach filial piety together with propriety and suggest specific patterns of behaviors that one should try to keep when one realizes one's natural feeling toward parents.

As the above-quoted passages imply, it is natural that the value and significance of these consanguineous affections are emphasized in picturing an ideal status of the relationship between family members. In addition, as many commentators have interpreted, filial piety and brotherly respect are regarded "not as the final goal, but as a starting point" for being humans and as practical contents of all human virtues. However, Qingpin Liu, in his recent article, examines the Confucian moral code as

---

[6] This also applies to the time when a son sees his father's wrongdoing.
[7] Paul Woodruff, *Reverence: Renewing Forgotten Virtue*, (Oxford University Press, 2001), pp.103-10.
[8] Paul Woodruff, ibid, p. 104.

being based primarily on consanguine affection rather than on the process of rational justification. He demonstrates the following critique;

> Filial piety as a point of departure may not lead to the realization of the ideals of individuality and sociality, but, conversely, may in fact ultimately obstruct their realization.[9]

As Liu suggests, more serious critiques of the Confucian idea of filial piety can be raised and are actually attempted regarding the following radical statements:

> The Duke of She told Confucius, "In my county there is 'Mr. Upright.' When his father stole a sheep, he bore witness against him." Confucius said, "The upright men in my country are different from this. Fathers conceal the misconduct of their sons and the sons conceal the misconduct of their fathers. Uprightness is to be found in this." (*Analects* 13:18)[10]

If we read this paragraph as an independent one without reading and considering the whole text, and keep focusing on the issue of a pattern of behaviors or moral rules that Confucians support, it might be surprising to know that Confucius, who pursues an ideal moral community, seems to support son's and fathers' mutual concealment of misconduct or serious crimes. But, it might not be surprising to many critics of Confucianism, as we see from the case of Liu's criticism. Mencius also seems to support Confucius' idea by offering the following conversation:

> T'ao Ying asked, "When Shun was Emperor and Kao Yao was the judge, if the Blind Man[11] killed a man, what was to be done?"
> Mencius said, "The only thing to do was to apprehend him."
> "In that case, would Shun not to try to stop it?"
> "How could Shun stop it? Kao Yao had his authority from which he received the law."
> "Then what would Shun have done?"
> "Shun looked upon casting aside the Empire as no more than discarding a worn shoe. He would have secretly carried the old man on his back and fled to the edge of the Sea and lived there happily, never giving a thought to the Empire." (*Mencius* 7A:35)[12]

---

[9] Qingping Liu, "Filiality versus Sociality and Individuality: On Confucianism as "Consanguinitism," in *Philosophy East and West*, vol.53, no.2 (2003), pp.236-237.
[10] *Source Book*, p.41, with slight modification.
[11] He is Shun's father.
[12] D.C. Lau, trans., *Mencius*, p.190. The passage, 5A:3 in *Mencius* should also be noted together regarding Mencius' idea of filial piety.

From these passages, obviously we recognize a moral conflict between a son's filial piety toward his father and his obligation toward society or social justice, between filial piety and loyalty, and so on. Regarding these paragraphs, Hsieh Yu-wei has once commented; "There is no simple solution to such conflicts, that is, no fixed general rule for settling them. . . .Thus the Confucian ethical point of view is that, in case of such conflicts, though there is no fixed rule, you should do what is proper in your heart." [13] This is an attractive but unclear answer to such a conflict, which could allow both negative and positive evaluations in terms of the question of whether it captures an understanding of a real Confucian intention.

Qingping Liu has an insight on this question, and points out that the statement "you should do what is proper in your heart" is a general rule and that, "in the Confucian value system, when conflicts occur, it is only by choosing consanguineous affection that a filial son can ultimately feel at ease."[14] From this analysis, he suggests to call Confucianism "filialism" or "consanguinitism" in the sense that "Confucianism is the sole doctrine that decisively assigns consanguineous affection a supreme position in ethical and moral practice."[15] He extends his analysis to claim that such a priority of consanguine affection over humane love is a main reason for social corruption.[16] His analysis and radical claim have initiated active debates particularly regarding the Confucian idea of filial piety.[17]

Against Liu's claim, Lijun Bi and D'agostino analyze the concealment case as an expression of worship for not only one's father but also one's ancestors: ". . .ancestor worship supplies one of the key reasons for the son to conceal his father's wrongdoing: to conceal the father's misconduct was

---

[13] Hsieh Yu-wei, "Filial Piety and Chinese Society," in *The Chinese Mind*, ed. by Charles Moore, (University of Hawaii Press, 1967), p.185, re-quoted from Qingping Liu (2003), *Ibid*, p.241.

[14] Qingping Liu (2003), *Ibid*, pp.241-242.

[15] Qingping Liu (2003), *Ibid*, p.246.

[16] Qingping Liu, "Confucianism and Corruption: An Analysis of Shun's Two Actions Described by Mencius," in *Dao: a Journal of Comparative Philosophy*, vol.6, no.1 (2007), pp.1-19.

[17] Such active debates are collected in *Contemporary Chinese Thoughts*, vol.39, no.1 (2007) and Guo Qiyong, ed., by, *Debates on Confucian Ethics: The Mutual Concealment among Family Members*, (Wuhan Jiaoyu Chubanshe 2004). In addition to the articles I examined in this paper, diverse insightful comments on Liu's claim are offered in *Dao: a Journal of Comparative Philosophy*, vol.7, no.1 and no.2 (2007).

to protect the reputation of the ancestors. . ."[18] A. T. Nuyen agrees with them and extends their point to interpret filial piety as respect for tradition.[19] Many other critiques of Liu's claim have focused on diverse interpretations of and/or re-emphasis on the conceptual priority of humane (universal) love to consanguine affection or filial piety based on it or the importance of filial piety in the Confucian philosophical system.

However, simply reiterating Confucian ideas of the relationship between filial piety and humane love can't rightly rebut Liu's claim if the question Liu implicitly and explicitly raises is not considered. Liu's question is, first, "What is the right thing to do in a moral quandary?," and, second, "On what basis do Confucians make judgment in such a conflict situation between filial piety toward one's father and one's social obligation toward social justice?" He is asking, "What are you or Confucians going to do in that moral situation?" If Confucians accept that his questions are appropriate for understanding the passages in the *Analects* and *Mencius*, they must accept that they *do* conceal their fathers' wrongdoing. No matter how much we interpret and add deep and elegant interpretations into the choice, it would probably be true that Confucians *do* put the priority of family love over any other ethical code.[20] This naturally leads to the next claim that such choices could be a main reason for social corruption.

Yet, Liu's examination missed an essential aspect of those passages. Confucius is not attempting to respond to questions such as "What is the right thing to do in a moral situation?," or "What choice is morally good or right?" Nor does he intend to insist that a son's covering up for his father is always right and can be applied to every similar case. Such questions already presuppose the dichotomies between right and wrong, good and bad, justice and injustice, and so on, independent of diverse moral contexts. Rather, Confucius is asking, "What does 'Upright' mean?" once again. The question lies in a conflict between whether one should remember and follow a certain rule, e.g., anyone who has stolen things

---

[18] Lijun Bi and Fred D'agostino, "The Doctrine of Filial Piety: A Philosophical Analysis of the Concealment Case," in *Journal of Chinese Philosophy*, vol.31, no.4 (2004), p.457.
[19] A.T. Nuyen, "The Contemporary Relevance of the Confucian Idea of Filial Piety," in *Journal of Chinese Philosophy*, vol.31, no.4 (2004) pp.433-450.
[20] Chu Hsi, who has been evaluated as a true completer of Neo-Confucianism in the Sung period, commented on the passage 13:18 in the *Analects* that the covering up that a father and son do for each other is the "apex of heavenly principle and human emotion,"[20] but his comment might be interpreted as supporting both defenders and critics of Liu's claim.

should be reported and arrested, and whether one should respond to each given context. It is not very difficult to suppose diverse contexts in which the father had to steal a sheep, the history of his son's growing up, the everyday moral practice of his family, the father's and son's moral character before (or after) the theft, the son's struggle to resolve the situation, the story and moral character of the owner of the sheep, and so on. Once again, Confucius is not claiming or justifying that the son's *action* of concealment is morally right or good. He tries to respond in a paradoxical way to the attempt of the Duke of She who defines the notion of "an upright man" in terms of action and rule and, by his definition, probably intends to attack Confucius' seemingly unclear and inconsistent teaching.[21] If Confucius had been asked to say whether the action of standing against one's father in the specific situation is upright or not, he might have agreed with the Duke of She. However, he is suggesting, by offering a different choice, that moral concern, judgment, and value should not be based on fixed rules and actions.

This intention has been further developed in the passage from *Mencius*. When he is asked to answer the question, "When Shun was Emperor and Kao Yao was the judge, if the Blind Man killed a man, *what was to be done?*" Mencius makes clear that in the situation "The only thing to do was to apprehend him," However, Mencius goes on to show that the sage, Shun, would have chosen to save his father by giving up the most honorable and highest social position of Emperor. Mencius' concern focuses not on a particular action of saving his father against the state's law, but on Shun's moral character and maturation, that is, the process through which this sage would struggle to resolve the conflict between a son's filial love toward his father and social justice as a ruler. Through this, Mencius also suggests, following his teacher, that morality should cover more than the issue of action and rule.

Along with this interpretation, one more different but old critique of Confucian family ethics and the idea of filial love in terms of rule and love should be noted here. Mo Tzu, the founder of Mohism and one of the

---

[21] It might seem that Confucius' teachings recorded in the *Analects* do not present any consistent system of moral philosophy. This is because he teaches different disciples through different statements and his cobnversations with his disciples are shaped according to the different qualities of the disciples and diverse moral contexts. It is also because the *Analects* is the collection of such teachings. However, as many commentators continue to demonstrate, this does not mean that his teaching does not have any consistent system at all although it might be true that the notion of 'system' should be approached differently from that of contemporary professional philosophy.

strongest critics of Confucianism, developed his own interpretation of humanity (*jen*) based on his utilitarian standard, and suggested the idea of *chien-ai* (commonly translated as all-embracing love, or universal love) as an essential Mohist moral code. One might note, merely from the translations of the word "*chien-ai*," the superiority and desirability of Mohist moral concern to that of Confucianism, because the idea of *chien-ai* seems to be contrasted to the Confucian idea of love with distinction (or graded love) and to pursue an altruistic perspective. According to Mohism, love should have in it no gradations of greater or lesser love. While Mohism emphasizes equality in loving others, Confucianism accepts that there should be degrees in love. The Mohist understanding of love has been systematized as a rule upon their utilitarian principle by which they should decide and evaluate their actions.

However, as A.C. Graham interprets, what the Mohists meant by *chien-ai* is not an emotional love, but an "unemotional will to benefit people and dislike harming them."[22] What is significant in the Mencian idea of love with distinction is not that one should practice different degrees of love toward different people. What Mencius means by love with distinction is that in addition to admitting that naturally I love my family more than my neighbors, I should extend this familial love to people in a broader community. Mencius emphasizes;

> Treat with respect the elders in my family, and then extend that respect to include the elders in other families. Treat with tenderness the young in my own family and then extend that tenderness to include the young in other families. . ." (*Mencius*, 1A:7)[23]

As Phillip J. Ivanhoe correctly points out, the process of extending one's natural love implies a mutual connection between familial and social lives in the sense that "one cannot extend a moral sense without knowing what it is to love and what it is to be loved in one's family and one cannot love one's family without knowing a deep concern for the society in which one lives."[24]

---

[22] A.C. Graham, *Disputers of the Tao* (Open Court Press, 1989) p.4.

[23] Translation is adapted from *Source Book*, p.61.

[24] Phillip J. Ivanhoe, *Confucian Moral Self-Cultivation*, 2nd ed. (Hackett Publishing, 2000), p.22. In this sense, it should be also noted that Ivanhoe gives the name, Development Theory/Model, to the Mencian argument for four beginnings/sprouts and self-cultivation, *Ibid*, pp.22 and 46. Here I briefly deal with the issues of Mohists' *chien-ai* and Confucian notion of graded love only in terms of my reflection on Liu's radical claim. For further reading of the debate between the two concepts, see David Wong's article, "Universalism versus Love with

An assumed conviction behind the Confucian vision is that the relationship between family as a small society and society as a big family should be approached as the most essential question in moral discussions. They can never be separated. Our moral concern should focus on self-cultivation and moral maturation of a person as a member of both one's family and community. From the Confucian perspective, the most dangerous behavior and judgment in our ethical lives would not be that a son conceals his father's wrongdoing after he struggled to fully consider both love toward parents and obligation toward his community, but that he stands against his father by blindly following a rule established independently of human natural emotion simply because that is an absolute and fixed rule to be obeyed.

This interpretation of those passages reminds us of recently increased ethical interest regarding the dichotomy between virtue ethics and rule/action-centered ethics. It is true that many contemporary commentators of the Confucian tradition have been attempting to re-value Confucian ethics as a version of virtue ethics. We may have a different but valuable discussion on the problems of Confucianism as a version of virtue ethics along with the examinations of the problems of contemporary virtue ethics, but such discussions are not the aim of this paper. At this point, I would just like to point out that those passages from the *Analects* and *Mencius*, which have been a main target of diverse critiques of the Confucian idea of filial piety and Confucian family ethics based on it, would rather be a good resource for suggesting a Confucian version of virtue ethics to contemporary moral discourses.

2

The Confucian emphasis on filial piety is not only a main target of serious critiques of Confucianism, but also a theoretical and practical basis for a new Confucian vision. In this section, I note a contemporary Confucian commentator's attempt to revalue Confucian ethics based on the notion of filial piety.

In his recent article, Professor Tu Wei-ming, who is one of the leading Confucian commentators and a representative of the movement of New Confucianism, re-emphasizes the Confucian idea of "humanity as embodied love" by "exploring filial piety in a global ethical

Distinction: An Ancient Debate Revived," in *Journal of Chinese Philosophy*, vol.16 (1989) pp.251-272.

perspective."[25] He regards the Enlightenment mentality as the most powerful and influential ideology the world has witnessed, and then diagnoses that, although traditional Confucianism has been rejected by Enlightenment universalism, The Enlightenment mentality is now in crisis.[26] He goes on to claim that the Enlightenment project can be enlarged and enriched by cultural resources springing from the Confucian tradition.[27] In support of this vision, he interprets that,

> Filial piety as embodied love is both a principle of differentiation and a principle of communication. As a principle of differentiation, it takes the relationship between parents and child as its point of departure. In this sense, the Confucian ethic demands that caring for one's parents takes precedence over social responsibility and political royalty. As a principle of communication, however, the Confucian ethic demands that we transcend not only selfish interests but also the private concerns of our families, communities, societies, nations, and species.[28]

His contention is that filial piety "can serve as a powerful critique of several modern ideologies, including excessive individualism, aggressive ethnocentrism, chauvinistic nationalism, religious exclusivism, and self-destructive anthropocentrism."[29]

I strongly support Tu Wei-ming's vision that Confucian ethics of the family with the core ethic of filial piety should be extended beyond a local norm to a universal and global moral value. However, I need to point out some problems with his vision as a candidate for a global ethical perspective. As some Confucian defenders do, he claims that Confucian ethics is based on a metaphysical idea of human nature. He overlooks that; 1) contemporary ethical discourses ultimately pursue a similar vision of an ideal, universal, and global community; 2) they are inspired by modern scientific rationality; 3) they do not welcome old metaphysical approaches to human nature,[30] especially the Confucian concern with the

---

[25] Tu Wei-ming, "Humanity as Embodied Love: Exploring Filial Piety in a Global Ethical Perspective," in *Is There a Human Nature*, ed., by Leroy Rouner, (University of Notre Dame Press, 1997) pp.172-181. As is well known, he has been keeping his efforts to reinterpret Confucian philosophical system and to incorporate Confucian ideas into contemporary discussion on moral problems.
[26] *Ibid*, pp. 173-174.
[27] *Ibid*, p.176.
[28] *Ibid*, P.173.
[29] *Ibid*, P.173.
[30] For an example, see Bernard Williams, *Ethics and the Limits of Philosophy*, (Harvard University Press, 1985) p.52.

normativity of human nature. In addition, it is a power of modern scientific rationality that diagnoses the crisis of the Enlightenment mentality and keeps up efforts to look for resolutions for the crisis. This power is a product of the Enlightenment project. I am not sure if, to such scientifically oriented efforts, it is persuasive or attractive to offer a new and grand vision based on an old format of a metaphysical approach to human nature.

I appreciate that Tu Wei-ming has re-explored the value, implication, and efficacy of filial piety by contrasting the huge framework of the Enlightenment project with a virtue of filial piety. However, there are too many issues and questions involved in the problems of the modern ideology. Tu's mottos that he has quoted from some Confucian texts for suggesting an anthropocosmic Confucian vision, such as "Heaven is our father and Earth is our mother," "we are filial children of Heaven and Earth," and so on, might sound "empty" under our anxiety of the complicated net of those serious and concrete modern problems. Ironically, just as in the 12th century Chu Hsi, the father of Neo-Confucianism, criticized his contemporary Buddhism simply as mystical, so does it seem to me that in the 20th and 21st century the anthropocosmic Confucian vision for a better millennium that Tu Wei-ming has suggested might sound "mystical" to contemporary philosophers.

3

In conclusion, I would like to attempt to re-shed light on the value of Confucian ethics with respect to the issue of ethics and the family, filial piety, and globalization, based on the two reflections on Liu's critique of and Tu's vision of Confucianism.

One of the reasons Confucianism has been a major target of criticism as an obstacle against desirable globalization is the assumption that, since Confucianism, as a local moral code based on consanguine affection, has been a cause for social corruption by contributing to the well-being of a limited social group, it will obviously become a stumbling block against universal values such as universal justice and peace. There have been both supports and critiques of this assumption from diverse perspectives, and such attempts should and will be continued. However, one point I would like to address here is that, if globalization implies a process of securing the universal values and does not exclude the implication of harmonious balance between universality and diversity of unique local cultures and moral codes, then, in order to pursue such a balance, it is more urgent to look for universal features of diverse local and particular codes than to blame them based on shallow levels of negative data against each of them.

Confucianism, especially Confucian ethics of the family could be one of the best candidates and resources for such an attempt. Confucianism does not simply insist on fixed rules that could work only for their own relevant times and spaces, but fully and highly considers the flexibility of practical applications of fundamental convictions. Confucius already encourages this, saying,

> It is the man that can make the Way (*Tao*) great, and not the Way that can make man great. (*Analects*, 15:28)

Such encouragement is available because Confucian convictions regarding our ethical lives are based on their deep concerns with fundamental, natural, and universal human conditions. Those concerns have matured through long discussions on the issues such as human nature, mind, emotion, family, society, history, and so on. I would define Confucianism as a philosophy of awareness in the sense that Confucianism is a philosophical system which ultimately pursues "learning for oneself" and moral practice with unending self-cultivation. It is the genuine aspect of the Confucian tradition which could still be appealing even to contemporary philosophical and scientific inquiries on human nature, mind, and ethical lives, and which I think should continue to be reiterated. In this respect, returning to the theme of this volume, the Confucian idea of filial piety should be re-considered not as a merely consanguine affection in a simply negative sense, but as a universal quality of human psychology from which our ethical discourses should start.

CHAPTER FOUR

FAMILY AND THE LARGER (MORAL) COMMUNITY

INTRODUCTION

It can be tempting to think of families as small, self-contained moral communities but of course nothing could be further from the truth. Every parent knows that we are constantly surrounded, even bombarded, by images of families that run the spectrum from idyllic to dysfunctional. But as central as families are to everyone's moral experience, their place in the larger moral community is somewhat less clear.

One reason for the uncertainty is the stress that many ethical theories put on the value of impartiality in making decisions about what to do. This makes a great deal of sense when thinking about how a government should treat its citizens, for example, but much less so when we think about the proper relationship between family members. It seems entirely wrongheaded to say that if a parent has a choice to save his or her child or a complete stranger that impartiality should matter at all. Understanding the nature of a family and a family's place in the larger community will tell us as much about ethical theory as it will about the family. The papers in this chapter attempt to shed some additional light on all of these questions.

From "Leave It To Beaver" to "Jon and Kate Plus Eight" to "The Adams Family" and "The Munsters", television has always been obsessed with exploring the drama of family life. More recent "reality" programming is no exception and in her paper "From 'Supernanny' to 'The Baby Borrowers': Reality television as family teacher", Kristie Bunton brings a journalistic perspective to examining the value of such programming in learning about the family. While such programs are by no means immune to criticism, Bunton takes the view that there is nevertheless much to learn from their depictions of families and their struggles.

But if society is a source of lessons about the family, this is mainly because what happens in the family has such a dramatic effect on the quality of society. Practices that improve family life thus deserve the utmost attention. In "The Application of Virtue Ethics in Family Processes to Facilitate Optimal Interaction", James Ponzetti uses the recent resurgence of interest in virtue ethics to describe some ways to improve familial interaction. He also argues that being on the front lines of moral education, the family has a necessary role to play in establishing the foundation of virtue in society.

The integration of modern ethical theory and family life does not always go hand-in-hand, however. As noted above, there is a tension between the impartiality valued by many theories and the inherently appealing partiality within familial relationships. Eric Silverman examines an attempt by David Velleman to reconcile our competing intuitions in his paper, "An Examination of One Strategy for Reconciling Familial Love and Impartial Morality". He finds much that is appealing about Velleman's Kantian approach, but ultimately finds it lacking features that most people would consider necessary to concepts of love and belovedness.

Diane Williamson also criticizes a Kantian perspective in her paper on "Emotional Intelligence and Familial Relationships". She identifies the Kantian thinking that we cannot be morally required to possess certain emotional states as undergirding the traditional thinking that family life occupies a "private" realm that should be largely outside the purview of public scrutiny. With a better theory of emotion and contributions from the ethics of care, she argues that we can and do have duties to take new responsibility for our emotions and develop emotional intelligence that guides us in familial relationships.

It is often said that one can choose one's friends, but not one's family. This presents a difficulty in moral theories that take autonomy to be central: if one does not choose one's familial relationships, how can one be morally bound by them? Taber flips the problem on its head in "A Value of Family: The Moral Significance of Involuntary Affiliations", arguing that the involuntariness of these relationships is actually the source of many of our obligations. Like the world at large, involuntary family associations make us appreciate that we are part of something bigger, which Taber argues is central to developing a moral life.

The final paper in this chapter, Jeff Buechner's "Are There Forms of Rationality Unique to a Family that Can Justify the Concept of 'Family Values'?", takes a different tack on what kinds of value are central to the family. Drawing on considerable resources from the philosophy of language and social philosophy, Buechner argues that there is a familiarity families create that may give rise to a unique form of rationality. From this form of rationality, we may find a whole different source for so-called "family values". If Buechner is right, the family is more than instrumentally valuable in creating the larger community; it is indeed valuable because it is a family.

From "Supernanny" to "The Baby Borrowers": Reality Television as Family Teacher

Kristie Bunton

Introduction

Many sources – TV critics and columnists, media literacy activists and parent educators – tell parents to be vigilant about the potentially harmful messages that television sends family members who watch its sex or violence. However, few of these same sources encourage families to pay careful attention to TV's potentially negative messages about families themselves. Yet such messages abound. One powerful stream of these messages about contemporary families is provided by television's "reality" genre. These programs, whether "Supernanny," "Nanny 911," "Wife Swap" or the controversial British import "The Baby Borrowers," provide viewers with entertaining messages about who makes up family and how they ought to behave.

Family reality shows present several ethical questions. For instance, is it ethically justifiable for television networks to exploit infants, children and troubled families for entertainment purposes? Do reality show producers violate child labor restrictions? Does the composition of the programs disproportionately suggest that two-parent families are more common than they are, or that families of particular racial, ethnic and class backgrounds are dysfunctional? It is ethically appropriate for viewers to take parenting tips from TV or to be entertained by other families' dysfunctions? Overall, what ethical lessons can be learned from reality shows about family?

This paper discusses several TV reality shows, using TV criticism and news reporting about those shows, to conclude that, with appropriate constraints, some reality shows may actually serve as powerful, positive teaching tools about family life.

Media messages about family have flourished
through the years

Reality TV shows are not the first sort of widely available national media content to tell families how to behave. Magazines have done so for years. "Since the 1740s, magazines have played a key role in our social and cultural lives"[1] and were the first mass medium to reach a truly national audience. Among the early nationally circulated and widely influential magazines in the United States was *Godey's Lady's Book*, which offered women across the country advice about fashion, etiquette – and families. Edited for 40 years by Sara Josepha Hale after its debut in 1830, *Godey's* was among the first magazines savvy enough to target women as a viable and distinct audience for both editorial messages and the national advertising that supported them. *Godey's* circulation hit 150,000 readers by 1860, and the magazine "played a central role in educating working- and middle-class women."[2]

In the years after *Godey's* success, a variety of magazines targeted parents – or, to be blunt, mothers – with messages about how to fulfill their roles. Some of these magazines' focus on family issues was evident from the very titles on their cover – think *Parents' Magazine* or *Family Circle*, for instance – while other magazines – think *Good Housekeeping* or *Better Homes & Gardens* – included a variety of family-related content. *Ladies' Home Journal* became one of the most popular magazines targeted at women. At the height of its influence at the turn of the 20th century, *Ladies' Home Journal* and its long-term editor Edward Bok "emphasized social concerns and the possibility of the breakdown of the American family."[3]

One article by Theodore Roosevelt, "The American Woman as a Mother," reflected concern for the growing lack of discipline of children, of the man who is not a good husband and father, and the woman who has "lost her sense of duty and is sunk in vapid self-indulgence." He claimed good morals and discipline at home would create a moral, disciplined nation.[4]

---

[1] Richard Campbell, Christopher R. Martin and Bettina Fabos, *Media & Culture: An Introduction to Mass Communication,* 6th ed. (Boston and New York: Bedford/St. Martin's, 2008), 313.
[2] Ibid., 316.
[3] Jean Folkerts and Dwight L. Teeter, *Voices of a Nation: A History of Mass Media in the United States,* 4th ed. (Boston: Allyn & Bacon, 2002), 249.
[4] Ibid.

In the 20th century, newspaper advice columns such as "Dear Abby" and "Ann Landers," written by eponymous twin sisters of Chicago, found enormous readership among Americans who turned to the columnists to learn what these women – who didn't purport to be experts—thought about everything from the effect of infidelity on marriages and families to how to cope with an unexpectedly pregnant teen or an alcoholic mother-in-law. "Abby" and "Ann" often pointed out to their readers that they were themselves mothers and wives, and occasionally shared their own families' disappointments, including the end of one sister's long marriage. The sisters also pointed out when they turned to a child psychologist, family counselor or clergy member to garner expert advice on a reader's sticky question. It is perhaps one measure of the columns' success with readers that after the 1964 presidential election, a national editorial cartoonist depicted the defeated candidate, Barry Goldwater, seeking advice from Dear Abby after his failure. "Abby" and "Ann" are long gone, but their legacy lives on, both in the "Dear Abby" column now written by her daughter, and in the many advice columns that have blossomed in newspapers and online ever since.

Looming over all media messages about family is television. Despite inroads made by the internet and other media formats, television "is still the one mass medium that delivers content millions can share simultaneously."[5] In 2006, television viewership averaged eight hours per day in American households, a 5 percent increase in viewing time in the typical U.S. home.[6]

From its earliest days, critics and scholars have tried to explain the powerful, magnetic role of television in the American culture. Former Federal Communications Commission chairman Newton Minow famously called television "a vast wasteland," while former FCC member Nicholas Johnson said of television, "It is the greatest communications mechanism ever designed and operated by man. It pumps into the human brain an unending stream of information, opinion, moral values and aesthetic taste. It cannot be a neutral influence."[7]

More than any other, television has been the one mass medium that family members of all ages had in common and that most often presented content that portrayed families. "From its hallowed living room perch, the magic box broadcast the first generation of domestic sitcoms, emblazoning idealized portraits of middle-class family dynamics into the national

---

[5] Campbell, Martin and Fabos, *Media & Culture*, 159.
[6] Ibid., 158.
[7] Folkerts and Teeter, *Voices of a Nation*, 491.

unconscious."[8]   Situation comedies, which establish a fixed set of characters in a domestic or workplace setting, are the only type of programming included in the year's top 10 television programs for every single year between 1949 and 2006.[9]

Sitcoms tell families who they should look like and how they should be composed, even if those messages are inaccurate. As family historian Stephanie Coontz points out, "Our most powerful visions of traditional families derive from images that are still delivered to our homes in countless reruns of 1950s television sit-coms."[10] Yet, as Coontz notes, the realities that face most families, whether in the 1950s or 2000s, are "far more painful and complex than the situation-comedy reruns or the expurgated memories of the nostalgic would suggest."[11]

Situation comedies often have gilded families with a gentle patina of nostalgia. They create a world in which, sometimes literally, "Father Knows Best." For instance, sitcoms for years have over-represented single fathers, when compared to their actual presence in the U.S. population. "My Three Sons" with Steve Douglas and his housekeeper Uncle Charlie, "Family Affair" with Uncle Bill and his stuffy British butler Mr. French, or "Full House" with Danny Tanner, his brother-in-law Uncle Jesse and friend Joey are just a few examples of the over-representation of single fathers on television sitcoms. Television situation comedies also routinely have under-represented families of color. Coontz observes that even from the earliest days of television, "real life was not so white as it was on television."[12] It wasn't until the 1970s that African American families were the central characters in such situation comedies as "Sanford & Son," "The Jeffersons" and "Good Times," and African American families didn't truly take television's center stage until the phenomenal success of "The Cosby Show" in the 1980s. No African American TV family since has reached the status and popularity of "The Cosbys," yet census data tell us African American families are a significant component of the U.S. population. Women have rarely taken charge of families on television, despite how frequently they play these roles in real life. In the 1970s, the depiction of single African American mother "Julia," played by Diahann Carroll, lasted just a few seasons before disappearing from the lineup, not to be replaced by a single mother of color for many years. Television

---

[8] Judith Stacey, "The Family Values Fable," *National Forum,* Summer 1995, 21.
[9] Campbell, Martin and Fabos, *Media & Culture*, 173.
[10] Stephanie Coontz, *The Way We Never Were: American Families and the Nostalgia Trap* (New York: Basic Books, 2000), 23.
[11] Ibid., 29.
[12] Ibid., 30.

situation comedy's depiction of working mothers garnered a previously untold level of national attention in 1992, when U.S. Vice President Dan Quayle used the unplanned pregnancy of unmarried career woman "Murphy Brown" to illustrate what he believed was a troubling decline in American family values. The attention paid to "Murphy Brown" during that year's presidential election campaign was so marked that the sitcom's screenwriters wrote Quayle's criticisms of the fictional character into the debut of the new season that fall.

Today, the situation comedy on television has been dethroned – or at least joined on its throne – by the "reality" show. The principal reason is that "unscripted" reality shows are cheaper to produce than scripted episodic series. Producers find no shortage of "average" viewers, wanna-be singers or has-been celebrities who are willing to work for little or nothing, in exchange for grabbing their 15 minutes of fame on television. That's a marked contrast to the hundreds of thousands of dollars per episode that must be paid to in-demand actors, writers and editors on scripted series. Television executives began to understand the advantages of unscripted series in the late 1980s, when the writers' guild went on strike.

But reality shows are not just about saving money. They're popular with television executives because they're popular with viewers. Why do viewers like them? Perhaps reality shows seem more authentic to viewers than stilted dramas and situation comedies. Some TV critics have suggested viewers enjoy reality shows because they like to watch other people be embarrassed or humiliated trying to perform a stunt on "Fear Factor" or sing a song that impresses the "American Idol" judges. Longtime *Washington Post* television critic Tom Shales has called some reality shows "exploitainment."[13] Yet other observers have suggested the shows are popular because they often ask viewers to weigh in on the fate of the programs' participants. For instance, "Dancing with the Stars" viewers get to help decide which contestants hang up their dancing shoes every week.

Since the debut of MTV's "Real World" reality soap opera in the early 1990s, a number of reality shows have attracted huge audiences. Contest-oriented reality shows such as "Survivor," "The Bachelor," "American Idol" and "Project Runway," celebrity-based shows such as "The Osbornes," "The Simple Life" and "The Surreal Life," and makeover-themed shows such as "Extreme Home Makeover," "The Swan" and

---

[13] Tom Shales, "A Case of Stolen Formula: 'Baby Borrowers' Follows the Reality Show Playbook," *Washington Post*, June 25, 2008, C-01.

"Celebrity Fit Club" have all found hundreds of thousands of viewers and thus generated high Nielsen ratings, which translate into the higher advertising rates that commercial television can charge for the ads that support it.

Among the longest-lasting family-oriented reality shows has been "Supernanny," a British import now in its fifth season on the ABC network. It has been imitated on other networks with such programs as "Nanny 911" and "Wife Swap." More controversial, perhaps, have been the CBS program "Kid Nation" and the NBC program "The Baby Borrowers." All have attracted many viewers, perhaps because the "antics of other people's children, and by extension, the flaws of other people's parenting, offer seemingly limitless entertainment value."[14]

Reality show production logistics raise ethical questions

"The Baby Borrowers," which was called "birth control" by the NBC network when it aired the show during summer 2008, housed five teen-aged couples in an Idaho cul-de-sac neighborhood and followed them for three weeks as they struggled to care for real infants, toddlers, adolescents and senior citizens.

Likewise, "Kid Nation," the controversial CBS reality show that aired in fall 2007 and that featured 40 children ages 8 to 15 struggling on their own to create and run a pioneer-era town, also filmed in the west, in this case New Mexico. It is perhaps no accident that both "The Baby Borrowers" and "Kid Nation" were produced in states that lacked stringent child-labor laws that would have protected children who were not members of the unionized actor's guild.

Legal is not by definition ethical. In these cases, it seems producers demonstrated some intent to circumvent legal protections for children as workers. After the shows aired, legislators in both New Mexico and Idaho considered measures that would make their states' child labor laws more protective of children.[15]

"The Baby Borrowers" and "Kid Nation" did secure the legally binding consent of the participating children's parents, but was that ethical? Should infants and children whose parents lack the good judgment to hesitate before exposing them to national television audiences

---

[14] Mary McNamara, "When Reality Bites – and Cries and Spits Up," *The New York Times*, June 25, 2008, E-11.
[15] James Hibberd, "NBC Net Nurses Reality 'Baby,'" *Television Week*, March 9. 2007, 2.

be protected by other, perhaps more rational adults? In the same way that the justice system provides a guardian ad litem for a child who lacks a parent or guardian capable of adequately representing him or her in a legal proceeding, should reality television be required to seek the advice of some sort of ethical guardian ad litem for these children? "Nanny 911" and "Supernanny" producers say they use psychological counselors to screen participating families and find those who are "fundamentally stable and secure."[16] That's a sound practice, but it's also a voluntary one that producers could abandon in any particular case. Several pediatricians told newspapers that they believed neither "Kid Nation" nor "The Baby Borrowers" would have survived the scrutiny of an institutional review board, if reality shows had an IRB-like process.[17] Some went so far as to suggest that the conditions created by the shows – such as letting teens drag a baby by the arm – amounted to child abuse that professionals in other settings would have been required by law to report to child protection authorities. Producers of both programs took pains to assure TV critics that nannies and medical professionals were standing just out of camera range at all times during production.

Children are vulnerable and deserve the utmost ethical protection. They are not fully mature and cannot clearly give informed consent before being portrayed on a reality program. Cincinnati pediatrician Deborah A. Borchers, who is a member of the American Academy of Pediatrics committee on early childhood adoption and dependent care, told *The New York Times* she was concerned about the lack of consent from children portrayed on reality shows such as "Supernanny" and "Nanny 911." "As the children get older, they'll watch the videotape of the shows of them being portrayed as brats, and they'll be embarrassed," she said.[18]

While most of the critics chastised "The Baby Borrowers" for getting parents of infants to lend their children to the production, many of those same critics seemed to forget to question the parents of the 18-year-old "borrowers" who were filmed sharing master bedrooms in those cul-de-sac homes. It wasn't clear whether the teens were encouraged by their own parents, or the show's staff, to practice safe sex while they lived together for three weeks during production.

Some families who fully consent to participating in a reality program don't always comprehend how the process of television production may

---

[16] Susan Gilbert, "Those Televised Supernannies May be Just a Bit Too Super," *The New York Times*, August 2, 2005, F-1.

[17] Linda Chassiakos, "TV Reality Shows Often Harm, Exploit Children," *Los Angeles Daily News*, July 15, 2008, A-17.

[18] Gilbert, "Those Televised Supernannies," F-1.

change their lives. One Minnesota family featured on "Nanny 911" said they consented to participating in the program but came to believe that the presence of television crews caused their children to act more wildly than they typically did. The family noted, for example, that the addition of lighting sufficient to film the show made their home uncomfortably hot, and the producers' request that the children not phone friends or spend time alone in their bedrooms put extra stress on the children. "That put them on a collision course that made for great television, but perhaps not complete 'reality.'"[19]

The "reality" of these family depictions is also affected by the locations where the programs are filmed. In its first years of U.S. production, British import "Supernanny" sought families who lived in small towns and rural areas, for simple reasons that had little to do with ethical responsibility in television programming and more to do with practical aspects of television production. "Supernanny" producers found it was easier to descend on a small town with vans and trucks of television equipment that could be parked outside a home for a couple of weeks than it would be to venture into a busy city or suburb, where disrupting the flow of traffic would create larger problems.[20] Even so, one "Nanny 911" family said neighbors in their small town resented increased traffic and the presence of cameras in the neighborhood.[21]

Early on, "Supernanny" producers thought it was easier to get small-town families to take their kids out of school and keep parents home from work for three to four days during a two-week "Supernanny" shoot. (By contrast, "Kid Nation" required children to miss a full month of school while it was being shot on a New Mexico ranch.) And following the formula that had worked for the British version of the program, "Supernanny" producers chose to portray the problems of intact two-parent families. Not until later did "Supernanny" include single parents or urban parents.

These logistical decisions translate into questions about the ethical duties of television for portraying American families responsibly. By focusing on families in small towns and rural areas, "Supernanny" over-represented people who live in such places. Urban families outnumber rural ones in the U.S. population, as do single-parent families, yet the world according to "Supernanny" originally was composed solely of

---

[19] Jon Tevlin, "After TV Nanny Leaves, Do Old Habits Return?" *Minneapolis Star Tribune*, March 17, 2007, 1-E.

[20] Lisa Joy LoMurray ("Supernanny" production assistant) in discussion with the author, November 2006.

[21] Tevlin, "After TV Nanny Leaves," 1-E.

married, heterosexual, white couples who owned homes and lived with their children in somewhat bucolic settings. It was not until several episodes into the show's tenure that "Supernanny" featured an African American family, and it wasn't until November 2008 that the program presented a family with parents in the throes of divorce. The principle of symbolic annihilation in the media tells us that people whose lives and characteristics are not represented in media messages may be symbolically erased from the minds of viewers and therefore disregarded as not relevant to the larger culture. "Supernanny" seems to have suggested some types of people matter more than others.

Too, "Supernanny" and "Nanny 911" typically presented families with small children, especially in their earliest episodes. Misbehaving children make for good television; after all, when a toddler hurls himself off the bed he's just been told to stay in or screeches at the top of her lungs to her parents, compelling audio and video result. Producers have found that many small children quickly forget the presence of camera and sound operators, and so go right back to misbehaving in dramatic ways on camera.[22] But the overwhelming focus on unruly small children potentially suggests that parents' hardest work occurs in the earliest years, although many parent educators believe too little attention is focused on the tough tasks involved in parenting teens and young adults.

In addition, the selection of families who are suffering from extreme discipline and control problems – so extreme that they turn to a TV nanny to get help – may suggest to viewers that troubled families are more common than they actually are. "The extent of the children's rudeness and wildness" on these reality shows is "unrealistic."[23] Many families do not take four hours every night to get their children to stay in bed and fall asleep, for instance, yet "Supernanny" and "Nanny 911" often spend significant portions of their programs helping parents learn a bedtime routine that will take minutes instead of hours.

Another ethical issue stemming from production logistics is raised when some reality shows offer compensation of a sort to get families to participate in the programs. While "Supernanny" never pays or compensates families, "Nanny 911" has offered participating families vacations.[24] "Kid Nation" paid its 40 participating children a $5,000 appearance fee, but more importantly, at the end of each episode the group of children chose one member to receive a "gold star" worth $20,000 that could be used as a college scholarship. As a pediatrics professor pointed

---

[22] LoMurray.

[23] Gilbert, "Those Televised Supernannies," F-1.

[24] Ibid.

out on National Public Radio's "Morning Edition," the stress of competing for money and national attention may be an unfair burden to place on children.[25]   The producers of "The Baby Borrowers" made a point of telling U.S. television critics that neither the child-lending families nor the borrowing teens had been compensated. Yet the producers' consciences cannot be entirely clear; surely those 18-year-old borrowers must have been at least partly lured into participating by the perceived glamour of television. Who knows how glamorous those same 18-year-olds felt when their emotional breakdowns and bad judgment were shown to national TV audiences?

Finally, ethical questions may be raised by the post-production decisions that television makes. In today's interactive media climate, networks routinely encourage viewers to weigh in online with their reactions to programs. Some families who say they fully consented to participate in a reality show, and learned how to better cope with their children as a result, nevertheless admit they were unprepared for the public scrutiny they faced after the programs aired. A Minnesota family who participated in "Nanny 911" said they didn't expect the nasty comments posted about them on the show's online chat room, where they were called bad parents by many viewers.[26]

Questions that stem from the shows' content

The "Supernanny" herself—Jo Frost, the soft-hearted but firm nanny who arrives at any home across the United States in an iconic London black taxicab and then proceeds to solve all a family's problems—did work as a nanny in the United Kingdom. However, Frost lacks formal training in child-rearing and discipline. The television program presents her as a credible authority, and her subsequent spin-off parenting books have been best-sellers. But are her recommendations – such as her now-famous "naughty corner" or "naughty step" – sound parenting practice? For the most part, yes, argues Certified Family Life Educator Dawn Cassidy:

> The methods introduced are basic parenting skills: establishing and sticking to a schedule, maintaining authority, rewards (typically praise) for good behavior and a "naughty chair" or "naughty mat," where acting-up children spend a few minutes in time-out. … [A]s a family life educator

[25] William Coleman, M.D., interview by Kim Masters, *Morning Edition*, National Public Radio, August 3, 2007.
[26] Tevlin, "After TV Nanny Leaves," 1-E.

and someone involved in promoting the field of family life education, I am thrilled that the concept of parenting education has come to prime time TV. While Nanny is a not a "parent educator," or a CFLE, alas, she uses mostly sound parenting techniques. I am sure she has introduced more than one viewing family to some plausible parenting techniques they can try in their own home.[27]

Several pediatricians and child-rearing experts interviewed by *The New York Times* agreed. They noted that many of the reality shows' parenting techniques – "especially the need to be consistent, to discipline without hitting and shouting, to reward good behavior and to set aside time for unstructured family play" – were especially sound and practical.[28]

Pediatrician Suzanne Dixon, who is editor of *The Journal of Developmental and Behavioral Pediatrics*, told *The New York Times* that one of the most helpful aspects of these reality shows occurs when adults are asked to explain on camera what they learned about parenting during the show.

"I write on prescription forms, 'Watch Supernanny,'" Dr. Dixon said. "I've been lecturing parents and professionals about managing disruptive behavior for more than 30 years," she said. "It's hard to create as vivid a picture in a clinical setting as 'Supernanny' is able to do with a video and a commentary from Jo, the nanny, as well as parents saying, 'I know I shouldn't have done that, but ...'"[29]

But some experts also criticized the use by both "Nanny 911" and "Supernanny" of the technique sometimes called "controlled crying," in which children who otherwise will not stay in bed at bedtime are allowed to cry themselves to sleep. Since controlled crying was popularized about 20 years ago, "parents and pediatricians have debated not only whether it works, but also whether it is a justified form of tough love or a Draconian method of discipline."[30] At the very least, it would seem reality producers should accept an ethical responsibility to point out to viewers when some of the programs' featured parenting techniques are considered debatable by pediatricians and parenting experts.[31]

---

[27] Dawn Cassidy, "Parent Education Comes to Prime Time TV," *CFLE Network*, Winter 2005, 1.
[28] Gilbert, "Those Televised Supernannies," F-1.
[29] Ibid.
[30] Ibid.
[31] Lucy Johnston, "NSPCC Attacks TV's 'Harmful' Baby Show: 'Bringing Up Baby' Advice 'Could Lead to Brain Damage,'" *Sunday Express*, October 14, 2007, 9.

Whatever the techniques advocated by "Supernanny" and "Nanny 911," perhaps their greatest positive impact comes in clearly suggesting that parenting is not simply an instinctive role, but one for which people should be educated. Says family life educator Dawn Cassidy: "The show provides an excellent platform for promoting the concept of family life education. More than one episode has shown distraught parents lamenting the fact that no one ever taught them how to be a good parent."[32] A Minnesota mother echoed that sentiment when she noted that simply seeing herself and her children on videotape was a more powerful corrective than any single technique they were taught by the TV nanny.[33]

"The Baby Borrowers" sought to be a corrective, too. Its producers said "The Baby Borrowers" program was intended to contradict media images that glamorize teen pregnancy. After all, this is a culture in which "American Idol" winner Fantasia Barrino, herself an unmarried mother at age 17, recorded a song titled "Baby Mama" that deems single motherhood "a badge of honor," in which the movie "Juno" made unplanned teen pregnancy the stuff of comedy and won an Oscar for screenwriting, and in which the heavily pregnant, unmarried, 16-year-old TV actress Jamie Lynn Spears was glowingly photographed for multiple magazine covers.

Some TV critics said the show provided exactly the corrective value its producers sought. "With no preachy subtext about chastity, 'The Baby Borrowers' presents a strong argument for shunning the path of Jamie Lynn Spears," noted *The New York Times*.[34] To its credit, "The Baby Borrowers" ended its summer 2008 run with a one-hour special that asked the participating teens and their families to put what they had learned into context several months after filming ended. The program also included interviews with some of the teens whose pregnancies came to light earlier in the summer when *Time* magazine reported on a "pregnancy pact" at their high school in Gloucester, Mass. The "pregnancy pact" story, later debunked as inaccurate, broke in *Time*'s June 18, 2008, edition and set off a frenzy of news reports that suggested as many as 17 young women in Gloucester deliberately agreed to become pregnant. "The Baby Borrowers" wrap-up show asked the teens and psychologists why they thought teens engage in sex without contraception. Certainly, after the media circus in Gloucester, the wrap-up episode was helpful in generating conversation about the realities of teen parenting. But the series itself may

---

[32] Cassidy, "Parent Education," 1.

[33] Tevlin, "After TV Nanny Leaves," 1-E.

[34] Gina Bellafante, "Test-Driving Parenthood Is Teenage Wake-Up Call," *The New York Times*, June 25, 2008, E-2.

not have been enough. For example, some Massachusetts teens were not
persuaded by the series. They said "The Baby Borrowers" taught more
about baby sitting than real parenting. They also said the show failed to
address the financial straits that face most teen parents.[35] And no teen
parent can walk off the job without consequences, as did at least one teen
on the show.

Questions that stem from audience responsibilities

While TV networks certainly should take responsibility for the
messages they broadcast, can all the fault for inaccurate or irresponsible
messages be laid at the feet of the networks? No. Rational parents cannot
simply take all their cues from television. They're responsible for turning
the television off, especially in the presence of their children, who may not
benefit from seeing other kids scream and cry.   Parents also are
responsible for seeking advice about rearing children from doctors,
counselors, religious figures, extended family and others, where
appropriate. And parents must be responsible for remembering that the
results typically portrayed on "Nanny 911" or "Supernanny" are rarely
achievable in the time frames used by the shows. "Nanny 911" visits a
troubled family for a week, while "Supernanny" spends two weeks with a
family, although Jo Frost herself is typically present for just five or so
days during those two weeks. As pediatrician Deborah Borchers told *The
New York Times*, that's unrealistic. "There's no way that a woman can
walk into someone's house and have the kids behaving in a week," Dr.
Borchers said. "The challenges are going to keep coming. There are no
quick fixes in parenting."[36]

It's incumbent upon families to place all these media messages about
parenting in context. Yet that's a difficult task. As Stephanie Coontz
argues, media messages that attribute all of society's failures to bad
parenting are hard to ignore. These media messages suggest that most
parents, particularly mothers, can never measure up to the challenges of
parenting healthy, well-adjusted children. Coontz suggests these pressures
on parents are overwhelmingly unrealistic and damaging.

> [W]e are fallible human beings in a society that expects us singlehandedly,
> or at most two-parently, to counter all the economic ups and downs, social
> pressures, personal choices, and competing demands of a highly unequal,

---

[35] Tenley Woodman, "Teens Say 'Baby' Barely Delivers," *Boston Herald*, June
27, 2008, E-17.
[36] Gilbert, "Those Televised Supernannies," F-1.

consumption-oriented culture dominated by deteriorating working conditions, interest-group politics, and self-serving advertisements for everything from toothpaste to moral value. We are expected to teach our children to sort through the claims or rival authorities without rejecting authority, to pursue self-reliance without abandoning commitment, and to resist the seductions of consumerism while preparing for jobs that will allow them to provide a better life for their own children.

It's a daunting proposition. … As a historian, I suspect that the truly dysfunctional thing about American parenting is that it is made out to be such a frighteningly pivotal, private, and exclusive job.[37]

Conclusion

On balance, I believe a show such as "Supernanny performs an ethical service. "Supernanny" offers families no incentives for participation beyond the goal of a calmer household, but it tells both participating parents and parents in the audience that it's OK to seek help and that it's possible to change dysfunctional family behaviors. Researchers in the United Kingdom suggest that shows like "Supernanny," which provide sound, practical tips on parenting, do actually make some adults better parents. A University of Manchester study of 740 parents found improved confidence and ability among its subjects.[38]

By comparison, no matter what parenting techniques they present, shows such as "The Baby Borrowers" fail to overcome the ethical hurdle of exploiting children who are not rationally able to give fully informed consent. TV critic Brian Lowry put it this way:

Since the genre arose in its modern form, each permutation of reality TV has demanded renewed scrutiny. With "Kid Nation" and "Baby Borrowers," the inquiry begins (and perhaps ends) by asking a simple question of every executive and producer responsible for such programs: Would you let your kid do it? Almost without exception, my guess is not in a million years.[39]

---

[37] Coontz, *The Way We Never Were*, 209-210.
[38] Ruth Smith, "Research Report: Parenting Support," *Children Now*, November 29, 2006, 17.
[39] Brian Lowry, "In Reality's New Wrinkles, the Kids Aren't All Right," *Variety*, May 28 to June 3, 2007, 13.

VIRTUE ETHICS AS THE BASIS FOR FAMILY INTERACTION

JAMES J. PONZETTI, JR.

Human beings exist within a moral ecology where they strive to live in a socially useful and fully developed manner.[1] As individuals grow from infancy to adulthood, they must learn the rights and responsibilities necessary to sustain harmonious relationships. Rights imply responsibilities consistent with constructive behavior necessary for mutual interaction.[2] [3] Virtue is vital to express these rights and responsibilities.

Virtue is required to facilitate behavior respectful of the rights and responsibilities needed to create amicable relationships. Accordingly, care and mutuality[4] are integral to ongoing interaction. For example, parents do not feed children because it is their right; rather parental care is simply the response to children's need. Virtue is fostered by incremental reciprocity in an interpersonal context.

Virtue is conducive to personal and collective well-being. It is the glue that holds communal life together. Individuals typically experience community in their families first. Families are influential in nurturing the qualities that constitute the basis of virtue. They serve as important mediators between individuals and the society writ large. [5] [6]

---

[1] Brinkmann, S. (2004). The topography of moral ecology. *Theory and Psychology, 14*, 57-80.

[2] Etzioni, Amitai (May, 1997). Education for intimacy. *Educational Leadership*, 20-23.

[3] Saunders, W. (1990). Education for interpersonal life. *Liberal Education, 76* (2), 11-12.

[4] Noddings, Nel (1984). *Caring: A feminine approach to ethics and moral education*. Berkeley, CA: University of California Press.

[5] Martone, Mary (1998). Developing virtuous children: A theological perspective. *Journal of Social Distress and the Homeless, 7*, 107-119.

[6] Walker, Lawrence (1999). The family context for moral development. *Journal of Moral Education, 28* (3), 261-264.

The purpose of this paper is twofold. First, the importance and relevance of virtue to quotidian existence is described. Second, virtue ethics is discussed as the basis for optimal family interaction.

What is virtue?

Virtue involves the full range of human functioning. The virtuous life is not simply defined by what people do because people are never just acting. Rather, they are always becoming better or worse people. A virtuous person is one who employs personal inclinations and character traits to do the moral thing, make an ethical choice, without necessarily asking how rules apply to the situation.[7] Virtue is not only necessary for proper actions (i.e., ethical behavior), but constitutive of respectable character (i.e., moral emotion and reason). People become virtuous by inculcating character that exhibit habitual responses indicative of virtue itself. Virtue is not innate; rather it is acquired over time.

Virtue prescribes ideals that are deemed morally exemplary. It provides standards for conduct that makes life go well for people. In other words, virtue is motivated by the emotional desire and willful intention to act well. The development of virtue is ambitious, especially when it confronts people with the painful reality of their imperfection, but virtuous striving can yield a more commendable life. Virtues are pivotal character strengths that enable individuals to perform moral actions easily and well.[8]

Virtue must not be construed as the imposition of anachronistic rules or strict moral codes. In fact, it can be contrasted with such rules or codes. Unlike the notion that a moral person primarily needs to know and follow specific rules to behave virtuously, virtue refers to the dispositions or capacity of people to perceive needs accurately and respond accordingly. So, rules and principles are derived from virtues. Rules or principles are directives that obtain their context from virtuous activity.

Virtue disposes one to act in ways indicative of optimal development. It directs people to think, feel, and act in ways that typically yield a commendable life; that is, it incorporates emotion, cognition, as well as behavior. It is the emotional desire to do what is moral, the intellectual decision to choose what is worthy, the volitional intent to act in a reputable

---

[7] Blaine J. Fowers (2005). *Virtue and Psychology: Pursuing Excellence in Ordinary Practices.* American Psychological Association Books: Washington, D.C.

[8] McCullough, Michael, and C.R. Snyder (2000). Classical sources of human strength: Revisiting an old home and building a new one. *Journal of Social and Clinical Psychology, 19* (1), 1-10.

manner, and the habitual practice of constructive behavior toward other people. The regular performance of virtuous acts is indicative of specific traits and inclinations that are possessed inchoately. Yet, a life lived in accordance with virtue is by no means devoid of tensions, conflicts, and difficult choices.

Discourse about virtue is not novel. Classical and contemporary philosophers have offered various descriptions of virtue in their writings. Three transcendent (or theological) virtues--faith, hope, and charity (love)—are traceable to St. Paul as traits acquired through grace. In *Nichomachean Ethics*, Aristotle wrote the first systematic virtue ethics. He divided virtue into those that were moral (i.e., having to do with character) and those that were intellectual (i.e., having to do with the mind). According to Aristotle, once people acquire moral habits, they are better able to make ethical decisions when faced with difficult choices.

Plato, in *The Republic*, offered a framework in which key virtues were identified as morally exemplary and thus worth cultivating. Thomas Aquinas subsequently adopted this framework with modifications. Four virtues were defined as cardinal because the Latin word cardo refers to a hinge, and all other virtues pivot on the cardinal virtues. The four cardinal virtues are prudence (or wisdom), justice, temperance (or moderation), and fortitude (or courage). The presence of one presumes the presence of the others.[9] [10] [11]

The cardinal virtues express what constitutes a virtuous person. Rather than being the last word on virtue, they are the first, providing the bare essentials of what it means to be a good person. The cardinal virtues empower and dispose one to act in ways indicative of human flourishing; that is, these virtues provide a framework for what people should fundamentally be and at what human action should basically aim. Moral actions hang on the cardinal virtues as integral to rightly ordered dispositions.[12]

Virtue is learned by observing and doing, by being aware of the reasons why a certain kind of action came about and the reasons for it. In

[9] Porter, J. (1993). "The Unity of the Virtues and the Ambiguity of Goodness", *Journal of Religious Ethics, 21*, 137-164.
[10] Terkel, S., & Duval, R. (1999). *Encyclopedia of ethics.* New York: Facts on File Inc.
[11] Harrison, R. K. (1992). Encyclopedia of Biblical and Christian ethics. Nashville, TN: Thomas Nelson.
[12] Oderberg, D. (1999). "On the Cardinality of the Cardinal Virtues", *International Journal of Philosophical Studies,* 7, 305-322

understanding virtue, the central challenge is to comprehend how people manage to override their own selfish inclinations and do what is exemplary instead. Virtue is acquired in a formative community, such as the family, rather than deduced through independent reasoning. Families provide one of the most influential settings in which individuals can learn (or fail to learn) virtue. Families and then schools teach children to not let their own wishes lead to actions that are detrimental to other family members, or their community. [13] [14] Scholarship in the empirical sciences, however, has ignored virtue as an important construct. Perhaps the perception that scientific investigation must be value-free has hampered the study of virtue and ethics.[15]

Family relationships are the primary context for socialization. Socialization processes involve subtle interaction that occur at different levels—intellectual, sensory and emotional as well as ethical. Families are instrumental in educating their members concerning the desired actions necessary for interpersonal relations. Indeed, parents are the first and perhaps most profound teachers of their children. Virtue is expressed in behavior consistent with healthy interaction and crucial to family well being. Thus, families constitute the moral center of personal life. Most individuals reside in familial settings where virtue reinforces the moral lifestyle essential for civil society. [16]

Alasdair McIntyre, in his seminal book on virtue ethics[17], claimed that contemporary social, political, and economic conditions are typically hostile to virtue. Put simply, modern circumstances encourage individuals and organizations to pursue external goods—money, possessions, fame, and power—to the detriment of internal goods, the satisfaction brought about by doing the right thing, by acting virtuously. The disposition to act well in everyday situations, in accordance with the internal goods conducive to daily interaction, provides the foundation of routine virtue.

---

[13] Okin Susan Moller, and Rob Reich (1999). "Families and Schools as Compensating Agents in Moral Development for a Multicultural Society", *Journal of Moral Education, 28* (3), 283-298.
[14] Pritchard, Michael (1992). "Families, Schools and the Moral Education of Children", *Denver University Law Review, 69* (3), 687-704
[15] Fowers, Blaine, & Alan Tjeltveit (2003). "Virtue Obscured and Retrieved: Character, Community, and Practices in Behavioral Science", *American Behavioral Scientist*, 47(4), 387-394.
[16] Halstead, J. Mark (1999). "Moral Education in Family Life: The Effects of Diversity", *Journal of Moral Education*, 28(3), 265-281.
[17] McIntyre, Alasdair (2007). *After virtue* (3rd edition). South Bend, IN; University of Notre Dame Press.

Quotidian virtue is largely hidden. Because it is exercised in the routine context of the private, rather than the public sphere, it goes largely unnoticed by others, often even by virtuous individuals themselves. Everyday virtue is part of the fabric of life, both in its personal as well as public dimension.

Shifting expectations of family relationships have weakened the pursuit of the internal goods that promote virtuous behavior. These changes undermine conventional moral directives concerning how far individuals should yield when selfish inclinations conflict with group needs for stable, harmonious relationships. Such involvement has become particularly poignant because families exist in a socially toxic environment[18] that is especially inhospitable to virtue. The actual practice of virtue within intense and sometimes volatile family relationships results from complex processes that often inadvertently promote vice. Virtue promotes interaction directed at the facilitation of family competence. Yet, family interaction has received only modest attention as a context for virtue.[19]

Virtues are widely regarded as important aspects of family relationships, but there is controversy as to which virtues should be espoused. Family life can be directed toward what is virtuous. A myriad of complex processes and practices foster virtue within intense and oftentimes volatile family relationships. Families are at least partially responsible for the presence of both virtue and vice.

The everyday existence of family members requires virtue to adjudicate competing interests or conflicting goals when they arise. The most enduring way to develop respectable character is to inculcate virtue. In other words, virtues are not only indicative of moral strength but provide the standard for right conduct in interpersonal contexts. Virtue is learned by doing and observing, by being aware of the reasons why a certain kind of action came about and of the reasons for it.

Virtue is widely regarded as paramount to close relationships but what virtues people should exemplify remains equivocal. These virtues command particular attention for optimal human interaction. In various cultures and societies around the world, certain virtues appear repeatedly, suggesting similar responses to the conundrum of living together. Granted many lists of virtues have been compiled; however, particular virtues have

[18] Garbarino, J. (1995). *Raising children in a social toxic environment.* San Francisco, CA: Jossey-Bass Publishers.
[19] Ponzetti, James (2005). "The Family as Moral Center: An Evolutionary Hermeneutics of Virtue in Family Studies", *Journal of Research in Character Education, 3*, 61-70.

been identified as cardinal because the tenacity of these virtues. The exposition of the cardinal virtues through word and deed within the familial context emphasizes and reinforces the importance these virtues hold in defining the fundamental aspirations of human beings. Through the lens of an evolutionary hermeneutic, the cardinal virtues constitute a curriculum for living in contemporary families.[20]

Unless justice and mutuality characterize family interaction and unless members are treated with respect and care, they are likely to be considerably hindered in becoming productive citizens. Unless they learn how to use prudence (or wisdom) when faced with conflicting options and opportunities, and make temperate (or disciplined) decisions in light of the impact of such decisions, they are likely to be disappointed in their intimate lives. In addition, unless they have the fortitude (or perseverance) to holdfast during times of trial and disappointment, they are not likely to navigate the daily challenges of family life successfully. Rather, than being one among many coequal institutions, families are the essential foundation of virtue.

Virtue ethics

As one of three major approaches in normative ethics, virtue ethics emphasizes the inner disposition or character of the person, in contrast to the approach which emphasizes duties or rules (i.e., deontology) or that which emphasizes the consequences of actions (i.e., consequentialism). Both deontological and consequentialist approaches articulate moral decision making that is episodic and intermittent, and not an integral part of everyday life. Contrary to virtue ethics, moral living is fragmented into a series of isolated decisions reserved for crisis situations. Neither approach considers the role of motives in the evaluation of moral decisions. Virtue ethics encourages people to desire certain outcomes and thus want to accomplish certain goals by their actions. Particular attention is given to the entirety of moral experience—perceptions, convictions, emotions, commitments, and actions. Ethical choices are woven into the web of quotidian moment-by-moment living.

The aim of virtue ethics is to help people develop habits conducive to interpersonal well-being. Having the proper disposition allows a person to accurately distinguish the right course of action from a wrong one. Most

---

[20] Ponzetti, James (2005). The family as moral center: An evolutionary hermeneutics of virtue in family studies. *Journal of Research in Character Education, 3*, 61-70.

ethical judgments do not involve issues that are already clearly right or wrong but instead are very nuanced, contain many different circumstances, and involve conflicting values. The contextual nature of virtue ethics occurs in the midst of everyday living, which is always relational.[21]

Virtue ethics was the prevailing approach to ethical thinking in the ancient and medieval periods. The tradition suffered an eclipse during the early modern period, as Aristotelianism fell out of favor in the West. The revival of virtue ethics in the latter twentieth century has been a timely reminder that living well involves many judgments and decisions previously thought to be too humble to attract attention.

Virtue ethics has regained popularity for several reasons. First, it provides an important contribution to understanding the central role of motives to ethical questions. To act from virtue is to act from some particular motivation; thus to say that certain virtues are necessary for correct moral decisions is to say that right decisions require virtuous motives. A second reason involves virtue ethics as a means of dealing with complicated moral calculations over what actions to take or duties to emphasize. Virtue ethics promises that once individuals are successful in creating the sort of person they want to be, arriving at correct moral decisions comes naturally. Rather than concentrate on specific acts or issues, virtue ethics focuses on the development of the whole person. This approach examines the tension between the person one is and the person one could be. It recognizes that acts have effects not only on the exterior world but also on the individual who performs them.

Virtue ethics offers a comprehensive approach for teaching moral living that attends to the development of the whole person within the social context in which he or she resides. It is particularly well suited in its application to family life and the socialization of virtuous children. From a virtue ethics perspective, virtue is learned incrementally by observing others within a particular context and not simply by following a set of abstract principles or procedures. Virtue ethics bridges the gap between abstract ethical theory and the moral demands implicit in everyday mundane situations. .[22] [23] [2425] Yet, the key question is how people realize such a life.

---

[21] Martone, Mary (1998). "Developing Virtuous Children: A Theological Perspective", *Journal of Social Distress and the Homeless, 7*, 107-119.

[22] Gould, J. (2002). "Better Hearts: Teaching Virtue Ethics", *Teaching Philosophy, 25*, 1-26.

[23] Van Hooft, Stan (2001). "Teaching Virtue Ethics: The Case of Love", *Teaching Philosophy*, 24(2), 143-154.

Families are schools of virtue in their role as one of the most formative environments for the individuals who comprise them. The family context presents a unique setting for daily intimate interaction that can facilitate moral growth.[26] Unless the adult interactions experienced by children are characterized by justice, and unless family members use prudence or wisdom when faced with the multiplicity of conflicting options and opportunities, and make temperate or disciplined decisions, they are likely to be considerably hindered in expressing virtuous character. And unless they have the fortitude or perseverance to holdfast during times of trial and disappointment, they are not likely to navigate the daily challenges of family life successfully.

Espousing virtue ethics endorses consideration of the whole person–thoughts, feelings, and behaviors–in context. Family educators tend to focus on behaviors that support relationships rather than the feelings or thoughts that reinforce these behaviors. For example, they may teach communication skills or investigate how to resolve conflicts rather than specific cognitions or emotions that promote the use of such skills. Skills *training* may have limited applicability in comparison to virtue *education* of similar skills in different situations. In other words, focusing on technical competence, although useful to a point, does not generalize across diverse contexts. Families educate rather than train its members how to care for one another and be productive citizens. If individuals are instructed and guided to internalize a virtuous disposition, then the emotions and thoughts that comprise this disposition facilitate moral action, even in circumstances in which specific skills were not learned. To be succinct, virtue ethics builds character in ways that skills training cannot.

Conclusion

Virtue ethics is the basis for family interaction. Individuals acquire their ways of living in their families. Family life is based on humble acts that represent a willingness to share ordinary occurrences, and find meaning in routine, familiar, unromantic tasks. Families depend on

---

[24] Holmes,A. (1991). *Shaping character.* Grand Rapids, MI: William B. Eerdmans.

[25] Hesch, J. (1992). "Fostering the Development of Compassion in Young Children", *Pastoral Psychology, 41*, 31-38.

[26] Hauerwas, Stanley (1985, Spring). "The Family as a School for Character", *Religious Education, 80* (2), 272-285.

finding value in simple and common things. They represent the discovery of the extraordinary in the midst of mundane activities of daily life.

The rhythms and bonding encountered and nurtured in families establish future life patterns. The early experiences of family life construct emotional environments that impact interaction in later life, e.g. confident rather than anxious, trusting instead of suspicious, contented rather than ambitious. The development of an optimal family environment can run its own course, sometimes leading to dysfunction; or family members can volitionally attend to creating a lifestyle guided by virtue.

The cardinal virtues offer an evolutionary framework for contemporary family life in realizing not only what virtuous life entails but also how to provide moral guidance. They are instrumental in modeling the compassion and care that emanate from virtue ethics.

RECONCILING FAMILIAL LOVE AND IMPARTIAL MORALITY: AN EXAMINATION OF DAVID VELLEMAN'S EFFORTS AND SOME ALTERNATIVE STRATEGIES[1]

ERIC SILVERMAN

One important ethical debate asks whether love in partial relationships can be reconciled with an impartial account of morality. The importance of this debate is well characterized in Bernard Williams's discussion of a man who can only save one of two drowning people, one of whom is his wife. What, if anything, ethically justifies the husband in saving his wife rather than the stranger? Williams concludes that partial attachments, such as romantic relationships, familial relationships, and deep friendships, will inevitably conflict with the demands of impartial morality. Yet, such attachments are an essential part of life, for "unless such things exist, there will not be enough substance or conviction in a man's life to compel his allegiance to life itself."[2]

David Velleman presents one model intended to bridge the gap between impartial morality and love. His account of love, modeled upon Kantian respect, construes it as a response to the objective personhood of the beloved. In doing so, he hopes to embrace the value of love and relationships without abandoning an impartial account of morality. His strategy for unraveling the partiality – impartiality dilemma is to separate the emotion of love itself from the desires and preferences that so often accompany love. The emotion of love need not contain a desire to benefit, care for, or protect the beloved. He explains, "Once we separate love from

---

[1] Sections of this essay are reprinted with permission from Silverman, Eric, *The Prudence of Love: How Possessing the Virtue of Love Benefits the Lover* (Rowman and Littlefield's Lexington Books, 2010).

[2] Bernard Williams, "Persons, Character and Morality," in *Moral Luck* (New York, New York: Cambridge University Press, 1981), p. 18.

the likings and longings that usually go with it, I believe, we will give up the assumption that the emotion is partial in a sense that puts it in conflict with the spirit of morality."[3]

While he makes an excellent effort to reconcile love and impartiality within the Kantian tradition, his account of love has counterintuitive implications. For example, it cannot explain normative experiences of love such as the perceived uniqueness and irreplacibility of the beloved. It is also unusually minimalist compared to most accounts of love. I proceed by outlining Velleman's account of impartial love. Finally, I conclude with an in-depth critique that rejects his account and offers some alternative strategies for reconciling impartial morality and familial love.

I. Velleman's Objective Basis For Love

In an attempt to reconcile love with the impartiality of morality Velleman construes love as an emotional response to the beloved's humanity, personhood, and rational capacities. Since the basis of love is generic personhood, all humans are appropriate objects for love. Love is an emotion that results from a person's awareness of a particular other's value as a person. His account focuses on mature adult loves, such as friendship and familial relationships, rather than irrational romantic love. He explains: "I do not want to claim that blind, romantic love has any special kinship with morality. When I say that love is a moral emotion, what I have in mind is the love between close adult friends and relations."[4] This love of friends is a morally valuable emotion since it is a response to the value of their personhood, which does not conflict with the demands of morality. He describes his strategy for reconciling love with impartial morality, "The way to bring love in convergence with morality is not to stop thinking of morality as impartial but to rethink the partiality of love."[5] He suggests that identifying an impartial basis for love is preferable to rejecting impartial morality.

Velleman claims love is similar to Kant's account of respect, which is also a response to the value of an agent's personhood. Both emotions are based upon the agent's awareness of another's personhood. He explains, ". . . reverence for the law, which has struck so many as making Kantian ethics impersonal, is in fact an attitude towards the person, since the law that commands respect is the ideal of a rational will, which lies at the very

---

[3] J. David Velleman, , "Love as a Moral Emotion," *Ethics* 109 (Jan 1999), p. 342.
[4] J. David Velleman 1999, p. 351.
[5] J. David Velleman, "Love as a Moral Emotion," *Ethics* 109 (Jan 1999), p. 342

heart of personhood."[6] Since the rational will is the essence of personhood, Velleman sees reverence for the moral law and love for others as paradigm examples of Kantian moral emotions. Both emotions have an impartial but personal basis.

Velleman explicates love and respect as second order negative emotions. Based on the second formulation of the categorical imperative, which prohibits treating persons as a means, he describes respect as a negative second order motive. It prevents one from having first order motives that treat persons only as means rather than ends. Respect is a second order motive because it is a motive pertaining to an agent's first order motivations. It leads the rational person to bring first order motivations in line with the second order guidance of respect. However, respect is also a negative motivation because it only prevents the agent from having morally unacceptable first order motivations. Respect for the moral law prevents an agent from immoral motivations such as greed, envy, hatred, and lust, which involve treating humanity as a means.[7]

Velleman claims that love, like respect, is also a negative second order motive, but one that has particular other persons as its object rather than all humanity. He asks,

> Could this model of a negative second order motive apply to love? Let me return to Kant's description of reverence as the awareness of a value that arrests our self-love. I am inclined to say that love is likewise the awareness of a value inhering in its object; and I am also inclined to describe love as an arresting awareness of that value.[8]

Respect deters immoral motives that treat a person as a mere means to some further goal. If love is a second order motivation, what first order motives will it restrain? Velleman claims love arrests a person's "tendencies toward emotional self protection from another person, tendencies to draw ourselves in and close ourselves off from being affected by him. Love disarms our emotional defenses; it makes us vulnerable to the other."[9] Thus, love is a second order motivation because it influences the loving agent's first order motives towards particular beloved persons. Love is a negative second order motivation because it restricts particular self-protective first order motivations. It restrains a

[6] J. David Velleman 1999, p. 348.
[7] Of course, it is possible to dispute aspects of Velleman's interpretation of Kant. However, my interest is examining his attempt to reconcile love with impartiality, so I will not comment on these interpretive issues.
[8] J. David Velleman 1999, p. 360.
[9] J. David Velleman 1999, p. 361.

person from acting upon self-protective motivations within relationships, such as fear, insecurity, and anxiety, allowing the lover to be open and vulnerable with the beloved.

Simultaneously, Velleman denies that love includes a desire to benefit or aid the beloved, rejecting such claims as 'sentimental fantasy.'[10] He explains, "Certainly, love for my children, leads me to promote their interests almost daily; yet when I think of other people I love--parents, brothers, friends, former teachers and students—I do not think of myself as an agent of their interests."[11] He believes these counterexamples demonstrate that love does not include a desire to care for or benefit the beloved. He perceives love's traditional association with benefiting the beloved as a source of its supposed conflict with impartial morality. If a desire to benefit the beloved is not an essential constituent of love, it is easy to see how love is compatible with impartial morality.

II. A Critique of Velleman

There are a numerous attractive features in Velleman's account of love. First, emotional vulnerability is a central normative experience of love in the broad range of loving relationships. One feature that unites love in friendship, marriage, families, etc. is a high degree of openness and emotional vulnerability. Second, his strategy eliminates much of the tension between partial love and impartial morality. Since love has nothing to do with benefiting the beloved, it is not connected with actions that conflict with impartial morality. Finally, he provides a compelling explanation for love's tenacity. Since love is based in an essential trait of the beloved, her personhood, it cannot be lost. Popular accounts of love that view the beloved's attributes as a basis of love such as beauty, personality, accomplishments, virtue, or even intelligence rely upon contingent personal attributes. These attributes come and go. Any emotion that is a response to these attributes should fluctuate just as easily, but love is thought to be tenacious. Passing fancy, infatuation, and lust may fluctuate easily, but love should not.

While Velleman's account has these positive traits, it is inadequate in other ways. One question raised by his account is why the lover cares for some people, but not others since they are all appropriate objects for love due to their personhood. Niko Kolodny develops an objection based on this problem, claiming that Velleman's account implies that since

---

[10] J. David Velleman 1999, p. 353.
[11] J. David Velleman 1999, p. 353.

personhood is the sole basis of love the lover ought to accept any other person as a substitute for the beloved. Yet, accepting such substitution is obviously incompatible with the normative experiences of love. Kolodny explains,

> In J. David Velleman's provocative and ingeniously argued proposal, the reason for love is the beloved's bare Kantian personhood, her capacity for rational choice and valuation. But no such non-relational feature works . . . . The claim that non-relational features are reasons for love implies, absurdly, that insofar as one's love for (say) Jane is responsive to its reasons, it will accept any relevantly similar person as a replacement.[12]

As Kolodny emphasizes, love is not transferable from the beloved to others simply based upon similar non-relational traits. This problem is particularly severe for Velleman's account since its reason for love is an attribute possessed by all persons. In an effort to ward off such criticisms, Velleman counters that we love some people rather than others based upon our ability to grasp their personhood.

> One reason why we love some people rather than others is that we can see into only some of our observable fellow creatures. . . . Whether someone is loveable depends on how well his value as a person is expressed or symbolized for us by his empirical persona. Someone's persona may not speak very clearly of his value as a person, or may not speak in ways that are clear to us.[13]

Velleman suggests we love some people rather than others, because we can only see into the personhood of certain people. If our interactions with another offer clear insight into his personhood, it is natural to respond to him with the love warranted by a valuable rational being. If we cannot see another's personhood, it is easier to be self-protective. Yet, this explanation seems strained and leads to unintuitive consequences.

The most serious problem with Velleman's explanation is its difficulty explaining the non-substitutability of the beloved and the various types of loving relationships. Since he believes love acts similarly in every loving relationship by merely restricting the agent's self-protective motivations the beloved becomes too easily replaceable. The lover may recognize the personhood of his classmate, his spouse, and his child, but the normative experience of love demonstrates that these relationships are fundamentally different and that these people cannot act as substitutes for one another.

---

[12] Niko Kolodny, "Love As Valuing a Relationship," *Philosophical Review* 112 (2003), p. 135.
[13] J. David Velleman 1999, p. 372.

Yet, it is difficult to see what reason Velleman can offer for not rejecting such substitutions, since the basis of love is identical in each case.

If love is impartial as in Velleman's account, it offers no reasonable basis for loving one person more than or in a distinct way from any other person. This implication is problematic since some aspects of love obviously differ from relationship to relationship. Love for a friend, a spouse, a child, and a parent, differ significantly and an account of love should offer some explanation for this common experience. A parent who is emotionally open to his child, but has no further desire, emotion, or action towards him falls short of love. Love between spouses requires more than emotional openness, such as ongoing relational commitments: to one another, to maintaining the relationship, and to sexual fidelity.

Velleman's account of love is also surprisingly minimalist. Love does not require a single positive action or motivation. He describes love as having an object in a particular other person, but no aim.[14] Instead of an aim, love merely restrains the lover's self-protection motives. Love need not be instantiated in any positive action or desire. Just as one may often carry out Kant's imperative to 'never treat humanity as a means only' by interacting very little with a particular person, one can be emotionally open without many actions typically associated within love. While this implication may be compatible with morality, the normative experiences of love suggest that interaction is at the heart of love. For example, Aristophanes' speech on love in Plato's *Symposium* depicts love in terms of an intense longing for one another. He says,

> And when one of them finds his other half, whether he be a lover of youth or a lover of another sort, the pair are lost in an amazement of love and friendship and intimacy, and one will not be out of the other's sight, as I may say, even for a moment: these are they who pass their lives with one another; yet they could not explain what they desire of one another. For the intense yearning which each of them has towards the other does not appear to be the desire of intercourse, but of something else which the soul desires and can not tell, and of which she has only a dark and doubtful presentiment.[15]

While this speech is hardly infallible and focuses upon a romantic type of love, the claim that love includes a desire for active closeness and intimacy is more compelling and is better supported by the normative experience of love than Velleman's alternative.

---

[14] J. David Velleman 1999, p. 354.
[15] Plato, *The Symposium*, Benjamin Jowett (trans.) (Mineola, NY: Dover Publications, 1993), 192b-c.

In contrast, Velleman rejects the idea that love requires a desire to be with another. He argues,

> But, surely, it is easy enough to love someone whom one cannot stand to be with. Think here of Murdoch's reference to a troubling relation. The meddlesome aunt, cranky grandfather, smothering parent, or overcompetitive sibling is dearly loved, loved freely and with feeling: one just has no desire for his or her company.[16]

At first Velleman's counter-examples may have some appeal. After all, he is correct that there are people that we love, yet whose company we do not enjoy. Yet, a failure to enjoy someone's company is not identical to failing to desire closeness and intimacy with that person. In fact, it is possible to desire closeness and intimacy with someone while being deeply frustrated that some aspect of their personality acts as an obstacle to intimacy.

Therefore, I suggest a better analysis of the 'troubling relations' counterexample is that we do desire closeness with beloved, but troublesome relatives. We merely wish they would change some non-essential traits so we could enjoy being close to them. Perhaps, their character flaws lead us to some self-protective behaviors, some guardedness in what we say in their presence, and some limiting of when and where we are willing to see them. Yet, if we didn't love these relatives we would simply distance ourselves entirely from them as we do from most people we find inordinately meddlesome, cranky, smothering, or petty. The fact that we maintain such relationships, that we keep in touch, and that we sometimes seek their company in spite of their flaws, is evidence of our love for them and that our love includes a desire for closeness with them.

Another problem with Velleman's account of love as emotional openness is that it implies that some relationships should be re-categorized as 'loving.' For example, a neurotic patient who pursues psychoanalysis faithfully, and has a personal connection resulting in emotional openness to his psychologist 'loves' his analyst on this account. Similarly, the new member of an Alcoholics Anonymous chapter who openly shares about his addiction with a room full of anonymous strangers and enjoys camaraderie in the exchange of the stories of their common struggles 'loves' them on this model. I do not suggest that such intimacy is worthless, but merely that it falls short of love.

---

[16] J. David Velleman 1999, p. 353.

Velleman's argument for divorcing love from a desire to benefit the beloved is also uncompelling. He concludes that love does not include a desire to benefit the beloved from the fact that love does not lead him to think of himself as a general agent of the interests of some people he loves including, 'parents, brothers, friends, former teachers and students.'[17] Yet, Velleman does not consider the possibility that love leads the lover to desire to benefit the beloved within a more specific scope, without the lover viewing himself as a 'general agent of the beloved's interests.'

In particular, it seems that the type of relationship the lover has with the beloved shapes how she desires to benefit the beloved.[18] For example, a loving teacher does not view herself as a general 'agent of her students' interests,' yet seeks to benefit her students by acting as a thoughtful instructor, helping them develop intellectual virtue, clearly communicating beneficial subject matter, wanting them to succeed academically, etc. A loving student benefits former teachers by appropriately crediting them with their role in his own success. A loving friend benefits other friends by encouraging them in their pursuit of life's goals and by being a confidante. Within many types of relationships, the ongoing relationship that the lover seeks with the beloved is itself a benefit to the beloved. Therefore, Velleman's purported counter-examples do not really establish that love does not include a desire to care for or benefit the beloved, but only that love does not necessarily entail becoming an unqualified general agent of the beloved's interests.

Finally, while Velleman works towards resolving the tension between impartial morality and love, his account ultimately circumvents the central issue of this debate. When ethicists worry about love's partiality, they aren't concerned with the partiality one shows through emotional vulnerability to friends, but by the practical benefits the lover offers the beloved. In Williams's illustration it is not the man's emotional vulnerability to his wife that is ethically troubling, but the husband's preferential treatment of her in saving her life rather than a stranger's. Velleman's ultimate response to William's illustration reveals that his account of love avoids rather than resolves the tensions between partial attachment and impartial morality. He explains,

> Of course the man in Williams' story should save his wife in preference to strangers. But the reasons why he should save her have nothing essentially

---

[17] J. David Velleman 1999, p. 353.
[18] I associate this insight with Thomas Aquinas' thought. *Cf.* Thomas Aquinas, *Summa theologica,* tr. The Fathers of the English Dominican Province, Second and Revised Edition (New York: Benziger Brothers, Inc., 1947), II-II q. 31 a. 3.

to do with love. The grounds for preference in this case include, to begin with, the mutual commitments and dependencies of a loving relationship.[19]

This response keeps love impartial by justifying the husband's partiality in terms of the mutual commitments and dependencies of a loving relationship, while denying these commitments and dependencies have any necessary connection with love. While it is trivially true that love understood as emotional vulnerability has no essential connection to marital commitments, this response does nothing to resolve the conflict between partial attachment and impartial morality, but merely separates the concept of love from partial attachment. While love no longer conflicts with impartial morality, the partial attachments formed from the mutual commitments and dependencies of loving relationships still have not been reconciled with impartial morality.

III. Conclusion and Alternative Strategies

David Velleman has offered an original and clever account of love modeled on Kantian respect. His account reconciles love with impartial morality by identifying an impartial basis for love in the beloved's personhood and by separating love from any desire to benefit or aid the beloved. However, his account is unusually minimalist and is not compatible with many normative experiences of love such as the irreplacibility, the uniqueness of the beloved, and the distinctions between the various kinds of loving relationships. Furthermore, while he successfully reconciles love with impartial morality, the problems posed by partial attachment reappear when examining the compatibility of loving relationships with impartial morality.

How then, might love be reconciled with impartial morality? The most obvious way would be to reconcile love and other partial attachments with a second-order rather than first-order type of impartiality. Moral theories require first-order impartiality if they require the moral agent to be impartial in everyday decision making. Second-order impartiality only operates in a special context where moral rules or principles are evaluated. Thus, a theory requiring second-order impartiality in establishing moral guidelines may be compatible with many expressions of everyday first-order partiality.

---

[19] David Velleman 1999, p. 373.

For example, traditional act-utilitarianism[20] requires first-order impartiality since the right action in any situation will be that which brings about the greatest happiness to all effected by the action. Therefore, one's family is not permitted to receive any special consideration at all. In contrast, rule-utilitarianism[21] only requires second-order impartiality since the right action is determined by whether a person is acting in accordance with impartially created moral principles that would result in the greatest happiness for all if everyone adhered to them. Therefore, rule utilitarianism might justify granting special consideration to one's family if a universally instantiated pattern of such partiality would result in the greatest happiness for all.

Yet, this type of strategy is not the only reasonable response to the tension between partial attachments and impartial morality. My preferred solution is to reconsider which traits hold moral significance that one ought to respond to impartially. Medieval thinkers such as Thomas Aquinas were quite aware of the competing demands of close relationships and impartial morality. Yet, the idea that certain types of relationships do not provide impartial moral justification for certain actions would never have occurred to them. They believed that there is a certain ideal structure to an agent's love that recognizes the existence of certain relationships as a moral justification for certain types of preferences.[22] Simultaneously, they were quite aware that all sorts of moral abuses stem from granting inappropriate preferences to those we care about.[23]

In this medieval spirit, I suggest that a person's relational traits have moral significance that ought to be responded to impartially. Since we are beings of limited capacities and resources, humans simply cannot benefit everyone equally. Among the possible guidelines for the ideal use of our limited resources to help others, one of the most sensible focuses upon giving some priority to close familial relationships marked by long-term proximity, mutual commitment, and detailed knowledge of one another. The existence of such a relationship should be viewed as an impartial factor in distributing certain types of benefits.

For example, the fact that another person is one's child (i.e. has the relational trait of being one's child) is morally relevant and should be

---

[20] Such as John Stuart Mill's well known theory outlined in *Utilitarianism* and J.J.C. Smart's contemporary utilitarianism outlined in *Utilitarianism: For and Against* (New York, New York: Cambridge University Press, 1973).
[21] Some thinkers who are often interpreted as rule utilitarians include George Berkeley, R.B. Brandt, and J. Harsanyi.
[22] *Cf.* Thomas Aquinas, ST II-II q. 26.
[23] *Cf.* Thomas Aquinas, ST II-II q. 63.

responded to regardless of the child's personality or the parent's personal preferences. We ought to give priority to our children's welfare in many situations even if we do not prefer to do so. This sort of moral reasoning seems to underlie the current practice of requiring mandatory child support payments from non-custodial parents. The fact of a parent-child relationship is used to justify taking money from even an unwilling non-custodial parent. Therefore, while relationships justify certain sorts of preferential treatment, this moral principle does not allow an agent's mere whims to dictate how she expends her resources. This approach is certainly preferential towards certain others, but it is not partial in the sense that it is based on the agent's mere subjective preferences. Furthermore, any morally acceptable preferential treatment that stems from a relationship should be universalizable. It must not apply to just one specific relationship, but all such relationships of the same type in similar circumstances.

While certain types of familial relationships justify some preferential treatment, there are limits to what is morally acceptable. For example, any morally appropriate preferential treatment within one relationship must be compatible with similarly appropriate preferential treatment within other relationships as well as a broad concern for the good of all humanity. Morally acceptable actions do not preference those closest to us in a way that ignores our obligations to others. This stipulation prevents callousness towards the needs of others, nepotism, and unfair favoritism in the public arena of life. Accordingly, the existence of a spousal relationship justifies some sorts of preferential treatment between two people including a substantial sharing of financial resources, time, and the sharing of sexual intimacy. Yet, there are other types of preferences that familial relationship do not justify, such as giving one's spouse preferential treatment when hiring for a non-family owned business.

To return to Williams' illustration, there is nothing ethically troubling in a husband saving his wife rather than a stranger if he cannot save both. After all, the husband did all the good that was possible by both saving a life and fulfilling the special commitments of his relationship. If he saved the stranger rather than his wife, he would do less good by failing to fulfill his spousal commitments. Ultimately, this solution is strikingly similar to Velleman's practical advice in the situation, but without the excessive redefinition of love that he believes is necessary to ethically support it. Reconciling loving relationships with impartiality requires neither the redefinition of love nor the rejection of impartiality. Rather we ought to acknowledge that certain kinds of relationships are morally relevant considerations; therefore, responding to them does not conflict with reasonable impartiality.[24]

---

[24] I would like to thank Daniel Haybron, Eleonore Stump, Fr. John Kavanaugh, Richard Beauchamp, and Jeremy Neill for their helpful comments on earlier versions of this paper.

FAMILIAL DUTIES AND EMOTIONAL INTELLIGENCE: A NEW FOUNDATION FOR THEORY AND PRACTICE

DIANE WILLIAMSON

In the United States, in the twenty-first century, we do not often hear about, or even think about the idea of, familial duties. Such is not to say that we spend any less time with our families than people of other cultures do, or that we feel any less guilt when we neglect our family members; we just do not think in these terms. It is not surprising, given our history of the ethos of rugged individualism, that we, as a culture, tend not to blame people who have neglected their familial duties. We feel plenty of sympathy for the victims of such neglect, but we also tend to have sympathy for the ones who have either pursued or have been bound by the constraints of their "own lives."

When we think of familial duties, we inevitably think of an earlier way of life. We perhaps think of other, non-Western, societies that are more in touch with their traditions. Cultural traditions are interwoven with families. For example, we see our families, or feel that we *should* see our families, on traditional holidays. People often become depressed when they are alone on the holidays even though this "family time" itself also causes anxiety, stress, and anger. It makes sense that reverence, or irreverence, for tradition and reverence, or irreverence, for parents and the elderly go hand in hand: the elderly, regardless of their own beliefs, come to be living symbols of that which is old and venerable (or old and resented).

One typical, intellectual model of familial duties comes from Confucianism. Confucius was concerned about preserving the traditional wisdom of Ancient Chinese society and about maintaining proper familial roles and relationships. Confucius saw the family as the most important human organization and the most privileged site of the cultivation of

humanity, *jen*, the cardinal Confucian virtue.[1] The relationships between
father and son, husband and wife, old and young are asymmetrical and
must be properly and carefully negotiated. Each, as with governmental
authority, should, on the Confucian world-view, involve tutelage through
moral rectitude. Aging is seen as a process of maturing and one's elders
occupy a superior position. The familial hierarchy grounds social and
governmental hierarchy and society is thusly stabilized. Yet, the
symmetrical and mutual relationship between friends is not fundamentally
dissimilar from the other four of the "five relationships" because the spirit
of equality can and should inspire affection between those who are
otherwise unequal.[2]

The last remark may be heard as an apology by Western ears, as we
perhaps, with our beliefs in democracy, cannot stomach any but the last
relationship. It is, perhaps, the paradigmatic relationship for us, offering a
guide for the regretfully inescapable inequalities of the family and the
government. For this reason, we have not embraced Confucianism as a
model for familial duties. Instead, Westerners tend to be skeptical of
Confucianism, viewing it as authoritarian, sexist, unfair, as well as
necessarily engendering fear, dependency, and hostility.[3]

Socrates, the person most often set up as the father of Western
philosophy, may or may not have had a family. We do not often hear about
it. Instead of striving to protect tradition, Socrates was accused of
dismantling it. He would often go off by himself to think, or to listen to his
daemon, his own personal god, and so we have been given the legacy of
the philosopher as the loner. Not coincidentally, in the *Republic*, we see
Socrates fantasizing about the total disillusion of the family. Two and a
half centuries later, the majority of philosophers are more concerned that
philosophy, and Western culture in general, is too individualistic. Care
Ethics has recently attempted to reconcile philosophy with the topic of the
family in a way that does not teleologically subordinate familial relationships

---

[1] See Tu, Wei-Ming, "Confucius and Confucianism" in *Confucianism and the Family*, Walter H. Slote and George A. DeVos (eds.), State University of New York Press, 1998. This volume offers various studies on Confucian family life.
[2] See Te, Wei Ming, "Probing the 'Three Bonds' and 'Five Relationships'" in *Confucianism and the Family*, Walter H. Slote and George A. DeVos (eds.), State University of New York Press, 1998.
[3] See Slote, Walter H., "Psychocultural Dynamics within the Confucian Family" in *Confucianism and the Family*, Walter H. Slote and George A. DeVos (eds.), State University of New York Press, 1998.

to individualism, and, in doing so, it has opened itself up to many of the same criticisms that have been lodged against Confucianism.[4]

In this paper I offer a way of thinking about familial duties that rises above this familiar dilemma between selfish individualism, on the one hand, and subordination and selflessness, on the other. Followers of Confucius will no doubt argue that what I propose is a renovation of the old idea that cultivating good familial relationships is the primary path of self-cultivation. I totally agree. Since I am critical of the hegemonic idea of natural superiority and do assume that relationships between adult family members are, or should be, most like relationships between friends (assuming that one has sufficiently caring relationships with one's friends) I may also appear to side with democratic individualists. In basing my approach to moral theory in Kant's *Metaphysics of Morals*, I hope to gain a place for thinking about familial relationships in Western philosophy and combat the common illiteracy in the arena. By bringing in work from contemporary psychology, I hope to ground renewed thinking about familial duties in the ways of thinking about the family with which we are already, at least partially, comfortable, as well as show that we cannot have a fully articulated moral theory without a good psychological grasp of the phenomenon of real familial relationships.

Working with the (young) tradition of care ethics, I start with the assumption that moral relationships must be recognized as personal, emotional relationships and that we must examine the moral dimension of our most intimate relationships or else we surely leave them vulnerable to immorality. Many assume that a Kantian care ethics is a contradiction in terms. Kant famously wrote that we have duties to act in certain ways, but cannot have duties to feel certain things. This idea, relying as it does on a simple dichotomy between the activity of thought and the passivity of feeling, is far too simple to be helpful for understanding emotional relationships, especially the complicated emotional relationships we have with our family members, and so it is commonly thought that Kantian moral theory could not possibly formulate duties to care. Yet, when we devote more careful attention to understanding Kant's theory of emotion we see that the duty to promote the happiness of others is an essential element of his moral theory. It is rather the case that this line of objection against Kant is a good representative of some of the general prejudice against the intelligence of emotions that we must face in considering the relationship between emotions and moral theory. Furthermore, in viewing

---

[4] See Bartky, Sandra Lee: *Femininity and Domination*, Routledge, New York, 1990, pp. 104-5.

this paper as a discussion with care ethics, we can see that it also poses some practical, psychological challenges to the ideal of caring, especially if we take the caring relationship to be divisible into the "one-caring" and the "cared-for."[5]

This discussion of familial duties does not offer a normative account of the emotions associated with family life; if anything, it significantly complicates the common accounts of these emotions. Instead, I argue that striving for emotional intelligence should be construed as a moral duty, especially with regard to familial relationships. I define "emotional intelligence" as understanding and working through one's own emotions in the service of psychological well-being. Emotional intelligence also involves openness to and literacy of the emotions of others. As we shall see, expressing the content of familial duties in this way makes more sense than arguing that we have a duty to love and/or respect our family members or that we have a duty to have good relationships with them. We cannot have a duty to have a good relationship: since having a relationship takes two and we only have control over our own part. Although, it is often the case that one person behaving well can significantly influence the other and go some distance toward establishing a happy relationship. Still, putting the focus on personal emotional intelligence makes it clear that we must each focus on our part in the relationship and the responsibilities we owe to ourselves. It also makes little sense to say that we have a duty to love our family members, since in the times that we do not, what matters is not so much *that* we do not, but that we take steps to improve the situation. In many cases, love will be entirely beside the point: it is the way that we work through conflict that is important. We might say that we have a duty to respect our family members, but only in a Kantian sense, keeping in mind that we also have a duty to respect ourselves and no respect can be true without this spirit of equality, even when the partners are not equals.

In what follows, I focus on the relationships between adults—grown children and their parents or grown siblings—not because children are somehow pre-moral, but because the focus of moral cultivation should be self-improvement, and *we* are adults. Furthermore, it seems most constructive to construe relationships with children as teleologically oriented toward relationships between adults. Therefore, it is important for us to have a good model of adult family relationships and work backwards from there, applying relevant knowledge about child development, to

[5] See Noddings, Nell, *Caring: A Feminine Approach to Ethics and Moral Education*, University of California Press, 1984. p. 69.

achieve a model for relationships between adults and children or between children. After all, if we do not provide a good model for our children, how can we teach them anything?

We like to think that when we are grown-up we have, hopefully, already developed a functional level of self-understanding and moral agency. As we have already seen, Confucius assumed that such is the case. In reality, though, we are not much different from children, especially in our familial relationships, and if cultivating emotional intelligence is a part of the Kantian duty to strive for self-perfection, as this paper argues, then it is never and can never be completed. Of course, the fact that many of us are transported back to the maturity level of children when we relate to our family members is the reason that talking about familial relationships makes many of us uncomfortable. It is quite common for people to dislike their family members entirely and not to want to have *any* relationships with them. Our dislike of certain family members may cause us to sever relations with them and demand: Do I really have a duty to this person? I did not choose to be in this relationship, so why should I sustain it?[6]

In the "Doctrine of Virtue" Kant writes that we have a duty to perfect ourselves and a duty to promote the happiness of others. By cultivating one's own perfection, Kant means that we should improve both theoretical and practical reason, or, we might say, as this seems to be closer to Kant's intention, both prudential reason and moral reason. Since Kant partially thinks about the term "happiness" hedonistically, he does not believe that we have a duty to promote our own happiness. He believes that such a duty would be redundant, since he believes that we naturally seek our own happiness, and mistaken, since happiness only has worth if it is subordinated to morality. We should promote the happiness of others, on the other hand, because we cannot set their ends for them, and must trust, within reason, that they will seek the good if they are given sufficient means. It is with providing those means that we must trouble ourselves, not attempting to meddle in their ends. Again, of course, meddling or not meddling must be restricted by proper reason, since it will obviously be necessary to sometimes explicitly prevent some one from doing something, such as killing another person, or to deny means when someone has clearly set immoral or unhealthy goals. Still, we do have a moral duty to promote the happiness of others, both because we are reciprocally dependent on others for such aid and because happiness, in another sense, promotes morality.

---

[6] In this light, Noddings' discussion of the natural impulse to care seems woefully insufficient.

The duties to perfect oneself and promote the happiness of others are wide, imperfect duties. A wide duty is a duty the content of which is imprecise: "the law cannot specify precisely in what way one is to act and how much one is to do by the action."[7] Moral theory cannot specify whom we are to help. We cannot possibly promote the happiness of everyone, at least not in any substantial way. Moral theory also cannot specify the exact content of the helping action: we may need to give food, or shelter, or a shoulder to cry on. Clearly, doing the wrong thing would be a failure to carry out the duty, offering a shoulder to cry on when someone needs food, for example. Still, this practical knowledge is situation dependent, and, as we shall soon see, requires a rather substantial degree of psychological acumen.

Kant does not have a lot to say specifically about familial relationships. We may think that he allowed them to fall into the realm of those things that happen naturally. If that is the case, we will need to provide our own basis for directing the duty to promote the happiness of others toward family members. My argument builds on Kant's formulation of our imperfect duties by showing that the duty to promote the happiness of others and the duty to seek one's own perfection are linked, especially in the case of cultivating healthy familial relationships. The fact that fulfilling our familial duties requires and contributes to the cultivation of self-perfection is reason to think that we do have a special duty to promote the happiness of our family members and should choose to direct our imperfect duty in this way.

Other ways of grounding familial duties seem to come up wanting. In thinking generally about the status of familial duties, it seems immediately clear that they are relative to our societies and cannot be based on biology. So, for example, if we lived in the kind of state that Socrates describes in the *Republic*, wherein all children are raised communally, and parents do not know their children, it makes little sense to say that grown children have any special duties to their parents or siblings. Familial duties are not based on biology. The example of adoption also gestures toward this conclusion. It seems to be the case that children who are given up for adoption do not have any duties toward their birth parents, and those biological parents cease having, or at least have very few, duties toward their biological children. At this point, however, we run the risk of making duties meaningless through tautology. Do we only have familial duties because we, as in the case of adoption, choose to take them on?

---

[7] TL 6:390

Perhaps there really are no familial duties at all. Rather what we take to be objective moral duties are merely social expectations, even legal expectations, that are in place for the sake of institutionalizing the necessary social functions of childcare and elder care. We might not want to call them duties because they seem so relative to a given society's social institutions, which are in flux. So, for example, with the origin of Medicare, grown children suddenly had less of a responsibility to care for their aging parents (which might help explain some of the religious opposition to governmental aid).

Such a conclusion, that there are no real moral familial duties but only responsibilities that are relative to society's institutions, would be based on an entirely overly abstract and vitiated notion of morality. Duties certainly can be relative to social needs, as they can be particular manifestations of the more general duty to live and cooperate socially. Surely the example from the *Republic* gets us started on the wrong foot. We are, after all, familial beings; just as we are "species beings" and "political animals." We do have families, and these relationships are already largely constitutive of our identities. The fact that it might, in a strange society, be otherwise should not detract from appreciating the importance these relationships do, in fact, have.

It is in accepting the fact that we are familial beings that we are given insight into a possible theoretical basis for familial duties, and, indeed, a new account of the content of these duties. Such an account would go beyond the needs of the recipient and focus instead on the relationships, and mutual, psychological needs. Not only must we reject a simple account of generational hegemony in order to make space for a good model of adult familial relationships, we also must reject the assumption of natural family feelings, such as "maternal instinct." Traditionally, we have thematized the family as the sphere of the private and natural, believing that "Nature" would miraculously take care of those things that we relied on her for, and, of course, it is no coincidence that Nature is a woman. As Julia Kristeva's Lacanian psychoanalysis emphasizes, as from the point of view of the child in her *Powers of Horror*, familial feelings trade in ambivalence from the very beginning.[8] We must accept this emotional ambivalence in order to achieve a good emotional comportment and cultivate good relationships. Oftentimes, the need to deny ambivalence is itself the cause of problems.

---

[8] Kristeva, Julia, *Powers of Horror: An Essay on Abjection*, Columbia University Press, 1982.

Psychologists are perhaps more at home in the arena of emotional ambivalence than ethical theorists. Harriet Lerner's work, especially her *Dance of Anger*, which itself draws from Bowen Family Systems Theory and Monica McGoldrick's *You Can Go Home Again*, can help us get a handle on some of the psychological patterns that are often at play in familial relationships.[9] Sharing insights from psychology with philosophy will put us in a better position to think realistically about familial duties in a way that does not risk being psychologically harmful to any member of the family.

The insight perhaps most exemplary and relevant to Noddings' model of the cared-for and one-caring is Bowen's idea of the common familial roles of the over-functioner and the under-functioner. In the spirit of Hegel's master and slave, these are reciprocal roles: the over-functioner, being ever competent in some area, needs the under-functioner to "care" for, and the under-functioner's self-image, as continually having problems in the over-functioner's area of expertise, is dependent on the over-functioner. Consider Lerner's example of the relationship between Lois and her brother. Lerner paraphrases Lois's statements of anger and exasperation at her brother, whom she describes as "a mess" and "screwed-up."[10] Her brother continually calls, in the middle of a personal crisis, asking for money and advice, which Lois gives but later resents. She continually tells him what to do, suggesting therapists, and staging interventions; nothing seems to work. Her brother seems to have no one else to help him. Lerner explains that this situations is neither the fault of the brother nor the fault of Lois: "Relationships are circular (A and B are mutually reinforcing) rather than linear (A causes B or B causes A). *Once a pattern is established in a relationship, it is perpetuated by both parties.*" Lerner suggests that Lois can and should change her move in the dance, since she is playing the role of the overfunctioner:

> The more she overfunctions, the more Brian [her brother] will underfunction—which means that the more Lois is helpful, the more Brian

---

[9] Lerner, Harriet, *The Dance of Anger: A Woman's Guide to Changing the Patterns of Intimate Relationships*, Harper and Row Publishers, 1985; Bowen, Murray, *Family Therapy in Clinical Practice*, Jason Aronson, 1994; McGoldrick, Monica, *You Can Go Home Again: Reconnecting With Your Family*, W.W. Norton and Company, 1997; see also the work of David Schnarch to apply this discussion to marriage, especially *Passionate Marriage: Keeping Love and Intimacy Alive in Committed Relationships*, Holt Paperbacks, 1998.

[10] Lerner, Harriet, *The Dance of Anger: A Woman's Guide to Changing the Patterns of Intimate Relationships*, Harper and Row Publishers, 1985, p. 140. The following paraphrase comes from pages 140-147.

will need her help. The more Lois fails to express her own doubts, vulnerability, or incompetence to Brian, the more Brian will express enough for both of them. The more emotional Lois gets about Brian's problems, the more he won't care enough about himself. Lois's big-sisterly sense of responsibility may have many positive aspects. Nonetheless, she is functioning at the expense of her brother's competence.[11]

In order to change the situation, the overfunctioner, or the caring-one, must change herself. The overfunctioner must share her own underfunctioning side. She will have to learn how not to be helpful. She will have to learn to refrain from giving advice. Doing this is extremely difficult for overfunctioners not in the least because their entire identity has been shaped around the role of caring. They have learned to silence their own needs, and getting in touch with these needs often causes depression at first since they are so unskilled in sharing vulnerability and seeking help. Gilligan seems aware of this phenomenon in her discussion of responsibility and responsivity to oneself. Lerner's discussion sheds light on one concrete form of, as well as the problem we may have in achieving, this responsibility.

From the dilemma between engrossment and independence, it may seem as though Lerner is advocating that Lois stop *caring* about her brother. If Lois were to simply cut her brother off emotionally, she would simply be going to the opposite extreme and would not be any closer to having a good relationship with him and promoting his happiness or her own perfection. One key concept from family systems theory is that of "hanging in" or guarding against emotional cut-offs. Just as divorce does not solve the problems in a marriage, cutting off ties with a family member does nothing to promote a good relationship. The overfunctioner must find ways to express caring that do not undermine the other person's competence and do not encroach on the other person's responsibilities to himself. Both members of the circular relationship will have anxiety about change, and, so the tendency simply to flee the situation by emotionally distancing:

> "Hanging in requires us to move against enormous internal resistance, which is most often experienced as anger ("Why should I get in touch with him when he's acting this way?) or inertia ("I just don't feel like taking the initiative").

---

[11] *The Dance of Anger*, p. 141.

The goal is not to cut-off the relationship, but to change it, and for the person who is trapped in a problematic and unhelpful mode of "caring" to better seek her own self-perfection. If it is the overfunctioner that wishes to initiate change, the most helpful thing she can do is to share her own underfunctioning side; if it is the underfunctioner who wishes to initiate change, the most helpful thing she can do is to get in touch with her own functioning. Of course, the person attempting to effect change will also have to face the counter-moves of the other person. Lois's brother will inevitably confront her with the biggest crisis ever, and her resolve will be tested. She can take comfort in the fact that her brother will never learn to take care of himself if she continually rushes in to do it for him. Furthermore, in continually putting herself in the superior position, she is also blocking mutual recognition and putting herself in an inferior position. It is not until she sees her brother as an equal and respects him as such that she will be able to respect and share the weaker parts of herself.

Here we see the importance of Kant's emphasis upon promoting the happiness of others, not their perfection. Kant was very aware of the dangers of paternalism. We must find ways to help that do not undermine the person's agency: just as Hoagland points out that caring relationships should aim at the cared-for's independence.[12] From Kant's discussion of virtue, we can take the idea that caring should directly promote the happiness of the other, not his or her perfection. Likewise, we cannot forget that a caring relationship should not undermine our own pursuit of perfection. We saw that, in the case of the overfunctioner, an unhealthy mode of caring actually reinforces certain types of failing to take care of and responsibility for oneself. It seems that, in this case, what is passing as care is not really care at all. If this is true, that a person's immediate caring impulse might be an imposter, then we cannot base a moral theory on caring. Instead, we need moral theory, hopefully a psychologically-informed moral theory, to help us spot imposter caring.

Any theory of morally-informed caring must have both feet firmly planted in the psychology of relationships. Following Lerner's work with family-of-origin studies, we can canvas some of the features of adult familial relationships. Doing so will lead us back to the argument that the foundation for familial duties lies both in the duty to promote the happiness of others *and* in the duty to promote our own self-perfection. First, we must note that it is often the case that familial relationships often

---

[12] Hoagland, Sarah Lucia, "Some Concerns about Nel Noddings' *Caring,*" *Hypatia* 5 (1), 1990, and "Some Thoughts about *Caring*" In Claudia Card, ed., *Feminist Ethics*. Lawrence, Kans: University Press of Kansas, 1991.

become stuck in certain patterns; these patterns then act, behind our backs, as a model for our other relationships. On the home front, problems in our relationships with our parents and siblings are replayed, although of course with meaningful variation, in our relationship to our kids.[13] The good news is that we are not fated to tragically replay the conditions of our upbringing, even though it often seems that we are. Still, the path to changing is a rocky road back through the original terrain. Our family is indeed the context in which we grow-up, if we can ever accomplish it. This process of achieving more mature relationships is a process of learning equality that then becomes the basis for all of our relationships. We might argue that we have a duty *as parents* to cultivate emotional intelligence regarding our relationships with our family members, so that we do not subject our children to the same problems, but I want to make the argument more broadly: so long as we fail to cultivate emotional intelligence regarding our relationships with our family members, we fail in our duty to cultivate our own self-perfection.

It may seem selfish for me to frame the issue in terms of *self*-perfection and benefiting *self*-understanding. We must understand that this focus is entirely removed from the way that we immediately encounter familial relationships and it is this shift toward thinking about ourselves and taking responsibility for ourselves that is necessary in those relationships that seem as though they might engulf us entirely. Perhaps it is the case that we normally think in terms of duties *to* family members because, in thinking about our important relationships, in which there is naturally some degree of tension, we automatically frame the problems in terms of the problems with the other people. It is therefore natural to view our family through the lens of considering all the help that everyone else needs. It is easier and most natural to focus on other people, the individual actors in the family, rather than the relationships and recurring patterns, and the role that we play in those patterns.

It is impossible for me truly to do justice to the topic of emotional intelligence and family relationships, but I can pass on some of Lerner's recommendations that can at least point us in the right direction.

1. Every person in the family needs to have a personal relationship with every other person in the family. It is all too easy to let alliances and gossiping undermine the respect we owe to each person as an individual.

---

[13] Lerner gives many examples of unresolved "family of origin" problems that surface in our relationships to our children, as we project our relationships with our parents and our siblings onto our relationships with our children (DA p. 180; MD p. 227)

As a general rule, in a conversation, focus on the lives of the two people in the conversation, and avoid keeping secrets from others.

2.Guard against cut-offs. Cutting off ties with a person is just another face of a fused identity, not a healthy act of independence. Plus it only guarantees that we will be forced to confront the problems in other relationships.

3. Change takes time. A hit and run confrontation of the "problems" with a particular relationship, even if it is based on genuine insight that takes responsibility for one's own role in the relationship patterns, cannot possibly work as a magic bullet to fix these problems once and for all. For every move toward change there will be counter-moves and the constant tendency to slip back into old patterns. It is important, also, that, while trying to make change, we stay connected in the relationship. Rising above problematic patterns does not mean that we should emotionally disengage or leave the relationship behind.

4. Keep in touch. Use low-crisis times as an opportunity to create the foundation for a good relationship. Use phone-calls, visits, or letters. Be suspicious of any impulse to retort that your family "means nothing" to you.

A discussion of familial duties can be more productive and psychologically astute if it takes emotional intelligence as its focus. Doing this shifts the attention away from asking about objective actions and duties, such as "what exactly does a daughter owe to her aging parents?" or "How much of her own pursuits should she sacrifice to take care of them?" These questions cannot have answers. Again, they refer to imperfect duties and require practical wisdom. The discussion also should not focus on relationships, asking questions such as "Do I have a good relationship with my father?" Achieving a relationship is not within the control of one person. We can do everything in our power to make a relationship possible, but we cannot make it happen. Instead the question should be "Am I standing up for what I believe in?," "Do I know why I'm acting like this?," "Am I taking this situation for what it is or am I reading more into it?," "Am I being forgiving and working toward resolution or am I being stubborn and selfish?" and "Am I respecting myself and others?" Even if we decide that we do specifically have duties to *care for* family members, we must remember that a caring relationship must be based on a healthy relationship in order to be truly caring.

In conclusion, I would like to briefly take up the old conundrum of the relationship between happiness and morality. What is the precise theoretical relationship between morality and emotional intelligence? I might be understood as having argued that it is (morally) good to promote good relationships with our family members because it is (pragmatically and psychologically) good for us. This direction of dependence threatens psychological egoism and may confuse us about the proper foundation of morality. Nevertheless, the fact of human needs, such as food and human connection, and their relative social manifestations, namely the psychological importance of family relationships, must play a role in moral theory: we have a moral duty to help people, all people, fulfill their needs. Kant believes that we do not have a duty to promote our own happiness because we do so naturally and because phrasing it that way might make us confuse selfishness and morality. Nevertheless, if we were somehow devoid of the natural inclination to promote our own happiness, it would be the job of moral duty to step in. We do have an *indirect* duty to promote our own happiness, insofar as happiness, and having our needs met, helps facilitate moral behavior. Greatly simplifying Kant, and ignoring the very real theoretical problems to which he points, let's just say that we have a duty to promote our true, morally worthy, happiness, the Happiness expressed in Kant's idea of the Highest Good. The idea of emotional intelligence, being related to psychological well-being and its connection to moral goodness, comes close to this Kantian ideal. It does seem to be the case that when we improve our relationships, they also become more morally righteous: we are more respectful, honest, self-aware and self-respectful. In fact, the old divide between morality and happiness seems less recalcitrant when we get a better, more psychologically accurate picture of happiness in the first place.

You may follow me this far but still be unconvinced that you owe anything more to your brother or sister than you owe to your best friend or a stranger on the street. If imperfect duties are wide, you might ask, why can't *I* choose whose happiness I want to promote? You might think that I have only succeeded in showing that it is useful for us to fulfill our wide duties in this way, not that we are morally obligated to do so. There is no magical, moral super-glue that holds families together, and yet these relationships do often seem to be different from other relationships: either we end up valuing them more or we feel more frustrated and ambivalent about them. It is this quality that makes them special sites for the development of self-understanding. It also makes the relationships and our behavior more important to the other person, our brothers sisters, parents, or children. They need us and we need them, not just for care (in all of its varieties), but for our personal development of happiness and self-understanding. If we choose to ignore these relationships, we are choosing to ignore the specificity of our duties to promote the happiness of others and our own perfection. Can we help one thousand strangers in order to equal the difficult task of talking to our father? Can we analyze every single one of our dreams and learn ten different languages in order to perfect ourselves, and still not understand why we always fight with our sister? No. Doing so would be like sending food to China while letting someone starve to death on our door-step. Just as we cannot choose our families, we cannot choose the particular contexts of our lives that, to a large degree, determine the demands we must negotiate and the patterns and conflicts we must understand and resolve. If we try to abstract the notion of moral duty from these identity-constituting relationships, the notion of duty becomes abstract and meaningless. We must engage in moral thought from the position in which we find ourselves. Plus, it is likely that we will find, that unless we do direct moral sensitivity to our relationships with our family members, we will lose our moral sensitivity entirely. We are not born fulfilling our moral duties, just as we are not born with emotional intelligence, or, for many of us, into happy relationships. It is foolish to think that progress on any of these fronts should be easy. If we will not be motivated by a moral calling, at least there is still the promise of happiness and familial love to keep us striving.

A VALUE OF FAMILY:
THE MORAL SIGNIFICANCE
OF INVOLUNTARY AFFILIATIONS

MICHAEL TABER

At the stage of life of most traditional-age, American college students, they strive to organize their lives more around friendships and romantic relationships than around familial attachments. This is understandable for a number of reasons, especially at residential institutions of higher education.

Yet these developing independent beings are still situated in families, and are usually still subject to family rules about such things as curfews, mealtimes, and laundry. And about family activities on vacations and holidays. These latter can be especially effective at fanning the flames of familial discord, because along with a family gathering's times for reacquainting, updating, laughing, and cooking, will come moments of feeling morally torn. Many will feel something like "Do I *really* have to go to Uncle Art's again? He can be so annoying. And such a bad cook. And tell such sexist jokes."

The surly teenage riposte, "I never *asked* to be born to this family," usually delivered with open contempt and folded arms, surely is correct.

Why should people have to put forth the effort to care about people with whom they have not asked to or sought out to become affiliated?

To sharpen my question, let me articulate a principle, and then ask some questions about it.

IFA (the involuntariness of our familial affiliations): Being a party to some family relationships is largely a matter not of one's choosing.

I say "some" because there are other family relationships that are predominantly voluntary, like forming a marriage or civil union, intentionally having a child, or adopting a child. I say "largely" in order to cover the existentialist objection that I can break any family relationship by committing suicide. Or by committing murder.

I take it that there is a philosophically important sense in which it is not up to us who our siblings, parents, in-laws, aunts, uncles, and cousins are.

Let me now distinguish some questions one might ask about IFA, so that I can discount what I am not after, in order to focus our attention on what I am after.

(A) Are there *facts morally relevant* to a person that stem from IFA?

Surely there are, both in terms of social expectations we develop ("How could you not visit your mother when she's sick?") and in terms of how one develops one's own moral sense ("My mother is the one who instilled in me a vivid sense of the importance of maintaining my moral relationships."). Even if my psychological identity as one caring has been created by the ways in which I have been one cared for, this is undeniably an important fact to know about me and my moral behavior or misbehavior, but it does not answer the question of why I *should* care about people with whom I have not asked to become affiliated.

It is not enough to point out that we *do* spend important developmental time in involuntary familial affiliations, or even to claim that these relationships formulate and constitute our very moral identities, for these claims, even if true, stop short of the heavy lifting needed for the normative enterprise. Even if this is the way in which my moral views have psychologically developed in me, what are the normative implications?

This problem is similar to that had by two other defenses of the centrality of familial relationships, which like the above, are both descriptive claims about the origin of our familial nature. We could answer (A) by citing the divine formation of the family; a god made us as familially affiliated beings, and wants us to honor our parents, siblings, and so even Uncle Art. Or we could answer it by appeal to a naturalistic grounding, claiming that we evolved as creatures of family relationships, and so we are built to strive to honor parents, siblings, and even Uncle Art).

(B) Are there valid moral claims upon a person that *endure despite* IFA?

Again, surely there are. The involuntariness of my being Art's nephew is not enough to extricate me from my duty to not lie to him, to call medical aid if he collapses, and the like. Even though it is not due to my volition that I am being asked directions by a stranger on the street, I am not morally permitted to lie. What Kant calls perfect duties cannot be overridden by the mere fact that the affiliation of the two parties is involuntary on the part of at least one of them.

Involuntariness does not provide a universal free pass on moral duties, but I wish to ask if this involuntariness might be a **source** of any moral duties.

(C) Are there valid moral claims upon a person that **stem from** IFA?

Might there be claims upon me that have their very *source* in the involuntariness of my affiliation? This is the claim I wish to investigate.

As Jacques Debille wrote, "Fate chooses our relatives, we choose our friends."[1] This difference no doubt accounts for most of the explanation of why, although fully one fifth of the *Nicomachean Ethics* is about friendship, you have to consult an index—and a very thorough one, at that—to find references there to family. It is not that Aristotle does not think that the family is philosophically important. He thinks it is the bedrock of political associations (*Politics* 1252b13), for example, and famously criticizes Plato for having dissolved the family (*Politics II*.2-5). And several times in his discussion of friendship, he uses the mother's disposition toward her children as the paradigm of the kind of helpfulness exhibited in the best friendships (*Nicomachean Ethics* 1159a28, 1166a6-9, and 1168a25-28).

If moral excellence (*arête*) lies on a mean involving choice (*prohaíresis*), then it is understandable, even if not ultimately justifiable, that a philosopher would think that relationships which one does not choose are not relationships that can reveal or develop *arête*.

Matters are similar with Kant. If the source of all moral value is the respecting of or enhancing of autonomy, both in oneself and in others, then it is difficult to see why I should give up my autonomy to do things for family members whom I heteronomously find to be parts of my life.

Much of our ethical deliberation is rightly about optimizing:
- to be the best persons (the most virtuous, the most filially pious) we can be
- to be as Christ-like as possible
- to never treat anyone as a mere means, and to foster people's being ends in themselves as much as we can, consistent with this
- to maximize pleasure for the greatest number
- to be the most caring without burning oneself out.

---

[1] Jacques Delille, *Malheur et Pitié* (1803), canto I

In each of these frameworks, there is an admirable restlessness, a valuable striving, and a noble refusal to accept not only the world as it is, but oneself as one is. It is doubtful that any ethical framework could omit any such optimizing, even though particular frameworks, understand the optimizing in different ways.

In fact, one could read the history of the range of ethical theories *as* the history of what it is that should be optimized. One could do worse than this, in finding a way to analyze the range of ethical frameworks proposed over the millennia.

Although optimization strategies are always looking to the horizon, to the greener pastures, another important element in our ethical relationships is our acceptance of where we are, our commitment to those in our lives. Virtues like commitment, loyalty, and immersion in another's life are not compatible with forever searching for, or even just forever being open to, greener pastures.

Consider the case of Socrates and the case of the protagonist in George Eliot's *Middlemarch*. Xenophon tells us that Socrates was drawn to Xanthippe because he found her argumentative. We are told, although by much later sources, and so likely apocryphally, that Xanthippe was a shrew, and that Socrates stayed married to her only because he knew that if he could endure her, he could endure anyone.

In *Middlemarch*, Dorothea Brooke marries Mr. Casaubon also for intellectual aspirations; she admires his erudition and wants to get an education through him and help him to complete his study, tedious though it is, on comparative mythology. She sticks with him even when it becomes clear to her that the marriage is cold and emotionally unfulfilling.

Now these are both fictional, the one apocryphal and the other in a novel. And they both concern marriage, which is not the clearest case of involuntary family relationships. A case better for my purposes would be if both Socrates and Dorothea had had an Uncle Art. Yet, their cases suffice to illustrate that there are times when you go forth in life with the affiliations you have, not the affiliations you wish you had.

Virtues like commitment and loyalty, whether to one's extended family, to one's romantic partner, or to one's friend, all require an element of checking at the door one's tendency to optimize, and instead to accept. Do I support my wife, daughters, friends or even colleagues because I believe them to be the single very best possible wife in the world for me, or best daughters in the world, or best friends or colleagues in the world? If I forever keep an eye open for pastures of greener affiliations, then to that extent I am not really able to have the virtues of commitment and loyalty to these people.

There are times in life—although not all times, I grant—in which a good person does not get to draw new cards, but instead has to accept the hand that unpredictable circumstances (in the cases of romantic relationships, friends, and colleagues) or ancestry (in the case on one's larger family) has dealt one.

This is not to say that they all need to be one's favorite people to spend time with. But it is to say that on joint projects, like caring for the cat or the kid (with one's life partner) or looking after the well-functioning of one's department (with one's colleagues), the project should be done with a minimum of resentment and an adequacy of pleasantness. The cat, the kid, and the department will benefit.

How does this apply to having to visit Uncle Art, when we share with him no household or department? Although there is, of course, a range of how tight family relationships are, each family *is* something of a joint project, and therefore there are times when the response "Because Uncle Art is family" is adequate, is justificatory and not simply descriptive.

There are times, however, when a person's behavior is so ethically noxious that spending time with the person is not ethically required—or even permissible. Commitment or loyalty to someone who is physically or emotionally abusive, whether the joint project is a family or a department of philosophy, is no virtue. The praiseworthiness of committing oneself to the task of helping those we find cast into our relational orbits by forces beyond our control is not categorical.

I suggest a slightly more extreme claim now, that it is not merely a concession to necessity to think that we sometimes accept the cards and people we are dealt in life, but that it can actually be ethically enhancing for us to have to work with what we have.

First, there is moral handicapping. If I can treat Uncle Art well, even when I would rather not be there, then I have succeeded at a challenge to improve myself.

Second, for me to accept that I am part of something larger than I, and something not of my own choosing, is for me to develop an accurate sense of how I should not expect that everything that befalls me is of my own choosing. The humility thus inculcated in me is a virtue.

Third, this sense of, and even appreciation for, one's own limitations (down to Uncle Art being the uncle we are stuck with) can lead to better fellow-feeling with others who have limitations, even if their limitations are very different from, and much more serious than, my own. Humans can be more empathetic than any omnipotent being can be. Humans with the flu, even more so. Humans with Uncle Art, ditto.

Although I do believe that what I have said here is true, I have no illusions about its being rhetorically successful with the surly teen. Or with most traditional-age American college students, for that matter. What eighteen-year-old, especially males, wants to hear about the virtues of accepting limitations on one's will?

I have a suggestion on this point, and it is not a merely rhetorical ploy. Our loyalty to Uncle Art, even if he is not the most interesting or good person in the world, is structurally similar to some other loyalties, like those to a sports team or to a high school alma mater.

In his 2001 article "The Ethics of Supporting Sports Teams," Nicholas Dixon argues that there are two kinds of sports fans, the purist and the partisan, and that the loyalty exhibited by the partisan is morally more admirable than that of the purist.[2] The purist fan roots for a team based on it exemplifying the most skill, and has an admiration for the game and how it is played best. But the purist will therefore have to have flexible allegiance, since which team is the most skillful will change over time.

The partisan fan roots for a team based on a personal connection, like geography or where one went to school. The partisan cares primarily for the well-being and success of the players of that team, whereas the purist cares primarily for the well-being of the sport. This is why, Dixon argues, although it might seem at first that the purist is the true fan, it turns out that the purist is no fan at all, since the purist's allegiance is conditional in a way in which the partisan's is not. He claims that either kind of fandom should be conditional upon the team rooted for not violating the letter or spirit of the rules, but the purist's allegiance to a team is additionally conditional, namely upon that team being the most skillful.

Traditional-age college students—especially males—can easily understand this argument, even if they do not all accept it. Uncle Art is like the Baltimore Orioles: neither is the best, but they are both *ours*.

There is, however, a point of disanalogy between what IFA requires and what is involved with rooting for sports teams: there is no clear sense in which rooting for a given sports team is involuntary.

I concede the point, but here is one way to offer a repair. Consider one's attachment to one's high school alma mater. One might be preferentially gladdened to hear of the approval of plans to add a much-needed wing to it, as opposed to other plans to add a just-as-much-needed

[2] "The Ethics of Supporting Sports Teams," *Journal of Applied Philosophy*, vol. 18, no. 2, 2001, pp. 149-158

wing to a different high school. One might participate in a fund-raiser for it, where one would not be inclined to participate in a fund-raiser for an equally needy high school.

In such cases, I am "rooting" for my high school only because it was mine, even though it was involuntarily mine (in the relevant sense). Uncle Art is like my high school: neither is best or most deserving, but they are both mine, and involuntarily mine.

But is my rooting for my high school in any sense *grounded in* or *added to by* its having been involuntarily mine? Although I do not think this is the way in which we would normally think of it, I do think there is something to be said for this suggestion. Maybe it was a one-high-school town and part of what I fondly remember is that we were all there, and all *had* to be there. It was before the days of magnet schools and charter schools, and other new-fangled notions. Part of the value of the experience was that there was not any option *to* the experience.

Or consider military service. I do not think that Alan needs to be an old fogey simply in thinking that he got some value from his experience in the service to which he was drafted, that was missing from Bob's otherwise identical experience in the service, but for which he enlisted. Part of what could have been transformative for Alan is that none of his group wanted to be there, and yet they persevered nonetheless. The development of commitment and loyalty to people who came into one's life through forces larger than one's own will can be a considerable virtue.

Although I would never say to Uncle Art's face that going to visit him is like being drafted into the military, I do think that there is a structural isomorphism. I also fully realize that bringing up the military draft is unlikely to be rhetorically successful against a surly teen or an eighteen-year-old American college student. But then part of what is involved in efforts to spread discussions of ethics across the curriculum is the courage to prefer deepening the discussion to winning on points.

ARE THERE FORMS OF RATIONALITY UNIQUE TO A FAMILY THAT CAN JUSTIFY THE CONCEPT OF 'FAMILY VALUES'?

JEFF BUECHNER

Family values

The idea of family values is one that is, historically, shot through with political, social, ethnic and cultural overtones. Given that is so, there is substantial disagreement among different groups as to what are actual instances of family values. Political conservatives in the Republican party endorse the nuclear family, religious commitment, traditional education, abstinence education, and oppose same-sex marriages, abortion, feminism, pornography, homosexuality, cohabitation. Liberals in the Democratic party endorse family planning, affordable child-care, maternity leave, access to contraception, abortion, increasing the minimum wage, sex education, and maternity leave. One right-wing organization, Support Our Families, lists the family values: responsibility, industry, morality, charity, humility, spirituality, loyalty and integrity.[1] Is there anyone who would argue with that? The issue for philosophers, though, is what family values are: what is their nature and are there any?

Family rationality and genes

One way of thinking about what is unique to families that is not shared by other social groups is that it is in families that its members reproduce— that is, have children. What is special about having children is that, from the gene's point of view, it is how genes are transmitted over time. Without the institution of families, transmission of genes would be random and sporadic. (That is not to say that within families gene transmission is not random and sporadic, but only that the degree and quality of

---

[1] See the website for Support the Family at http://fami.ly/

randomness differs, though this largely a question about the mathematics of family networks.) Of course, it is rational from the gene's point of view to have the institution of the family. But that is not a line which we will pursue here, since our aim is to look at the family from the point of view of the family members and not from the point of view of genes found in the family members. It is the family members who are agents capable of rational actions and we wish to discern the kinds of values that fall out of patterns of rational activity that are unique to families and not to any other kind of social group. It makes little sense to say that genes pursue rational courses of action and are committed to distinct moral values. In the following, I will propose a radical view of family values. It is the family that is the primordial social group and the family is qualitatively different from any other kind of social group. We learn how to form plural subject s (that are not families) by first having the experience of constituting a family as a plural subject. The conception of a plural subject that Margaret Gilbert has articulated[2] is an attempt to show how social groups are not merely the sum of the individuals who constitute them and that actions that are rational for a social group may be irrational for individuals. I will first look at the problem for individual rationality that the plural subject conception addresses and then raise a fundamental problem for Gilbert's conception of the plural subject. I will argue that a solution to the problem is the notion of the family as a special kind of plural subject—the plural 'me.' Some family values can be seen as a means to sustain the family and, in particular, the relation that constitutes the plural 'me,' while other family values can be seen as certain moral obligations that arise from the very nature of a plural subject, in this case, the family. I end with some speculations on a linguistic mechanism for sustaining the family as plural subject.

A problem for individual rationality: conditions under which a unique best point is unreachable

Intuitively, it strikes one as patently obvious that where all rational agents desire the same outcome and each desires that outcome more than any other outcome available to any of the agents, that each of the rational agents know that all of the other rational agents know this fact (that is, this fact is common knowledge among all of the rational agents), and that the fact that each agent is rational is also common knowledge, then by reason

---

[2] Margaret Gilbert, *On Social Facts* (Second edition), Princeton University Press, 1992.

alone each agent will see what to do and that each agent will get what he
most desires. (Call such a situation, in which everyone gets what they most
desire, a unique best point.) After all, if everyone desires the same thing,
and each person knows that everyone desires the same thing and is
rational, how could things not turn out that each gets what they most
desire? If someone chose irrationally—perhaps they are motivated by a
desire to thwart the actions of their friends or, indeed, of perfect
strangers—we could easily see how everyone would not get what they
most desire. But where everyone is rational, how could things go wrong?

Margaret Gilbert has argued persuasively[3] that there are decision
situations in which things go wrong even though the agents, in being
confronted with a decision problem, conform to all of the conditions noted
above. Let's now closely examine the kind of case she presents, since
there are several lessons we can learn from it in thinking about how
families differ from other social groups and from individuals acting on
their own. Suppose that two individuals, Jack and Jill, have heard that one
of their colleagues at their office will be fired on the basis of false
accusations against him. The false accusations were started by an
anonymous employee. Both Jack and Jill want to alert other people in the
office to this fact so that all can pressure the boss to change her mind. If
everyone confronts the boss, she will infer that the accusation is false and
not fire the company employee.

The false accusation is (now) secret knowledge known only to Jack
and Jill. Each sees that the best way to proceed is to send e-mails to all of
their office workers. But it is now the weekend, Jack and Jill are unable to
communicate, and the firing will take place first thing Monday morning.
Once that happens, there is little chance (owing to the peculiarities of the
company by-laws) of the firing being rescinded. If only one sends out e-
mails, while the other does not, company employees will think the sender
is making false accusations, tell the boss and, for creating trouble, will be
fired. If both send e-mails, that will convince everyone to confront the
boss. If neither sends any e-mails, they both keep their jobs, but their
colleague loses his job. The decision problem that each is confronted with
is the following: If each sends e-mails to all fellow employees, their
colleague will not be fired. Suppose the payoff for this action has value 8.
If neither sends any e-mails, their colleague will be fired. This payoff for
this action has value 2. If one sends an e-mail, but the other does not, then
the one who does not send the e-mail is fired (as well as the colleague).

[3] Margaret Gilbert, "Rationality, Coordination and Convention," *Synthese*, 84
(1990), 1-21.

The payoff for this action is 0 for the one who does not send the e-mail and -10 for the one who does send the e-mail.

There is certainly a unique best point in this choice situation. It is for each to send e-mails to all of their fellow employees. Moreover, it is common knowledge between Jack and Jill, as is the fact that each is rational. Notice that if Jack decides to do his part in securing the unique best point, it can only be that he has reason to think that Jill will also do her part in securing the unique best point. We examine Jack's reasoning in deciding whether Jill will choose what will secure the unique best point. That reasoning will involve the process of putting oneself into the shoes of another to determine how they will reason about their choice, what Margaret Gilbert calls[4] "reason-replication." Let's see what Jack's episode of reason-replication will look like. In putting himself in Jill's shoes, he sees that, like himself, Jill will know that if Jack sends e-mails, so should she. If so, the unique best point is secured. But then Jack wonders: What exactly can Jill figure out about what I—Jack—will actually do knowing this is so?

How could Jill figure out that Jack will send everyone e-mails if Jack's decision to send e-mails depends upon knowledge of Jill's decision to send e-mails? That Jill will send e-mails depends on whether Jack will send e-mails. The basis for each decision is determined by the other's decision. Thus, there is an intrinsic circularity to the process of deciding whether to send e-mails and so there is no rational basis for making the decision. Reason-replication is a useless procedure in this context.

The problem that both Jack and Jill face is that neither knows what the other will do, even though each knows the other is rational and wants to do what will secure the unique best point. The situation is not unlike Prisoner's Dilemma, where although the two prisoners are both rational and each knows that and each wants to secure the unique best point, neither knows what the other will do. Given that neither knows what the other will do, the rational thing to do is to opt for the next best thing, since if either chooses what will help in securing the unique best point while the other does not, then the outcome is the worst thing. Rationality is a useful guide to action, but in these kinds of cases, it cannot provide actual knowledge.

That raises the important question: just what could provide the knowledge that would be needed in order for the unique best point choice in Prisoners Dilemma type choice situations to be rational? The most obvious answer is one that does not happen (or, if it does, happens with a

---

[4] Gilbert, op. cit., p. 5.

probability that is negligible). Namely, that each agent is able to read the mind of the other agent. Clearly, in that case, each would know what the other agent intends to do. Unfortunately, direct mind reading is certainly not a reliable procedure and could not secure knowledge in any agents who attempt it unless they already know that they will be successful in doing it. Indirect mind reading is something less reliable, though it can be entirely reliable under the right circumstances. The speech of a human being and their bodily expressions (especially facial expressions) are the indirect ways by which we read the contents of their mind. However, the kinds of choice situations we are considering here are ones in which the agents do not have access to the speech or bodily expressions of one another. Thus the only way they can determine the contents of another's mind is by engaging in reason-replication and, as we have already seen, such reasoning cannot secure reliability and thus cannot secure the knowledge that is necessary for it be to rational to choose that action which secures the unique best point.

What is rational for a group might be irrational for an individual

We will now look at how groups in general might surmount some of the problems that individuals in such choice situations encounter and how families in particular can surmount the same problems in ways that groups (excluding families) cannot. One simple solution to the unique best point choice problem that could be employed by members of a group that is not available to individuals acting outside any group structure (including all 2-member group structures) is to develop within the group protocols of solidarity, such as training sessions in which members of the group engage in practice sessions in Prisoners Dilemma type choice situations. The idea is that if any two members of the group were involved in such a situation, they would have the training that would help in deciding which course-of-action to pursue. In particular, it is the training that would provide the information, in addition to that of reason-replication, which is needed to provide knowledge of what the other agent will do. The problem with such a method, though, is that it is not reliable enough to provide knowledge, since any agent in a Prisoners Dilemma type-situation will have reasons to believe that the other agent might not respect the protocols of solidarity, since the situation might be one in which there are motivating influences that would deter the other agent from respecting such protocols. Indeed, each agent will quite reasonably think that the other agent might be confronted with such motivations, and thus not respect the solidarity protocols. So a solitary decision-maker wonders: do I *really* know who she is? Do I really know what she will do?

So the end result of reason-replication augmented with group training is that the agent does not have the knowledge necessary for choosing that action which will secure the unique best point. (This is not to say that there are no group protocols that would result in knowledge in Prisoners Dilemma type-situations. For instance, a group might sanction extraordinary penalties for those who defect from choosing the unique best point action. However, if this is the case, then the penalties will have to be built into the Prisoners Dilemma choice situation and this would change the basic payoff structure of the game.)

Gilbert has argued that one kind of group principle for actions—notably a social convention—gives us reasons to believe that each would choose what will secure a unique best point, if we express together our willingness to so regard something as 'our principle.' Then—for Gilbert—we are rational to proceed in accordance with it in choice situations. Unfortunately, there are motivations to break such agreements that cannot be foreseen and against which there is, within the framework of the agreement, little or no protection other than post hoc penalties. But then we would have to reason about the deterrence effectiveness of penalties and reason replication would reveal we cannot do much with that. However, Gilbert presents another way into the problem—this is her conception of the plural subject. It is Gilbert's claim that in constituting a plural subject, all individual wills are bound simultaneously and interdependently, from which it follows that certain obligations and duties are incurred and that reasons for acting in the absence of knowing with certainty what the other will do can fall within these obligations and duties. I do not disagree with this important consequence of constituting a plural subject. What I will argue, though, is that the very act of constituting a plural subject recreates the same problem revealed by replication reasoning in the context of a Prisoner's Dilemma type choice situation. I will then argue that it is the family that is the means by which the problem can be effectively dissolved.

Gilbert's Plural Subject

An ongoing debate in sociology has been over the issue of whether social groups are nothing more than the set of individuals included in them or whether social groups are something more than just that set of individuals. On the first view of a social group, it is the individual intentions of the individual actors that determine which actions the group should perform and what are and are not moral obligations of each of the group members. On the second view of a social group, there are group intentions, as to what actions the group should perform, which are not either the individual intentions or the individual intention that wins (under some voting scheme). There are also group moral obligations.

Gilbert has provided a careful analysis of the constitution of a social group, using her original concept of a plural subject, as a means to navigate the analysis. The plural subject conception of a social group is in line with the second view, above, of a social group. In "Walking Together: A Paradigmatic Social Phenomenon,"[5] she elucidates the nature of the plural subject in the activity of two people going for a walk. Her aim is to reveal the logically necessary and logically sufficient conditions for the constitution of a plural subject.

Consider two people going for a walk together. Each expects the other to do various things, such as not walk so fast that they are soon far ahead of the other person. However, these expectations about what the other person will do are not sufficient to generate the kinds of moral entitlements that would underlie the ascription of moral obligations to each person on the walk. Expectations that the other person will do something are based on evidence acquired from observing the other person and the inferences that can be rationally and reliably made from that evidence. But this is not to say that a moral obligation has been incurred. The question, then, is how the analysis of a plural subject allows for an inference from the evidence that the two walkers use to infer expectations about what actions the other will perform to the obligations to perform those actions. It is here that Gilbert brings in the notion of the plural subject: "in order to go for a walk together, each of the parties must express willingness to constitute with the other a plural subject of the goal that they walk together along in one another's company."[6] In expressing such a willingness (not necessarily verbally), each person sees that they must act "as would the parts of a single person or subject of action in pursuit of the goal."[7] What kind of person is this, though? Gilbert does not brooch the issue. Here is one way of thinking of plural subjects: they are generic persons constituted purely in terms of a goal that the individual parts (that is, the actual individuals in the social group) pursue. In the case of two people on a walk

---

[5] Margaret Gilbert, "Walking Together: A Paradigmatic Social Phenomenon," in *Living Together: Rationality, Sociality and Obligation*, Rowman and Littlefield, 1996, 177-194.

[6] Gilbert, op. cit., p. 184.

[7] Gilbert, op. cit., p. 184.

together, the plural subject in constituted in terms of a goal that each pursues qua member of the plural subject.

Gilbert employs a remarkable description of what the commitment of one's will to the plural subject consists in: "each person expresses a special form of conditional commitment such that only when everyone has done similarly is anyone committed... All wills are bound simultaneously and interdependently."[8] Gilbert's description is remarkable, since it *appears* to resolve the problem of replicative reasoning. Recall that the replicative reasoning that one in a Prisoner's Dilemma-type situation engages in fails to secure knowledge of what the other will do, for the simple reason that the other will have to know what the one now engaged in replicative reasoning as to what the other will do, will do. There is a circle that cannot be broken without the addition of knowledge about what the other will do that neither has and that cannot be acquired from replicative reasoning. Notice that this kind of problem that replicative reasoning cannot resolve arises for those who wish to bind their wills in a plural subject. That is, if each member of the soon-to-be-created plural subject commits her will to the plural subject conditional upon everyone else committing their wills to the plural subject, and each member knows that everyone else knows this, there will not be a time at which there is an actual (as opposed to conditional) commitment, since no one will know that the others have committed their wills. In the same way that in Prisoner's Dilemma type-situations one will not know what the other will do, so too, in creating a plural subject, one will not know that the other has actually committed their will to the creation of the plural subject.

To say, then, as Gilbert does, that wills are bound simultaneously and interdependently, is essentially to beg the question. The question is: how this is accomplished? To say that it has been done is not to say how it can be done and, thus, whether it can actually be done. Gilbert remarks "If 'we' refers to a plural subject of a goal, it refers to a pool of wills dedicated *as one* to that goal... a premise about 'our goal' is as effective as one about 'my goal' in establishing a reason for action for a participating individual."[9] This remark recapitulates the question begging move in the description of binding individual wills into a plural subject, since it is only if we know how it has been done—how the wills are bound simultaneously and interdependently—that one can go from a reason for me to a reason for the plural subject of which I am a part. I don't see how Gilbert escapes the circle that is the basis for her begging the question: an individual is

---

[8] Gilbert, op. cit., p. 185.
[9] Gilbert, op. cit., p. 186.

bound as a plural subject provided that everyone else is bound as a plural subject. Thus, a is bound only if b is bound only if a is bound (where 'a' and 'b' are names of individuals attempting to establish a plural subject).

I will now make a bold claim. There is no circle, and thus no question begged in Gilbert's account, because we learned how to go from 'my' to 'our,'—we learned how to bind our wills simultaneously and interdependently—in families. In my view, families are the primordial form of social group and it is the special blood ties in family life that are necessary for making the inference from 'my' to 'our.' Gilbert does not make any intrinsic distinctions between families and other socials groups other than to distinguish between plural subjects committed to goals or beliefs or principles of action. I will, however, make a distinction. There are (at least) two different notions of plural subject: the sort introduced by Gilbert and the plural subject found in families. For want of a better term, I will call the plural subject in family life "the plural 'me.'"

The plural 'me'

In Gilbert's conception of a plural subject we have a generic subject that is constituted in terms of the wills of individuals in the group to pursue some goal, share some belief or share some principle for action. In families, the plural subject is not a generic subject, but one that has a flesh-and-blood identity. What does this mean? It is a fact of family life that is so much on the surface that it escapes critical reflection: namely, we see ourselves in our parents and our parents see themselves in us. To put it somewhat coarsely, I am part of my father and I am part of my mother. Moreover, my father is part of me and my mother is part of me. Similarly, I am a part of my sibling and my sibling is a part of me.

What follows from this? The first is that there is a qualitative difference between the kinds of part-whole relationships in social groups that are not families and families. Whereas the part-whole relation in a social group that is not a family is "I am part of the plural subject—the collection of wills with goal X (or belief X or directions for action X)," the part-whole relation in the family is "I am part of an extended me." Thus, there are distinctly different kinds of plural subjects.

The second is that the part-of relation between family members has the formal structure of an equivalence class. This is easy to demonstrate. Clearly, "I am part of me" is true, so the part-of relation is reflexive. "I am part of my father and my father is part of me," establishes symmetry. Finally, from "I am part of my brother" and "My brother is part of my mother," we get "I am part of my mother," which establishes transitivity.

Since the part-of relation for families is reflexive, symmetric and transitive, it is an equivalence relation. Thus all family members belong to an equivalence class in virtue of satisfying the part-of relation. Since all of the objects in a formal equivalence relation are "equivalent" (with respect to the relation of part-of), any single object in the class can represent the entire class of objects. Thus any family member can represent the entire family.

It is this fact about the part-of relation that reveals how the inference from 'my' to 'our,'—which is the inference central to the constitution of a plural subject—can be made. Given that I am a member of the family and that I can stand as surrogate for any other family member under the aegis of the equivalence relation, I am, so to speak, the whole class of objects. That is, the inference from 'my' to 'our' is founded on the fact about an equivalence class that any single member can stand for the whole. An immediate objection to my claim is that it is absurd to think that typical families are familiar with the idea of a formal equivalence relation. In which case, the inference from 'me' to 'our' would not be made in a typical family. The objection can be met, however. I will not contest that typical families are not familiar with formal equivalence relations. That, however, does not mean that we are unable to recognize such relations, especially when we exhibit them in our family structure. One does not have to have a formal theory of arithmetic in order to recognize that '1 + 1 = 2' is a truth of elementary arithmetic. Similarly, one does not have to have a formal theory of equivalence relations to recognize that all family members are equivalent in terms of the part-of relation each instantiates with respect to every other family member.

The objector might accept these points, but continue his objection: a typical family member will surely not recognize that all family members are equivalent in terms of the part-of relation. In response to this, it need not be the case that the recognition is an explicit and conscious recognition. Rather, it is undoubtedly a recognition that occurs at a subconscious level of cognitive processing, just as the parsing of sentences in a natural language, the representation of speech sounds as phonemes and the depiction of three-dimensional structure in visual scenes are accomplished at a subconscious level of cognitive processing.

Each family member might think of the family as a 'composite me,' or as an 'extended me.' Phenomenologically, the experience of being a family member is a "me in her and her in me," and "me in him and him in me" experience. A plural subject in Gilbert's view is a collection of wills that act together without each will having to reason whether the other wills will (or will not) act in unison toward a common goal (or having a common belief or a common policy for action). A family is that and more, however. It is a plural subject which is a collection of 'me's.' It is a plural me. An objection against the idea of a plural me can be raised: individual family members are individuals, and they recognize they are distinct from the other family members. Indeed, adolescence is a painful recognition of the individuality of a given family member. However, such an objection fails to be cogent, since it presupposes as the ground for the objection that there is a bond—of some kind—between family members that the adolescent rebels against. That bond is the plural 'me.' Moreover, the idea of an equivalence class is not logically incompatible with there being differences of all kinds between individual members of the family. It is only with respect to the part-of relation that there is an equivalence relation and the consequent powers of being a surrogate for all family members, of being a part which provides the whole.

It is also easy to see how all wills are bound in the plural subject (that is the family) simultaneously and interdependently (given that any one family member is a surrogate for the entire family) without either begging the question—as in Gilbert's account of the constitution of the plural subject—or presupposing knowledge about what the other will do which one does not, in fact, have. Since any one family member is a surrogate for all of the others, his or her decision to commit to the plural subject commits all to the plural subject. Since each family member will be a surrogate for all, then all commit simultaneously and interdependently. It might be objected that such episodes of constitution of the plural subject must be reenacted whenever new children are born into the family and, on that account, there is never a unique plural subject that is the family, but one which changes over time. This objection is misguided, since the only change that occurs is the mere addition of a new member into the family and not any of the essential features of the plural subject that is the family. Another objection is that there is not a specific time at which wills are bound into the plural subject that is the family. This, too, is misguided, since families, unlike non-family social groups, are not constituted by various people assembling in a specific place under a specific organizational rubric at a specific time. Rather, the constitution of the family members as a plural subject is a process (though not an explicit and conscious one) that is continually repeated throughout the duration of the family. The family meal is just one instance of the process that is the constitution of the plural subject that is the family.

Since a family is a plural subject, all of the moral obligations that are in effect for plural subjects are in effect for families. As Gilbert points out, being rational and accepting that one is committed to the plural subject will entail a number of obligations on the part of all members of the plural subject, as well as other kinds of actions, which, though not morally obligatory, are necessary for the proper functioning of the group. (She employs the distinction H. L. A. Hart drew between being obliged and having an obligation to distinguish the kinds of actions that are obligatory and those that are non-obligatory but necessary for the group to achieve its goals.[10]) However, the specific obligations and duties may differ from one social group to the next. This raises the question: which family values are morally obligatory and which are not obligatory, but necessary for the proper functioning of the family? Certainly, it would be nice if those values that sustain the part-of relation that is central to the constitution of the family as a plural subject are also necessary for the proper functioning of the family. Why is that? No doubt, where a family is dysfunctional, the part-of relation is jeopardized. The feeling of being "me in him" and "him in me" will be painful where a father is alcoholic and violent. I think that we will not have a clear view of what are family values until we have a clear picture of the kinds of mechanisms that are in place to sustain the part-of relation for families.[11] The following sections are somewhat

---

[10] Gilbert, op. cit., p. 181.

[11] In her valuable commentary on this paper (read at the 2009 Third Annual Felician Ethics Conference, April 18th, 2009), Carrie-Ann Biondi charges that the model of family unity proposed here succumbs to biological reductionism: the familial resemblances are a matter of shared DNA. I disagree; it is not biological reductionism, since the equivalence relations are defined, not over biological properties, but rather over the phenomenology of resemblance between family members. Certainly, how it is that the phenomenology is manifested in us could be a biological matter, but that would be irrelevant for defining the equivalence relations, since these relations are definable only at a higher level than the biological level. Biological properties of a human being can provide some features that are necessary for the phenomenology to occur, but they are not features in terms of which the inferences constituting the equivalence relation are drawn. In some families, there is no resemblance, since the children are adopted. Would this family be one where the equivalence relation could not be inferred? No, since the concepts of being a sibling, of having (or being) a parent, build in the phenomenology (even if there is no obvious resemblance between family members). Notice, as well, that the equivalence relations are not a matter of establishing personal identity. Indeed, personal identity and the equivalence relations are in tension, and adolescent rebellion is just one way in which personal identity trumps the equivalence relations. However, I do not claim that my proposal is the last word on what the family bond comes to—there are deep issues about whether there is a form of family bond that precedes the equivalence relations or whether the equivalence relations generate the family bond. As Professor Biondi pointed out, how we develop trust in voluntary social

speculative, but they offer my view as to how the part-of relation for families is sustained through a linguistic mechanism.

De re and *de dicto* propositional attitudes toward numbers and toward family members

There is a well-known distinction in the philosophy of language between *de re* and *de dicto* propositional attitudes, which has roots in medieval philosophy. The basic idea of the distinction is that attitudes toward sentences are different from attitudes toward actual objects and their properties.[12] Take the *de re* sentence: '(3x) Ralph believes that x is a spy' and the *de dicto* sentence 'Ralph believes that (3x) and x is a spy.' In the first case, the sentence is true if there is an actual person x of whom Ralph believes that he (or she) is a spy. In the second case, the sentence is true if Ralph believes the proposition (or dictum) that there are spies (even though he may believe of no one that he (or she) is a spy). Notice that the *de dicto* sentence can be true, while the *de re* sentence is false. But it is unlikely that the *de re* sentence could be true and the *de dicto* sentence false, since if Ralph believes of Jack that he is a spy, then surely Ralph believes that there are spies. Another example: I can believe that the shortest spy is a spy, even though I do not believe that there is any spy. If I believe, of someone, that they are the shortest spy, then it follows that I believe that there is a shortest spy. But I can believe that someone is a spy without believing of anyone that they are a spy, let alone the shortest spy. Before we can take these lessons to the family, we need to examine ways of designating objects and their relevance to the distinction between *de re* and *de dicto* propositional attitudes toward numbers and toward the family.

One way I can designate the person who killed Alexander Hamilton is "the killer of Alexander Hamilton." This is not useful information, though, if my goal is to find the killer of Alexander Hamilton. That description does not give me direct access to the killer.[13] On the other hand "Aaron Burr, who lives at 21 Silver Street, shot Alexander Hamilton" gives me

---

relationships is an important problem that is left open by my proposal, to the extent that my proposal leaves open what the true nature of the family bond consists in.

[12] W. V. Quine, "Quantifiers and Propositional Attitudes," *Journal of Philosophy*, 53 (1956), 177-187.

[13] David Kaplan, "Demonstratives: An Essay on the Semantics, Logic, Metaphysics, and Epistemology of Demonstratives and Other Indexicals," in *Themes From Kaplan*, J. Almog, J. Perry and H. Wettstein (eds.), Oxford University Press, 1989, 481-563.

direct access to the killer of Hamilton. Now consider ways of designating natural numbers. We can do this in different systems of notation. For instance, we can use a base two notation which employs only two distinct symbols, (namely, '0' and '1'). Or we can use a base 10 notation, which employs 10 distinct symbols ('0' through '9'). How we designate a natural number can make an important difference when we ask whether we know what number it is. We have much experience with base 10 notation, but little with base 2 (unless we write code for compilers). When confronted with the natural number 12, I know what number it is. I do not have to make some kind of calculation before I know what number it is. But when the same natural number is represented in a system of numerical notation that I am not familiar with, or not that familiar with, I will have to make a calculation before I know which number it is. Do you know which number 1100 is?

The point to carry away from this discussion of *de re* and *de dicto* attitudes is that how we designate the objects that we directly experience can matter enormously in determining whether we know what object it is. If we designate an object in an unfamiliar way or in a way that is trivial, we will not know what object it is. Thus, if we designate '25' as 'the number that is the solution to the equation '$x^3 + 49 = 15,576$,' we will not know what number it is unless we make a calculation. How about people? If we designate "Jones' as "the guy who has a small mole on the bottom of his left large toe," we cannot determine which person Jones is until we find the actual person who has that property, but it is not clear we will know who Jones is even then, since it's not clear that the description "the guy ..." gives us direct access to Jones. The base 10 numeral 12 gives us direct access to the natural number 12. 1100 does not give us direct access to 12. What will give us direct access to a human being? One answer is that the proper name of a human being gives us direct access to them, since a proper name is a rigid designator. This, though, cannot be right, since 1100 is a rigid designator, but does not give us direct access to 12.[14] Here is a radical proposal: we have direct access to people when they are family members and we designate them as family members via descriptive properties of various kinds. The question, then, is what is the designation of family members by which we have direct access to them? I don't claim to have an answer to this question, but only a sketch of an answer. My proposal is that we designate family members in terms of certain phenotypic properties: facial expression, facial physiognomy, body

---

[14] Saul Kripke, "Logicism, Wittgenstein and *Dr Re* Beliefs About Numbers," Whitehead Lecture II delivered at Harvard University, May 5, 1992, forthcoming in *Collected Papers, VolumeTwo*, Oxford University Press.

posture, moles, hair color, eye color, wrinkles and so on. Question: Why don't we do the same for non-family members and have direct access to them that goes beyond that provided by their proper names? In which case, there is no distinction between family and non-family members that would support the claim that we have direct access to one, though not the other. We use a constellation of properties that are satisfied more by family members than by non-family members. But that is not the only means by which we achieve direct access. There is also the plural 'me,' the plural subject that is constituted by the part-of relation that creates a formal equivalence relation in which I am the surrogate for all of the other family members (and, similarly for them). It is the conception of 'he in me' and 'me in him,' that allows family names to provide direct access to their bearers—but only when those names are used by other family members. In that sense, the names are highly contextualized. If a non-family member uses the name, it will not achieve direct access to the extent that a family member using the name achieves. (This is, then, a case of what Russell meant by knowledge by acquaintance and is reference by acquaintance.[15])

There are various conjectures as to why we have direct access to 12 through the numeral 12 and not through the numeral 1100, but it is still a puzzle. Here, too, it is a puzzle that, if my claim about having direct access to family members by names and various descriptive properties is correct, needs to be addressed. But waiving the question of how direct access to family members is accomplished, what work could direct access do in resolving the problem that reason-replication is not sufficient (and possibly not even necessary) to acquire knowledge about what another person in a choice situation will do if the joint goal is to secure the unique best point. What we get from direct access to numbers via a notational system is knowledge of what number it is. If 12 is the answer to a problem in arithmetic, then we do not know the answer when we encounter 1100, but we know the answer when we encounter 12.

Facts from psychology and evolutionary psychology about choice of spouses

One problem for the claim that each family member is a surrogate for all under the equivalence relation established by the part-of relation between family members is that husbands and wives are not related by blood lines. Thus, it is not the case that a wife is part of her husband, or that a husband is part of her wife, in that they share common genetic

---

[15] Bertrand Russell, *The Problems of Philosophy*, New York, Holt, 1912.

material. But it has been shown that prospective mates typically select one another on the basis of both similarity in appearance and similarity in genetic stock (though determining that someone else has a similar genetic make-up is obviously not something done consciously). Moreover, there is also a literature on the ways in which familiarity with someone (or something) creates preferences for that person (or object), all else being equal. For instance, Robert Zajonc's 'mere exposure' effect would explain why it is that husbands and wives will come to think of themselves as more similar to one another than to their friends and colleagues.[16]

A number of studies have shown that we prefer mates who most resemble either us or our parents. (Indeed, we prefer as pets dogs that most resemble us.) The great ethologist Konrad Lorenz's notions of filial imprinting and sexual imprinting[17]—and recent fMRI studies have identified where in the brain imprinting occurs[18]—provides strong evidence that we have such preferences for mates who most resemble our parents. Other studies provide strong evidence that we have such preferences for mates who most resemble ourselves.[19] Other studies have found that resemblance enhances trust.[20] (There are interesting questions about whether such preferences compete and whether measuring one kind of preference—for mates resembling oneself—is really an expression of a preference for mates resembling one's parents.)

If these preferences are true of us and humans have been making them for countless generations, we should expect the typical family to consist of members who resemble one another. What could follow from this about knowing how a family member would reason in a Prisoner's Dilemma type choice situation? It is this: just as we know which number 12 is without having to perform a calculation (and do not know which number 1100 is unless we perform a calculation) because we were brought up on the base 10 notation for natural numbers, so too we know how a family member would reason in a Prisoner's Dilemma type choice situation

---

[16] Robert Zajonc, "Attitudinal Effects of Mere Exposure," *The Journal of Personality and Social Psychology*, 9 (#2, pt. 2) (1968) 1-27.

[17] Konrad Lorenz, *Here I Am—Where Are You?: The Behavior of the Greylag Goose*, New York, Harcourt Brace Jovanovich, 1988.

[18] G. Horn, "Visual imprinting and the neural mechanisms of recognition memory," *Trends in Neuroscience* 21 (1998), 300-305.

[19] Robert Zajonc, P. Adelmann, S. T. Murphy, and P. M. Niedenthal, "Convergence in the physical appearance of spouses," *Motivation and Emotion*, 11 (1987) 335-346.

[20] L. M. Debruine, "Facial resemblance enhances trust," *Proceedings of the Royal Society of London*, Biology, 269 (2002), 1307-1312.

because family members look like us and we believe, on that basis, that they will think like us in such situations. (There are probably some interesting studies to be done on human inferences about inter-species and intra-species mental contents and reasoning abilities.) If such beliefs are hard-wired into us, then we have what appears to be an easy solution to reason-replication without group regimentation and without group principles, such as social conventions. (But appearances can be deceiving. Wittgenstein's problem for hard-wired accounts of rule-following would play havoc with reason replication.) Suppose, however, that they are not hard-wired into us. We do not think that choice of base 10 notation is hard-wired into us, since there have been cultures that have used other base notations of representing the natural numbers. But it is the knowledge that something is the number that it is that we get from base 10 notation and not from other base notation. Similarly, with the proper choice of descriptive predicates, we know who our sibling is, knowing that they will think the same way as we do in such choice situations. That they will think the same as us in choice situations might either be an obligation or a necessary but non-obligatory value that arises in the constitution of the plural 'me,' or even a value that sustains the plural 'me.' Knowing who our family members are just is to have direct access to them in our references to them and in our use of descriptive predicates about them. I suspect that 'knowing who' is a linguistic mechanism that sustains the family as plural 'me,' primarily because it has important uses in choice situations encountered in everyday family life.

An objection: Prisoner's Dilemma type choice situations are rarely encountered

Here is the picture of the family as plural 'me,' and the reasoning needed to secure the unique best point in Prisoner's Dilemma type choice situations. As we have seen, the family constituted as a plural subject provides the knowledge that is necessary for securing a unique best point. I conjecture that it is the usefulness of the family as plural subject in securing unique best points (in various choice situations) that sustains the family as plural subject. That is, one mechanism by which the family as plural subject is sustained is its usefulness in securing unique best points.

However, it can be reasonably objected that we are rarely (if ever) in Prisoner's Dilemma type choice situations. When was the last time you were held incommunicado with a friend (or family member) in a jail? If human beings are rarely in such choice situations, it would make little sense for nature to provide a facility in the human brain for making conclusions about how family members would reason in such situations. But to think we rarely encounter such situations is false. Indeed, we encounter them frequently, even though they are not actual Prisoner's Dilemma situations. Rather, they have the formal structure of such choice situations, but have different payoffs and different choice descriptions. There are also other kinds of choice situations, not with the exact formal structure of Prisoner's Dilemma, but close enough to it (which economists and political scientists have catalogued).

Here is an example of a Prisoner's Dilemma type choice situation we encounter frequently. Jack and his sister Jill are in different parts of a city neither has visited before and neither has any way of communicating with the other. (Suppose their cell-phone batteries are dead.) They need to meet at 5 PM (and each knows that). Where should they meet? Another example: Jack and his sister Jill are in different parts of the house and each hears the doorbell ring. It might be a thief. If both answer the door, the thief will be deterred. If neither answers, the thief cannot get in. If only one answers, the thief can overpower them (and then overpower the other, unless they run away). There are also examples involving buying gifts vs. not buying a gift, where if one buys a gift, but the other does not, there is extreme humiliation. Whenever there is a coordination problem where there are no communication links between the agents, it can easily meet the conditions of either a Prisoner's Dilemma type choice situation or of other choice situations structurally close to Prisoner's Dilemma. Coordination problems occur throughout everyday life (and David Lewis was famous for arguing that use of language involves solving complex coordination problems[21]). Mundane coordination problems, such as who washes dishes, the actual washing of the dishes with another person, use of the toilet and shower, what to see on television and when and when not to have it on, arise in everyday family life. So coordination problems, Prisoner's Dilemma type problems and problems that are structurally like, but nonetheless distinct from Prisoner's Dilemma problems, pervade everyday life and provide countless opportunities to reinforce the picture of the family as the plural subject.

Family rationality, group rationality and individual rationality

It is rational for a family member to make their choice of a unique best point, since they have direct access to other family members. Even though

---

[21] David Lewis, *Convention*, Harvard University Press, 1973.

reason-replication does not provide knowledge necessary to show it is rational to choose what will secure the unique best point, having direct access to a family member does provide that knowledge. Moreover, having direct access to a family member is facilitated by each family member being a member of a plural subject that is the family.

It would not be rational for a member of a non-family group to do the same, since they do not have such direct access to members of their group. The difference between the two is like the difference between accessing the natural number 12 through the numeral 12 or through the numeral 1100. Similarly, it would not be rational for an individual not in any group, though in a Prisoner's Dilemma type choice situation, to do the same, since the individual would not have direct access to the other person. So there is a distinct form of rationality unique to families that is not appropriate for non-family social groups and not appropriate for individuals (outside the context of their families). Which kinds of moral obligations and duties follow from this form of rationality will determine only some of the kinds of family values discussed in the literature. Other family values will be determined by what kinds of values are necessary for sustaining the family as plural subject. But where a purported family value fails the test of either flowing from the form of rationality unique to a family or sustaining the family as plural subject, there is, then, no good reason to take it to be an authentic family value. It may well have political expediency, but that is not an adequate criterion to take it to be an authentic family value.[22]

---

[22] Which family values are justified (and which are not) in terms of the equivalence relations that constitute the family bond will depend upon a number of features that are a matter of evolutionary adaptation, although such features cannot tell the whole story, since the normative aspects of family values will run orthogonal to them. However, using such features as guides to the kinds of values that count as authentic family values is a useful heuristic, just as using information from evolutionary psychology can be a useful heuristic in moral theory, though no substitute for discerning its normative features.

CHAPTER FIVE

FAMILY PRACTIONERS, LAW, ETHICS, AND EMERGING TECHNOLOGIES

INTRODUCTION

Recent advances in the medical and legal fields create new ethical challenges for both families as well as the professionals that serve them. Questions concerning decisions and responses that should be made as the result of these changes often demand that we as a society address the notion that "just because we can, does not mean that we should".

Decisions regarding reproductive technologies are among the most ethically challenging for families and health care providers. Single women can become mothers through sperm donation, raising the question of "fairness" to the children, who will be raised by one parent rather than the traditional two, and will have either no or limited knowledge of their biological father. Genetic testing allows parents to discover their risk of passing on genetic disease or chromosomal abnormalities before conception, or to have a biological "blueprint" of a child during pregnancy, as well as the opportunity to terminate if problems are found.

Fertility drugs and Invitro fertilization (IVF) allow couples struggling to conceive to often have not one, but multiple children, even resulting in "mega-births" as seen recently in the media craze surrounding "Jon and Kate Plus Eight" and Nadya Suleman, who gave birth to octuplets after using IVF. The question of ethics emerges as a result of the risks to both mother and children when there are multiple fetuses, including premature birth, long-term developmental delays, and death. Many question whether it is ethically appropriate for a doctor to insert more than two or three embryos, while others debate whether or not selective reduction should be employed when multiple embryos implant. Some call these multiple births "miracles", while others describe them as irresponsible. Should there be a limit on the maximum number of births in a given pregnancy, and if so, what is the number? How do we enforce this? The overarching question becomes who makes these decisions, parents, medical professionals, or policy makers?

There are other critical issues surrounding reproductive technologies and ethics. Doctors have developed a technology to select the gender of a child by sorting male and female sperm before conception. This begs the question, should parents be allowed to select the gender of their children, and if so, what implications does this have for society as a whole? In this chapter, Elizabeth Meade examines some of the issues at stake in the new technologies of gender selection in "Choice's Challenge: Feminist Ethics and Reproductive Autonomy". In particular, she examines whether these technologies are properly seen as part of the broader array of reproductive technologies that have tended to find support in feminist ethics. Meade also considers the use of gender selection abroad, where it has led to dangerously skewed gender ratios, as well as in the US, where it is used primarily for reasons of "family balance."

Further ethical considerations focus on the use of medical technologies in children. In "Superkid or Frankenchild: Ethical Issues in Chemically Enhancing the Next Generation", Steven Weiss explores the use of biotechnical and pharmacological interventions, such as human growth hormone and Ritalin, to improve the lives of otherwise normal, healthy children. He argues that if such drugs are deemed safe and offer the possibility of improving performance in children, then parents should be able to utilize these pharmaceuticals to help their children learn better, behave better and perform better.

In addition to ethical issues surrounding reproductive technologies and the use of pharmaceuticals in children, end-of-life decisions are among the most controversial within the medical community. Again, a critical argument arises over who has the final say in such matters: the individual, family, medical professionals, or someone else. In "Organ Donation Impasse and Family Rights", Robert Muhlnickel examines the double-veto organ donation policy, wherein two decision-makers have the authority to refuse organs from being taken after their relative's death, even if the deceased has indicated willingness to donate their organs after their death.

Child serving professionals often encounter ethical dilemmas that must be addressed when working with this population. Paul Newhouse examines "Conflicting Ethical Duties? The Dilemma of the Best Interests Attorney", particularly as between duties to the legal system and duties to the child, resulting in an interesting contrast between the case of the 'best interests" attorney and the litigation attorney. Similarly, in "Ethical Dilemmas and a Decision-making Process for Child Welfare Practice", Karen Rice considers an ethical quandary that results from the dual relationship between professional and child, and professional and family, that child welfare workers encounter in their work. She addresses how this complicates the decision making process, as the outcome often benefits only one member of the family.

As technologies in the medical field continue to develop and legal and professional changes are made in the child serving field, new ethical questions will emerge, needing to be addressed. Whose best interests are and should be served in these cases will need to be examined by all of those who desire to serve individuals and families in an ethical manner.

CHOICE'S CHALLENGE: FEMINIST ETHICS AND REPRODUCTIVE TECHNOLOGY

ELIZABETH M. MEADE

A cornerstone of feminist ethics for over 30 years has been the preservation of reproductive autonomy. What few today seem to remember is that the commitment to reproductive autonomy is part of a larger concern with the promotion of full corporal autonomy: the belief that women deserve the right to full control over their bodies, free from any sort of economic, physical or sexual coercion. The advent of the first technologies for assisted reproduction in 1982, with the first successful birth from in vitro fertilization, began a debate among feminists and ethicists alike about the potential impact of these technologies on women's reproductive autonomy. There were those who saw these technologies as increasing the hegemony of the male medical establishment over women's bodies on one side of the debate, and those who saw the technologies as increasing women's control over their own bodies and reproduction. Over time, the latter perspective has dominated, especially as reproductive technologies have enabled alternative families to produce children: single mothers, gay and lesbian couples and older women in particular.

More recently, a new set of technologies has emerged which require us to reconsider the question of whether reproductive technologies enhance or restrict reproductive freedom. This paper seeks to explore the ethical issues at stake with the new technologies of gender selection, in terms of three questions: Is gender selection itself morally objectionable? Is gender selection itself inherently oppressive? And, finally, is it justified to see these technologies as part of the larger array of reproductive choices open to women?

Traditionally, feminists have been staunch defenders of reproductive choice. If gender-selection is legitimately understood as part of the array of reproductive technology, one would expect broad support for it from feminists. But the technologies of gender-selection may possibly be the instruments of gender ideology and gender oppression. In India and China, for example, the ratio of males to females has already become dangerously skewed as a result of aggressive gender-selection, leading some to observe increased violence toward women as the stock of potential wives dwindles, and others to predict increasing pressure on women to fulfill their traditional roles of wives and mothers at the expense of other ambitions. Hence, gender selection poses a considerable challenge to the notion of reproductive choice as traditionally defended by feminists.

The first question, whether gender selection is in itself morally objectionable, has no easy answers. For many, the ethics of gender selection are primarily dependent on the method employed. For example, few find anything morally objectionable about following the so-called Shettles method, which makes recommendations about optimal foods to eat to produce the desired gender, as well as optimal sexual positions and times in the ovulation cycle for sexual intercourse. But the primary post-conception methods concern many, especially those on the pro-life side of the abortion debate. Post-conception gender-selection, the first methods of sex-selection available (apart from infanticide or infant abandonment, both of which have been widely practiced throughout history and can be found around the world even today) are the result of the development of pre-natal testing that can reveal the gender of the fetus. These techniques currently consist of ultrasound imaging, amniocentesis and chorionic villus sampling. Some ultrasound technicians claim that imaging can reveal the sex with some degree of accuracy as early as the 12th week of pregnancy, while others state that one needs to wait until 16-20 weeks. It is never 100% accurate. Amniocentesis, which involves taking a sample of the amniotic fluid and testing it for genetic abnormalities or for gender, reveals the gender with 100% accuracy, and can be done only after the 16th or 17th week of pregnancy. It also involves an increased risk of miscarriage. Chorionic villus sampling is a technique that can be done between weeks 10 and 12 of the pregnancy. It involves taking a small sample of the placenta and testing it for genetic abnormalities or gender. It carries an even higher risk of miscarriage than amniocentesis and is done less frequently than amniocentesis.

To be used as a gender-selection technique, the testing is followed by an abortion when the fetus is determined to be the "wrong" gender. In the U.S., where the abortion debate shows no signs of quieting down, this presents some serious issues, as abortion after the 12th week of pregnancy or in the second trimester tends to be more heavily restricted. And of course, for those opposed to abortion at any time in a pregnancy, gender selection would hardly justify it. Even some who are less opposed to abortion may find it objectionable when used for gender selection. They may find abortion justified for people who feel economically or emotionally unprepared to raise a child, but less so for people who want to raise a boy only or a girl only.

Another method of post-conception gender-selection involves the creation of embryos through in vitro fertilization techniques. This is known generally as pre-implantation genetic diagnosis or PGD. As is the case with ultrasound, chorionic villus sampling and amniocentesis, PGD was developed not for gender selection, but for the early detection of genetic defects or other abnormalities. In PGD, prior to implantation, the embryos are tested to determine the presence of any genetic defects or diseases. Gender can also be determined at this time, and may be the only thing to be determined in some cases of severe sex-linked diseases. Then the embryos of the desired genetic make-up or gender are implanted. Initially, PGD was used solely to assist couples with a family history of sex-linked diseases, but while it has not become a routine part of in vitro fertilization, it certainly can be and is being used to select the gender of one's child. This is an expensive method, as IVF currently costs around $13,000 per cycle.[1] It also involves the ethically problematic issue of what to do with the embryos that are not of the desired gender. Couples can choose to preserve the additional embryos (although they cannot be preserved indefinitely), they can choose to discard the embryos, or they can choose to donate the embryos to another infertile couple or to medical research. This issue is complicated in the U.S. by the fact that creating embryos one does not intend to implant is seen by many as the moral equivalent of abortion. For those opposed to abortion, PGD is not ethically permissible because it involves the almost inevitable destruction of human embryos.

There is a third method of gender selection just beginning to be available to American couples, currently the only reliable method of pre-conception gender selection. It involves separating X-bearing sperm from Y-bearing sperm, since X-bearing sperm are 2.8% heavier than Y-bearing sperm. In this technique, known as flow cytometry, "laser beams are passed across a flowing array of specially dyed sperm in order to separate the . . . heavier X- from Y-bearing sperm to produce an X-enriched sperm sample for insemination."[2] After separation, the woman is inseminated using the techniques of artificial insemination.

---

[1] Debora L. Spar, *The Baby Business: How Money, Science and Politics Drive the Commerce of Conception.* (Boston: Harvard Business School Press, 2006), p. 213.
[2] "Preconception Gender Selection for Nonmedical Reasons," Ethics Committee of the American Society for Reproductive Medicine, in *Fertility and Sterility, Vol. 75, No. 5, May 2001.*

Currently, this technique is most effective for producing the X-enriched sperm, and so can primarily assist in the conception of girls. The USDA has licensed the technology to a company in Virginia that has been using the technique on carefully selected couples, to gather data. The criteria for inclusion in the trial is that the couple already have a child, want a child of a specified gender only for family balancing reasons, and commit to loving and raising the child no matter which gender. The company's website reports 73% success in achieving boys and 88% success in achieving girls.[3]

Apart from issues linked to the abortion debate, the primary ethical issue posed by gender selection is the fact that it commodifies children, turning them into high-end, customizable luxury goods. Selecting the gender of an embryo prior to implantation is just a baby step away from selecting for other traits (hair color, eye color, musical ability), leading to the specter of designer babies that ethicists have been warning about for several decades now. There are a number of potential ethical problems here. I believe it will be very damaging for families, subtly altering the attitude of parents to children from loving them for who they are, to expecting them to be what the parents paid for. It will also narrow the range of acceptable physical traits, leading to an affluent class of people who are more physically homogenous, meeting their own self-designed standard of beauty and perfection.

Turning now to the second question, of whether gender selection is inherently oppressive to women and families, we ask: Why have people invested so much time, effort and now money into pre-determining the gender of their child? Historically, it is fair to say that the phenomenon has been the result of gender ideologies preaching the value of one gender (usually the male) over the other. Gender ideology becomes deeply embedded in a culture and its practices, so that having a boy, for example, becomes a matter of economic necessity. In cultures in which only boys may inherit property, it is essential to have a male child to keep property within a family and even to provide support for unmarried female relatives. In many countries only male heirs have been allowed to inherit titles and positions, as is currently the case in Japan where the Crown Princess has given birth to two girls, with the assistance of fertility experts, but nonetheless failed to provide an heir to the throne. There are many other similar examples, but all such practices are founded upon the assumption that females are of less value, are less truly members of a

---

[3] http://www.microsort.net. Accessed 8/15/08.

family, or are incapable of such responsibilities as owning and managing property.

Ideologies about an ideal family, requiring a balance of genders, may also be a significant factor. It is very common in the U.S. to assume that a woman expecting her second child wants a child of the opposite gender, or to assume that a couple with all boys or all girls feels some deprivation at the gender imbalance. And, in fact, in the U.S. a desire for gender balance is the most frequently cited reason for seeking out the various techniques of gender-selection. People may also have opinions about birth order, feeling it important to have either a boy or a girl first. The concern with family balance or birth order reflect fairly deeply held gender stereotypes: that a girl or a boy will bring a certain set of traits into the family or will provide a certain kind of companionship to the parents or siblings. Consequently, it is fair to conclude that the desire to select the gender of one's child is rooted in gender stereotypes or ideologies. Of course, many people expecting children "hope" for one gender or another, motivated by a similar set of largely unconscious stereotypes, so is it really so very bad to have people act on those desires for sons or daughters?

One very clear negative consequence to gender selection is the possibility of gender imbalance. When you conceive a child, your chance of getting a boy or a girl is 50/50 every time. Presumably nature has a good reason for maintaining this ratio: some studies have even shown that where there is a higher infant mortality rate for one sex in the first year of life, the sex ratio at birth can compensate, to produce an even number of boys and girls after the first year.[4] In India and China, where gender selection in favor of boys has been aggressively practiced for several decades, we see a significant imbalance in the gender ratio. India in particular has made aggressive use of medical technology for gender-selection, in particular, ultrasound imaging and amniocentesis, followed by sex-selective abortion. Currently it is estimated that the gender ratio in India is 927 girls for every 1000 boys.[5] In China, where infanticide and infant abandonment are the preferred methods, the ratio stands at 117 boys for every 100 girls, although in some areas of the country the imbalance is far greater.[6] The harm posed by such gender imbalances is very real:

---

[4] Radhika Balakrishnan, "The Social Context of Sex Selection and the Politics of Abortion in India," in *Power and Decision: The Social Control of Reproduction* (Cambridge: Harvard School of Public Health, 1994), pp. 267-286. In her article, she cites Miller, 1981.

[5] *Christian Science Monitor*, February 9, 2005.

[6] *The Baby Business*, p. 124.

from the millions of girl babies dead and abandoned, to the larger societal harm of a generation of men being unable to find wives.

In the U.S., the ratio of males and females is roughly equal and likely to remain so. The ideology that influences gender-selection is gender balance rather than a desire for boys over girls. In fact, it tends to be used most often by women wanting girls. There are many who argue that gender-selection as practiced in the US is not sexist or oppressive of one gender over the other. There has been a great deal of sympathy in the medical community, and even in the feminist community, for the desire to gender-select for the purposes of gender variety or gender balance. There seems to be broad support for the idea that a couple with 3 sons might want a daughter. Is such a desire inherently sexist? It seems to me that the desire for gender variety can quite easily be sexist, but is not necessarily. It can be, when what is desired is not the variety of gender, and hence of child-rearing experiences, but a set of gender-stereotyped characteristics.   In reading about women seeking gender-selection techniques such as flow cytometry, it is clear that such a factor is present. Women seeking a daughter after having one or more sons are looking for gendered companionship. A woman wants a daughter to go shopping with, to dress in pink. A man might want a son to play football with, to pass on the family name. This attitude is, I argue, both sexist and potentially damaging. It reinforces such stereotypes that girls like to shop and boys don't, that boys like to play football and girls don't, that only a male heir can carry on the family name.

While people have these preconceptions about children whose gender is selected by nature, I am concerned about the damage done if the children born to couples who pay for gender-selection fail to live up to these gender stereotypes. If one has invested such time and money into producing a son for the purpose of carrying on a family name, what recriminations might result if he chooses not to have children? What will be the effect when a woman invests money, effort and the emotional cost of these procedures to produce a daughter for female companionship, but ends up with a girl who prefers baseball to shopping and overalls to frills? I believe that sex-selection, even for the most benign reasons, poses a real barrier to seeing individuals as individuals and not as representatives of a particular gender. In reality, women do experience companionship with sons and men with daughters. It may have more to do with the right combination of personalities than with compatibility of gender. I do believe that it is possible to have a gender preference that is not tied up in gender stereotypes. But even when one's personal desire to select the sex of one's child is not inherently sexist, the practice taken as a whole most certainly is.

The final ethical question I want to address is whether it is justified to see gender-selection as part of a larger array of reproductive choices that are available to women and that should be defended by feminists (and others) on the grounds of reproductive and bodily autonomy. I have come to believe that the techniques of gender selection are fundamentally different than other forms of reproductive technology. The various techniques of birth control, abortion and assisted reproduction enable women to determine whether and when to have children. Margaret Sanger wrote in 1920 that "[n]o woman can call herself free who does not own and control her own body. No woman can call herself free until she can choose consciously whether she will or will not be a mother."[7] The technologies that allow women to prevent pregnancy and those that enable pregnancy fit this description of corporal autonomy. Gender selection does not. Having a child born who is not of a desired gender or does not have desired genetic traits or perfect health is not an infringement of one's reproductive autonomy. Autonomy implies control over one's own body. I do not believe we can extend that autonomy to imply control over one's children.

---

[7] *The Boundaries of Her Body: The Troubling History of Women's Rights in America*, Debran Rowland. (Naperville, IL: Sphinx Publishing, 2004), p. 41.

SUPERKID OR FRANKENCHILD: A PLEA FOR CHEMICALLY ENHANCING THE NEXT GENERATION

STEVEN D. WEISS

Good parents want what is best for their children and often make great sacrifices of time, energy and resources to offer them every opportunity to succeed and flourish. But now in addition to taking their children to tennis and violin lessons, enrolling them in private schools, and paying for expensive SAT prep classes, neuroscience and psychopharmacology offer parents another way to help their children meet difficult challenges and achieve goals. This paper explores the ethical issues surrounding the use of psychotropic drugs for enhancing cognitive performance in normal, healthy children. The first part of the paper reviews some of the standard drugs currently prescribed for enhancing cognition and mental functioning in both adults and adolescents diagnosed with various cognitive deficits and disorders. Since clinicians and researchers recognize that these drugs are equally safe and effective in enhancing mental functioning among healthy individuals–children included–the natural suggestion is that these pharmaceuticals could be used beyond their present therapeutic context to make us "better than well"–to borrow a phrase from the title of Karl Elliot's book.[1] The second part of the paper draws from the 2003 Report by the President's Council on Bioethics (chaired by Leon Kass, M.D.) entitled *Beyond Therapy: Biotechnology and the Pursuit of Happiness*, to present a battery of objections to providing cognitive enhancement drugs to healthy children.[2] The ethical issues raised by the report include concerns about social control and conformity, moral education and

---

[1]. Carl Elliot, *Better Than Well: American Medicine Meets the American Dream* (New York and London: Norton & Co., 2003).
[2]. A Report by the President's Council on Bioethics, *Beyond Therapy: Biotechnology and the Pursuit of Happiness,* Leon Kass, et. al. (New York, NY: Harper Collins Publishers, 2003); available at www.bioethics.gov/reports/beyondtherapy.

medicalization, and the meaning of performance. The final section of the paper counters each of these worries and makes a case for using pharmaceuticals to help children learn better and perform better as they make their way in the world. There is little reason to suppose that the Superkid of the future will resemble a Frankenchild abomination.

Better Living Through Chemistry

The term "cognition" typically includes skills pertaining to attention, learning, memory, language, complex motor behaviors and the executive functions involving decisionmaking, goal setting, planning and judgment. Methylphenidate (brand name Ritalin) and amphetamine (Adderall) are two stimulants that can improve memory and learning for those suffering from attention deficit disorder, frequently marked by hyperactivity and difficulty in focusing attention. (Methylphenidate is actually a synthetic derivative of amphetamine.) Acting on various neurotransmitter systems of the brain, these stimulants have been very successful in improving the performance of ADD/ADHD students in school, where this illness is thought to affect up to 10 percent of children in the United States.[3] Furthermore, Kass's own report acknowledges that these stimulants are able to boost alertness and concentration in children who show absolutely no symptoms of ADD/ADHD.[4] There is also clinical evidence that in small doses amphetamines enhance neural plasticity and accelerate motor learning and are especially helpful for recovering stroke victims when combined with training which, as researcher Anjan Chatterjee M.D. observes, raises the possibility that these stimulants could aid normal subjects in fine-tuning their motor skills as they learn to swim, ski, or play the piano.[5]

Martha Farah, director of the Center for Cognitive Neuroscience at the University of Pennsylvania, captures the professional consensus when she observes that not only are Ritalin and Adderal effective in treating ADHD but when taken by normal individuals "induce reliable changes in vigilance, response time and higher cognitive functions, such as novel problem-solving and planning."[6] She goes on to note that thousands of healthy children and adults have discovered the same, and that these drugs

[3]. Peter Whitehouse and Eric Juengst, "Enhancing Cognition in the Intellectually Intact," *Hastings Center Report* 27, issue 3 (May/June 1997): 14-22.
[4]. Kass, *Beyond Therapy,* 76.
[5]. Anjan Chatterjee, M.D., "Cosmetic Neurology," *Neurology* 63 (2004): 968-974.
[6]. Martha J. Farah, "Emerging Issues in Neuroscience," *Nature Neuroscience* 5, no. 11 (Nov. 2002): 1123-1129 at 1124.

have become wildly popular across college campuses as healthy students use them to boost their academic performance.[7] The same appears to be true at many high schools and elite prep schools. When a *New York Times* reporter convened a forum of 13 precocious, over-achievers from private high school across the city to discuss the use of stimulants among their contemporaries, she learned that Ritalin and Adderall were readily available and extremely popular among many non-ADHD students who used them to stay on top academically.[8] Chatterjee opines that it is all but impossible socially to prevent healthy individuals from using cognitive enhancement drugs originally developed to treat those who are learning disabled,[9] and neurologist-researcher Michael Gazzaniga agrees:

> Just as Ritalin can improve the academic performance of hyperactive children, it can do the same for normal children. It is commonly thought to boost SAT scores by more than 100 points, for both the hyperactive and the normal user. Many healthy young people now use it that way for that purpose, and quite frankly, there is no stopping the abuse.[10]

Of course social inevitability does not constitute an ethical argument, but it does raise the question of what the appropriate social policy should be in light of the apparently wholesale abuse of stimulants within the healthy population.

Ritalin and Adderal are just two psychotropes in the wide-wide world of cognitive enhancement drugs that show promise for healthy individuals. Researchers also have evidence that the drug donepezil (trade name Aricept), a long-standing treatment for slowing progressive memory loss in Alzheimer's patients, improves cognitive functioning and memory in normal subjects. Using a flight simulator, researchers trained two groups of pilots for thirty days where half the subjects received a placebo while the other half were given 5 milligrams of donepezil (less than the prescribed dose for Alzheimer's). During their simulator training, both groups were required to perform complicated maneuvers and respond to emergency in-flight situations. Both groups of subjects were tested once again in the simulator a month after their initial training to determine how well they could recall and implement what they had learned. Researchers

[7]. Martha J. Farah, "Emerging Issues in Neuroscience," 1124.
[8]. Anemona Hartocollis, "High School Chemistry," *New York Times* (Feb. 13, 2005); available at http://www.nytimes.com/2005/02/13/nyregion/13colm.html
[9]. Chatterjee, "Cosmetic Neurology," 972.
[10]. Michael Gazzaniga, "Smarter on Drugs," *Scientific American Mind* 16, no. 3 (2005): 33-37 at 34.

discovered that those who took donepezil performed significantly better than the placebo group, as demonstrated by their enhanced performance on the landing approach and their handling of emergencies. One of the lead researchers of the study, Jerome Yesavage of Stanford University, noted that "if cognitive enhancement becomes possible in intellectually intact individuals, significant legal, regulatory, and ethical questions will emerge."[11] Commenting on the findings of this study, Michael Gazzaniga foresees the possibility that donepezil could become the new Ritalin for college students, and he states that very little can be done to stop this development.[12]

Another psychoactive drug that has caught the attention of individuals in the enhancement-seeking healthy population is modafinil (marketed as Provigil), a drug that was approved by the FDA in 1998 for the treatment of narcolepsy, a condition thought to affect about 125,000 American. But with annual sales now reaching $200 million each year, it's apparent that this drug is being prescribed off label by psychiatrists to treat a range of other disorders such depression and fatigue due to certain medical conditions. Clinicians report being barraged by requests from healthy people for modafinil to allow them to stay awake longer and work harder.[13] Two Cambridge University researchers set off a vigorous debate within academe when they reported in a December 2007 edition of the journal *Nature* that twelve of their colleagues admitted to regularly using both Provigil and Adderall to improve their academic performance.[14] Chattergee also mentions modafinil within the context of his discussion of cognitive enhancement drugs that look promising for improving memory, attention and learning for healthy individuals, noting that "modafinil improves arousal and ameliorates deficits of sustained attention associated with sleep deprivation."[15]

Just Say No to Enhancement Drugs

What's wrong with parents giving healthy children cognitive enhancement drugs if doing so helps them learn better, perform better, and remember better? Certainly these drugs alter biochemistry, but so does

---

[11]. Stephen S. Hall, "The Quest for a Smart Pill," *Scientific American* 289, no. 3 (Sept. 2003): 54-65.

[12]. Gazzaniga, "Smarter on Drugs," 34.

[13]. Hall, "The Quest for the Smart Pill," 58.

[14]. Barbara Sahakian and Sharon Morein-Zamir, "Professor's Little Helper," *Nature* 450, no. 20 (Dec. 2007): 1157-1159.

[15]. Chatterjee, "Cosmetic Neurology," 969.

good food and nutrition. The question is not whether enhancement drugs alter biochemistry, but whether they do so in a way that is safe: if these drugs do not have a proven safety record, they should be used for neither therapeutic nor nontherapeutic reasons. Also, while the associated risks and side-effects of these drugs might be acceptable when it comes to treating disease, it is reasonable to ask whether incurring these risks is warranted in the case of boosting performance in healthy children. In response to this worry, however, we realize that it is impossible for parents to expose their children to a range of enriching opportunities and activities that are entirely risk free. And so parents enroll their children in gymnastics and karate classes and let them play soccer and football knowing the attending risks of bodily injury–or worse. These parents are not acting irresponsibly but rather recognize that the potential benefits of these activities–the development of talents and abilities–outweighs the risks. So what are the risks of cognitive enhancement drugs? In the case of Adderall and Ritalin, Kass' report acknowledges that "the preponderance of the evidence shows a remarkably low incidence of side effects when the stimulants are used, in low doses, in treatment of ADHD and allied conditions."[16]   The report goes on to argue, however, that even if enhancement drugs are safe and effective, there are compelling reasons why parents should refrain from giving these agents to healthy children in order to boost their performance.

The first general concern raised by the Kass report focuses on issues of social control and conformity. The initial worry is that by directly altering a child's neurochemistry, we risk infringing upon a basic natural and social liberty of children that limits the degree to which they may be coerced or restricted. While recognizing that children are not fully competent to make autonomous decisions regarding important life matters, the report claims that children "display certain traits of personality and forces of will that ought not simply be repressed by others."[17]   The assertion is that, whether bold or cautious, docile or assertive, independent or dependent, there are certain defining characteristics that touch upon the core personality or identity of a child and therefore should be "off limits" to the controlling power of psychopharmaceuticals. A second and related worry is that the interjection of these drugs into child-rearing may change the fundamental nature of childhood which dictates that, in some important sense, children should be allowed to be children. The alleged danger is that psychoactive drugs may dampen the natural rambunctiousness

---

[16]. Kass, *Beyond Therapy,* 86.
[17]. Kass, *Beyond Therapy,* 89.

of boys and girls in order to better control them–to make them more pliable, tractable, and sociable. Additionally, while these drugs make children more attentive and therefore more teachable, their use may pressure even more children to resort to these chemical enhancements just to keep up with their classmates.[18] A final concern raised under the rubric of social control and conformity has to do with the power of behavior-modifying drugs to diminish the diversity of traits, stifle individual differences in temperament and character, and remold unique personalities to conform to conventional standards of normality–all in the name of promoting better performance.[19]

A second reason cited by the Kass report for resisting the use of enhancement drugs for healthy children has to do with the shift away from the language and methods of moral education to the discourse and methods of medicine. Children who genuinely suffer from ADHD lack impulse control and are unable to moderate their behavior in appropriate ways; in these cases stimulants help bring them up to level of normal functioning where they can learn to regulate their own behavior. By contrast, normal children learn self-control without drug intervention by being exposed to the moral instruction and guidance of parents and teachers who, by serving as role models and benevolent sources of praise and blame, help children slowly master their own impulses and actions. And while it is appropriate to alter the neurochemistry of ADHD children to restore them to levels of normal functioning where they can learn to exercise self-control, the concern raised by the Kass report is that using stimulants for healthy children to modify their behavior bypasses moral education altogether and ignores the difficult character-building struggle of learning how to develop self-mastery and impulse control. The implicit message sent to children is that character development and self-control are as easy as swallowing a pill. Thus, the modification of children's behavior through psychoactive drugs risks being purchased at the expense of genuine self-mastery. All of this, it is claimed, may seriously erode a child's sense of selfhood and identity by suggesting that who and what she is is more a matter of her biochemistry than her moral beliefs, judgments and decisions that spring from an understanding of what is right and wrong. The medicalization of normal childhood behavior threatens to diminish the emerging sense of moral responsibility and agency so important for children to develop.[20]

---

[18]. Kass, *Beyond Therapy,* 90.
[19]. Kass, *Beyond Therapy,* 90-1.
[20]. Kass, *Beyond Therapy,* 92-3.

The Kass report finally warns that the use of enhancement drugs will distort the meaning and significance children will come to assign to the ideas of performance and the development of their abilities. The argument is this. The sense of achievement and self-worth children develop has much to do with how well they meet the challenges laid out before them; performance does matter and it is important that children acquire the skills and abilities they need to succeed. The reward of this difficult rite of passage for children is found in the improved skills and heightened self-confidence that comes from hard work, practice and study. The introduction of enhancement drugs into this process, however, sends the entirely wrong message to children. The Kass report acknowledges that, while "artificial enhancement" can improve children's abilities and performance, it does so by driving a wedge between achievement and effort, and in so doing deprives children of the sense of self-worth that comes from individual effort–and further teaches them that it is acceptable to succeed "by artificial, even medical means."[21]   In the process, the meaning of performance is distorted for children by placing too much emphasis on achievement while under-emphasizing "the integrity of genuine ability and unaugmented merit."[22]

Neurofreedom for Children

The Kass report first objects that providing cognitive enhancement drugs to healthy children will make them vulnerable to the forces of social control and conformity in ways that violate their liberty, alter intrinsic features of childhood, and diminish the diversity of character traits and temperaments. But the argument that children possess certain core personality traits that are off limits to any kind of alteration is difficult to make out. How are we to determine which traits are protected by the so-called inviolable liberty of children? Even if we could identify a set of traits that captures a child's deep personality, it may turn out that we *should* attempt to alter or redirect some of them, as in the case of a strong propensity toward selfishness or aggression. A second objection charges that enhancement drugs may make children more pliable, tractable, and sociable so that attentiveness is chemically substituted for natural rambunctiousness. What the Kass report seems to have in mind is that Adderall and Ritalin not only heighten concentration and alertness but also

---

[21]. Kass, *Beyond Therapy,* 93.
[22]. Kass, *Beyond Therapy,* 93.

dampen unruly behavior in both learning disabled and normal children.[23] But it is a gross overgeneralization to suppose that *all* cognitive or performance enhancement drugs work this way. There is no evidence that the drug donepezil does anything other than improve memory, or that modafinil, which increases alertness, might somehow make individuals pliable. Rather than increasing social control and conformity, cognitive enhancement drugs may actually boost intelligence in ways that make children more sensitive to how social standards and conventions should be challenged. The objection that enhancement drugs will stifle the diversity of innate traits, inclinations, and personality types in order to make children better behaved and educable also overgeneralizes: not all enhancement drugs modify behavior in the same way as Adderal and Ritalin. As a class, cognitive enhancers are more likely to sharpen the diversity of traits among individuals than they are to level them out. Further, even if some enhancement drugs increase performance at the expense of dampening rambunctiousness, it may be a tradeoff well worth making; as a rule developing or strengthening one trait means that some other trait or set of traits must take a back seat.

The charge that cognitive enhancement drugs will short circuit moral education and diminish a child's sense of moral agency and responsibility is a red-herring argument. In laying out this objection, the Kass report drops all talk of "cognitive enhancement drugs" and instead refers only to "behavior-modifying agents," limiting its discussion to how these "agents" work directly on the brain to improve impulse-control rather than allowing children to develop self-control through effort and moral guidance. The message these drugs will send to children, it is warned, is that character is simply a matter of outward behavior which can easily be controlled by a pill; and, as a result of this creeping medicalization of moral education, children will come to think of themselves and their actions more in terms of their neurochemistry, thereby weakening their sense of responsibility and moral agency. In response to this overwrought argument, it must be pointed out, once again, that most cognitive enhancement drugs have little or nothing to do with impulse-control or dampening unruly behavior. A review of the clinical literature shows that cognitive enhancement research is directed primarily toward the development of psychoactive agents that will improve either attention or memory.[24] There is little reason to suppose that boosting attention and memory in children will somehow undermine their moral education or weaken their sense of moral

---

[23]. Kass, *Beyond Therapy,* 83.
[24]. Whitehouse and Juengst, "Enhancing Cognition in the Intellectually Intact," 14.

responsibility and agency. Furthermore, the Kass report implicitly assumes that thinking about human behavior in neurochemical terms diminishes our sense of ourselves as moral agents who confront difficult situations and exercise choice. This assumption ignores sophisticated compatibilist positions that make room for notions of ethical choice and responsibility while also acknowledging the physicalist basis of our makeup and behavior.

The worry that enhancement drugs will diminish the value and meaning of accomplishment for children by weakening the link between achievement and effort is, once again, much-to-do-about-nothing. The cognitive enhancement drugs currently available or on the horizon are not wonder-drugs that will suddenly transform our children into little Einsteins. These drugs do focus attention and sharpen concentration, they allow us to work longer and harder without the usual associated fatigue, and they improve memory–but they do so only in conjunction with *our* effort and energy. Enhancement drugs do not replace effort or diminish its importance; rather, they allow us to put our effort to better use, to work more efficiently, and to accomplish more. The suggestion that there is something amiss with using pharmaceuticals to improve performance taps into the ancient bias against enhancers we *take* as opposed to the ones we invent or earn.[25] But the Kass report seems to depend upon just this unsupportable prejudice when it refers favorably to "the integrity of genuine ability and unaugmented merit" while calling into question achievement that has been enhanced by "artificial, even medical means."[26] But why should drugs be regarded as "artificial" and therefore illicit forms of enhancement when other means of enhancement, now commonly used by one and all, are not? If giving children access to enhancement technologies such as computers and calculators does not diminish the value of their accomplishment or sever the bond between effort and achievement, it is difficult to understand why allowing them to use cognitive enhancement drugs would be any different. Even if we could sort out the distinction between artificial versus natural forms of enhancement, it is not obvious why the former is necessarily bad while the latter always good. The fact that we *take* enhancement drugs as opposed to *using* some other form of enhancement technology we have invented hardly constitutes a morally relevant distinction.

The drug enhanced child of the future (or the local middle- or high school) is unlikely to be a Frankenchild who will usher us into a

---

[25]. Whitehouse and Juengst, "Enhancing Cognition in the Intellectually Intact," 14.
[26]. Kass, *Beyond Therapy,* 93.

posthuman dystopia of chemical zombies. It is wildly unrealistic that a pharmaceutical equivalent of Nozick's experience machine will be developed that will allow our offspring to become instantly brilliant and high-performing at the pop of a pill. But the enhancement drugs currently on the market offer real cognitive improvements that benefit both individuals and society. Given the relative safety and efficacy of these drugs, the same liberty that responsible parents now enjoy to do what they take to be in their child's best interest should be extended to these chemical agents as well. It is certainly important to proceed with caution, monitoring both the short- and long term effect of these drugs, but there is every reason to believe that this evidence-based approach will bear witness to the benefit of these drugs for our prodigy.

ORGAN DONATION IMPASSE AND FAMILY AUTHORITY

ROBERT L. MUHLNICKEL

Introduction

Suppose someone dies whose organs could be taken for transplantation or research and the dead person's preference and the dead person's family's preferences are incompatible. Some policy is needed to resolve the impasse resulting from the incompatible preferences. This paper is about the morally best policy for resolving the impasse. Current policy in the United States gives both the dead person and their family members authority to refuse the donation and gives either decision-maker's refusal greater weight than the other's preference for donation.

Taking the organs from a person's body, even postmortem, is a morally serious act, so moral reasons should support any policy that permits doing so. The deaths and suffering that result from insufficient donated organs to meet the need for transplantation are morally serious, so any policy that results in such death and suffering requires moral reasons to support it. Current U.S. policy about taking organs from the dead is a response to different moral reasons, the value of the dead person's self-direction and the value of the family members' relation to the dead person. If either the dead person has refused to donate or if the family refuses to allow organs to be taken, health care professionals working in organ procurement teams do not take the organs. This is called the *double-veto policy* because both the dead person and family members are authorized to veto taking organs from the dead person's body. The double-veto policy is the source of the *organ donation impasse* of my title.

I explain the reasoning that yields to the double-veto policy in Section 1. In Section 2 I show that the double-veto policy is incoherent when one considers the usual reasons offered to support it. However, T. M. Wilkinson has recently defended a different version of the double-veto policy. In Section 3 I show that Wilkinson's defense combines consequentialist and deontological elements. In a crucial move, Wilkinson argues that although the dead person has right to offer his organs for donation, health care professionals may accept his organs conditional on the family members' agreement with the donation. He argues that family members acquire legitimate authority to decide when health care professionals make their acceptance of offered organs conditional on family members' agreement. In Section 4 I show that the argument fails. There are better reasons for accepting the dead person's organ donation than for complying with the family members' refusal to donate the organs.[1]

In view of the great good that would result from transplantation and research using organs taken from the dead and the small number of organs donated relative to the number of persons who would benefit, a moral policy should encourage organ donation. Given the risk of coercion and exploitation of the vulnerable, some measures are necessary to assure organs are removed only with the prior consent of the person from whose body they are taken. The best overall policy is a system of mandated choice that requires every adult to communicate a choice about organ donation, so that the preferences of the dead person are known to transplant teams. My goal is to show that reasons given to support the double-veto policy fail to do so. They fail because they support inconsistent moral conclusions, resulting in an incoherent policy. Since the policy is incoherent it should be abandoned, and its advocates should instead support mandated choice.

1. Moral Reasons and the Double-Veto Policy

A moral policy is justified by the moral reasons that support it. Moral reasons cite factors that, when not overridden by factors supporting an alternative course of action, justify morally the action or policy under consideration. The double-veto policy reflects the prominence of two factors in thinking about organ donation: the identity of the authoritative decision-maker and the content of the decision. It is plausible that the dead person is the authoritative decision-maker because it is her body from which organs could be taken and she has authority of what is done to her body. One plausible reason for the family being the authoritative decision-maker is that family members have an interest in what is done with the

---

[1] I assume families are unitary decision-makers throughout this paper. Although the assumption excludes important moral issues, cases where family members are divided among themselves about preferences for donation or refusal add another complicating factor.

body of their dead relative.[2] The second moral factor is the content of the preference: to permit organs to be taken or to refuse permission. Either permission or refusal could be considered weightier. If permission is weightier than refusal, then a decision to permit taking organs takes precedence over refusal, and vice versa.

These two factors provide moral reasons. Say the factor that provides stronger reason takes precedence over the other and the factor that provides weaker reason is subordinate to the other. Combining the two factors and the precedence-subordination relation yields four possible policies:

(1)   Permission or refusal by the dead person takes precedence;
(2)   Permission or refusal by family members takes precedence;
(3)   Permission by the dead person overrides refusal by the family and permission by the family overrides refusal by the dead person;
(4)   Refusal by the dead person overrides permission by the family and refusal by the family overrides permission by the dead person.

In policies (1) and (2) the identity of the authoritative decision-maker takes precedence over the content of the preference, the permission or refusal. In (1) the fact that the dead person is the decision-maker takes precedence over the content of the preference. In (2) the fact that the family of the dead person is the decision-makers takes precedence over the content of the preference. In policies (3) and (4) the content of the preference takes precedence over the identity of the decision-maker. In (3) the fact that the preference is permissive takes precedence over the identity of the decision-maker. In (4) the fact that the preference is a refusal takes precedence over the identity of the decision-maker. Whether the family member or the dead person is the decision-maker is subordinate to a preference for refusal.

Position (4) is the double-veto policy that is the current U. S. policy. Supporters of (4) argue that it gives correct weight to personal autonomy and the importance of family members for deciding on the disposition of the body of a dead person.[3] Both the dead person and his family members

---

[2] A second reason for thinking the family should be the authoritative decision-maker is that family members presumably know better than others the dead person's values, interests, and beliefs, and this gives them better justified beliefs about what the dead person would have preferred. This is not relevant here, in cases where even if family members know the dead person's preferences, they disagree with them.

[3] Childress (2006); Wilkinson (2005)

have the authority to veto taking organs, regardless of the other decision-maker's preference.[4] The dead person's decision to refuse donation takes precedence over the family members' permissive preference and the family member's decision to refuse takes precedence over the dead person's expressed preference for donation.

However, the double-veto policy is difficult to reasonably defend. Defending it requires reasons to think that each decision-maker individually has the authority to veto the other's preference for permission and that the reasons for each decision-maker's authority to veto do not undermine the reasons for the other's when the other's preference is refusal. T. M. Wilkinson shows the most commonly given reasons for the decision-makers individually having such authority undermine the other's authority. Wilkinson also argues that his account restores the coherence of the double-veto policy. This means that his account eliminates the threat of incoherence that results from each decision-maker's authority to veto undermining the other decision-maker's authority. Wilkinson claims his account avoids what I call mutually undermining reasons.

2. Mutually Undermining Reasons

The usual reasons for the double-veto policy result in incoherence. Incoherence results because the content of the decision, its being a refusal, takes precedence over the identity of the decision-maker whether the decision-maker is the dead person or the family members. Wilkinson asserts that reasons usually given for the family member's authority, namely averting family members' distress, the inability of the dead to consent, the desires of the living having greater weight than the desires of the dead, defective standardized consent procedures threaten to undermine the double-veto policy. I demonstrate in greater detail than Wilkinson does that these reasons undermine each other. I also show that a reason often given for complying with the dead person's preference undermines the double-veto policy. Individual arguments based on each reason are inconsistent with the double-veto policy. Collectively, they support the claim that the double-veto policy is incoherent. The purpose of explicitly displaying these arguments is to press the case that the double-veto policy is incoherent and undeserving of support.

Consider first the argument that averting family distress is reason to comply with family members' preference not to take the organs of the dead person.

---

[4] Wilkinson (2005) coins the name 'double-veto policy.'.

Averting Family Distress Argument

(1)   S gives permission to take S's organs and S dies.
(2)   If taking S's organs averts family distress, then it is impermissible for health care professionals to take S's organs.
(3)   It is impermissible for health care professionals to take S's organs.
(4)   S refuses permission to take S's organs and S dies.
(5)   If not taking S's organs averts family distress, then it is permissible for HC professionals to take S's organs.
(6)   It is permissible for health care professionals to take S's organs.

The Averting Family Distress Argument is inconsistent since it supports both the permissibility and impermissibility of taking S's organs, seen in lines (3) and (6). The argument is based on the idea that morally relevant factors that outweigh S's permission also outweigh S's refusal. Since permission and refusal are results of giving or withholding consent, and giving or withholding consent is the morally relevant factor, permission and refusal should have the same weight in moral reasoning. If averting family distress outweighs permission, then it also outweighs refusal, since both refusal and permission are results of giving or withholding consent. Averting family distress is an equally strong reason whether S gives permission or S withholds permission to take S's organs. If averting family distress justifies not taking S's organs when S has given permission to take S's organs, then averting family distress justifies taking S's organs when S has refused permission to take S's organs.

Claims about consent appear in arguments for the view that the family member's refusal outweighs the dead person's permission to take his organs. These arguments variously claim that the dead cannot consent, that the desires of the living outweigh the desires of the dead, and that standardized procedures for consent are defective. However, if permission and refusal are equally weighty factors in moral reasoning, the result is a contradiction: both the family member's refusal outweighs the dead person's permission to take their organs and the family members' permission to take the dead person's organs outweighs the dead person's refusal.

Consider an argument based on the view that the dead are unable to consent:

The Dead are Unable to Consent

(1)   The dead are unable to consent.
(2)   S has given permission for S's organ's to be taken, S dies, and S's family refuses permission for S's organs to be taken.
(3)   If (1) and (2), then the family's refusal overrides S's permission for S's organs to be taken.
(4)   The family's refusal overrides S's permission for S's organs to be taken.
(5)   If (4), then it is impermissible for health care professionals to take S's organs.
(6)   It is impermissible for health care professionals to take S's organs.
(7)   S has refused permission for S's organs to be taken, S dies, and S's family gives permission for S's organs to be taken.
(8)   If (1) and (7), then the family's permission overrides S's refusal to permit S's organs to be taken.
(9)   The family's permission overrides S's refusal to permit S's organs to be taken.
(10) If (9), then t is permissible for HC professionals to take S's organs.
(11) It is permissible for HC professionals to take S's organs.

Again, the result is an argument that yields contradictory claims, that it is both impermissible and permissible to take S's organs.

Another argument concerning consent holds that the desires of the living deserve greater weight than the desires of the dead in moral reasoning. This argument also yields inconsistent results.

The Desires of the Living Outweigh the Desires of the Dead

(1)   The desires of the living outweigh the desires of the dead.
(2)   S has given permission for S's organ's to be taken, S's permission expresses S's desires, S dies, S's family refuses permission for S's organs to be taken, and S's family's refusal expresses their desires.
(3)   If (1) and (2), then the family's refusal overrides S's permission for S's organs to be taken.
(4)   The family's refusal overrides S's permission for S's organs to be taken.

(5) If (4), then it is impermissible for health care professionals to take S's organs.

(6) It is impermissible for health care professionals to take S's organs.

(7) S has refused permission for S's organ's to be taken, S's refusal expresses S's desires, S dies, S's family gives permission for S's organs to be taken, and S's family's permission expresses their desires.

(8) If (1) and (7), then the family's permission to take S's organs overrides S's refusal of permission for S's organs to be taken.

(9) The family's permission to take S's organs overrides S's refusal of permission for S's organs to be taken.

(10) If (9), then it is permissible for HC professionals to take S's organs.

(11) It is permissible for HC professionals to take S's organs.

The arguments above assume that the dead person's preference is known and not in doubt. However, family members disagree with the dead person's clearly known preference. Another kind of argument results from family members attempting to determine what the dead person preferred, given lack of complete information about the dead person's preference. Doubts about the preferences of the dead person sometimes arise due to the use of standardized procedures to communicate refusal or permission.

Many standardized procedures for communicating refusal or permission for organ donation are added to bureaucratic procedures, such as renewing a driver's license or filing income taxes. Ordinarily, one does not carefully deliberate about organ donation in line at the local Department of Motor Vehicles office or when filing income taxes. The means of communicating permission or refusal is a check mark or signature. These features support worries that consent given by means of standardized procedures is defective. Since consent is not coerced in these cases, the claim is that consent in standardized procedures is inadequately informed or insufficiently reflective due to the circumstances of the standardized procedures.

An argument based on defective standardized procedures follows below:

Standardized Procedures for Consent are Defective

(1) Standardized procedures for consenting for organs to be taken are defective.

(2)   S gives permission for S's organs to be taken in a standardized procedure, S dies, and S's family members refuse permission for S's organs to be taken in a valid consent.

(3)   If (1) and (2), then S's family members refusing permission overrides S's permission in a standardized procedure for S's organs to be taken.

(4)   S's family members refusing permission overrides S's permission for S's organs to be taken in a standardized procedure.

(5)   S refuses permission in a standardized procedure for S's organs to be taken, S dies, and S's family gives permission for S's organs to be taken.

(6)   If (1) and (5), then S's family members giving permission overrides S's refusing permission in a standardized procedure for S's organs to be taken.

(7)   S's family members giving permission overrides S's refusing permission in a standardized procedure for S's organs to be taken.

Again, the claim yields the contradictory claims that it is impermissible and permissible to take S's organs.[5]

Wilkinson discusses arguments like those above but gives less attention to arguments based on reasons for the dead person's refusal. However, arguments based on reasons given for the dead person's refusal also threaten the coherence of the double-veto policy. Consider the Autonomous Control Argument:

Autonomous Control Argument

(1)   Autonomous control of one's body includes sole authority to determine what is done to one's body after one dies.

(2)   S refuses permission for S's organs to be taken after S's death, S's refusal expresses S's autonomous control, S dies, and S's family gives permission for S's organs to be taken.

(3)   If (1) and (2) then S's refusal for S's organs to be taken overrides S's family's permission for S's organ to be taken.

---

[5] One might argue that the procedure by which family members give or refuse permission is also defective. The family members are experiencing the emotional response to death, often in a hospital unit or emergency room, after having the option presented to them by a stranger using moral and legal concepts that are unfamiliar except to specialists. The view that both the dead person's and the family members' consents are defective is plausible. However, it is beside the point of this paper.

(4)   S refusal of permission for S's organ to be taken overrides S's family's permission for S's organ to be taken.

(5)   Hence, it is impermissible for health care professionals to take S's organs.

(6)   S gives permission for S's organs to be taken after S's death, S's permission expresses S's autonomous control, S dies, and S's family refuses permission for S's organs to be taken.

(7)   If (1) and (6), then S's permission to take S's organs overrides S's family's refusal to permit S's organ to be taken.

(8)   S's permission to take S's organs overrides S's family's refusal to permit S's organ to be taken.

(9)   Hence, it is permissible for health care professionals to take S's organs.

The Autonomous Control Argument states that the person has sole authority to determine what is done to her body after her death. That personal autonomy implies such control over what is done to and in one's body has been widely accepted since Judge Benjamin Cardozo asserted it in 1914.[6] It is a moral factor that requires very good reason to override. Despite complaints that the prominence of personal autonomy skews many widespread views in medical ethics, autonomy is widely thought to be authoritative with regard to control of one's body. It is controversial whether personal autonomy implies *sole* authority over what is done to one's body after one's death. However, this claim or something close to it is the basis of the view that health care professionals and others are obliged to comply with the dead person's desires or preferences after their death. For the purposes of this paper it is more significant to note that the Autonomous Control Argument undermines the family veto of the double-veto policy. If the value of personal autonomy is the basis for compliance with the dead person's refusal of permission to take her organs when the family wants to permit taking her organs, then it is sufficient for compliance with the dead person's permission to take her organs when the family members want to refuse permission.

---

[6] "Every human being of adult years and sound mind has a right to determine what shall be done with his own body; and a surgeon who performs an operation without his patient's consent commits an assault for which he is liable in damages." Schloendorff, v. The Society of New York Hospital, Court of Appeals of NY; 211 N.Y. 125; N.E. 92.

3. Wilkinson: Negative Rights and Effects on the Family

The arguments for the double-veto policy evaluated above appeal to different kinds of moral reasons to support each decision-maker's authority to decide whether to take the dead person's organs. Averting Family Distress appeals to consequentialist reasoning. The argument identifies a consequence of taking organs from someone who has given permission for them to be taken but whose family members refuse permission: the distress that taking the person's organs would cause the family members. The value of that consequence is thought to outweigh the value of the consequences of the alternative, taking the organs. Taking the organs has the positively weighted consequences of complying with the dead person's preference, research, and extended or better lives for transplant recipients. According to the argument, the negative value of averting family distress is greater than the values of the other consequences, so it is impermissible to take the organs. Other arguments appeal to deontological considerations. They appeal to rights or some version of individual autonomy. Arguments that the dead are unable to consent and that the consent is defective appeal to reasons that autonomy is compromised in some way. These arguments assume that were autonomy not compromised, compliance with the dead person's decision would be morally required. Arguments based on autonomous control merge with rights-based arguments where rights are conceived as protected zones of decision.

One could make a consequentialist argument based on the effects of the double-veto policy. Instead of a rule-consequentialist view, it would be a policy-consequentialist view. The argument for the view would claim that the combined values of all the effects of the policy are greater than the values of alternative policies. The empirical claims embedded in the argument are very detailed. It would take substantial inquiry to evaluate them. Wilkinson rejects the policy-consequentialist argument for the Double-Veto Policy because of this difficulty. He suggests instead an argument that combines negative rights with other moral considerations. Let us consider his view combining negative rights and other moral considerations.

Wilkinson appeals to negative rights to support the view that the dead person is the legitimate decision-maker with regard to his body after his death. If both the dead person and the family each have a negative right against their preference being overridden, then the ability of each decision-maker to veto taking the organs is justified, though we have a case of conflicting rights. However, he rejects the notion of family rights, since families are not agents and causing them distress is not the basis for a right.[7]

Wilkinson suggests a modified argument in which the dead person has a negative right against her organs being taken without her permission and other reasons justify health care professionals' compliance with the family member's preference not to have the dead person's organs taken. He suggests that "there are moral reasons which are neither based on nor have the force of rights" and that these moral reasons justify compliance with the family's decision to refuse permission to take the dead person's organs.[8] He mentions averting family distress and avoiding bad publicity as reasons, though he recognizes that his defense of the double-veto policy is coherent only if "the reasons really are strong ones."[9] Wilkinson's proposed defense is tantamount to a mixed proposal: it combines negative rights, a deontological consideration, and the effects of not complying with family members' preference, a consequentialist consideration.[10]

If averting family distress is actually a strong enough reason to comply with the family members' refusal to permit organs to be taken, then it should be a negative consequence that is as weighty as a rights violation though not itself a rights violation. However, this position is coherent only if the negative consequences are as strong as rights claims, so they must be stronger than reasons that do not "have the force of rights." That is, we must have moral reasons that are at least as weighty as rights claims. If the only reasons are less weighty than rights claims, then reasons for compliance with the dead person's decision to donate his organs are stronger than the countervailing reasons.

Wilkinson does not describe a class of reasons he thinks are as weighty as rights claims. He asks us to suppose that we do have such weighty reasons and gives averting family distress and avoiding bad publicity as examples. Wilkinson sets aside arguments from positive effects as too complex and subject to empirical disqualification, as noted above.

---

[7] Wilkinson (2005), p. 589. A theory that assigns right to families though they are not agents is conceivable. The most plausible theory would require assigning rights to families in virtue of their value as a form of social organization rather than their capacity for agency. Even in this theory the family would possess instrumental value as the procreative and educative instrument of what is intrinsically valuable, whether the bearers of intrinsic value are persons or properties of persons.

[8] Wilkinson (2005), p. 589.

[9] Wilkinson (2005), p. 589.

[10] Set aside reasons of bad publicity. Such reasons are more speculative than the others considered and do not yield the impasse with which we are concerned.

However, after setting aside consequentialist reasons and asking us to suppose we have unidentified reasons that are as strong as rights claims are usually taken to be, Wilkinson introduces consequentialist reasons.

Averting family distress is a consequence of an action by a medical professional. My reasoning is as follows. Suppose S has given non-defective consent to have S's organs taken after S's death, S has died, and the family would experience great distress at S's organs being taken. The distress it would cause the family to take S's organs has greater value than the value of taking the organs, so the transplant team is morally required to refuse S's organs. The family members' distress would be a consequence of taking the organs, if the health care team were to take the organs.

Wilkinson blurs the difficulty by arguing that even if S has given non-defective consent to have S's organs taken, this entails no obligation on the part of the transplant team to take S's organs.[11] This follows from standard rights theories. But this line of reasoning only makes the problem more pressing. If rights claims cannot be overridden except for the most serious reasons, then he should give some description of the class of reasons that are strong enough to override rights claims. Wilkinson does not describe any class of reasons but cites the positive effect of averting family distress. If averting family distress is reason not to comply with the dead person's preference for organ donation, something more must be known about the intensity, duration, and object of that distress. The object of the family distress might be (a) the family member's death; (b) the prospect of organs being taken; (c) organs actually being taken; (d) beliefs about what would be done to the organs if they were taken.[12] The duration and intensity of family members' distress are qualitative factors admitting of great variation. Family distress varies greatly, depending on the interactive effects of these various aspects of distress. A case of family distress that is of short duration and low intensity would be a weaker reason not to comply with the dead person's preference than a case of lengthy, high intensity distress. But these comparisons are obscured by the variety of cases classed as family distress. Appeal to averting family distress is a less weighty reason than it first appears.[13]

Wilkinson claims it is coherent for the transplant policy to accept averting family distress as a reason they should refuse to comply with a

---

[11] He repeats this claim in Wilkinson (2007). See my criticism in Section 4 below.

[12] Beliefs about what would be done to organs once taken are numerous, so I do not list them here.

[13] Wilkinson (2007) acknowledges the ambiguity of family distress more fully than his (2005). However, the structure of his view is the same in both accounts of the double-veto policy.

non-defective consent to donate organs but fails to say why that is a good enough reason to refuse. He does not think family distress involves an appeal to rights and he rejects consequentialist reasons. Wilkinson's defense of the double-veto policy is threatened with incoherence because it combines a deontological constraint, negative rights, with a consequentialist consideration, averting family distress. The conflict of consequentialist reasons and rights claims is not resolved by Wilkinson's assertion that "distress is a bad thing in itself."[14] Though the intrinsic badness of the family members' distress is reason to consider rejecting the dead person's preference for donation, it is not decisive by itself. Wilkinson's suggestion to consider the intrinsic badness of distress is an invitation to consider the consequences of the decision not to take the dead person's organs. Among those consequences is the distress of those who suffer loss and death at not having transplants from those who would donate their organs. These bad consequences give us reason to comply with the dead person's preference, despite the family members' distress, which is arguably shorter and less intense than that of those who suffer illness and die from lack of transplantable organs.

Wilkinson's mixed argument for the double-veto policy introduces the consequentialist element by appealing to family members' distress. However, the family members' distress at having the dead person's organs taken is outweighed by the harm to those who would suffer distress and loss of life were the organs not taken. The consequentialist element in Wilkinson's argument fails to make the double-veto policy coherent. Let us now turn to consider the rights-based element of his defense of the double-veto policy.

4. How Family Members Acquire the Authority to Decide

The rights-based element in Wilkinson's defense of the double-veto policy is based on the claim that although the dead person has the right to offer his organs for donation, it is morally permissible for health care professionals to accept his organs conditionally. That is, the health care professionals accept them only if the dead person's family members do not refuse permission to donate. I show that Wilkinson's rights-based element is not supported for two reasons. The first is the failure of his argument by analogy between the health care professionals' role and the role of parents to whom someone cedes authority to decide on a marriage proposal. The second is that when health care professionals consider substantive reasons

---

[14] Wilkinson (2007), p. 33.

for refusing an organ because family members oppose the dead person preference for donation, as Wilkinson acknowledges they should, the reasons for complying with the family members are not compelling.

Wilkinson argues for the rights-based element of his defense of the double-veto policy by analogy with a marriage proposal. A's proposal to marry B is analogous to S's offer to donate his organs. B's parents and the health care professionals who are responsible for taking and transplanting organs can conditionally accept the offers. The analogy is as follows. A's offer to marry B is A's right. B's refusal or acceptance is B's right. B's acceptance contingent on B's parents' approval is B's right.[15] S's offer of S's organs is S's right. The health care professional's refusal or acceptance is their right. The health care professional's acceptance contingent on the family's approval is their right.

If it is permissible for B to refuse A's marriage offer upon B's parent's refusal to give permission, it is permissible for the health care professionals to refuse S's offer of organ donation upon S's family members' refusal to give permission. The force of the analogy derives from the parallel between B's authority over B's life and the health care professionals authority over the organ transplant system. The rights-based element in defense of the double-veto policy is formal in the sense that it is not based on substantive reasons regarding the preference of either decision-maker. Rather, it is based on the authority of the decision-makers to make decisions they believe fitting.

I show that the analogy between the conditional acceptance of marriage proposal and the conditional acceptance of organ donation fails. The analogy is inapt because of differences in the role of health care professional and the role of parent. There are inherent obligations in the role of health care professional that are not inherent in the parent role. The health care professionals' obligations are not merely to S and his family. The health care professionals' obligations are to potential transplant recipients and to the beneficiaries of research that could be conducted using S's organs. The health care professionals' obligations to ease suffering and extend lives are the result of their professional role. Health care professionals have obligations to many patients, not merely to the patients with whom they currently are engaged. For health care professionals who work in organ donation, their other patients include transplant recipients and beneficiaries of research. These obligations are inherent in the professional role. The health care professionals' acceptance

---

[15] In these examples assume that B's contingent acceptance is voluntary.

or rejection of the offer is constrained by these moral obligations to other patients.

B's parents are not constrained by obligations inherent in the parental role. In some circumstances, B's parents' approval might legitimately be constrained by obligations to assure that B manage a family business or care for dependent relatives for whom B could not care if married to A. But such constraint is highly variable across cultures, family structures, religious groups, and legal requirements. The obligation to take others' well-being into account when making decisions about B varies while the health care professionals' obligation to take other patients' well-being into account is a fixed part of the health care professional role.

The difference between the health care professionals' obligations and B's parents' obligations becomes apparent when we ask why it is that B is at liberty to accept A's offer contingent on parental approval. I submit that it is because B's acceptance or rejection of A's offer is largely a matter of B's conception of B's happiness and how marriage would influence B's happiness. B's parents are obliged to give some weight, no matter how little, to B's happiness in their decision-making. B has ceded to B's parents' judgment of what constitutes B's happiness. In contrast, health care professionals who consider accepting or refusing S's donation of her organs make a decision that is not determined by their judgment about S's happiness. S has already determined that deciding to donate her organs makes her happy and after S's death, S's happiness is not relevant. It is true, as Wilkinson mentions, that the health care professionals are responsible for managing the organ procurement and donation system. But the authority deriving from this responsibility is not analogous to B's parents' authority to determine whether marriage to A would make B happy. The health care professionals have an obligation inherent in their role to consider the benefit to others that is not inherent in B's parents' role.

The case for complying with the family members' preference to refuse donation is further weakened when health care professionals evaluate the family members' substantive reasons for refusal. Wilkinson admits that considerations other than the family's preference itself are relevant to the considering the moral permissibility of complying with the family members' preference. This is an admission that some substantive reasons can override the formal authority of the decision-makers. Wilkinson cites families that use unjust procedures for deciding whether or not to authorize taking the dead person's organs. For example, a procedure that excluded competent adult family members from participation due to gender would be unjust. These unjust procedures "would not be worthy of respect as procedures," he writes, "even if the decisions they make might be right on independent grounds."[16] The clearest sense of procedures not being "worthy of respect" is that others are not obliged to comply with the preferences that result from those procedures. If this is so, then the health care professionals decision whether to accept organs offered for donation is not contingent merely on the family members' approval, as the case of B's acceptance of A's proposal is contingent merely on B's parents' approval. It is also contingent on the justice of the reasons for the decision or preference, which does not seem to be a factor in the double-veto policy. This admission of substantive reasons tells against complying with the family members' preference when they refuse to donate the dead person's organs when the reason is the family members' distress.

Wilkinson's admission that substantive reasons can make the results of unjust procedures impermissible seems intended to apply to procedures used by a family that are unjust to some members of the family. However, obligations to others are inherent in the health care professionals' role, so decision procedures used by health care professionals should do justice to those to whom health care professionals have obligations. Among those to whom health care professionals working in organ procurement have obligations are those in need of organs for transplantation. Family members who refuse to comply with a dead relative's preference that his organs be donated due to their distress at the time of the relative's death use an unjust procedure for deciding whether or not to take the dead person's organs. In the procedure in question, temporary distress at the loss of a loved one is given greater weight than the preservation of life and relief of suffering that would result from complying with the dead person's preference. The family members' distress is temporary and there is good reason to believe it will subside. The harms done by not taking the dead persons' organs are permanent decline in health, bodily function, and at the extreme, death by organ failure. These are good reasons for health care professionals to accept the dead person's offer of organs and to refuse to comply with family member's refusal based on their distress.

Conclusion

Many people would suffer less and live longer if they could receive an organ transplant. At the same time, many die without donating organs that could reduce suffering and extend lives. The number of cases in which the dead person and their family members have incompatible preferences

---

[16] Wilkinson (2007), p. 36.

about taking the dead person's organs is small. However, the issues raised by cases of incompatible preferences derive from an incoherent policy that gives authority to family to decide that the dead person's organs should not be taken despite the dead person's preferences. This paper has shown that the double-veto policy is incoherent and that Wilkinson's recent defense of the policy fails to sustain it against criticisms.

Arguments for the double-veto policy based on usual reasons yield inconsistent moral directives. The arguments based on family distress are shown to be less plausible when the ambiguities of family distress are examined. Wilkinson argues that the family acquires legitimate authority by health care professionals' contingent acceptance of the dead person's offer of organs. The analogy with the recipient of a marriage proposal fails for the reasons given above. In addition, unjust decision procedures are good reasons for refusing to comply with family decisions. Since unjust decisions procedures are good reasons for refusing to comply with family decisions, health care professionals have good reason not to comply with family members' refusal to allow organs to be taken from their dead relative when their reason is to avert distress. Wilkinson's admission of substantive reasons undermines the formal account of family authority on which the double-veto policy is based. Such substantive reasons are more plausible than acceding authority to family members and show that the double-veto policy is undeserving of support.

CONFLICTING ETHICAL DUTIES? THE DILEMMA OF THE BEST INTERESTS ATTORNEY

PAUL F. NEWHOUSE

In Maryland, as in other jurisdictions, mental health care providers, such as psychiatrists, psychologists, and social workers, are obligated to maintain the confidences of their clients. This confidentiality is required by the standard of care as well as the ethics of these professions. Many jurisdictions, including Maryland, also provide for an evidentiary privilege, to protect the confidential communications between mental health care providers and their clients from being divulged in legal proceedings. The ethical duty of confidentiality owed by a mental health professional to his client does not by itself preclude the disclosure of that confidential information in a judicial proceeding; the existence of an applicable privilege may preclude such disclosure.

Privileges are subject to exceptions of several types, primarily waiver. For example, the holder of a privilege arising from a psychotherapeutic relationship may waive the relevant privilege by executing a writing to that effect. He may also waive his privilege as a matter of law (without signing any writing) by bringing a civil action in which he places his own mental state at issue (for example, by alleging psychological damage in a tort case, or lack of capacity to contract in a contract case).

The purpose of this paper is to examine apparently conflicting ethical demands upon an attorney appointed by the court to represent a child in a custody, visitation rights or support action, where the issue is whether to waive the privilege the child enjoys with regard to any psychotherapist the child has seen or is seeing for therapeutic rather than forensic purposes. These attorneys, known as "best interest attorneys" (hereafter referred to as "BIA"), are appointed pursuant to Maryland Family Law Code, § 1-202, which provides as follows:

(a) In an action in which custody, visitation rights, or the amount of support of a minor child is contested, the court may:

(1)(I) appoint a lawyer who shall serve as a child advocate attorney to represent the minor child and who may not represent any party to the action; or

(II) appoint a lawyer who shall serve as a best interest attorney to represent the minor child and who may not represent any party to the action; and

(III) impose against either or both parents counsel fees.

(b)   A lawyer appointed under this section shall exercise ordinary care and diligence in the representation of a minor child.

The words "ethical demands" used in the preceding paragraph are intended to refer to ethical obligations which can be defended as such by appeal to an ethical theory. This is to be distinguished from those so-called ethical obligations which are imposed upon a professional by his licensing board, and are not truly ethical, but only "obligatory" in the sense that failure to discharge them may result in sanctions against the professional's license. In this latter sense, as the term is frequently and loosely used, certain "ethical" duties imposed upon professionals may actually require them to act immorally. I intend consistently to use the term "ethical duties" to refer only to true ethical duties, or those duties, obligations, imperatives, and the like, which can be defended by reference to a recognizable ethical theory.

In 1983, the Court of Appeals of Maryland (Maryland's highest court) held that when a minor child possesses a privilege arising from treatment for a mental or emotional disorder and the child is the subject of a custody action, the determination of whether that privilege shall be waived must be made by an attorney, rather than the child's parents. The attorney is to be guided by the best interests of the child.[1] The court's reasoning was that the parents faced a conflict between their interests and those of the child, and could not be relied upon to make a decision about the waiver in an unbiased manner.

What is the moral status of the directive that the BIA's decision concerning privilege is to be governed by the best interests of the child? One might see it as a deontological rule, issuing from legitimate authority, and adopted by the BIA as action-guiding when the BIA accepts appointment to his particular social role with respect to the court action in question.

---

[1] *Nagle v. Hooks*, 296 Md. 123, 460 A.2d 29 (1983).

In the alternative, one could adopt the view taken by the Court of Special Appeals of Maryland in the case of *Kovacs vs. Kovacs*:[2]

> The failure of a chancellor to exercise independent judgment with respect to matters concerning the best interests of children constitutes a neglect of the duty of *parens patriae* entrusted to the circuit court. As the representative of the State, the chancellor's responsibility to ensure the best interests of the children supersedes that of the parents.

The source of the court's ethical duty to children could easily be social contract theory. It appears likely, however, that more could be said to support the rule from an ethical (rather than purely legal) perspective.

One obvious approach would be to examine the consequences of the "best interests of the child" rule. The interests affected by any rule adopted to guide the BIA in making his decision concerning waiver are the following: the interests of society in general; the interests of the psychotherapeutic professions; the interests of parties to the case or persons married, formerly married, or to be married to such parties (for example, the biological parents or step-parents (actual or prospective), and even third parties (including foster-parents) who may have developed an emotional bond with the child as a result of rendering care in the absence of biological, or foster-parents); and the interests of the child whose privilege it is.

Surely it cannot be denied that there is immense utility in the creation, acceptance and enforcement of the relatively simple and straightforward rule of the "best interests of the child." Having such a rule fosters the uniformity of results in litigation concerning custody, visitation, child support, and other related matters, and such uniformity is an important aspect of the rule of law. The "best interests of the child" rule is much easier to apply than any possible competitors, because it does not require the BIA to calculate the consequences of waiver and non-waiver to anyone other than the child whose privilege it is. No calculation of consequences is necessary for society as a whole, the psychotherapeutic professions, or other persons involved in the action.

Further, it may plausibly be claimed that acting in the best interests of the child generally creates more utility for the entire society than any alternative, and that acting in the best interests of some other interested party (one of the biological parents, for example) will likely fail to produce as much utility in the long run. These conclusions follow from the importance of custody, visitation and support in the formation of a

---

[2] *Kovacs v. Kovacs*, 98 Md. App. 289, 633 A.2d 425 (1993).

future citizen (the child), as opposed to the relatively secondary economic and psychological interests of, for example, the biological parent in a custody, visitation or support arrangement which is *not* in the best interests of the child.

The utility created by adopting a rule which restricts the interests the BIA must take into account when making the waiver decision must, of course, be weighed against the disutility of ignoring the interests which the rule instructs him to ignore. I do not intend to explore this issue exhaustively, but it cannot be ignored.

One of the most obvious of such interests is that of the society in what I shall, for the purposes of this paper, call "truth-in-litigation."

A fundamental principle of jurisprudence in the common law tradition is that "[t]he public has a right to every man's evidence."[3] This is a useful principle, and the ability to compel a witness's testimony has been available in chancery since the late fourteenth century, and at law since the mid seventeenth century.[4] As a general principle, such compulsion is certainly valuable in the hands of a plaintiff or the prosecution (*i.e.*, those with the burden of proof). Fairness decrees that a defendant, civil or criminal, also have a right to every man's evidence, lest the courts "become themselves the instruments of wrong."[5] I take it as obvious that any well-functioning adversary system of justice will admit reliable and probative evidence, and *compel* it if necessary.

It may have been inevitable that along with the ability to compel testimony came "privilege," from the Latin *private lex*, a prerogative given to a person or class of persons.[6] With the creation of privilege came a conflict: "[A] privilege is a derogation from the general rule that all relevant evidence is both admissible and compellable before a court or tribunal."[7]

It is not the purpose of this paper to argue whether the adversary system of justice is best, or whether there is some competing system that might be more just or better in some other way (for example, less demanding on society's resources). For better or worse, we are wedded to the adversary system, and the fact that some particular rule of law serves the adversary system I take to be an ethical argument in favor of the practice embodied by the rule.

---

[3] *Trammel v. United States*, 445 U.S. 40, 50 (1980)
[4] Auburn, *Legal Professional Privilege: Law and Theory*, Hart Publishing, 2000, p. 7
[5] *Jaffee v. Redmond*, 518 U.S. 1, 19 (1996) (Scalia, J. Dissenting)
[6] Auburn, p. 1.
[7] Auburn, p. 1.

Nor is it the purpose of this paper to determine whether the goal of the adversary system is the discovery of truth. There are those who accept this as given[8] and those, like myself, who question whether this is the case. For present purposes, I am content to accept that the determination of truth is at least *one important goal* of our adversary system of justice.

That privilege may interfere with the judicial search for truth is thus not a trivial consideration, because it can preclude the introduction into evidence of information that may be relevant, reliable and probative. This fact is irrelevant to the BIA, because his imperative under *Nagle v. Hooks* is to act in the best interests of his client, the child, and, by implication, to ignore any other interests. The exclusion of relevant, reliable and probative evidence due to the exercise of privilege is not, however, irrelevant to members of society insofar as the existence and strength of the rule of law is determined in part by the extent to which the application of the society's laws to individual cases is consistent with the goals and values of the society, and those goals and values in our society include truth-in-litigation. Further, the exclusion of privileged information is highly relevant to all persons who have an interest in the outcome of specific litigation concerning custody, visitation or support. These persons may be frustrated by the assertion of the psychotherapist - client privilege as they attempt to attain their ends in the litigation.

Nevertheless, the BIA is not subject to a conflict of ethical duties here. At the very minimum, he is entitled to ignore truth-in-litigation when deciding whether to assert or waive his client's privilege because he is bound by a deontological rule which he is obligated to respect. In addition, there is reason to suppose that the "best interests of the child" rule is not merely a deontological rule which owes its origin to precedent only, nor merely a rule deriving from rational considerations of harmonious co-existence. The "best interests" rule is also adequately supported by considerations of rule-utilitarianism, both on the abstract level which is concerned with the existence of any rule whatsoever, as well as the level concerned with the content of such a rule.

Accordingly, I shall assume in what follows that the BIA need not concern himself with the possibility that his assertion of the psychotherapist privilege on behalf of his client may conflict with the social goal of achieving truth-in-litigation. This, however, does not mean that there is no truth-in-litigation issue which must be confronted by the BIA, for the BIA must sometimes still choose between asserting the

---

[8] For example, Justice Scalia in his dissenting opinion in *Jaffe v. Redmond*, above, where the Supreme Court created, as federal common law, a privilege applicable to a social worker.

psychotherapist - client privilege on behalf of his client and adducing evidence favorable to the best interests of that child which may be otherwise unavailable, as, for example, when the child has disclosed to his psychotherapist some act by a parent for which no other evidence is available.

In each of the following examples, let us suppose a BIA has been appointed for the purpose of determining whether his client's psychotherapist - client privilege should be waived, and that he has, as he ought, spoken with the psychotherapist. (This conversation, I should mention, is governed by the ethics of confidentiality, which permit it to occur; its content is both confidential and privileged because the BIA represents the child.) In the various cases, the BIA has learned that the child has said the following:

A. "I don't want to live with my mother. I am afraid of her. She yells at me a lot, calls me stupid, and is mean to me."
B. "My father drank a lot of beers again last night. He passed out on the floor, and I couldn't get him up. He did wake up just as I was calling for help. This is the second time this month."
C. "I hate my father. He used to hit my mother, and I'm afraid he will hit me if I am living with him."
D. "My father usually comes home from work and goes to bed and sleeps. He isn't interested in me or what I do at all. He hardly eats anything, and we never do anything fun."

This is not a paper on the law of evidence. I will assume that a competent lawyer will find a way to get these statements (which suffer from obvious hearsay problems) into evidence, sometimes using the psychotherapist as his witness and sometimes using the psychotherapist's written progress notes, whether as impeachment of the child's testimony, to refresh the child's recollection, as the basis for expert opinion, or as part of a series of direct examination questions directed to the child that narrowly avoids an objection on the grounds of "leading" the witness. It cannot be doubted that at some point the child will be made aware that the source of the information was his psychotherapist. In each case, the BIA must choose whether to waive the child's privilege, and require the psychotherapist to testify. What considerations must the BIA entertain to discharge his duty to act ethically in the best interests of the child?

One might reasonably assume that the decision of the BIA should arise from an initial state of equipoise as between waiver and non-waiver, comparing the consequences to the child of both alternatives. I argue that this is not the case.

It is important to be clear about what is to be considered by the BIA: The general social good of maximum truth-in-litigation is *not* considered. The contest is between the child's interest in maintaining confidentiality (arising from the potential harm of waiver), and the utility to that child of maximizing true information at trial, leading (hopefully) to the decision which is in the child's best interests, based on the fullest, most complete set of true facts concerning the child, his needs, his relationship with his parents, and his innermost hopes and fears.

It is at this point that we do well to remember the caution voiced by the authors of *The Best Interests of the Child*:

> The law is, after all, incapable of effectively managing, except in a very gross sense, such delicate and complex relationships as those between parent and child and those between parent and parent.[9]

We cannot expect, as a general rule, that routinely waiving the child's privilege in order to maximize the information upon which a custody decision will be made will result in a higher percentage of decisions which truly reflect the best interests of the child. This demands too much of our legal system, and ignores factors such as the life experiences, values, beliefs, and expertise (or lack thereof) which characterizes the particular judge to whom the case has been assigned. In short, the most defensible way of deciding what in a given case is in the best interests of the child (one of the subjects of *The Best Interests of the Child*) is inconsistent with the position that it is always better for the court to have more information about the child, regardless of how it is obtained. This is to be contrasted with cases in which a specific bit of significant information would likely not come to light absent a waiver of the privilege.

In order to resolve this issue adequately, it is useful to examine the reason for applying the psychotherapist - client privilege to children, and to compare this reason with the reason for adopting an attorney - client privilege generally. Let us begin with the latter.

One way of approaching the attorney - client privilege (as it relates to litigation) is to take the position that genuine assistance of counsel demands knowledge by that counsel of the facts with which he will be confronted at trial. Candor on the part of the client is thus seen as a necessary condition for the effective operation of the profession, and it is believed by many that privilege is essential to that candor (or at least the lack of privilege will detract from that candor). A second, related reason for the existence of the attorney - client privilege is based upon the role of

---

[9] Goldstein, *et al. The Best Interests of the Child*, The Free Press 1996, pg. 7.

the attorney as an advisor independent of the official machinery of justice, and one who owes his loyalty to his client. Here, the privilege protects the client from betrayal and divided loyalty on the part of his attorney. This loyalty is limited only by the prohibition against an attorney's assisting his client to deceive the court. As an "officer of the court," an attorney may not utilize perjured testimony in order to prevail in litigation. Thus, if a client admits to his attorney that he did, in fact, commit the crime of which he is accused, the attorney may not permit his client to testify and deny his guilt.

In contrast, the psychotherapist - client relationship is not primarily intended to encourage candor on the part of the client with respect to truths concerning the objective world. The initial goal of psychotherapy is seen by many mental health care providers as the creation of a psychotherapeutic relationship in which trust, not truth telling, is the most critical ingredient.[10] The important thing in a psychotherapeutic relationship is not that the client tell the truth about what happened to him and around him, but rather that the client freely communicate his fantasies, misperceptions, exaggerations, feelings, projections and incorrect beliefs. This requires enormous confidence on the part of the client in the integrity and discretion of the psychotherapist, and the primary concern of the privilege is the preservation of this trust, not the search for truth. Thus, rather than candor as a necessary condition for the professional's ability to carry out his professional tasks as a psychotherapist, what is required is *trust*.

The centrality of trust is particularly important in the case of children, who cannot understand notions such as confidentiality and its limitations, privilege, waiver, and informed consent,[11] but certainly do understand when they have been betrayed. The maintenance of this trust between a

---

[10] *Jaffee v. Redmond*, majority opinion.

[11] Ordinarily, a psychotherapy client must be informed at the outset of therapy concerning the limits of confidentiality. This is a part of the requirement that clients give "informed consent," a requirement which itself is open to debate concerning its net utility. For example, it may be criticized because of its potential "chilling effect." Furthermore, it may serve as a roadmap which the client may use to avoid disclosure by not transgressing the stated boundaries of that of which it is permissible to speak. However this may work itself out in the adult realm, at least the adult client cannot complain of complete breach of loyalty and betrayal on the part of the psychotherapist. The difficulty is that "informed consent" of this type cannot be obtained from younger children, and it is difficult to state when a child is sufficiently intellectually mature to appreciate the idea of informed consent, to say nothing of understanding the concepts of "privilege" and "waiver."

child and his psychotherapist requires that the child's confidentiality not be compromised, for two reasons: (1)   protecting the children from experiencing betrayal, which would destroy the psychotherapeutic relationship and preclude further fruitful psychotherapy with the psychotherapist who testified; and (2) concern that if the psychotherapeutic bond is broken between a child and his psychotherapist, the child may have a much more difficult time establishing a new relationship due to lack of trust which is seen as the inevitable result of the betrayal involved in testifying concerning the child's confidences.

We are now in a position to assess whether the most accurate description of what the BIA does is to balance the good or harm of waiver against the good or harm of asserting the privilege– a sort of act utilitarian evaluation in each case, wherein the initial position is equipoise and the only standard is the best interests of the child whose privilege it is– as well as to examine the factors which a BIA might consider in reaching his decision as to whether to waive his client's psychotherapist - client privilege.

It appears to me that the consequences to the child of the betrayal of his trust are so devastating that they cannot easily be compared with the negative utility entailed by forgoing any of the evidence to be found in examples (A) through (D). The child cannot properly be prepared for the possibility that his words to his psychotherapist will be used in court, to the disadvantage of one of his parents. In addition to the destruction of the important relationship between the child and his current psychotherapist, the experience of betrayal could well cause harm by rendering it impossible for the child to establish a similar relationship in the future with *another* psychotherapist.   There will also likely be harm to the relationship with the parent whose custody aspirations are affected negatively by the information elicited from the psychotherapist.

These reasons suggest that simple balancing from an initial position of equipoise is not an appropriate model for making the waiver decision. The magnitude of the potential injury to a child's sense of trust in the adult world in general and in psychotherapists in particular so far outstrips the possible benefits of some particular bit of evidence that it is simply not accurate to maintain there is a weighing of alternative consequences starting from an initial position of equipoise. It would be more accurate to approach the situation along the following lines (of which I prefer the second to the first):

(1) Adopt as an overarching principle the maxim to do no harm by one's decision as a BIA concerning waiver. This is a very difficult standard to meet, and would appear to eliminate the possibility of ever

waiving the privilege, except in those very unusual circumstances in which the child was able to give informed consent and would not see the waiver as betrayal.

(2) Adopt a presumption that the privilege will not be waived, and require a very substantial magnitude of net positive utility to be achieved by waiving the privilege.

The recognition of a presumption favoring the privilege does not conclude the inquiry. Each of the examples A through D above presents the germ of a very serious objection to an award of custody to the parent referred to:

A. The child's words in example A suggest a poor if not destructive relationship with her mother which is likely to have an impact upon any custody decision.

B. The father in example B may suffer from serious alcohol addiction– a condition which would likely make him unfit to have custody of his child.

C. The statement quoted in example C would give anyone concern about the possibility of future child abuse, and would be a serious objection to custody on the part of the father.

D. The father in example D may suffer from severe clinical depression, which, if untreated, would make him unfit to have custody.

The BIA ought to take into account the following considerations when making his decision concerning the privilege:

1. The presumption of non-waiver should be taken very seriously. In other words, waiver is not appropriate in order to obtain marginally superior evidence. This is contrary to the litigation lawyer's instinct, which is to seize every advantage and utilize every bit of helpful evidence. Although this behavior is generally considered part of what it means to represent one's client zealously, it can in this context be contrary to the best interests of that client.

2. Each case must be examined closely to determine whether there is any evidence to be obtained by waiver of the psychotherapist - client privilege which is clearly relevant to the case to be presented, not redundant or cumulative, reliable and credible, as well as highly probative. In short, the evidence must be good evidence, and not easily rejected or ignored by the court.

3. It should be impossible or very unlikely that the evidence could be obtained from any other source. The privilege should never be waived simply because that is the easiest way to get the needed information. With regard to all of the examples A through D, it would be remarkable if the only way of obtaining the evidence about the various impediments to

custody with regard to the parent referred to was through the child's psychotherapist. If the problems are real, there should be other witnesses who could testify concerning them.

4.   The evidence should clearly support a custody outcome that the BIA believes is definitely superior. The goal is not the perfect trial, but the best interests of the child.

Hopefully, answering these questions will dispel any remaining ethical issues with regard to the decision of waiving the psychotherapist - client privilege. Nevertheless, even after answering these questions as well as they can be answered in the circumstance, it may still be the case that the BIA must confront a genuine ethical conflict and exercise ethical judgment. I can only hope that the issues will be clearer and the decisions a bit easier and more defensible.

ETHICAL DILEMMAS AND A DECISION-MAKING PROCESS FOR CHILD WELFARE PRACTICE

KAREN M. RICE

Ethical conduct requires professionals to respond with maturity, judgment, discretion, wisdom, and prudence.[1] Child welfare caseworkers hold a unique and confidential relationship with the families with whom they work in that they are active participants in the change process. This reciprocal relationship is complicated however due to the power inherent in the professional obligations of the child welfare worker which often leads to ethical dilemmas. Child welfare caseworkers are charged with ensuring the safety, permanency, and well-being of children with whom they work, yet also have a responsibility to provide all necessary services to the children's family in order to maintain or reunite the family.[2] This dual relationship complicates decision making as often the outcome benefits only one member of the family. Additionally, the services provided may run counter to a family's desire for services as specific mandates are imposed upon families involved with the child welfare system. The purpose of this paper is to explain the use and function of the National Association of Social Workers Code of Ethics[3], identify the principles that support ethical decisions, highlight the complexities of the caregiver/caseworker relationship, elucidate common ethical traps made by child welfare caseworkers, and discuss an ethical decision making framework and ethical principles screen to utilize when faced with ethical dilemmas.

---

[1] Corey, Gerald, Marianne Schneider Corey, and Patrick Callanan. *Issues and Ethics in the Helping Professions, 5th ed.* Pacific Grove: Brooks/Cole Publishing Company, 1998.
[2] Department of Public Welfare, *Adoption and Safe Families Act, Public Law 105-89*. Washington, DC: GPO, 1997.
[3] National Association of Social Workers (NASW), *Code of Ethics*. Washington, DC: NASW Press, 1999.

National Association of Social Workers Code of Ethics

Purpose of the Code

The National Association of Social Workers (NASW) Code of Ethics outlines the values, principles, and standards that should guide professional social work practice.[4] "Professional social work ethics are intended to help social work practitioners recognize the morally correct way of practice and to learn how to decide and act correctly with regard to the ethical aspects of any given professional situation"[5]. Remaining entirely objective in all professional situations is impracticable due to firmly held, sometimes conflicting personal and professional values. Additionally, the dual role conflict inherent in child welfare further complicates the issue. The Code of Ethics allows social workers to check and balance their own feelings, values, and expectations with those of the profession. Yet the adherence to one principle or standard may produce noncompliance with another. When such a quandary occurs, the Code of Ethics provides no set rule on which standards outweigh others, and this inherent ambiguity is a major limitation of professional ethical codes.[6]

Principles of the Code

The code of ethics does proffer a set of behavior ideals derived from the profession's values. The six principles include 1) helping individuals in need and addressing social problems, 2) challenging social injustice, 3) respecting the inherent dignity and worth of the individual, 4) recognizing the importance of human relationships, 5) behaving in a trustworthy manner, and 6) practicing within one's area of competence and developing and enhancing one's professional expertise.[7] All social work students are instructed in these principles throughout their education and are expected to act accordingly. These ethical principles are what direct the professional social worker's practice with others.

---

[4] NASW, 1999.
[5] Loewenberg, Frank, M., Ralph Dolgoff, and Donna Harrington. *Ethical Decisions for Social Work Practice, 6th ed.* Itasca, Illinois: F. E. Peacock Publishers, Inc., 2000.
[6] Beth Haverkamp, and Judith C. Daniluk, "Child Sexual Abuse: Ethical Issues for the Family Therapist," *Family Relations 42* (1993): 134-139.
[7] NASW, 1999.

Complex Caregiver/Caseworker Relationship

Child welfare caseworkers hold a unique and confidential relationship with the families with whom they work. The caseworker is not just the change agent for the family but also the "control agent" for society.[8] They balance the professional duty of helping the family with the legal responsibility of protecting the child, one of society's most vulnerable members. This competing role between child safety and family preservation complicates the caregiver/caseworker relationship.

Often, as the caseworker is an active participant in the change process, a mutual relationship ensues. However, due to the inherent power differences and professional obligations of the caseworker, case decisions are often complicated. On the one hand, the caseworker may feel compelled to do the "right thing" for the family[9], or on the other hand, feel called to "make a statement" in the name of child protection. For example, caseworkers may empathize with a parent's struggle with addiction and wish to support him or her through the recovery process, yet the caseworkers' legal mandate compels them to petition to terminate a parent's parental rights when significant progress is not made within a specified amount of time. In either case, intuitively driven decisions not based on a sound ethical process can positively or negatively influence case outcomes. As a result, child welfare caseworkers must conduct themselves with maturity, judgment, discretion, wisdom, and prudence.[10] This requires knowledge in ethical professional conduct.

Unethical conduct can have serious repercussions in the lives of those it touches.[11] Caseworkers are often revered as the "expert" on the family and their input in case decisions are valued and desired. This is especially true during court proceedings when the input from the caseworker is factored into the judge's decision. As a result, it is further commanded that considerable thought be afforded each decision as the consequences may be grave.

Although the principles outlined in the NASW Code of Ethics is meant to guide and aid the social worker in his or her practice, the complexities

---

[8] Richard D. Parsons, *The Ethics of Professional Practice.* Boston: Allyn and Bacon, 2001.

[9] Parsons, 2001.

[10] Corey, 1998.

[11] Cynthia Crosson-Tower, *Exploring Child Welfare: A Practice Perspective, 4th ed.* New York: Allyn and Bacon, 2007.

of the code may produce ethical dilemmas[12], two or more conflicting professional obligations, as no set guideline on the ranking of principles exist. Regardless, encountering ethical dilemmas is inevitable as there are no straightforward solutions, especially when the competing obligations are "right" when examined separately. Lamentably, social workers attempting to resolve ethical dilemmas often resort to one of four ethical traps.[13]

Common Ethical Traps

Commonsense or Objectivity Trap

The commonsense or objectivity trap occurs when social workers believe commonsense, objective solutions exist for all ethical dilemmas and thus consultation is not warranted.[14] Caseworkers, like most social workers, enter the helping profession with the goal to help others. Therefore, understandably, their decisions should be based on what is best for the individual. However, with nothing guiding those decisions, the caseworkers are left to intuition which is guided by personal values. Despite the claim of practicing objectively, answers to specific situations lie within the individual caseworker based on the premise that all helping professionals act ethically.[15]

The "Values" Trap

When social workers substitute their personal values, morals, or religious convictions for the provisions of their professional ethical code, they are committing the "values" ethical trap.[16]

Values are derived from our past experiences, perceptions, and attitudes.[17] Prior research has shown how caseworkers' values influence

---

[12] Steinman, Sarah, O., Nan Franks Richardson, and Tim McEnroe. *The Ethical Decision-making Manual for Helping Professionals.* Pacific Grove: Brooks/Cole Publishing Company, 1998.

[13] Steinman, 1998.

[14] Steinman, 1998.

[15] Steinman, 1998.

[16] Steinman, 1998.

[17] Tatum, B.D., B. Harro, W.J., Blumenfeld, and D. Raymond. 2000. *Readings for Diversity and Social Justice: An Anthology on Racism, Anti-Semitism, Sexism, Heterosexism, Ableism, and Classism.* New York: Routledge.

their behavior. Lundgren, Schilling, Fitzgerald, Davis, and Amodeo[18] reported the negative attitudes of child welfare caseworkers regarding methadone maintenance was inhibiting women IV drug users from seeking such treatment for fear of losing custody of their child.

In a study examining caseworkers' views of kinship care, Peters[19] found that ambivalent attitudes affect a workers' behavior. Although caseworkers reported kinship care being a positive resource, their negative attitudes created biases and resulted in unfair and harsh treatment toward the family members.[20] Further, this led to a lack of trust and an adversarial relationship between the caseworkers and family members.[21] Therefore, despite good intentions, caseworkers' attitudes were more predictive of how they would respond to the family member. It is apparent that this trap has the potential of causing serious negative consequences as outcomes in child welfare can permanently separate all ties between parents and their children.

The "Circumstantiality" Trap

Social workers commit this particular ethical trap when they believe the circumstances under which the behavior occurred should be weighed in the decision making process.[22] Opposite from the commonsense/objectivity trap, caseworkers committing this ethical trap spend much time considering the details of a situation prior to making a decision. Too often irrelevant information is processed resulting in a muddling of the key dilemma. In fact, behavior is usually right or wrong according to professional ethical standards regardless of the circumstances under which they occurred.[23] For example, child welfare caseworkers are charged with protecting all children from potential harm even when the individuals of threat to the children are themselves children. Factoring in the age of the individual creating the threat ignores the ethical, and in this scenario, the legal mandate to protect the safety of the children in danger.

---

[18] Lena M. Lundgren, Robert F. Schilling, Therese Fitzgerald, Kathy Davis, and Maryann Amodeo, "Parental Status of Women Injection Drug Users and Entry to Methadone Maintenance," *Substance Use & Misuse 38,* no. 8 (2003): 1109-1131.

[19] Jay Peters, "True Ambivalence: Child Welfare Workers' Thoughts, Feelings, and Beliefs about Kinship Foster Care," *Children and Youth Services Review 27,* no. 6 (2005): 595-614.

[20] Peters, 2005.

[21] Peters, 2005.

[22] Steinman, 1998.

[23] Steinman, 1998.

The "Who Will Benefit" Trap

Many ethical dilemmas result in taking a stance among two or more conflicting interests resulting in a "winner" and a "loser".[24] When social workers deliberate over whose interest is paramount, they commit the "who will benefit" trap. Of all the ethical traps presented, this is probably the trap child welfare caseworkers will risk committing most. Caseworkers find themselves in unique situations of needing to simultaneously meet the needs of the parent and the child. However, protecting the interests of parents may not coincide with what is in the best interest of the child.

Parental substance abuse is a factor in 50-80% of children entering foster care.[25] The Adoption and Safe Families Act (ASFA) mandates a petition to terminate a parent's parental rights be filed when a child has been in foster care for 15 out of the past 22 months.[26] Throughout the literature, it has been noted that these timeframes are incompatible with those of drug and alcohol recovery.[27] Consequently, an ethical dilemma is created as the caseworker struggles with the filing of a termination of parental rights petition knowing the parents were not afforded adequate time to recover from their drug and alcohol addiction. Although the child may "win" as a result of obtaining permanency, the parents "lose" as all their parental ties to the child are indefinitely severed.

To avoid committing this trap, caseworkers must consider the long-term and not just the short-term interests of their clients.[28] Nevertheless, the alternatives may continue to create an ethical dilemma. Should this occur, it is imperative that the caseworker utilize a rank-ordering approach to assess the effectiveness of the potential outcomes.[29] Ethical dilemma decision-making frameworks exist to aid caseworkers through this process to avoid committing all of the aforementioned ethical traps.

---

[24] Steinman, 1998.
[25] Christine E. Grella, Yih-Ing, Hser, and Yu-Chuang, Huang, "Mothers in Substance Abuse Treatment: Differences in Characteristics Based on Involvement with Child Welfare Services," *Child Abuse & Neglect 30,* no. 1 (2006): 55-73.
[26] Adoption and Safe Families Act, 1997.
[27] Child Welfare League of America, *Research Roundup: Family Reunification,* http://www.cwla.org/programs/r2p/rrnews0203/pdf
[28] Steinman, 1998 .
[29] Loewenberg, 2000.

Ethical Dilemma Decision-Making Process

As previously stated, the NASW Code of Ethics provides no guidance for preference in conflicting principles. Rather, social workers are advised to align their decisions and actions "with the spirit as well as the letter of" the Code.[30] This vagueness demanded the need for an ethical decision-making process to guide the social worker through complex, ethical issues. The ethical dilemma decision-making framework of Reamer[31, 32] and Loewenberg et al.[33] will be applied to ethical dilemmas common within child welfare.

Reamer[34,35] and Loewenberg and associates[36] provide a general decision-making model to aid social workers in processing ethical dilemmas that arise within their practice. This model entails social workers maneuvering step-by-step through a series of actions ending with the implementation, monitoring and evaluation of the decision made. The specific steps include: 1) identification of the problem, 2) identification of all individuals involved in the problem, 3) determination of individuals to include in the decision making process, 4) identification of values, personal and professional, relevant to the problem, 5) identification of goals and objectives which may resolve the problem, 6) identification of alternative intervention strategies, 7) assessment of the effectiveness and efficiency of each alternative, 8) selection of the most appropriate strategy, 9) implementation of the strategy selected, 10) monitoring of the implementation, and 11) evaluation of the outcomes.[37]

The decision-making can create ethical dilemmas; however, Loewenberg and associates'[38] framework is implemented in an ethical context where dilemmas are resolved through the rank-ordering of the ethical principles. This framework is particularly useful in child welfare because caseworkers have an obligation to protect the rights of their clients and the interests of society while at the same time ensuring the least amount of harm is

[30] NASW, 1997.
[31] Frederic G. Reamer, *Ethical Dilemmas in Social Service: A Guide for Social Workers, 2nd ed.* New York: Columbia University Press, 1990.
[32] Frederic G. Reamer, "The Social Work Ethics Audit: A Risk-management Strategy," *Social Work 45,* (2000): 355-372.
[33] Loewenberg, 2000.
[34] Reamer, 1990.
[35] Reamer, 2000.
[36] Loewenberg, 2000.
[37] Loewenberg, 2000.
[38] Loewenberg, 2000.

caused. These obligations may generate different alternative intervention strategies (Step 6 in the above decision-making model). Nonetheless, this decision-making framework rank orders the ethical principles which clearly elucidate the order of priority for each alternative intervention strategy.

In their Ethical Principles Screen (EPS), Loewenberg and associates[39] hierarchically position seven ethical principles so that ethical principle one is superior to ethical principles two through seven, ethical principle two is superior to ethical principles three through seven, and so on. Ethical principle one specifies the protection of all human life as the paramount obligation which overrides all other principles.

The second ethical principle is often applied in child abuse cases. Loewenberg et al. suggests "equal persons have the right to be treated equally and nonequal persons have the right to be treated differently if the inequality is relevant to the issue in question"[40]. Therefore, it is acceptable, and in fact expected that the protection of a child from abuse overrides the right of alleged abusers to confidentiality on the basis that the child is not in an equal position of power with the adult.

Ethical principle three states "social workers should make practice decisions that foster a person's autonomy, independence, and freedom"[41]. However, an individual's decision to abuse or exploit a child should not be ignored as ethical principle two takes precedence. As already stated, child welfare caseworkers are often faced with ethical dilemmas that have the potential for causing harm. When this occurs, Loewenberg et al. outline in ethical principle four that "social workers should always choose the option that will cause the least harm, the least permanent harm, and /or the most easily reversible harm to all individuals"[42].

Ethical principles five, six and seven suggest social workers choose options that promote a better quality of life for individuals, make decisions that protect confidentiality, and disclose relevant information to clients, respectively. Equipped with these guidelines, upon identification of alternative intervention strategies to a particular ethical dilemma, child welfare caseworkers will be able to classify the alternatives into one of the seven principles on the EPS (Step 7). Assessment of the EPS will then elucidate the higher ranked alternative to select as the most appropriate strategy (Step 8).

---

[39] Loewenberg, 2000.
[40] Loewenberg, 2000.
[41] Loewenberg, 2000.
[42] Loewenberg, 2000.

Conclusion

Ethical dilemmas are unavoidable but how to respond should be purposeful.

Careless reactions may create devastating outcomes, especially in child welfare practice. The ethical conduct of child welfare caseworkers is paramount. Utilization of an ethical decision making model ensures caseworkers' personal values are subtracted from the decision making equation.

INDEX